Virtues and Economics

Volume 1

The series is dedicated to virtue ethics and economics. Its purpose is to relocate economic theory to a domain where the connection between the virtues and economic decisions, as that connection is actually experienced in everyday life, is an organic component of theory rather than some sort of an optionally added ingredient. The goal is to help develop a virtue-based economic theory which connects virtues with the contents of economic activities of individuals, unincorporated and incorporated economic agents. The primary context is Catholic Social Teaching but other faith traditions (especially Judaism, Islam, Hinduism, Buddhism, and Confucianism) will also be explored for their construction of virtues in economic action. Special attention will be made to regulatory and policy issues in promoting economic justice.

The series connects virtue ethics with the core of economic theory and practice. It examines the basic and irreducible intentionality of human activities concerned with the production, distribution and consumption of goods and services. It considers the incommensurability of values as the central problem of economic decision making and examines whether that problem can be overcome by any means other than practical reason.

This series will cover high quality edited volumes and monographs.

More information about this series at http://www.springer.com/series/15627

Peter Rona • Laszlo Zsolnai
Editors

Economics as a Moral Science

Springer

Editors
Peter Rona
Blackfriars Hall
University of Oxford
Oxford, UK

Laszlo Zsolnai
Corvinus University of Budapest
Budapest, Hungary

European SPES Institute
Leuven, Belgium

ISSN 2520-1794   ISSN 2520-1808 (electronic)
Virtues and Economics
ISBN 978-3-319-53290-5   ISBN 978-3-319-53291-2 (eBook)
DOI 10.1007/978-3-319-53291-2

Library of Congress Control Number: 2017936974

Printed on acid-free paper

This Springer imprint is published by Springer Nature
The registered company is Springer International Publishing AG
The registered company address is: Gewerbestrasse 11, 6330 Cham, Switzerland

Preface

The book is an attempt to reclaim economics as a moral science. It argues that ethics is a relevant and inseparable aspect of all levels of economic activity, from individual and organizational to societal and global. Taking ethical considerations into account is needed in explaining and predicting the behavior of economic agents as well as in evaluating and designing economic policies and mechanisms.

The unique feature of the book is that it not only analyzes ethics and economics on an abstract level but puts behavioral, institutional, and systemic issues together for a robust and human view of economic functioning. It sees economic "facts" as interwoven with human intentionality and ethical content, a domain where utility calculations and moral considerations co-determine the behavior of economic agents and the outcomes of their activities.

The book contains selected papers from international workshops that we co-organized with the European SPES Institute in Cambridge, Oxford, and Leuven. The first workshop, entitled *The Economic and Financial Crisis and the Human Person*, was held at the Von Hügel Institute, St Edmund's College, University of Cambridge, in 2013. It addressed the need to rebalance material and spiritual values in economic policy and business functioning. The second workshop, entitled *Teleology and Reason in Economic and Social Affairs*, was organized at Blackfriars Hall, *University of Oxford*, in 2014. It explored Catholic social teaching for analyzing today's pressing economic and financial problems. The third workshop, entitled *Virtues and Vices in Economics and Business*, was held at the Catholic University of Leuven in 2015. In applying the tradition of virtue ethics, participants discussed new models for encouraging virtuous action in business and economic policy.

This book is the first of the series of volumes under the general title *Virtues and Economics* dedicated to exploring the connection between virtue ethics, economy, and theories about the economy. The series is an attempt to redefine the domain of economics so as to provide the foundation for reestablishing the spiritual nature of man when acting as economic agent.

The book employs the personalist approach that sees human persons – endowed with free will and conscience – as the basic agents of economic life and defines human flourishing as the final end of economic activities. The book intends to demonstrate that economics can gain a lot in meaning and also in analytical power by reuniting itself with ethics.

Oxford, UK Peter Rona
Budapest, Hungary Laszlo Zsolnai

Acknowledgment

The editors would like to acknowledge the financial support provided by the Mallinckrodt Foundation of the workshop held at Blackfriars Hall in 2014.

Contents

Part I Introduction

1 **Why Economics Is a Moral Science** ... 3
Peter Rona

2 **Issues and Themes in Moral Economics** ... 11
Laszlo Zsolnai

Part II The Moral Foundations of Economics

3 **Economics as if Ethics Mattered** ... 21
Stefano Zamagni

4 **Teleological Reasoning in Economics** ... 43
Luk Bouckaert

5 **Economic Rationality Versus Human Reason** ... 57
Laszlo Zsolnai

6 **Rediscovering a Personalist Economy** ... 69
Hendrik Opdebeeck

7 **Happiness and Human Flourishing** ... 79
Knut J. Ims

8 **Understanding Financial Crises: The Contribution of the Philosophy of Money** ... 95
Antoon Vandevelde

9 **Economics and Vulnerability: Relationships, Incentives, Meritocracy** ... 107
Luigino Bruni

Part III Companies and Their Management

10 Ethics, Economics and the Corporation 131
Peter Rona

11 Are Business Ethics Relevant? 163
David W. Miller and Michael J. Thate

12 Economy of Mutuality 175
Kevin T. Jackson

13 Economic Wisdom for Managerial Decision-Making 199
Mike Thompson

Part IV Economic Policy and Economic Development

14 Catholic Social Thought and Amartya Sen on Justice 215
Johan Verstraeten

15 The Theological Virtue of Charity in the Economy: Reflections on "Caritas in veritate" 225
Helen Alford

16 Ethics of Development in the Age of Globalization 233
Zsolt Boda

17 Transdisciplinarity, Governance and the Common Good 249
François Lépineux and Jean-Jacques Rosé

Part V Conclusions

18 Agenda for Future Research and Action 271
Peter Rona and Laszlo Zsolnai

Index 275

About the Editors

Peter Rona is fellow of Blackfriars Hall, University of Oxford, where he teaches courses in economics and the philosophical foundations of the social sciences. He obtained his BA degree in economic history (cum laude) from the University of Pennsylvania and his law degree from the University of Oxford (first class) in 1964. He was an associate of the Washington, D.C., law firm, Arnold & Porter, and a counsel to the US Department of Commerce before becoming the personal assistant of Lord Richardson, governor of the Bank of England. He joined the Schroder Group in 1969 as the general counsel of its operations in the USA and became the president and chief executive of the IBJ Schroder Bank & Trust Co. in 1985. In 2003, he joined the faculty of Eötvös Loránd University where he taught public international law, and in 2006, he was made an honorary professor there. His published articles include a study of the Euro and an examination of the philosophical foundations of economics.

Laszlo Zsolnai is professor and director of the Business Ethics Center at the Corvinus University of Budapest. He is president of the European SPES Institute in Leuven, Belgium, and co-chair of the Future Earth Finance and Economics Knowledge-Action Network in Montreal. Laszlo Zsolnai's recent books include *The Palgrave Handbook of Spirituality and Business* (2011. Houndmills, UK, New York, NY: Palgrave Macmillan), *Beyond Self: Ethical and Spiritual Dimensions of Economics* (2014. Peter Lang Academic Publishers, Oxford), *The Spiritual Dimension of Business Ethics and Sustainability Management* (2015, Springer), *Post-Materialist Business: Spiritual Value-Orientation in Renewing Management* (2015, Palgrave Macmillan), and *Ethical Leadership: Indian and European Spiritual Approaches* (2016, Palgrave Macmillan). His website is http://laszlo-zsolnai.net.

About the Authors

Helen Alford is professor and former dean of the Faculty of Social Sciences at the Pontifical University of St. Thomas ("Angelicum") in Rome. She originally trained as a manufacturing engineer at Cambridge University, UK, and her PhD thesis concerned human-centered technology and its potential for the humanization of work in manufacturing. She is the author with Michael Naughton of *Managing as if Faith Mattered: Christian Social Principles in the Modern Organization* (2001, University of Notre Dame Press). Her more recent book, edited with Francesco Compagnoni, is *Preaching Justice: Dominican Contributions to Social Ethics in the Twentieth Century* (2007, Dominican Publications, Dublin, 2007). Helen Alford is author of numerous articles and papers in the areas of human-centered technology, Catholic social thought, corporate social responsibility, and business.

Zsolt Boda holds an MA in economics and a PhD in political science. He is director of the Institute of Political Science, Hungarian Academy of Sciences, and associate professor at the Business Ethics Center, Corvinus University of Budapest. He has coedited and written books in Hungarian on corporate ethics, political theory, and environmental politics and policy. He has published several papers in academic journals and books on international ethics involving the fair trade problematic, trade and environmental issues, and the politics of global environmentalism.

Luk Bouckaert is emeritus professor of ethics at the Catholic University of Leuven, Belgium. He is a philosopher and an economist by training. His research and publications fall within the fields of business ethics and spirituality. In 1987, he founded with some colleagues the interdisciplinary Centre for Economics and Ethics at the Catholic University of Leuven. In 2000, he started the SPES Forum (Spirituality in Economics and Society) and in 2004 the European SPES Forum which he chaired as president until 2014. His recent publications in English include *Spirituality as a Public Good* (coedited with L. Zsolnai, 2007), *Frugality: Rebalancing Material and Spiritual Values in Economic Life* (coedited with H. Opdebeeck and L .Zsolnai,

2008), *Imagine Europe* (coedited with J. Eynikel, 2009), *Respect and Economic Democracy* (coedited with Pasquale Arena, 2010), and *The Palgrave Handbook of Spirituality and Business* (coedited with L. Zsolnai, 2011).

Luigino Bruni is professor at LUMSA University in Rome and serves as international coordinator of the Focolare Movement ("Economy of Communion"). His recent books include *The Wound and the Blessing: Economics, Relationships, and Happiness* (2012, New York, New City), *The Genesis and Ethos of the Market* (2012, London, Palgrave Macmillan), *In the Beginning: An Economist Reads the Book of Genesis* (2016, London, Palgrave MacMillan), and *Handbook of Research Methods and Applications in Happiness and Quality of Life* (with P. Porta, 2016, Cheltenham, Edward Elgar).

Knut J. Ims is professor in business ethics at the Department of Strategy and Management at the Norwegian School of Economics. He has a PhD from the School of Economics and Legal Science, Gothenburg University, Sweden. He is a member of the Business Ethics Faculty of the CEMS – Global Alliance in Management Education. His recent publications include *Business and the Greater Good: Rethinking Business Ethics in an Age of Crisis* (with L.J.T. Pedersen, 2015, Edward Elgar, Cheltenham, UK, Northampton, MA); "Product as Process – Commodities in Mechanic and Organic Ontology" in *Ecological Economics*, 110 (2015) pp. 11–14 (with Ove Jakobsen and L. Zsolnai); and "Deep Ecology and Personal Responsibility" in L. Zsolnai (Ed.): *The Spiritual Dimension of Business Ethics and Sustainability Management* (Springer, 2015).

Kevin T. Jackson is professor and Daniel Janssen chair at the Solvay Brussels School of Economics and Management in Brussels, Belgium. He is a scholar in international business ethics, global economic governance, and legal philosophy. His research papers have been published in Business Ethics Quarterly, Journal of Business Ethics, Brooklyn Journal of International Law, Harvard Journal of Law and Public Policy, and Law and Philosophy. His Charting Global Responsibilities: Legal Philosophy and Human Rights (University Press of America, 1994) was presented as a gift to His Holiness the Dalai Lama by the US State Department.

François Lépineux is professor at Rennes School of Business, France. After graduating from HEC Paris School of Management in 1990, he has carried on various research and consulting activities. He received his PhD in management science at the Conservatoire National des Arts et Métiers (CNAM) in Paris. He has coedited two books with Professor Henri-Claude de Bettignies: *Finance for a Better World: The Shift Toward Sustainability* (2009. London, Palgrave Macmillan) and *Business, Globalization and the Common Good* (2009. Oxford, Peter Lang Academic Publishers).

David W. Miller is director of the Princeton University Faith and Work Initiative. He also serves as president of the Avodah Institute. Before joining Princeton, his previous appointment was at Yale University, where he served as the executive director of the Yale Center for Faith and Culture and taught at both the Divinity School and School of Management of Yale University. David Miller brings an unusual "bilingual" perspective to the corporate world and the academia. Before receiving his PhD in ethics, he spent 16 years in senior executive positions in international business and finance. He is the author of *God at Work: The History and Promise of the Faith at Work Movement* (2006, Oxford University Press). Alongside his work at Princeton, David serves as an advisor to CEOs and senior executives in matters pertaining to ethics, values, leadership, and faith at work.

Hendrik Opdebeeck is professor of philosophy at the University of Antwerp (Belgium) where he is affiliated with the Centre for Ethics. He studied philosophy and economics at the universities of Leuven and Ghent where he obtained a PhD with a dissertation on E.F. Schumacher. His research interest is focused on the cultural-philosophical backgrounds and effects of globalization. Opdebeeck is member of the Board of the European SPES Institute. His recent publications include "Responsibility in a Globalised Environment" *Journal of Global Responsibility* (2012, 3(1), p. 111–120), "The Wisdom of Mercy as the Foundation of Business and Peace" in L. Bouckaert and M. Chatterji (Eds.): *Business, Ethics and Peace* (2015, Emerald), and *The Point of Philosophy: An Introduction for the Human Sciences* (2015, Peter Lang, Brussels).

Jean-Jacques Rosé is researcher at the Norbert Elias Center, EHESS – CNRS, Marseille, France. He is a former associate professor at Paris-Sorbonne University and former CEO of ID FORCE – FCA communications consulting. He is now vice-president of the Association for the Development of Education and Research on Corporate Social Responsibility (ADERSE). He is particularly interested in the application of lexical analysis methods to business ethics, corporate social responsibility, and sustainable development literatures.

Michael J. Thate is research associate at the Faith and Work Initiative, Princeton University. Prior to coming to Princeton, he was a lecturer of New Testament Interpretation at Yale Divinity School. His research interests revolve around the formation and reception of discourses, particularly religious and scientific. His books include *Remembrance of Things Past?* (2013, Mohr Siebeck). For 2016 and 2017, he is a recent recipient of the Alexander von Humboldt fellowship in Germany.

Mike Thompson has served alongside entrepreneurs throughout his career. His business and academic career has focused on responsible leadership and corporate governance. His books are Wise Management in Organisational Complexity (edited with David Bevan, 2013) and Suited Monk Leadership (with Raf Adams, 2014). Mike Thompson is visiting professor of practice at the China Europe International Business School (CEIBS) in Shanghai and at the University of Victoria in Canada.

He serves on the boards of Good Leaders Online (GLO) and GoodBrand, the sustainable enterprise consultancy.

Antoon Vandevelde is professor at the Centre for Economics and Ethics and the Institute of Philosophy of Catholic University of Leuven, Belgium. He served as dean of the Institute of Philosophy between 2006 and 2013. Formerly, he was teaching at the University of Antwerp and Erasmus University of Rotterdam. He was guest professor at the universities of Tilburg and Nijmegen (the Netherlands), Bandung (Indonesia), and Stellenbosch (South Africa) and at the Université Nationale du Rwanda. He published many articles, mainly in the field of economic ethics and political philosophy, for instance, about philosophy of social security, migration policy, responsibility for future generations, altruism and the logic of the gift, liberalism, and communitarianism. His books include *Is Inheritance Legitimate?: Ethical and Economic Aspects of Wealth Transfers* (with G. Erreygers, 1997, Springer), *Gifts and Interests* (2000, Peeters), *Autonomy & Paternalism: Reflections on the Theory and Practice of Health Care* (with Th. Nys and Y. Denier, 2007, Peeters), and *Justice, Luck & Responsibility in Health Care* (with Y. Denier and C. Gastmans, 2013, Springer).

Johan Verstraeten is professor of social ethics at the Faculty of Theology and Religious Studies, Catholic University of Leuven (Belgium), where he is coordinator of the Research Unit Theological and Comparative Ethics. He teaches Christian social and political ethics, ethics of peace, war and international relations, business ethics, leadership, and spirituality. He was extraordinary professor of business ethics at the Tilburg University from 1995 to 1997. His recent publications include "Spirituality as Source of Inspired, Authentic and Innovative Leadership" in P. Nullens and J. Barentsen (Eds.): *Leadership, Innovation, and Spirituality* (2014, Peeters, pp. 81–97) and Language and Silence. Towards Leadership Without Fear (in Dutch, 2014, Averbode).

Stefano Zamagni graduated from Catholic University of the Sacred Heart in Milan in 1966. He received his PhD from the University of Oxford. From 1973 to 1979, he was a professor at the University of Parma. Since 1979, he has been a professor at the University of Bologna. His additional activities involved include serving as a visiting professor at Bocconi University (Milan) since 1985 and as an adjunct professor at Johns Hopkins University (Bologna Center) since 1983. Zamagni is the author of several books, including *History of Economic Thought* (1995 and 2005); *Living in the Global Society* (1997); *Non-profit as Civil Economy* (1998); *Economics: A European Text* (2002); *Multiculturalism and Identity* (2002); *Relational Complexity and Economic Behavior* (2002); *The Italian Non-profit at the Crossroad* (2002); *Civil Economy* (2004); *A Civil Economic Theory of Cooperative Firm* (2005); *Markets, Money and History: Essays in Honor of Sir John Hicks* (with R. Scazzieri and A. Sen, 2008); and *Dictionary of Civil Economy* (with L. Bruni, 2009).

Part I
Introduction

Chapter 1
Why Economics Is a Moral Science

Peter Rona

Abstract The paper argues that the attempt to relocate economics from the domain of the moral sciences to one closer to that of the natural sciences necessarily meant that free will, intentionality and moral judgment were excluded from its purview. However, the resulting surrogate reality has proven to be less than satisfactory because economic life is simultaneously about what should be as well as what is. Because economic life is lived with a purpose in mind, economic 'facts' are interwoven with intentionality.

Attempts to reconstruct economics as a moral science show how utility calculations and moral considerations co-determine the behavior of economic agents, and throw light on the deep connection between virtue ethics and all levels of economic activity as well as the deleterious consequences when that connection is impaired or severed.

"Moral sciences" as a designation of a field of inquiry came into widespread usage following the Scottish Enlightenment, reached the peak of its popularity during the last third of the nineteenth century, and – despite the important efforts of John Maynard Keynes and Kenneth Boulding among others to revive it – the term, together with the concept behind it virtually disappeared by the middle of the 20th. Limited interest in its meaning resurfaced only in the last decade or so. This collection of essays is concerned with reconsidering economics as a moral science in place of its present configuration as a particular form of applied mathematics.

Despite the frequent use of the term, the precise scope and meaning of moral science had not been given much systematic attention. In its early career it tended to echo the distinction between natural and moral philosophy, and to rely on the generally accepted contrast between corporeal and incorporeal reality with the moral sciences occupying the latter domain. However, the curriculum actually specified for the tripos in Moral Sciences at Cambridge University provides a fair picture of the scope and content of this subject, and, perhaps more significantly, places economics as the object of inquiry in a context it has lost upon gaining its status as an

P. Rona (✉)
Blackfriars Hall, University of Oxford, Oxford, UK
e-mail: pzrona@gmail.com

P. Rona, L. Zsolnai (eds.), *Economics as a Moral Science*,
Virtues and Economics 1, DOI 10.1007/978-3-319-53291-2_1

autonomous discipline. The revival of interest in economics as a moral science may be due to the pervasive sense that, as an autonomous science, economics has helped create an unsatisfactory and unjust world despite its contribution to the dramatic betterment of the material existence of many. It has brought about an unwelcome change in the very nature of human existence as it has coerced us to change who we are and who we would like to be in order to conform to its ill-conceived ideals of economic rationality, built on a diminished, severely reductionist notion of our humanity. The scientism of modern economics, it is felt by many, rests on a mistaken conception of the subject matter of this discipline. In sharp contrast with the claims of leading economists, economics is seen as inherently not about what is, but, rather, what ought to be, and its pretence to 'objectivity' as just a smokescreen for the advancement of an agenda. In what way is the subject matter of modern economics misconceived?

The hallmark of the natural sciences is the ability to measure the object under study with methods and devices that are both constant and independent of that object. The natural sciences concern themselves with objects that exist independently of human thought. But economics, unlike the natural sciences, does not have an ontologically objective subject, because economic life, unlike matter, is the product of human intentionality. The objects of economics, such as 'employment', 'interest', 'money', 'utility', 'supply', or 'demand' like the object or purpose of economic activity – the production of monetarily measurable value, in short, exchange value – are objects of thought that come into being through language and perception that posits them as its objects. The tool-based language of modern economics, expressed in the form of models, – notwithstanding the claim to the contrary – constitutes the reality that is its object and does not represent some objective reality outside it; a clear distinction between theory and its subject cannot be drawn because the subject is the product of theory. Lionel Robbins' definition of economics as the "science which studies human behavior as a relationship between ends and scarce means which have alternative uses"[1] fails to meet the minimal requirements of a science because 'ends' and 'scarce means' are socially constructed objects with a purpose. They do not exist outside language. To borrow Thomas Hobbes' brilliant phrase, they are "made with words"[2] and, as such, are inherently purposeful. Physical objects, such as the chemists' elements, do not have a purpose, an end, a telos. The purpose with which they may be endowed, the use to which they are put is not a property of these elements. The difference between physical objects and the incorporeal, socially constructed objects of economics was noted by Keynes in his famous letter to Roy Harrod:

> In chemistry and physics and other natural sciences the object of experiment is to fill in the actual values of the various quantities and factors appearing in an equation or a formula; and the work when done is once and for all. In economics that is not the case, and to convert a model into a quantitative formula is to destroy its usefulness as an instrument of thought...

[1] Robbins, L. "An Essay on the Nature and Significance of Economic Science" p. 15.

[2] The phrase in the title of Philip Pettit"s important book, *Made with Words, Hobbes on Language, Mind and Politics* (2008) Princeton University Press.

> I also want to emphasize strongly the point about economics being a moral science. I mentioned before that it deals with introspection and with values. I might have added that it deals with motives, expectations, psychological uncertainties. One has to be constantly on guard against treating the material as constant and homogeneous in the same way that the material of the other sciences, in spite of its complexity, is constant and homogeneous. It is as though the fall of the apple to the ground depended on the apple's motives, on whether it is worth while falling to the ground, and whether the ground wanted the apple to fall...[3]

In interpreting this passage, the question is whether economics for Keynes was still an apple except that, unlike Newton's, it has motives, that, following Mill, can be regarded as "disturbing causes", or, to the contrary, the analogy with the apple does not hold at all because economic actors, unlike apples, act pursuant to a conscious purpose. Keynes' ambiguity is the fundamental dilemma of modern economics. To pretend that its objects are like apples "the actual values of the various quantities and factors (of which) can be filled in an equation or a formula" is a conceit that puts an end to the sort of thinking the subject requires. But to take the other road, and acknowledge that there are no apples in economics would terminate the quest for scientific status. The history of economic thought from the early part of the nineteenth century has been the history of the attempt to reify the stuff of economic life, to turn intentionality into an object that can be measured and quantified. The idea that economics has some sort of a hard core factual domain capable of being freed from the subjectivity of the economic actor and expressible in the language of mathematics, to which ethical precepts are nothing more than optional add-ons has been with us at least since Helvetius and it is the axiom driving John Stuart Mill's thought, who expressed the point as follows:

> If there are some subjects on which the results obtained have finally received the unanimous assent of all who have attended to the proof, and others on which mankind have not yet been equally successful; on which the most sagacious minds have occupied themselves from the earliest date, and have never succeeded in establishing any considerable body of truths, so as to go beyond denial and doubt; it is by generalizing the methods successfully followed in the former enquiries and adapting them to the latter, that we may hope to remove this blot on the face of science.

This line of thought was carried to its logical conclusion by Leon Walras:

> ...the pure theory of economics is a science which resembles the physico-mathematical sciences in every respect... the physico-mathematical sciences, like the mathematical sciences, in the narrow sense, do go beyond experience as soon as they have drawn their type concepts from it. From real-type concepts, these sciences abstract ideal-type concepts which they define, and on the basis of these definitions they construct a priori the whole framework of their theorems and proofs... the pure theory of economics ought to take over from experience certain type concepts, like those of exchange, supply, demand, market, capital, income, productive services and products. From these real-type concepts the pure science of economics should abstract and define idea-type concepts in terms of which it carries on its reasoning. The return to reality should not take place until the science is completed and then only with a view to practical applications. Thus, in an ideal market we have ideal prices which stand in exact relation to an ideal demand and supply...

---

[3] Letter to Roy Harrod, of 10 July, 1938 (misdated 16 July) in *Collected Letters of John Meynard Keynes*.

Remarkably, he adds:

> After that they (the scientists) go back to experience not to confirm it, but to apply their conclusions.[4]

Economics then is not a science dedicated to the study of a reality independent of it, but, rather, a scheme for crafting human behavior to accord with a predetermined, axiomatic criterion.

The search for the common element of wealth among its innumerable forms – ranging from land, art objects, stocks, bonds, cash, intellectual property to precious metals – has not been successful because value is not a property of any of these objects in the sense the valance of an element is the property of that element. Their respective values are socially constructed separately and distinctly from each other. It may be said that the value of a plot of land is dependent on the use to which it is put, but that use is a social construction that changes with the ceaseless reconstruction of social reality. Not surprisingly, unlike physicists, chemists and biologists, economists do not employ measuring instruments because none can be fashioned for the measurement of any reality with which economists are concerned. Measuring instruments cannot be devised for phenomena consisting of incommensurable components, and where, to make matters even more difficult, these incommensurate components are highly reflexive. Reflexivity in economics is compounded because the variables of economic events affect each other through the agency of human beings, who are both the objects and the subjects of those events.[5] Economic phenomena are always necessarily incommensurate because they occur in historical time and space. Reflexivity reinforces their incommensurability, because the effects of reflexivity are unlikely to be the same at different points in time or space. If, for example, labor is measured in units of man-hours, in what units should capital be measured so as to make any mathematical representation of the two in, for example, an equation meaningful and empirically truthful? So, when economists write, as they do:

$$O = f(L,C)$$

where L is the quantity of labor, C the quantity of capital and O is the rate of output, what is the unit of L and the unit of C such that the combination of the two can give us a meaningful and truthful O?[6] What is that C, that may be represented by a number? The original paid-in capital, market capitalization, break-up value, etc. and on what day of the week are we to undertake its measurement? Accordingly, it is a

---

[4] Walras, L. (1926) *Elements d'Economie Politique Pure ou Theorie de la richesse sociale* translated as Elements of Pure Economics or the Theory of Social Wealth (1954) George Allen and Unwin Ltd., London, p. 71.

[5] For a detailed explanation of the concept of reflexivity and the causal circularity it generates, see Soros, G. (1987) *The Alchemy of Finance,* Wiley.

[6] The question was first raised by Joan Robinson in her essay "What is Capital?" Solow's answer – that capital can be defined in service hours – as Solow himself subsequently acknowledged –, does not work.

conceit to assume that the techniques available and appropriate for the natural sciences are appropriate for an understanding of intentional, purposeful human behavior. Those techniques are crafted to be applied to an ontologically independent object. Economics seeks scientific status through the construction of a surrogate reality consisting of objects that are produced through a process of reification, in short, on the basis of objects made with words. But the theoretical knowledge constructed with this strategy, – employed by corporations and policy makers – is at odds with the practical knowledge with which people make their economic decisions. The result is an unsustainable tension between the behavior prescribed by corporate and political policy makers and the every day morality of human beings. In the name of the overriding superiority of theoretical over practical knowledge, modern economic theory has therefore forced a paradigm on society that is at odds with how people make decisions about their material needs in line with their conscience. What then is the difference between theoretical and practical knowledge, and to which of the two does the stuff of economics belong?

Practical knowledge[7] is the human capacity for the reflective and critical evaluation of our reasons for action. It is the totality of all of our capacities – including feelings, tastes, knowledge, experience, impulses and rational reasoning – ordered and filtered by our ability to critically evaluate these sources of our lives we engage and deploy in making decisions. It is, in short, the knowledge we deploy when deciding what is to be done. Theoretical knowledge, in contrast, disconnects these sources, and, instead, gains knowledge of objects and phenomena that exist and function independently of human intention. The objects of practical knowledge are profoundly different from the objects of theoretical knowledge. It may be true, as Hilary Putnam has it,[8] that the rigid separation of fact from value has become untenable,[9] but the collapse of that distinction does not diminish the difference between theoretical and practical knowledge. As Putnam himself recognizes:

> I think that Aristotle was profoundly right in holding that ethics is concerned with how to live and with human happiness, and also profoundly right in holding that this sort of knowledge ('practical knowledge') is different from theoretical knowledge. A view of knowledge that acknowledges that the sphere of knowledge is wider than the sphere of 'science' seems to me to be a cultural necessity if we are to arrive at a sane and human view of ourselves or of science.

Modern economic theory, a deeply positivist discipline, regards practical knowledge – if it regards it as any sort of knowledge at all – as exogenous to its concerns, as a form of knowledge that may perhaps exist prior to the formation of economic

---

[7] The terms 'practical knowledge' and 'practical reason' are largely interchangeable, although Aristotelian and Thomist inspired thought tends to use the former, while Kantians seem to prefer the latter. The former tends to base practical knowledge on internal normativity as a given human capacity, while the latter places greater emphasis on the connection between 'practical reason' and rationality.

[8] Putnam, H *The Collapse of the Fact/Value Dichotomy.*

[9] For a contrary view see, for example, Kincaid, H. (1996) *Philosophical Foundations of the Social Sciences,* Cambridge University Press.

objects, such as preferences. It posits preferences as objects capable of ordinal ordering, and, as such, separable from what went into their formation. But preferences have no intelligible meaning if deprived of the intentionality and the purpose with which they are formed. Goods can be ordered ordinally only if they are commensurable on some common basis, and they can be rendered commensurable only by eliminating the intentionality inherent in any choice. In real life there are no Pareto optimal outcomes because the objects without inherent intentionality with respect to which such outcome can be determined do not exist. Mill's famous axiom to the effect that 'a greater gain is preferred to a lesser one' is, at heart, a tautology, one that is true if and only if the greater and the lesser gain both consist of material that is, in Keynes' words, 'constant and homogeneous', and if and only if the context in which they are commensured is constant and identical. The 'greater', in other words, must be of the same stuff as the 'lesser' and must not contain, in Mill's own words, 'disturbing causes'. But the objects of economics, given that they do not exist in nature, are necessarily 'caused' by human intentionality, and it is economic theory, rather than some intrinsic property of the object, that determines which causes should be deemed 'disturbing'. If either one of these requirements is not met, if, for example, the greater gain entails a lesser honor (e.g. because it is obtained with dishonest intent) and the lesser gain a greater honor, the preference for the former cannot be formed on Mill's quantitative basis.

Virtually all of the debate about the ethical content of economic life and the objects of economics, – constructed so as to permit a claim of scientific status for the discipline – has been epistemological, and has disregarded the ontological characteristics of the objects under study. Modern economics has assumed that its objects are ontologically objective, but this assumption is unwarranted, and the problem is much more serious than the epistemological fact/value dichotomy. Economics cannot be the subject of theoretical knowledge, because, whichever definition one chooses from among the many on offer, its objects are mind-dependent, ontologically subjective contrivances; it is necessarily about what should be done, and, as such, it is a form of practical knowledge.

The essays in this book reassess the domain of economics from a range of perspectives with a view to showing, that economics is indeed a moral science. The cost of divorcing the discipline from practical knowledge is that economic events and decisions are deprived of all moral meaning. The consequence of this violence, at best, is that the decisions taken along the lines prescribed by theory are amoral, at worst, that they are very bad decisions with serious consequences. With the cultivation of this end, economists take on the words given to Werhner von Braun in the Harvard mathematician and part-time song writer Tom Lehrer's song about the great German scientist:

> Once the rockets are up,
> Who cares where they come down,
> That's not my department,
> Says Wernher von Braun.

Whether one prefers Lehrer's mordant humor or the profound wisdom of Pope Francis' *Evangelii Gaudium* (in particular paragraphs 55, 62 and 206), the fundamental point – namely that *all* human deeds have an irreducible and inalienable moral content – remains constant. Morality is not something we add to a model constructed without it; one built without morality as its integral component is an unsound structure. Restoring economics to its former habitat as a moral science, a science of practical knowledge, cannot be evaded.

Chapter 2
Issues and Themes in Moral Economics

Laszlo Zsolnai

Abstract This chapter summarizes the main issues and themes of the book and shows its contributions to the development of moral economics.

Zamagni suggests that we can harness market interactions by re-defining the market in a non-individualistic way, as a network of mutually beneficial relations, along the lines suggested by the civil economy paradigm. Bouckaert underlines that thinking of economics as a relational dynamic opens a space for human creativity without losing the embeddedness in a system of meaning and purpose.

Following Amartya Sen economic reason can be understood as reasonableness of preferences, choices and actions. Zsolnai argues that reason requires that economic activities are achieved in ecological, future-respecting and pro-social ways. But Peter Rona warns that the corporation was born as the device for severing the unity between the act and responsibility. He concludes that positivist economic theory, when combined with the function performed by the corporate veil destroys the unity between the action, the actor and the moral responsibility for the action with the result that the corporation must do without the basis for a morally authentic life. Helen Alford suggests that economics needs to be more reflective about its underlying ideas. Whereas the tradition of jurisprudence is well established in the legal field, economics has no equivalent tradition of self reflection.

Following the tradition represented by Kenneth Boulding (1969), Amartya Sen (1987), Amitai Etzioni (1988), Daly and Cobb (1989), Atkinson (2009) and more recently DeMartino and McCloskey (2016) this book constitutes a manifesto for reclaiming economics as a moral science.

This chapter summarizes the main issues and themes of the book and shows its contributions to the development of moral economics.

In his paper "Economics as if Ethics Mattered" Stefano Zamagni (University of Bologna) states that mainstream economics is founded on the paradigm of axiological individualism according to which economic actions originate from subjects

L. Zsolnai (✉)
Corvinus University of Budapest, Budapest, Hungary

European SPES Institute, Leuven, Belgium
e-mail: zsolnai@uni-corvinus.hu

P. Rona, L. Zsolnai (eds.), *Economics as a Moral Science*,
Virtues and Economics 1, DOI 10.1007/978-3-319-53291-2_2

whose features and purposes are those of the utility maximizing Homo oeconomicus. This stance makes it conceptually impossible for the economic-scientific discourse to meet with ethics. Zamagni suggests that we can harness market interactions by re-defining the market in a non-individualistic way, as a network of mutually beneficial relations, along the lines suggested by the civil economy paradigm.

Zamagni argues that virtue ethics has the capacity to resolve the opposition between self-interest and interest for others, by moving beyond it. The virtuous life is good not only for others but also for the actor. Zamagni warns that there are cases when the conscious pursuit of one's self-interest is incompatible with its attainment. In several instances a seemingly "irrational" response based on the principle of reciprocity leads to better results than the one conforming to the canons of the exchange of equivalents paradigm. This paradox is the opposite of the one exemplified by the Invisible Hand.

Zamagni believes that the discipline of economics needs the relational perspective. A relation of reciprocity considers the force of "between" as Buber (2000) suggests. In economics this is captured by the concept of relational good. It is urgent to abandon the assumption of homogeneous motivation for all economic agents. The economic world is inhabited by a plurality of types of subjects: some are anti-social (the envious or the malicious) while others are pro-social (who act with the public interest in mind). The personal dispositions of agents matters. Gift as gratuitousness always counterposes its logic of overabundance to that of equivalence, typical of contracts.

Zamagni refers to Akerlof and Kranton (2000) who emphasize the importance of identity in economic interactions. Identity means to recognize oneself and be recognized. The self-recognition dimension implies self-knowledge, the memory of oneself and one"s own experience of life; the dimension of being recognized recalls the need of every person to be inserted in a network of relations facilitating self knowledge thanks to information provided by those with whom the person interacts.

Zamagni underlines that reciprocity occupies the intermediate position between exchanges and pure altruism. With Kolm (2000) he suggests an understanding of reciprocity as a series of bi-directional transfers, independent of each other and at the same time interconnected. Independence implies that each transfer is voluntary, i.e. there is no external obligation capable of acting on the mind of the agent. In reciprocity there is much more freedom than in the market exchange where the transfer in one direction becomes obligatory by the transfer in the opposite direction. The bi-directionality of the transfers characterizing reciprocity is what differentiates it from pure altruism, which consists in one-directional transfers. Zamagni argues that reciprocity is important because it can stabilize pro-social behavior and/or modify endogenously the preference orderings of the agents.

In his paper "Teleological Reasoning in Economics" Luk Bouckaert (Catholic University of Leuven) recalls Aristotle's Politics as the prime example of the teleological approach to economics. Aristotle defines economics as the art of creating the material and social conditions for the survival of the *oikos* or household. Simultaneously, Aristotle integrates economics in a social matrix that subordinates economics to politics and ethics.

Bouckaert notes that modern economics is anti-Aristotelian and anti-teleological. Modern economic actors are supposed to be driven by autonomous preferences and free choices. The market functions as an equilibrium mechanism that promotes welfare for everyone in an unintended way. Adam Smith interpreted this effect of the market as the 'Invisible Hand'.

In his paper Bouckaert explores how a personalist approach to economics can overcome some of the failures of modern economics. Thinking of economics as a relational dynamic opens a space for human creativity without losing the embeddedness in a system of meaning and purpose.

In his paper "Economic Rationality versus Human Reason" Laszlo Zsolnai (Corvinus University of Budapest and European SPES Institute, Leuven) analyses the rationality assumptions of mainstream economics and shows that they are empirically misleading and normatively inadequate. He argues that the world ruled by self-interest based rationality leads to 'unreason' from a wider ecological and human perspective.

Amartya Sen (2004) suggests that economic reason can be understood as reasonableness of preferences, choices and actions. Zsolnai argues that reason requires that economic activities are achieved in ecological, future-respecting and pro-social ways. Intrinsically motivatedeconomic agents who balance their attention and concerns across diverse value-dimensions are able to do this. Organic agriculture, the Slow Food movement, ethical fashion, fair trade initiatives and ethical banking show the viability of true economic reason under the circumstances of present day "rationally foolish" economic world.

In his paper "Rediscovering Personalism for Economics" Hendrik Opdebeeck (University of Antwerp) suggests that we can rediscover the personalist philosophy in searching for new models for business and economic actions. At the core of Jacques Maritain's "Humanisme intégral" (1936) is the idea that man is a person who is spiritual in nature, endowed with free will, and thus autonomous in relation to the world.

For Maritain the community is central: the true goal of the temporal order is thus more than the mere tallying up of individual needs. It concerns the good life of the entire community—the common good or *bonum commune*. But the temporal *bonum commune* is not the ultimate goal, as it is subordinated to what transcends temporal-welfare —the attainment of freedom and spiritual perfection of the human person.

In his paper "Happiness and Human Flourishing" Knut J. Ims (Norwegian School of Economics – Bergen) explores the concept of human flourishing drawing on two traditions, the Aristotelian–Thomistic virtue ethics tradition and the new research tradition of positive psychology. These traditions may seem very different in origin, but they have some fundamental similarities. Martin Seligman, one of the founders of positive psychology has summed up human flourishing using the acronym PERMA, where each letter indicate one element; **P**ositive emotions, **E**ngagements, **R**elationship, **M**eaning and **A**ccomplishment. Seligman emphasizes the problems of hedonic pleasure and "happyology" in describing human flourishing.

Knut Ims concludes that the Aristotelian and Thomistic ethics capture the dyadic aspects of human wellbeing: the wellbeing that people experience as they live their lives, and the judgment they make when they evaluate their life. Both employ a virtue ethical perspective, which means that they are concerned about the importance of good character and how to build good characters as part of living in a good society.

"Understanding Financial Crises: The Contribution of the Philosophy of Money" Toon Vandevelde (Catholic University of Leuven) remind us that the origin of money lies more in the religious and legal sphere than in the economic realm. Money was used in the exchange between men and goods and in order to compensate for manslaughter, rather than for facilitating the satisfaction of material needs. 'Vergelding', the conversion of guilt into debt was a means to prevent revenge and violence. But soon unease cropped up: the possibility to express everything that is valuable in monetary terms was felt as a form of violence against the soul of men and things.

Aristotle has tried to fit money in a teleological view of the world, but he was faced with the ambivalence of money. Money was deemed to be good as a unit for calculation and as a means of exchange, but it was distrusted as a astore of value. However, Vandevelde argues that it is impossible to separate the three functions of money, as many utopian reformers of the monetary order have tried to do.

Toon Vandevelde underlines that nowadays we experience the violent potential of money in the coercion to pay back our debts. Debts have to be repaid, otherwise the debtor will be destroyed as an autonomous subject. The conflict between various categories of debtors and creditors is the most prominent form of "class struggle" we face in our society. It is also a clash between various conceptions of distributive justice.

In his paper "Economics and Vulnerability: Relationships, Incentives, and Meritocracy" Luigino Bruni (Lumsa University – Rome) warns that a significant body of philosophical work in virtue ethics is associated with a critique of the market economy and economics. The market depends on instrumental rationality and extrinsic motivation; market interactions therefore fail to respect the internal value of human practices and the intrinsic motivations of human actors. By using market exchange as a central model, mainstream economics normalizes extrinsic motivation, not only in markets but also in social life more generally; therefore economics appears as an assault on virtues and on human flourishing.

Luigino Bruni argues that this critique is flawed, both as a description of how markets actually work and as a representation of how classical and neoclassical economists have understood the market. He shows how the market and economics can be defended against the traditional critique from virtue ethics, and crucially, this defense is constructed using the language and logic of virtue ethics. Bruni proposes an understanding of the purpose ("telos") of markets as cooperation for mutual benefit, and identifies traits that count as virtues for market participants. His conclusion is that the market need not be seen as a virtue-free zone.

In his paper "Ethics, Economics and the Corporation" Peter Rona (Blackfriars Hall, University of Oxford) argues that the corporation was born as the device for severing the unity between the act and responsibility. Henceforth responsibility is coterminous with legal liability or the management of competing interests among shareholders and other stakeholders. He examines the philosophical foundations of this paradigmatic change and concludes that positivist economic theory, when combined with the function performed by the corporate veil – in effect the institutional device for the removal of ethical considerations from economic decision making apart from those embodied in legally binding norms – destroys the unity between the action, the actor and the moral responsibility for the action with the result that the corporation must do without the basis for a morally authentic life.

In their paper "Are Business Ethics Relevant?" David W. Miller and Michael J. Thate (Princeton University) notice that the relevance of business ethics can be a question of utility, which considers profits, cultural concerns, and social capital regarding organizational health. But there are underlying suspicions regarding the relevance of business ethics. First, in corporate contexts, "ethics" is often conflated with compliance, and becomes the domain of compliance and risk management. Miller and Thate's point is not to disparage compliance officers or their departments. Rather, the point is that there are limits of assigning "ethics" and the valuation of actions as "ethical" to a place or office within corporate contexts. Such approaches will necessarily be reactive to and driven by law, code, and policy.

Another suspicion concerns the relevance of one's personal ethics within what Miller and Thate refer to as an "ethical field." The ethical field is where diverse ethical agents, with differing ethical contexts and convictions, inhabit space. The effect and influence of one's ethical actions or convictions depends on where one lives within a given ethical field. This field approach to ethics stresses that an agent's ethical actions and convictions are enmeshed within social relations. And, of course, power relations within any given field are always asymmetrical.

Miller and Thate emphasize that religious ideas can help shape and inform the ethics of peoples and business cultures. Attentiveness to that is an impactful way to engage business school students and business people to think afresh about ethics as character and culture. Thinking about ethics through the lenses of the "Right", the "Good", and the "Fitting" can help guide people through ethical grey zones, informing them toward richer and wiser ethical decisions.

In his paper "Economy of Mutuality" Kevin Jackson (Solvay Brussels School of Economics and Management) posits the concept of economy of mutuality as a mediation space for shifts in emphasis between market and social structures. He develops a triad of business archetypes. In each archetype, alternative emphasis goes to elements of profitability and financial independence on the one hand, and poverty alleviation and solidarity on the other.

Archetype 1: Business enterprises conducted primarily as for-profit institutions to the end of financial sustainability. Financial self-reliance is a precondition of a firm's survival and for remaining capable of continuously expanding products or services to new clientele. Archetype 2: The social and financial missions of business enterprises are merged; a coordination of social and financial functions is at the heart of the "promise" of the company as a sustainable enterprise. Archetype 3:

Businesses are run with principal allegiance to social missions – outreach to the poor, environmental rectitude, and other facets of sustainability.

Jackson argues that the trio of archetypes also serves as alternative teleological exemplars of the purpose and nature of business. Archetype 1 presupposes the essence of business as profit maximization. Under Archetype 2, business is a means for creating varieties of value for a broad range of stakeholders. For Archetype 3, the purpose of business is serving the common good, with profits secondary and derivative.

In his paper "Economic Wisdom for Managerial Decision-Making" Mike Thompson (GoodBrand, London, CEIBS Shanghai and University of Victoria, Canada) argues that Aristotle's "phronesis" can be explained as social practice wisdom, a discursive system linking mind and social practice to produce wellbeing and human flourishing. Mike Thompson uses the contemporary conceptualization of phronesis and its related metatheoretical construct of wisdom principles to bring a practical dimension to wise decision-making.

The chapter first reviews progress in the understanding of wise leadership within leadership studies and the principles of wisdom proposed by McKenna et al. (2009). Against this taxonomy it then recontextualizes the numerous calls in leadership literature for qualitative, research. It presents samples and interprets the resulting theory based in original material from interviews with 184 managers generated by the Wisdom Project.

Michael Thompson concludes that an economic wisdom is present in the minds of managers. Economic wisdom could offer resources for management education and development across all business domains to address the challenges of the VUCA world with a more realistic, holistic and planet-friendly approach.

In his paper "Catholic Social Thought and Amartya Sen on Justice" Johan Verstraeten (Catholic University of Leuven) states that Sen's (2009) "Idea of Justice" is not only the most inspiring and reasonable response to Rawls' (1971) "Theory of Justice" but also an important challenge for Catholic Social Thought. Verstraten underlines that Catholic Social Thought and Sen's Idea of Justice have much in common.

Verstraten argues that despite the emphasis on individual freedom in Sen's capability approach, the convergence between his approach and Catholic Social Thought is strong. Verstraten articulates several points of resemblance: the role of indignation and emotion, the implications of a realistic anthropology ("seeking institutions that promote justice rather than institutions as themselves manifestations of justice"), freedom as responsibility, human rights as rooted in our shared humanity, valuing religious wisdom in justice theory.

In her paper "Charity and Money: Reflections on Caritas in veritate" Helen Alford (Pontifical University of St. Thomas Aquinas – "Angelicum", Rome) addresses the problem of charity as a theological virtue in relation to money. She uses "Caritas in veritate" (Benedict XVI, 2009) as a basic reference. The central message of the encyclical is as follows: "In order to defeat underdevelopment, action is required not only on improving exchange-based transactions and implanting public welfare structures, but above all on gradually increasing openness, in a world context, to forms of economic activity marked by quotas of gratuitousness and communion." In line with this reasoning Helen Alford warns that three aspects of development should be considered: "exchange-based transactions", "public welfare structures" and "quotas of gratuitousness and communion".

"Caritas in veritate" places man before the astonishing experience of gift. Gratuitousness is present in our lives in many different forms, which often go unrecognized because of a purely consumerist and utilitarian view of life. The human being is made for gift, which expresses and makes present his transcendent dimension. Helen Alford recalls that today we tend to ignore the gratuitous dimension of human life; we think we can sort out our own problems without reference to the transcendent. The cause of this is very definitely identified in the encyclical as sin, and original sin in particular. As a result, we deprive ourselves of hope.

Helen Alford concludes that economics needs to be more reflective about its underlying ideas. Whereas the tradition of jurisprudence is well established in the legal field, economics has no equivalent tradition of self reflection. But this is gradually changing. In "Caritas in veritate", however, we are challenged to go further than philosophy, to see what light theological reflection can throw on economics.

In his paper "The Ethics of Development in the Age of Globalization" Zsolt Boda (Institute of Political Science, Hungarian Academy of Sciences and Corvinus University of Budapest) employs the ideas of Goulet (1995) that "development" is a normative and value-laden concept which refers to a multi-dimensional phenomenon. Development should include improvements of material welfare, but also of social conditions, political empowerment, the cultural foundations of self-esteem and ecological conditions.

Boda argues that despite some of its achievements the current development model fails to meet important challenges, like the environmental one. However, this is not accidental: development led by global business is unable to embody the necessary social, cultural, and environmental aspects. An ethical development requires the transformation of global business and economic regulatory rules (for instance those set by the World Trade Organization), but it also needs a complex social, political, and institutional infrastructure that can ensure the translation of the different dimensions of development into decisions and practice.

In their paper "Transdisciplinarity, Governance and the Common Good" François Lépineux. (Rennes School of Business) and Jean-Jacques Rosé (Centre Norbert Elias EHESS-CNRS, Marseille) state that humanity has entered into a stage of world unification where many issues become global and the preservation of global common goods is challenging. They argue that the era of globality calls for a complex and transdisciplinary approach. Their main argument is that multi-level governance mechanisms should be developed to preserve global common goods based on the principle of subsidiarity. The global water crisis is a crucial example of the need for developing such mechanisms.

References

Akerlof, G., and S. Kranton. 2000. Economics and Identity. *Quarterly Journal of Economics* 65 (3): 715–753.

Atkinson, A.B. 2009. Economics as a Moral Science. *Economica* 76 (Suppl 1): 791–804.

Benedict XVI, 2009. *Caritas in veritate*. Vatican City: Libreria Editrice Vaticana.

Boulding, K. 1969. Economics as a Moral Science. *American Economic Review* 59 (1969): 1–14.

Buber, M. 2000. *I and Thou*. New York: Scribner.

Daly, H., and J. Cobb. 1989. *For the Common Good. Redirecting the Economy Toward Community, the Environment, and a Sustainable Future*. Boston: Beacon Press.

DeMartino, G.E., and D.N. McCloskey, eds. 2016. *The Oxford Handbook of Professional Economic Ethics*. New York: Oxford University Press.

Etzioni, A. 1988. *The Moral Dimension*. New York: The Free Press.

Goulet, D. 1995. *Development Ethics: A Guide to Theory and Practice*. New York: Apex Pr.

Kolm, S. 2000. Introduction to the Economics of Reciprocity, Giving and Altruism. In *The Economics of Reciprocity, Giving and Altruism*, eds. L. Gerard Varet, S. Kolm, and J. Mercier Ythier. London: MacMillan.

Maritain, J. 1936. *Humanisme Intégral*. Paris: Aubier.

McKenna, B., D. Rooney, and K. Boal. 2009. Wisdom Principles as a Meta-Theoretical Basis for Evaluating Leadership. *The Leadership Quarterly* 20 (2): 177–190.

Rawls, J. 1971. *A Theory of Justice*. Cambridge, MA: Harvard University Press.

Sen, A. 1987. *On Ethics and Economics*. Oxford: Blackwell.

———. 2004. *Rationality and Freedom*. Cambridge, MA: Harvard University Press.

———. 2009. *The Idea of Justice*. London: Allen Lane.

Part II
The Moral Foundations of Economics

Chapter 3
Economics as if Ethics Mattered

Stefano Zamagni

Abstract After discussing the main reasons why the thesis of the axiological neutrality of economics is indefensible, the paper provides a thorough critique of the standard economic approach to human behavior. It then takes position in favour of the adoption of the relational paradigm in economic discourse. The paper supports the introduction of the principle of reciprocity within economic theory in order to expand its grasp on reality. Reference to the civil economy paradigm and to its salience is offered.

The paper argues that virtue ethics has the capacity to resolve the opposition between self-interest and interest for others, by moving beyond it. The virtuous life is good not only for others but also for the actor. The paper suggests that the discipline of economics needs the relational perspective. The economic world is inhabited by a plurality of types of subjects: some are anti-social (the envious or the malicious) while others are pro-social (who act with the public interest in mind). The personal dispositions of agents matters. Gift as gratuitousness always counterposes its logic of overabundance to that of equivalence, typical of contracts.

3.1 Introduction

The relationship between economics and ethics is a major issue today that calls into question the foundations of economic discourse. It is well-known that mainstream economics continues to be founded upon the paradigm of axiologic individualism according to which economic action originates from a subject whose features and purposes are those of the utility maximizing *homo oeconomicus*. This stance makes it conceptually impossible for the economic-scientific discourse to meet with that of ethics. There is an evident absence of any trace of such contact in economic literature; the economist does not feel the urge, *qua* economist to deal with the question of the relationship between her science and morality. Indeed, once the concept that values and value judgments stand only at both ends of the scientific process (the

S. Zamagni (✉)
University of Bologna, Bologna, Italy

Johns Hopkins University, SAIS Europe, Bologna, Italy
e-mail: stefano.zamagni@unibo.it

P. Rona, L. Zsolnai (eds.), *Economics as a Moral Science*,
Virtues and Economics 1, DOI 10.1007/978-3-319-53291-2_3

choice of the problems to investigate and the utilization of the results obtained) one is brought to subscribe to the "thesis of the great division", between knowing and evaluating, i.e. between truth and values. This is a widely disseminated thesis in contemporary culture whose origin is usually traced back to David Hume – a thesis denying the truth foundation of value judgments, which would simply express decisions, imperatives, at best as subjective preferences (Atkinson 2009).

Many economists today share the feeling that a radical change is necessary even though it is not clear which is the course that should be taken. It is a fact that the epistemological stances of the past have unduly restricted the ability of the economist to deal with many of the problems of his subject matter. It is time economists should realize that what is urgent for them is to free intellectual energies from unnecessary shackles. After all, giving up old illusions does not imply a desire for regression, nor a choice of nihilistic diagnoses. It simply means a recognition of the fact that results of great significance are achieved all the time from "unacceptable" positions. Moreover, economists have come to realize that the reality studied by them is not fixed like that of the natural sciences. This implies that more important than the peculiarities of the object under study are those of the scientists themselves. There is no doubt that the cultural background and the "vision" of the scientists have a strong effect on their research activities; and still more determinant are the common ideas and values accepted by the scientific community which decrees the problems to be studied, establishes the directions in which solutions should be sought and, ultimately, decides which theories are acceptable. The literature dealing with the foundations of the economic discourse in the last two decades clearly reveals how uncomfortable it is to move with a Nessus jacket on, a jacket that demands belief in the alleged neutrality of scientific knowledge. On the contrary, it is obvious to most that economic theories are no neutral tools providing knowledge about human behavior since they always somehow guide specific behavior in human beings. That is, they do not only convey the results of simulations or experiments, but are also directly or indirectly instrumental to the alteration of existing set-ups. This is why economic science cannot progress if severed from ethics.

Indeed, "progress" in science has to do with views, perspectives. Scientific theories are not discovered in the same way as an explorer discovers a new land; they are inventions of the human mind. This is why, the "view" is not merely an expository device. It is of fundamental use if the task is to understand the whole of the mountain range, not just to climb single peaks. Today, we have come to the point where even the most "abstract" of the economists cannot but admit that if we want to attack the main problems of our society – such as the endemic aggravation of inequalities, the scandal of human hunger, the emergence of new social pathologies, the clashes of identity adding to the traditional clash of interests, the paradoxes of happiness, the ecological crisis, and so on – research simply can no longer confine itself to a sort of anthropological limbo. One must take a position on the matter.

If it is true that every theory is a specific view of reality, it is impossible to theorize, without selecting a standpoint from which to scrutinize reality. Otherwise, economics will continue to advance, to enrich its technical and analytical apparatus, but if it does not escape self-referentiality it will be less and less capable of actually grasping reality. For fear of publicly endorsing a precise anthropological option, a good many economists have taken shelter in analysis, dedicating ever greater intellectual resources to the deployment of more and more sophisticated logical-mathematical instruments. But there can never be a trade-off between the formal rigor of economic discourse – which is in any case essential – and its ability to explain, to interpret economic events. We must never forget that the production of economic knowledge, while it helps to shape or modify the cognitive maps of economic actors, also acts on their propensities and their motivations, or – as Alfred Marshall preferred to say at the end of the nineteenth century – their character.

K. Boulding, in modern times, was the first to re-introduce the expression "economics as a moral science". He wrote: "We cannot escape the proposition that as science moves from pure knowledge toward control,... what it creates becomes a problem of ethical choice and will depend upon the common values of the societies in which the scientific subculture is embedded. Under these circumstances science cannot proceed at all without at least an implicit ethic" (Boulding 1969: 3).

3.2 The Indefensible Thesis of the Axiological Neutrality of Economics

The argument supporting the thesis of the ethical neutrality of economic science goes as follows: there is a sphere of social relations – those that run through the market – that need not be subjected to moral judgment since the purpose of economic activity is per se good. Economic action differs from any other kind of human action in that it escapes moral imperatives without negating them. In fact, current observation, while informing us that individuals tend to satisfy self-interested preferences, also shows that individual performances exert a positive influence upon the community even though this is not part of their intentions. How can such a harmony of individual and collective interests be achieved? Quite simply by taking for granted the identity of individual and social economic objectives. The competitive, acquisitive attitude of man is seen as a given natural feature. On the other hand, self-centered passions directed by the Smithian invisible hand necessarily attain a degree of coordination permitting the fulfillment of general interest without any need for external interventions stemming from a moral (or political) authority alien to the market.

It is therefore unnecessary to submit self-interest to superior goals since the socialization of human passions occurs through that automatic and impersonal mechanism, the competitive market, that is the offspring of a natural human inclination to the division of labor, hence to exchange.

It is generally believed that we owe to Adam Smith the first clear and explicit "demonstration" of the assertion according to which the market, as a forum in which all agents act parametrically (they take price as a datum) and atomistically (everybody only cares about him/herself), is the only institution necessary and sufficient to ensure the harmonization of individual and social purposes. However, for this harmonization to take place all those involved in the market process must conform to a definite behavioral code, the so-called code of "mercantile morality" whose main features are moral sentiments such as sympathy, trust, benevolence. In short, all that is required to achieve social harmony and the common weal is self-interested behavior, a mercantile morality code and a well organized legal system enforced by the State.

The birth of modern economic thought chiefly appears as a description of invisible hand mechanisms to which the fate of well-being and progress is entrusted. The hypothesis implicit in such a construction is that, regardless of the actual motives of economic agents, figuring the worst would produce the most robust explanation. Should we in fact assume that agents are inspired by virtues like prudence, reciprocity, benevolence, sense of solidarity, observable phenomena such as cooperation in the private provision of public goods could be explained *ex ante*. If instead we succeed in demonstrating that a satisfactory social order is achievable by self-interested and self-regarding agents, we will have supplied a truly fundamental explanation. To be sure, this is the arrival point of a long tradition of thinking. When the systematic analysis of actual market functioning was started in the seventeenth century, scholars of economic matters made as traumatic a discovery as that made by Machiavelli and Montesquieu in political thought. I am not here referring only to Mandeville's celebrated paradox of private vices which by stimulating luxury trade would produce public benefits. As early as the middle of the seventeenth century some profoundly religious French thinkers – Pascal among them, to name but the most prominent one – realized that a well-ordered society could exist and survive even without love and charity as its fundamentals. As they found out, another principle could fulfill the function of social organizer: self-interest. We all know the amount of embarrassment this discovery caused its authors, above all the alarming enigma it eventually created: since a society that is not "built" upon love is sinful, how can it so admirably perform as to make it seem as if Providence had a hand in it? (Ythier 2011).

It will take another century for Adam Smith to succeed in dispelling these anxieties. However, the way Smith's conceptualization was and is being approached by orthodox economic theory is unsatisfactory. If for example we take the celebrated Ronald Coase interpretation of the market according to which the market is more than a perfect substitute of the Smithian benevolence – in that by reaching farther than benevolence it can achieve much more than the latter – we notice that this is ultimately an aporetic interpretation. On the one hand, Coase acknowledges that to function properly a market presupposes the practice of benevolence and compliance with the code of mercantile morality by all agents; on the other hand, he maintains that market outcomes depend solely upon the self-centered interest of those acting in it. Which is tantamount to saying that for the market to exist specific virtues should be practiced, but these practices are totally irrelevant as far as the outcome of the market process is concerned: a really striking paradox. Why should rational subjects practice virtues like benevolence if the results obtained through market interaction are independent of those practices? (One should remember that unlike a scarce resource, virtue is reproduced by its use and is exhausted by its non-use). What is true, instead, is that we can choose to harness market interactions by redefining the market in a non-individualistic way, as a network of mutually beneficial relations, along the lines suggested by the civil economy paradigm (Bruni and Zamagni 2016a).

Amartya Sen argued that "economics has had two rather different origins, but related in rather different ways, concerned respectively with ethics on the one hand and what may be called 'engineering' on the other" (Sen 1987: 2) and suggested that a closer contact with the "ethics-related tradition", which "goes back at least to Aristotle" can enrich economic theorizing (Sen, A. 1987: 3). But which ethical theory is adequate to the purpose? My answer is virtue ethics, as Adam Smith, on the heels of the line of thought inaugurated by the civil humanists in the fifteenth century, elaborated in his fundamental work *The Theory Moral Sentiments* (1759). The institutional structure of society – says Smith – must favor the dissemination among citizens of the civic virtues. If economic agents don't already embody in their structure of preferences those values that they are supposed to respect, there isn't much to be done. For virtue ethics , in fact, the enforceability of the norms depends, in the first place, on the moral constitution of individuals; that is of their internal motivational structure, much before any system of exogenous enforcement. It is because there are stakeholders that have ethical preferences – that attribute, that is, value the fact that the firm practices fairness and works for the dignity of people *independently* of the material advantage that can be derived – that the ethical code could be respected *also* in the absence of the mechanism of reputation. And that there are subjects endowed with ethical preferences is, today, a fact documented by a dispassionate observation of reality, in addition to experimental research.

The point worth highlighting in particular is that the key to virtue ethics is in its capacity to resolve the opposition between self-interest and interest for others, between egoism and altruism, by moving beyond it. It is this opposition, child of the individualistic tradition of thought, that prevents us from grasping that which constitutes our own wellbeing. The virtuous life is the best not only for others – like the various economic theories of altruism would have it – but also for us. This is the real significance of the notion of common good, which can never be reduced to a mere sum-total of individual wellbeings. Instead, the common good is the good of being in common. That is, the good of being inserted into a structure of common action, which is exactly what is required in order to sustain nature.

A common action is one characterized by three elements. The first is that it cannot be concluded without all those who take part being conscious of what they are doing. The mere coming together or meeting of many individuals is not enough. The second element is that each participant in the common action must retain title, and therefore responsibility, for that which he does. It is exactly this element that differentiates common action from collective action. In the latter, in fact, the individual's identity disappears and with him disappears also personal responsibility for that which he does. The third element is the unification of the efforts on the part of the participants in the common action for the achievement of the same objective. The interaction among many subjects in a given context is not yet common activity if they follow diverse or conflicting objectives (For an elaboration, see Zamagni 2015).

The specific value that virtue ethics offers, is that of liberating us from the obsessive Platonic idea of good, an idea that says there is an a priori good from which an ethic is extracted to be used as a guide to our actions. Aristotle – the initiator of virtue ethics – in total disagreement with Plato, indicates for us instead that the good is something that happens, that is realized through activities. As D. Lutz (2003) puts it, the most serious problem with the various ethical theories stemming from the individualistic tradition of thought is that they are not capable of offering a reason for "being ethical." If it's not good for us to behave ethically, why do what is recommended by ethics? On the other hand, if it is good for us to "be ethical," then why would it be necessary to offer managers incentives for doing that which is in their own interest to do? The solution to the problem of moral motivation of decision makers is not that of setting constraints (or providing incentives) for acting against their self-interest, but to offer them a more complete understanding of their own wellbeing. Only when ethics becomes part of the objective function of the agents does moral motivation cease to be a problem, because we are authentically motivated to do that which we believe is best for ourselves. This is why cultivating civic virtues is the undeniable task not only from the point of view of citizenship – something known for a long time – but also from the point of view of sustaining nature.

The difficulties and risks inherent in the practical carrying-out of a strategy as the one here indicated are obvious to everyone. It would be ingenuous to think that the diversity of the interests involved do not mean high levels of conflict. But the task is unavoidable if we wish to overcome the affliction of a rhetoric at all costs (a rhetoric that often ends up by appearing nihilistic), as well as a clear-eyed optimism of those who see in technical, scientific and economic progress a sort of triumphal march of humanity towards its fulfillment. The responsible person cannot fall victim to traps of this kind.

Economics is inextricably a part of ethics because humans are not aloof islands of exchange; rather, they live, work and thrive in social settings. Humans have innate dispositions *for* self, *for* others, and *against* others that serve useful functions, yet whose claims must be internally adjudicated by a moral agent. Understanding individual and social conceptions of "right" and "wrong" is essential for the environmental problematic. There is nothing to marvel at here. When one acknowledges the looming crisis of our civilization one is obliged to abandon any dystopic attitude and dare to seek out new paths of thought. As T.S. Eliot once observed, you can't build a tree; you can only plant one, tend it and wait for it to sprout in due time. You can, however, speed its development up with proper watering. For, unlike animals, which live in historic time but have no historic time, human beings have the ability to alter their times (For an illuminating account of biblical teachings on the economy, see Barrera 2013).

3.3 A Critique of the Economic Approach to Human Behavior

Economics has always been considered the 'queen' of social science thanks to its alleged superior ability to explain human behavior by rigorous and mathematically elegant reasoning. This stated superiority has been producing in the last few decades a more and more hegemonic attitude on the part of economists, who, on more than one occasion, ambitiously attempted a "colonization" of research areas traditionally the domain of other social sciences. In his *Models as Economies,* Townsend (1998) for example, insists that the variety of social frameworks and institutions as evidenced by socio-cultural anthropological research, are but contingent expressions of the aggregation of optimizing individual choices, ruled by self-centered objective functions subject to appropriately specified constraints. The most extreme expression of this research strategy is undoubtedly Gary Becker's. In the course of his long scientific career he examined and described through the lens of the theory of rational choice, phenomena such as marriage, fertility, criminal behavior and law enforcement, addictions, social interactions, to mention but a few topics. Becker's straightforward argument is that human behavior can be explained by a logic which compares ad hoc defined costs and related benefits of every possible option accessible to the decision-maker, with the ensuing selection of the option offering the prospect of the highest reward. It follows that those choices the non-economist is accustomed to consider as prompted by deep emotional urges and by definition remote from any logic of rational calculation, in fact reveal themselves as shaped by sophisticated utilitaristic considerations whose extent, as Becker's interest in sociobiology demonstrates, may include instinctual urges dictated by the 'selfish gene'.

The adoption of Becker's vision is tantamount to accustoming oneself to consider each aspect of one's life in market terms: there will be a market for marriage, one for the enforcement of law, one for social exchanges with our friends, colleagues, even with the outcasts we meet in the street who beg for our alms. Becker's working hypothesis is the hypostatization of a hyper-individualistic concept of behavior seen as rational 'translation' of a preference system representing the deep essential level of human identity. According to this vision the disappointments and frustrations of daily life are the ultimate result of our limited ability to abide by the economic canon of rationality for our decisions. If for example we often go out with a partner whose clothes we dislike, the 'rational' approach to the problem is to provide an appropriate incentive scheme so as to persuade her to dress in a way that suits better our wishes. By the same token, our partner will conform with our wishes if the incentives we have provided more than compensate the material and psychological costs incurred to adjust her clothes to meet our requirements, and so forth.

The application of Becker's logic to human behavior *tout court* tends however to produce a profound feeling of incongruity. The problem is that *homo Beckerianus* is a perfect specimen of a social idiot: a subject so completely devoted to the rational pursuit of its own preference as to be unaware that in order to do so it has to manipulate, systematically and explicitly, other people's behaviors and choices. This is precisely the point: in a hyper-individualistic perspective, we see the 'other' as a mere *instrument* for the attainment of our utilitarian goals. But a large number of social interactions and major practical decisions acquire significance due to the lack of instrumentality and are desirable only as such. The meaning of a generous action towards a friend, one's child or *partner* lies in it being gratuitous. If we were aware that it is prompted by a precise utilitarian and manipulative logic, it would acquire a totally different aspect and substantially alter the way it is received and the behavioral responses it elicits. However there can be no room for this vision within a conceptual perspective in which the social dimension is the sum of the individual ones, whence the need to include behavioral purposefulness in a sort of individual accountancy. *Homo Beckerianus* is profoundly lonely, even and all the more so when she worries about others, in that this solicitude is but an idiosyncrasy of *her own* preferences, and is as valuable as other people's idiosyncrasy, say, for stamp-collecting.

The reduction of human experience to the 'accountancy' dimension of economic rationality is not just an act of intellectual arrogance: it is sheer methodological naivety. The deep reason for this unsatisfactory situation lies in the fact that economic theory focuses on a description of human behavior almost completely centered on *acquisitive* purposes as if the only valid theory of human action were the theory of intentional action. Indeed, we know that most human actions have, at their beginning, not only intentions but also dispositions. So, the danger of applying the canons of rationality solely to intentional actions is that actions carried on in adherence of dispositions such as those prompting the principle of reciprocity are judged as irrational by standard economic analysis. Yet we know that in quite a few cases the conscious pursuit of one's self-interest is incompatible with its attainment: in several instances an "irrational" response based on the principle of reciprocity leads to better results than the one conforming to the canons of the exchange of equivalents paradigm. One should notice that this paradox is exactly the opposite of the one exemplified by the Smithian invisible hand (Donati and Archer 2015).

The fact is that an effective characterization of economic rationality cannot do without a careful consideration of the cultural matrix of the environment in which the agents are embedded. The acknowledgment of this fact, however, brings about a crucial question: to what extent agents' choices are conditioned by the preexisting social environment rather than by explicit optimizing calculations? It is clear that, to a certain (substantial) degree, individual choices are conditioned by the preexisting social environment, as convincingly argued by the sociopsychological literature and that these social conditionings are not completely traceable back to individual optimizing behavior. On the other hand, it is implausible to postulate that individuals are never able to recognize that some courses of actions are relatively more rewarding than others and to opt for the more rewarding ones. In other words, the trade-off between social conditionings and individual optimizing motivations must not be shaped unilaterally as far as the modeling of the determinants of human actions is concerned.

A first step toward a correct understanding of such interplay calls for a theoretical set-up able to: (i) explain how the two forces (i.e. social and cultural factors versus optimization) interact and how this interaction feeds back on the ongoing social relations; (ii) explain how the structure of this interaction tends itself to be modified by ongoing social relations. The key notion in this respect seems to be that of coevolution: individual behaviors and social norms evolve jointly as micro and/or macro changes in the latter prompt adjustments in the former and vice versa. Evolutionary game theory in its actual standard form, while it seems to be the right tool for studying the "short run" dynamics of social conventions (i.e. point (i) above), proves to be inadequate to deal with the co-evolution of norms themselves (i.e. point (ii) above). In fact, the relationship between observables like economic institutions and basically unobservables like individual dispositions is a two-way one, i.e. institutions and dispositions co-evolve through a complex – typically non-linear – process which is history dependent.

It follows that the basic modeling choice of standard economic theory of a "dualistic" framework in which norms act as mere external constraints on behaviors is missing at least one half of the feedback loop that is actually at work. What one needs is a "unified" framework where behavior contain "hidden" norms that freeze and become salient whenever the corresponding behavior spread over the population of agents. In turn, such a unified framework calls for a deep rethinking of the rational choice model and, ultimately, of the postulate of methodological individualism on which it is built. It is not asked to abandon methodological individualism altogether, but rather to go beyond it, since the core elements on which purposeful individual choices are based (i.e. preferences) evolve as a consequence of repeated social interactions.

An immediate application of the argument above is that of moral responsibility in a time of accelerated globalization like the present one. Traditional ethics claims that moral responsibility can be direct, indirect or adiaphoric. (In ancient Greek, "adiaphora" designated "indifferent things" to denote things outside moral law). Now, while it is relatively easy to identity direct moral responsibility, the same cannot be said when economic action is undertaken with the intention of harming no one, yet causes negative effects. Given what global markets are in reality today, the agents' greed, along with their bounded rationality and unforeseen contingencies, entails opportunistic and imprudent behavior that generates negative externalities for the whole economic system. This is particularly the case with pecuniary externalities, not to be confused with technological externalities (e.g. environmental degradation). To understand the nature of pecuniary externalities, it might be of interest to recall what Adam Smith wrote in *The Wealth of Nations* on the consequences of the discovery of America and the passage of the Cape of Good Hope – "The two greatest and most important events recorded in the history of mankind" (Smith 1950: 141). Dealing with the consequences of these events, Smith remarked: "What benefits or what misfortunes to mankind may hereafter result from those great events, no human wisdom can foresee. By uniting, in some measure, the most distant parts of the world (...) their general tendency would seem to be beneficial. To the native, however, both of the East and West Indies, all the commercial benefits which can have resulted from those events have been sunk and lost in the dreadful misfortunes which they have occasioned. At the particular time when these discoveries were made, the superiority of force happened to be so great in the side of the Europeans, that *they were enabled to commit with impunity every sort of injustice in those remote countries*. Hereafter, perhaps, the natives of those countries may grow stronger, or those of Europe may grow weaker and the inhabitants of all the different quarters of the world may arrive at that equality of courage and force which… can alone overawe the injustice of independent nations into some sort of respect for the rights of one another" (Smith 1950: 141; italics added). I consider this passage a remarkable anticipation of the argument according to which nowadays we need a more prudent (and wise) approach in order to acknowledge both the gains and losses from globalization. Indeed, if it is certainly true that we enjoy today enormous "gains from trade", it is also the case that we are facing "pains from trade". It is not acceptable on moral ground that only the first component is taken into consideration in economic theorizing.

3.4 The Return of Relationality in Present-Day Economic Discourse

For some time now the discipline of economics has begun to feel the need for the relational perspective in order to transcend the clash between the holistic and individualistic paradigms. Why is this? Actually, reference should be made to the individualistic paradigm, for the simple reason that the holistic one has been practically abandoned by now. Indeed the line of thought running from Ricardo and Marx to Polanyi and Sraffa, in which that paradigm was embedded, has ceased to offer a real alternative to the intellectual hegemony of neoclassical thought in its countless versions. Note that the relational perspective I am considering here is not that of exchange but that of reciprocity. Exchange is instrumental in nature: it is obvious that every time I initiate an exchange I am entering into a relation with someone, but this relation is merely instrumental, a means to my end. A relation of reciprocity, by contrast, considers the force of "between" as Martin Buber (2000) suggests; in economics, this is captured by the concept of relational good (Zamagni 2005a).

One reason why economists are now more or less obliged to adopt more sophisticated behavioural axioms than that of "economic man" and thus open to the relational approach, is the observation that the so-called additive hypothesis fails to find confirmation in the real world; in fact, it is regularly and systematically contradicted. Let me clarify the point. The fundamental assumption underlying the "standard" theory of economic behaviour is that extrinsic motivations – monetary or other – are added to, and reinforce, intrinsic motivations, i.e. those that flow from the personal identity of the agent. By this seemingly innocuous manoeuvre, mainstream economics manages to restrict its field of inquiry to extrinsic motivations alone, leaving to moral philosophy, psychology, or sociology, the study of motivations. In this view, the criticism that *homo oeconomicus* is a poor representation of human behaviour because it ignores intrinsic motivations can be disregarded as irrelevant. For no serious mainstream economist will ever deny the explanatory importance of ethical values, religious beliefs, and the intrinsic motivations of economic agents generally. Rather, he or she will assert that since extrinsic motivations are added to and reinforce the intrinsic ones, what economics is supposed to do is to give attention to extrinsic motivations in order to augment their efficacy. Hence the insistence of economic research on identifying the most effective incentives for directing people's choices in a particular direction.

However, the additive hypothesis has been found to be untenable, because of pervasive "crowding out" and "crowding in" phenomena between the two types of motivation, which calls into question the very foundations of what had long been deemed a perfectly solid edifice. The British sociologist Richard Titmuss (1970) was the first to alert social scientists that the offer of payment to blood donors reduced both the number of donations and the quality of the blood. Today the empirical and theoretical literature on the crowding-out effect is simply huge (Frey 1997; Janssen and Mendys-Kamphorst 2004). The explanation of the phenomenon is clear: economic incentives not only diminish self-determination and the range of possibilities for personal self-expression but undermine the very basis of what Adam Smith called self-esteem. That is, being paid for an act that the person would have performed anyway diminishes the social reward. What is more, an incentive always conceals an unequal power relationship, because it implies that there is no valid reason for you to do what is asked of you so that your behaviour must be "bought."

B. Gui and R. Sugden (2005) after setting out the empirical evidence of the countless links between the economic sphere and that of interpersonal relations, ask how far the dominant economic paradigm can actually satisfy the need for relationality. Their answer is trenchant: not only to an inadequate extent but –what is more – in a distorted way. It is not hard to see why. In fact, what do we find at the bottom of the "received view"? Nothing but the theory of rational choice that claims to explain economic behaviour solely on the basis of agents' preferences and beliefs, as if inclinations, motivations and moral sentiments were useless adornments with no explanatory power. This is tantamount to saying that "rational choice" bears exclusively on the cognitive dimension of interactions between persons, not the affective and moral dimension. Yet recent evolutionary game theory and behavioural economics have demonstrated that the importance of the affective component of decision-making – such as emotional states that are reflected in signals that the agent has trouble controlling but that are readily perceptible to those with whom he interacts – must not be underestimated. The truth is that interpersonal relations activate mechanisms of information transmission that the theory of rational choice precludes. Moreover, the fact that persons whose behaviour is not strictly self-interested are active in the market invalidates a good many of the conclusions achieved by rational choice theory insofar as it assumes all agents to be self-interested.

But how can we be sure that there actually exist, in reality, people exhibiting prosocial behaviour? A meta- study of C. Engel (2010) examines results from around 328 different dictator games experiments for a total of 20,813 observations. The result is that only around 36 percent of participants follow Nash rationality and give zero and more than half give no less than 20 percent. A further interesting results is that students are those who are closer to the homo oeconomicus behaviour (40 percent), while only 20 percent of children, 10 percent of middle aged players and almost no one of the elders behave in this way. Engel's final comment is that: "while normally a sizeable fraction of participants does indeed give nothing, as predicted by the payoff maximization hypothesis, only very rarely this has been the majority choice. It by now is undisputed that human populations are systematically more benevolent than homo oeconomicus" (Engel 2010: 24).

Let us get rid of one possible objection. Even the theory of rational choice, it could be argued, admits that there are some altruistic people, and others who are averse to injustice. This is the position of Gary Becker and his followers. Yet his broadening of the conventional theory does not lead far, for the evident reason that all it does is to extend the range of preferences of actors, or at the very most alter the form of their preference function. The motivational system, that is, remains one of self-interest, even though this can now be "enlightened." The real challenge, which rational choice theory cannot take up, is the study of interactions between people at the level of their motivational and dispositional structures. Indeed, it is certainly true that relations are acted by individuals, but they also have an independent existence, so much so that individuals increasingly come into conflict with the relations themselves, and not only with other individuals. What is rational in a relation? What does it mean to study the economy as a fabric, of inter-personal relations? What route can we take, then, to overcome the paralyzing reductionism of "received economic theory"?

Scholarly responses to these and similar questions are differentiated, not convergent, but there is consensus on one point: it is urgent to abandon the assumption of homogeneous motivation for all agents. Note that this does not mean simply banishing *homo oeconomicus*, because there are in fact *a-social* persons in the world who neither "help" nor "harm" others. What we need to do is to recognize that the economic world is inhabited by a plurality of types of subjects. Some are *anti-social* (the envious, for example, who in order to inflict harm or suffering on someone else is willing to sustain a cost that he knows will produce no material benefit for himself; or the malicious, who takes pleasure in other people's ill fortune); others are *pro-social* (such as the numerous consumers who support and sustain the fair trade and the ethical finance movements; or the businessmen, who are instituting democratic governance stakeholding in their own firms; or benefit-corporations). Pro-social acts, it should be noted, are such not because they are actually in the public interest but because they are performed with the public interest in mind.

What is entailed in assuming motivational heterogeneousness? First of all, it implies that before tackling the problem of choosing the optimal course of action, one has to face the problem of addressing the personal dispositions of agents. Now, since dispositions respond to institutional changes, the problem becomes that of designing institutions that operate as a mechanism for selecting groups with various motivational systems, not merely as an incentive mechanism to favour one group or another of subjects, as is done in the current literature. The second implication is that one can no longer keep the category of relationality outside of the economic domain. The fact that human beings live partly in a symbolic dimension leads unavoidably to the idea of relationality and to the notion of relational good.

The person in relation to others is what is missing in standard economic theory, which appears not to see that what is relevant to people is not to be found only in people themselves, but also in what happens among them. An economic science that assumed *all* agents to be asocial, and failed to consider that the person *qua* person matters would be a poor science indeed, and ultimately of little use. Even the "new social economics" of Durlauf and Young (2001) – certainly an interesting line of thought – offers late and quite often simplistic answers, because it posits an "economic man" who, like the mushrooms Hobbes talked about in *De Cive*, comes onstage already full formed. The self comes before the social relation, so that the latter becomes strictly instrumental. This is why this literature fails to account for the importance of reciprocity, which is regularly interpreted as the "special case" of an exchange of equivalents relation, in which the agents pursue enlightened self-interest.

The culture of modernity is responsible for this reductionist stance, whereby contracts and incentives (plus, of course, a well defined institutional arrangement) would be all that the economy needs. This means refusing to see that gift as gratuitousness always counterposes its logic of overabundance to that of equivalence typical of contracts. It is known that there are moral traditions like the Puritan which considers actions complying with duty superior to those stemming from love. As Max Weber wrote in the *Protestant Ethics:* "a higher ethical value is attached to the accomplishment of duty without love than to sentimental philanthropy" (Weber 1967: 202). Why? Because while the Kantian morality seeks universal principles independent of social ties, (and market exchange seeks equivalence also independent of those ties), things tend, on the contrary, to be embedded in social ties. They circulate embedded in a social relationship; not in the name of an abstract principle. The gift is an invitation to a relationship, since when one receives a gift it induces an impulse to give. Economic theory needs to think of an agent who can combine freedom of choice with relationality, for if human relations alone would produce an equivocal communitarianism, freedom of choice by itself would resume all the shortcomings of axiological individualism.

A phenomenon that has contributed greatly to bringing the relationality principle back into economic discourse is the happiness paradox, or "Easterlin's paradox" (after the American scholar Richard Easterlin who proposed it in 1974). Pascal (*Pensées,* nol. 425) observed that "All men seek happiness. This is without exception. Whatever different means they employ, they all tend to this end. … This is the motive of every action of every man, even of those who hang themselves." Now as long as economic doctrine was able to convince that "to be" happy was the same thing as "to have" happiness, it succeeded in masquerading utility as happiness and persuading people that maximizing utility was not just rational but reasonable, i.e. an act of wisdom.

The problems came to a head just when it was discovered empirically, that the relation between per capita income – as an indicator, albeit rough and ready, of utility – and subjective well-being (happiness) can be graphed as an inverted "U" (a parabola concave upwards). That is, above a certain level further increases in per capita income actually diminish the subjective perception of well-being. I do not intend to dwell on the countless explanations suggested for this paradox. They run from the psychological (the treadmill effect) through the economic (positional externalities) to the sociological (based on the notion of relational goods). The literature is vast and deep-rooted (Bruni and Zamagni 2016b).

In another work I have dealt with the peculiar characteristics of relational goods and their meaning in today's advanced societies (Zamagni 2005b). Here, let me add that the main reason the individualist paradigm can never treat relational goods adequately is that with these goods it is the relation as such that constitutes the good; that is, the interpersonal relation does not exist independently of the good, which is produced and consumed at the same time. This means that my knowledge of the identity of the other with whom I have a relation is indispensable for there to be a relational good at all. By contrast, the assumption underlying the exchange of equivalents is that it is always possible to replace the person or persons on whom my well-being depends with other persons. (If I am not satisfied with my regular butcher, I can always go to another. But I cannot replace the person who provides me with a service of care without altering my own index of happiness.) As Philip Wicksteed (1910) saw clearly, the primary foundation of the capitalistic market is not egotism but "non-tuism," because business is better done with people whose personal identity one does not know. From the relational perspective, however, the relationship with another person presupposes recognition and receptiveness: welcoming a presence that, in its humanity, is common to me and in its otherness, distinct from me. No easy task, certainly – "Hell is other people," as Sartre said in *No Exit* – but essential if we want to overcome the severe shortage of relational goods that typifies our society. Individualism is a useful guide for utility that depends on goods and services that can be enjoyed even in isolation. But it is a poor maestro for happiness, given that true happiness requires being at least two in number, as Aristotle wrote. To quote Scripture, "The Lord God said, it is not *good* that the man should be alone" (Genesis 2:18, King James version).

The fact is that I need the other to discover that it is worth preserving myself; in order to flourish, as in the Aristotelian "*eudaimonia*". But the other too needs me to recognize him/her as someone whose flourishing is good. Since we need the same recognition, I will act towards the other as if before a mirror. Self-fulfilment is the result of that interaction. The original asset that I can put at the disposal of the person in front of me is the capacity to recognize the value of that person's existence – a resource that cannot be produced unless it is shared. What matters here is to see that this implies recognition of the other – not just her *right* to exist but of the *necessity* that she exist as a condition for my own existence, in relation to him/her. Recognizing the other person as an end in himself and recognizing him as the means for my own fulfilment are reunified, which resolves the reductive dichotomy between Kantian morals, which require that we see others strictly as an end in themselves, and a theory of instrumental rationality in which others are seen as the means to one's own ends. The good of self-fulfilment is attained when there is reciprocal recognition. Note that the fact that my recognition of the other person brings with it the reciprocal recognition that I myself need does not make this disposition merely instrumental. For the self is constituted in part by the recognition conferred by others.

3.5 Reciprocity Versus Exchange of Equivalents

Economics has known for quite some time that social interaction produces externalities and that the latter tend to delay the movement towards socially advantageous equilibria. This follows from the fact that there is a basic difference between social decisions (those that influence the utility of others) and individual decisions (those whose effects remain limited to the sphere of the agent). To clarify the point: whereas the quality and the intensity of my relationships with friends are not affected by my decision to consume, say, bananas instead of apples, my decision to get married or not, to obtain a degree, or not, has direct effects of marked relevance to others. In fact, decisions of this kind help to define my identity and thus influence my relationships with others. It may thus happen, as G. Akerlof (1997) notes, that the main determinant of my choice is the impact I imagine my decision will have on the network of my relations with others; whereas the evaluation of the direct effects of my choice on my level of utility – which is what the standard theory restricts itself to considering – could be of secondary importance.

In recent times, a theory of social interactions, explicitly taking into account the externalities associated with social decisions, is the one stemming from the huge amount of empirical research on the principle of reciprocity. The work of Kahnemann and Tversky on economic psychology, that of Bewley on labor economics, that of Sudgen on the voluntary contribution to public goods, that of Fehr and others on the enforceability of contracts, clearly shows that reciprocating behavior cannot be explained in terms of self-interested preferences and behavior oriented to results. It is by now certain that reciprocity is something different from the so-called reciprocating altruism or from direct reciprocity, as exemplified by the tit-for-tat strategy R.M. Axelrod (2006) speaks of. The reciprocating altruist, in fact, is prepared to reciprocate only if some recompense is expected in the future from his action. Such a recompense can emerge as an equilibrium solution in games infinitely repeated or else in finite games with complete information. Furthermore, this kind of behavior is perfectly compatible with self-interested preferences, since the prospect of future gains (or the credible threat of future punishments) can induce selfish but patient agents to make momentary sacrifices in contexts of repeated games.

Reciprocity, on the other hand, is a behavioral answer to "perceived courtesy" – as Falk and Fischbacher (2001) put it – where the term courtesy is taken to mean both the sense of distributive justice and the intention to behave fairly. The motivation of those who have reciprocating preferences is not based, then, on any kind of prospect of future gain. An individual of this kind is disposed to make material sacrifices in favor of those who are similarly disposed, and to punish those who are not. For example, to punish unfair iniquitous behavior in a game like ultimatum, is a form of reciprocity. Again, in games of coordination, most of the laboratory experiments show that the players, first, tend towards an inferior equilibrium and then, unexpectedly, change their strategy and converge to the dominant equilibrium. For this inversion to take place it is necessary that several individuals choose actions that are not best replies to the results of the moves that occurred immediately beforehand. In other words a certain number of players "make sacrifices" in the short run to teach the other players the way to coordinate on the dominant equilibrium.

Two conceptions of the principle of reciprocity are present in the literature. One, which remains within the consequentialist perspective, is founded on aversion to the sense of injustice: it is aversion to unfair distributions that stimulates the reciprocating response. The other notion, based on the principle of perceived courtesy, takes into account not only the consequences of the action, but also the intentions behind it. (In ultimatum game, for example, a certain offer of money is rejected by the other player much more often if the person making the offer is evidently not well-intentioned than if the same offer signals a good intention – let us say because the proponent finds herself in a particular situation of need). Needless to say, the second notion represents an interesting development within the theory of reciprocity, since it allows to represent the utility of the agents as a function not only of the pay-offs of the original game, but also of the term expressing the response to the courtesy perceived – a term that Falk and Fischbacher (2001) rightly call "utility of reciprocity". But on reflection, the explanatory power of the theory is a good deal lower than the expectations it initially aroused. To me, the reason is that both versions of the standard theory of reciprocity presuppose the same individualist framework that is also basic to the theory of altruism. In both cases, in fact, individuals possess interdependent preferences; in other words, they are interested in some way in others' pay-offs as well as their own. The difference between the two approaches, in the final analysis, lies in the different specification of the interdependence of the preferences, but the conceptual structure behind it remains the same.

Indeed, the declared purpose of this literature is to show that the preferences for reciprocity are compatible, despite appearances, with the individualist statute. The idea, in short, is that when information is incomplete – and therefore the preferences cannot be observed – preferences that are not individualistic are not credible and hence end up by being dominated by individualistic preferences, since the agents, though they know the relative frequency of the various types in the population, do not know the preferences of those with whom they find themselves interacting. The conclusion is therefore that within big groups and in the presence of incomplete information, there can be no doubt at all that evolution favors individualistic preferences in agents that operate in social contexts like a market economy.

It is not difficult to see the basic weakness of a line of argument of this kind. The point is that in this literature the meaning of the term reciprocity is being juggled with. Whereas, reciprocity postulates the knowledge of the identity of others, and above all the readiness on the part of the agent to be in relation with others, the mainstream approach reduces reciprocity – which is a relation – to a mere preference. It is therefore obvious that if others do not know who I am, i.e. they do not know my identity in the sense of Akerlof and Kranton (2000), they are led to behave individualistically towards me, since it is precisely this mode that emerges as the one evolutionarily stable among all those generated by any other kind of "mutant". The fact is that identity means to recognize oneself and be recognized. The self-recognition dimension implies self-knowledge, the memory of oneself and one's own experience of life; the dimension of being recognized recalls the need of every person to be inserted in a network of relations facilitating self knowledge thanks to information provided by those with whom the person interacts. Precisely because identity belongs to being, rather than having, it is not negotiable.

In view of this I believe the conceptualization of reciprocity proposed by S. Kolm (2000) to be more relevant. To him, reciprocity is a series of bi-directional transfers, independent of each other and at the same time interconnected. Independence implies that each transfer is voluntary in itself, i.e. free; in other words, no transfer constitutes a prerequisite for putting the other into action, since there is no external obligation capable of acting on the mind of the agent. It is precisely this characteristic which differentiates reciprocity from relations based on the principle of the exchange of equivalents, relations that are also constituted by a set of bi-directional transfers, but in which the voluntariness is, so to speak, global in the sense that it is applied within a set of transfers, and not to each single transfer taken by itself. In other words, the transfers implied by the relation of exchange of equivalents are each the prerequisite of the other, so that a third party (for example, a judge) can always intervene to render contractual obligations enforceable. Nothing like this happens with reciprocity, even if it remains true that exchanges of equivalents and reciprocity, to the extent that both postulate voluntariness, are opposed to command relation. At the same time, however, there is much more freedom in reciprocity than in the exchange of equivalents, where the transfer in one direction becomes obligatory by the transfer in the opposite direction. The bi-directionality of the transfers characterizing reciprocity is what differentiates the latter from pure altruism, which consists in one-directional transfers. On the whole, it may be said that reciprocity occupies the intermediate position between exchanges and pure altruism.

In view of the above, it may be concluded that the relation of reciprocity requires some form of balancing between what one gives and what one *expects* to obtain, a balancing, however, that is not expressed in a defined relation of exchanges (i.e. in a relative price), since it may vary according to the intensity with which moral dispositions such as sympathy, benevolence, or the feeling of solidarity are put into practice by the agents involved in the relation. At any rate, it is true that reciprocity in some way refers to the strategic dimension of interaction between individuals: if those who receive my transfer do not give me some sign of reciprocation, I shall be induced to break off relations with them. So where does the difference lie with what happens in the exchange of equivalents relations? The answer lies in a dual order of circumstances. In exchanges the determination of the exchange ratio (i.e. the equilibrium price) logically precedes the transfer of the item exchanged – only after the purchaser and seller have agreed on the price of the house which is the object of the transaction can the exchange take place. In the relation of reciprocity, on the other hand, the transfer precedes, both logically and temporally, the counter-transfer, about which the agent who begins the relation cannot claim any right, but only an expectation. Secondly, the reciprocity nexus can modify the results of the game itself, whether because the practice of reciprocity tends to stabilize pro-social behavior in agents who find themselves interacting in contexts of the prisoner's dilemma type, or because the culture of reciprocity tends to modify endogenously the preference orderings of the agents. As the results of the basic trust game, if I find myself needing the help of others in circumstances in which I cannot credibly bind myself to some commitment for the future, a rational agent in the sense of the theory of rational choice, though capable of helping me, will certainly not do so if, knowing that I am also a self-interested agent, he conjectures that I will not have the slightest interest in reciprocating the favor received. But this is not the case if my potential helper knows that I am someone who practices reciprocity (Kolm 2000).

It is now possible to understand why, unlike what happens with the principle of exchange (and with coercion), reciprocity cannot be explained in terms of *self-interest only*: motivations and the attitude towards others are a fundamental component of the concept of reciprocity. This is why standard economic theory, hinging on the scheme of rational choice, fails to explain the notion of reciprocity adequately: the latter being a relation cannot be confused with reputation – which is an intangible asset.

3.6 Conclusion

The reductionist path taken by economic science over the last 50 years has ended up disarming critical thought, with the effect that are now evident to all. Having believed that scientific rigor assumes a sterile neutrality, and that research, in order to be scientific, must free itself from ethics, has led to accepting libertarian individualism as a sort of pre-analytic assumption that, as such, requires no justification whatsoever, since it is believed to be a natural condition. We know however that this in and of itself is a very strong value judgment. Indeed, for individualism the individual is the only judge who attributes value to things and relationships in which one finds oneself. Since objective values do not exist, the individual is always the one who decides what is right or wrong, just or unjust, what is good and what is not.

But individualism alone would not be sufficient to account for the current state of "civilization and its discontents" (Freud) if it were not tightly coupled with libertarianism, by those who think that grounding liberty and responsibility requires recourse to the idea of self-actualization. Only a self-actualized agent is wholly free, or as expressed by Galen Strawson (2004), one who is *causa sui*. And so, the idea derived from libertarian individualism – the real signature trait of the current individualistic revolution (the first was the Enlightenment) – that liberty assumes the dissolution of all bonds, and that every individual has the right to expand to the limits of his potential. In erroneously equating the notion of "bond" with "constraint," the conditionings of liberty (i.e. constraints) are confused with the conditions of liberty (i.e. bonds).

Reinterpreting the recent events of the economic and financial crisis through this conceptual lens allows us to go beyond the flood of tautological explanations produced so far. Michel Foucault was one who, with rare perspicacity, understood this serious contradiction in second modernity. Confronting the problem of access to truth, he questioned whether it is true that we live in a time in which the market has become a "site of truth," a place where the entire lives of those involved are subsumed to economic efficiency, and where the market still ensures that for a government "to be a good government" it must operate according to this site of verediction – "The market must tell the truth; it must tell the truth in relation to government practice. Henceforth, and merely secondarily, it is its role of verediction that will command, dictate and prescribe the jurisdictional mechanisms, or absence of such mechanisms, on which [the market] must be articulated" (Foucault 2008: 32).

Actually, Foucault's and others' agitated preoccupation has profound roots. In his inaugural lecture for the new academic year at Oxford in October 1829, Richard Whately, the influential chair of political economy, stated for the first time the NOMA principle (*non-overlapping magisteria*) (See Emmett 2014). Whately's thesis was that if economics aspires to the status of a science it must separate itself from both ethics and politics. He divided the tasks as follows: ethics, the sphere of values, has the task of defining the norms that guide human behavior; politics, the sphere of goals, has the task of democratically defining the objectives that society wants to attain; economics, the sphere of means, has the task of researching the most efficient ways to achieve those objectives with respect to those values. What need is there then for economics to maintain close ties with the other two spheres? For the economist, as a technician of means, the criterion of efficiency suffices as a guide for acting. Actually, Whately sought to mitigate the NOMA principle by speaking of distinctions between the spheres rather than separations, but with little success. Despite the objections of many non-influential voices, all successive economic thought more or less embraced this principle. Even today the majority of economics textbooks repeat with only minor variations Lionel Robbins's famous definition: "Economics is the science which studies human behavior as a relationship between given ends and scarce means which have alternative uses" (Robbins 1932: 16).

The most obnoxious consequence of a narrow-minded (and obsolete) notion of the market, still predominant to this day, is to lead us to believe that a behavior inspired by values other than non-tuistic self-interest inexorably drives the economy to disaster. By encouraging us to expect the worst of others, such vision eventually brings out the worst in us. Moreover, in the end it immensely hampers the exploitability of such inclinations as trust, benevolence, reciprocity, since that vision perceives these inclinations as merely inborn peculiarities of human nature, unrelated to the civilization process in progress in our societies. In the absence of actual – not just virtual – competition among different types of firms, the citizen-consumer will be left with a reduced space of freedom. One might end up living in a more and more affluent society, more and more efficiently inundating us with commodities and services of all sorts, but more and more "indecent" and, ultimately, desperate. Indeed, the reduction of human experience to the "accountancy" dimension of utilitarian calculus is not just an act of intellectual arrogance; it is disclaimed by actual experience in the first place.

Today, we have come to the point where even the most "detached" observer cannot but admit that if we want to attack the new problems of our society, research simply can no longer confine itself to a sort of anthropological limbo. One must take a position on the matter, selecting a standpoint from which to scrutinize reality. Otherwise, economics will continue to spread, to enrich its technical and analytical apparatus, but if it does not escape self-referentiality it will be less and less capable of actually grasping reality, and thus of suggesting effective lines of action. There is no denying that this is the true risk that economics as a scientific discipline runs today.

References

Akerlof, G. 1997. Social Distance and Social Decisions. *Econometrica* 65 (5): 1005–1027.

Akerlof, G., and S. Kranton. 2000. Economics and Identity. *Quarterly Journal of Economics* 65 (3): 715–753.

Atkinson, A.B. 2009. Economics as a Moral Science. *Economica* 76 (1): 791–804.

Axelrod, R.M. 2006. *The Evolution of Cooperation*. New York: Basic Books.

Barrera, A. 2013. *Biblical Economic Ethics*. Lanham: Lexington Books.

Boulding, K. 1969. Economics as a Moral Science. *American Economic Review* 59 (1969): 1–14.

Bruni, L., and S. Zamagni. 2016a. *The Challenge of Public Happiness: An Historical Methodological Reconstruction, World Happiness Report,* 2016.

———. 2016b. *Civil Economy*. London: Agenda Pu. Co..

Buber, M. 2000. *I and Thou*. New York: Scribner.

Donati, P., and M. Archer. 2015. *The Relational Subject*. Cambridge: Cambridge University Press.

Durlauf, S., and H.P. Young. 2001. *Social Dynamics*. Cambridge, MA: MIT Press.

Emmett, R.B. 2014. Economics and Theology After the Separation. In *Christianity and Economics*, ed. P. Oslington. Oxford: Oxford University Press.

Engel, C. 2010. *Dictator Games*. MPI Collective Goods Preprint No 7/2010.

Falk, A., and U. Fischbacher. 2001. A Theory of Reciprocity. *Games and Economic Behavior* 54 (2006): 293–315.

Foucault, M. 2008. *The Birth of Biopolics*. Palgrave.

Frey, B. 1997. *Not Just For The Money*. Cheltenham: Elgar.

Gui, B., and R. Sugden. 2005. *Economics and Social Interaction. Accounting for Interpersonal Relations*. Cambridge: Cambridge University Press.

Janssen, M.C.V., and E. Mendys-Kamphorst. 2004. The Price of a Price: On the Crowding Out and In of Social Norms. *Journal of Economic Behavior and Organization* 55 (2004): 377–395.

Kolm, S. 2000. Introduction to the Economics of Reciprocity, Giving and Altruism. In *The Economics of Reciprocity, Giving and Altruism*, ed. L. Gerard Varet, S. Kolm, and J. Mercier Ythier. London: MacMillan.

Lutz, D. 2003. Beyond Business Ethics. *Oikos* 2003 .

Robbins, L. 1932. *An Essay on the Nature and Significance of Economic Science*. London: Macmillan.

Sen, A. 1987. *On Ethics and Economics*. Oxford: Blackwell.

Smith, A. 1950 [1776]. *An Inquiry Into the Nature and Causes of The Wealth of Nations*. (Edited by Edwin Cannan) London, Methuen.

Strawson, G. 2004. Free Agents. *Philosophical Topics* 32 (1/2): 371–402.

Titmuss, R. 1970. *The Gift Relationship*. London: Allen & Unwin.

Townsend, R.M. 1998. Models as Economies. *The Economic Journal* 98 (390): 1–24.

Wicksteed, P.H. 1910. *The Common Sense of Political Economy: Including a Study of the Human Basis of Economic Law*. London: Macmillan.
Ythier, J.M. 2011. Ethics and Economics. mimeo, University of Paris
Zamagni, S. 2005a. La svolta antropologica in economia. *La Società degli Individui* 2 : 2005.
———. 2005b. L'economia civile e i beni relazionali. In *La nuova economia*ed, ed. R. Viale, Milano, Il Sole 24 Ore, 2005.
———. 2015. Beni comuni e economia civile. In *Beni comuni e cooperazione*, ed. L. Sacconi and S. Ottone. Il Mulino: Bologna.

Chapter 4
Teleological Reasoning in Economics

Luk Bouckaert

Abstract The prime example of a teleological approach to economics can be found in the first part of Aristotle's Politics. He defines economics as the art of creating the material and social conditions for the survival of the *oikos* or household. Simultaneously, he integrates economics in a social matrix that subordinates economics to politics and ethics. Modern philosophy and economics is anti-Aristotelian and anti-teleological. Modern economic actors are supposed to be driven by autonomous preferences and free choices. The market functions as a causal equilibrium mechanism that promote welfare for everyone as an unintended byproduct. Although Adam Smith interpreted this unintended teleological effect as an 'invisible hand', he was one of the first moral philosophers to underpin this order with a non-teleological substratum. After him, the deconstruction of teleology pursued its logic giving way to the idea of economics as a process of 'creative destruction' (Schumpeter). The paper explores how thinking economics as a relational dynamic opens a space for human creativity without losing the embeddedness in an ecological system of meaning and purpose.

Teleological reasoning explains and helps understand phenomena by referring to their ultimate purpose and design. Modern positive science avoids teleological reasoning because of its controversial, metaphysical implications. Instead, causal analysis is its hallmark. Despite many efforts in economics to become a 'pure science', teleological reasoning has always paid a substantial role. Discussing e.g. the aim of business *ipso facto* implies a teleological mode of reasoning. Even if we do not agree in defining that purpose, at least we agree that a company has a purpose or *telos*. In a similar way we cannot fully understand the role of markets unless we explain their social utility and functioning. Hence the question 'Do we need a teleological model of economics?' seems to be trivial because the answer can only be in the affirmative. The more relevant questions are: why do we differ in defining the purpose of business and economics? Which teleological model should be prioritized

L. Bouckaert (✉)
Catholic University of Leuven, Leuven, Belgium

European SPES Institute, Leuven, Belgium
e-mail: luk.bouckaert@kuleuven.be

P. Rona, L. Zsolnai (eds.), *Economics as a Moral Science*,
Virtues and Economics 1, DOI 10.1007/978-3-319-53291-2_4

in our context of today? Why do some of us define the aim of business as maximizing profit and others as realizing a set of stakeholder values or even serving the common good? Answering these questions refers us to the meta-stories of philosophical and normative views on economics, politics and ethics as well as to the historical context in which these views are embedded.

In this paper we will identify four meta-stories or paradigms of teleological reasoning in economics and business. These models are historically dated but their relevance is still operative in current debates and arguments. The first section explains briefly Aristotle's model of natural teleology in economics. The second deals with the modern shift from natural to market teleology and refers to Adam Smith the 'father of economics' (which I call Smith I), while the third section explores the hybrid teleological model that combines ethics and economics and which is related to Adam Smith as a moral philosopher (Smith II). The last section explores the emerging paradigm of a spiritual-based teleology in business and economics.

4.1 Aristotle's Natural Teleology

In the first part of his *Politics*, Aristotle defines the *oikonomiké technè* as the art of securing the material and social conditions for the survival of the *oikos* or household. However, it is important to realize that *telos* for philosophers as Socrates, Plato and Aristotle and many other ancient philosophers does not only mean a *goal* to be realized but predominantly a *limit* that must be respected. Without this sense of limit, we will never reach a situation of *eudaimonia* or public happiness, which is the ultimate aim of the natural order. Aristotle's economic theory is not a program for ambitious entrepreneurs taking the sky as their limit. It contains a set of common sense guidelines clarifying what should not be done rather than what should be done. In Book 1 of his Politics, he points out four basic distinctions in order to limit the economy to its so-called natural *telos*.

The first distinction differentiates the art of managing the *oikos* (oikonomikè technè) from the art of accumulating wealth (chrèmatistikè technè). Accumulating wealth results from activities such as hunting, fishing, and farming but also from piracy and slave raiding which are more or less taken for granted in the ancient world. Notably, the accumulation of wealth must be limited in function of the satisfaction of the material and social needs of the household. If it transgresses this limit, wealth accumulation will create a moral and social disorder. Therefore exchange of goods in order to increase satisfaction of needs is allowed but trading solely for moneymaking is not acceptable.

The second distinction deals with the difference between money and economics. For Aristotle money can only be an instrument for facilitating a moderate exchange of local products. The monetized economy must be strictly kept under control. If there is no limit to the creation of money and credit, money might become itself a valuable good and desirable as such. In parallel with the acquisition of wealth, the infinite accumulation of money turns out to destroy the natural sense and limit of economics. Therefore a strict prohibition of charging interest is necessary to restrain the use of money and credit. A capitalist interest-and-money-driven growth economy is in his view an aberration and not compatible with a moral and flourishing society. Marx admired Aristotle for his anti-capitalist view on economics.

Aristotle's third distinction defines the relationship between economics and politics. While the natural purpose of economics is to secure the survival of the *oikos* as a private good, the aim of politics is to organize and ensure the good life as a public good for free citizens. According to Aristotle we need a watertight demarcation between economics and politics in order to avoid the economization of politics.[1] Economics is subservient to politics but not the other way around. On the one hand, the polis needs an efficient system of *oikoi* that enables the privileged 'citizens' to be freed from manual work and to invest time and money in public life and debate. But on the other hand, economic management should not be transferred to the political sphere. Aristotle 's concept of politics is far removed from the modern idea of a welfare state that promotes economic growth, redistributes wealth and stimulates job creation. This set-up would be unnatural and would lead to the economization of politics.

The fourth Aristotelian distinction deals with the difference between economic and political leadership. An economic leader has to be a *despotes,* a master in managing the household. The Greek word *despotes* has the same etymological origin as the Latin-based word of manager: *despotes* refers to domos (house) and posis (acting) and the Latin-based word *manager* to managium (household) or mansus (manor) and agere (acting). Management is a technical skill and very different from the moral wisdom or the *fronesis* that inspires a political leader. The major task of a good *despotes* is the management of human resources, which were mainly slaves. This was not an argument for an unbridled exploitation of slaves. As Aristotle remarks, if we could replace slaves by technological devices, this would create a complete new situation for the survival of the *oikos* and a possibility to liberate slaves. For Aristotle slave management was considered as unavoidable, based on the laws of necessity and efficiency and therefore technocratic and non-democratic in its functioning.

So far Aristotle. Even in his time, the Aristotelian model was not applicable. Commercial activities and trading were intense. There was also a kind of State economy that used slaves and foreigners. The Aristotelian model was not a description of the actual state of the economy, but a normative view that aimed at freeing the polis from the grip of economics and connecting politics with an ethical concept of the good life. It is this warning against the economization of the social and political sphere that makes Aristotle appealing today. In his exhortation *Evangelii Gaudium* (2013), Pope Francis, in condemning the current economy of money follows the Aristotelian argument. Also, conservative politicians who advocate strong budgetary control and hard restrictions on money and debt creation, can find an ally

[1] Just as there is a strict demarcation and hierarchy between the celestial/divine and the terrestrial/human sphere, there must be a clear demarcation and hierarchy between politics and economics.

in Aristotle. However we must keep in mind that the intention of Aristotle never was to save a financial system from bankruptcy but to claim the priority of politics over economics.

4.2 From Natural to Market Teleology

The rise of the modern economy runs parallel with an intellectual process of cleaning up Aristotle's natural teleology. The scholastic philosophers in Salamanca and Leuven already softened and liberalized some of the Aristotelian limits. For example, they drastically transformed the Aristotelian prohibition of interest into a moderate interest theory making space for financial markets. Yet modern economics officially started with Adam Smith's Wealth of Nations (1776), and more precisely with Smith's presentation of the self-regulative mechanism of market processes. It is the idea of self-regulation that made the imposed limitations of natural teleology redundant and opened the door for a new way of teleological reasoning in economics.

Smith did not invent the concept of markets. Local and global markets always have been a vital part of flourishing economies, ancient as well as medieval. They were places of human exchange, commerce and barter. The new thing in modern economics was the discovery of equilibrium cycles within markets. The *Tableau économique* of F. Quesnay and the ideas of the Physiocrats in France inspired Adam Smith. But Adam Smith applied the new idea of self-regulation to the emerging industrial economy. Parallel to what scientists such as Galileo and Newton achieved a century earlier in the field of physics, a generation of economists shifted their focus from the *causa finalis* to the *causa efficiens* and from common sense analysis to empirical and mathematical reasoning. As most of the new modern thinkers were Christians, they still believed that the mechanisms of self-regulation in physics and economics were part of a divine order. But the divine design was no longer needed to explain or justify the *modus operandi* of the system.

In Chapter 7 of the first book, Smith explains how the market mechanism creates an optimal equilibrium around the natural price which covers the cost of production. If there is too much of something that people do not want, the price and profit rate will decrease and it will become unattractive for future entrepreneurs to invest money and time in that market segment. On the other hand, if there is a growing demand for some products, or an emergent market for a new product, creative entrepreneurs and investors will become interested and try to make a profit out of it.

Smith's social justification for the 'marketization of economics' is widely known as 'the invisible hand' argument. Through its equilibrium mechanism, the market aligns individual needs with the general welfare without any reference to a natural teleology or to moral feelings and reasoning. The only condition for the adjustment mechanism is a context of free and transparent competition. Hence the government has to ensure a space of free competition. Although Adam Smith is far from a free-market fundamentalist, he did open the door for a paradigm shift in that direction.

He approved of the marketization of economics but not yet of politics and socio-cultural life. Smith and many economists after him are still aware of the limits of the market economy. But the perceived limits no longer derive from a natural, ontological design but from the fact that the conditions of free exchange and transparent competition are not always realized or desirable. Modern economists do not speak about 'moral failures' as did Aristotle but about 'market failures'.

It is striking how Smith's fascination with self-regulation is also present in his moral philosophy. His principle of sympathy that coordinates our moral feelings and judgments within society is not informed by common sense and natural teleology but by the psychological and social need to be acknowledged by other people. The psychological need for social recognition is 'the invisible hand' behind ethics. It explains our capacity for empathy and why we adjust our feelings to the feelings and expectations of other people projected in an ideal outside spectator. Even a criminal person accepts some moral rules in order to be recognized and accepted by at least his peer group. Yet in contrast with economic market-regulation driven by self-interest, moral self-regulation is motivated by the desire of social acceptance and moderates our self-interested economic ambitions. But Smith was well aware that this moral regulation of economics was more fragile than the self-regulating teleology of free markets which promote prosperity without limiting economics. The four limits set up by Aristotle became redundant and were gradually discarded. We get a complete new agenda for modern economics.

There is no longer a reason to be concerned about wealth accumulation in the context of a positive-sum game of market exchange because overproduction can only be a temporary mismatch between supply and demand. The right remedy to overcome the mismatch is to dismantle the natural and social barriers to free competition in order to restore the optimal equilibrium.

A similar argument based on the self-regulating power of financial markets is put forward to promote the nearly unrestricted creation of money and credit. "Authorities should not interfere with the pollinating bees of Wall street' is a nice quote of Alan Greenspan from his biography.

The third limit separating economics from politics is no longer valid because the constitution and *modus operandi* of markets require at least some well-designed political action and regulation. A free market economy is part of the broader scope of political economy. Because the market combines rational with *free* choice, modern economics overcomes theoretically the Aristotelian fear of losing political freedom through the expansion of economics.[2] The economic man is not a slave but a free and rational individual.

The agenda of the Aristotelian manager or *despotes* is no longer restricted to the economy. Because all human activities are characterized by scarcity of time and resources, the rational manager is needed in all sectors of life. All human problems

[2] In a social context with many rational actors and managers, the free market offers a solution. Instead of claiming a super rational manager who transforms the state into a despotic regime, the market introduces a system of free exchange where all rational actors can try to make a benefit without manipulating the other or imposing his/her will.

need rational management to be solved. Hence the growing and despotic power of technocratic management in all fields of human action.

In many ways the modern belief in the self-regulating power of the markets has been proven to be naïve. The current financial crisis is a good example. The idea that financial markets are self-regulative and efficient implies that genuine bubbles cannot occur, that the asset prices always reflect the underlying economic fundamentals and that we do not need regulation by governments or central banks. These assumptions make us blind for reality. But even today, the belated 'conversion' of some neoliberal economists need not imply a fundamental shift in their way of reasoning. Of course, some measures have been taken to reduce the oligopolistic power of banks too big to fail and to make financial markets more transparent, but the computer models and the minds of the actors on the stock exchange didn't change that much. The corrections are mainly perceived as corrections of 'market failures' (more transparency, less monopolistic power) which are necessary but do not address the deeper economic paradoxes of our economic system.

4.3 Adam Smith's Moral Teleology

For many economists Adam Smith represents the transition to modern rational economics. But there is of course another Adam Smith as well. Besides the Adam Smith who discovered the self-regulating capacity of the market economy, there is also the Adam Smith as promoter of the role of virtue in economic life (Smith 1759). We can safely assert that for Smith economics remained part of a broader moral and political science. The self-regulating efficiency of markets must be evaluated and embedded within the framework of a political economy and an ethically designed teleology .

The economic man in Smith's work who produces the 'wealth of nations' is not the Aristotelian *despotes* nor the modern *homo economicus*. It is the industrious man driven by the virtue of prudence. A modern economist will be inclined to interpret Smith's virtue of prudence as the expression of rational long term self-interest. But for Adam Smith, the motivation behind the virtue of prudence - and behind all moral virtues - is not primarily self-interest. Neither is it altruism. A prudent person looks at his action from the empathic point of view of an impartial spectator who evaluates an action as good if and only if the action seems intrinsically appropriate (propriety) and deserves respect and recognition from a moral community (merit). Of course, the consequences of our actions (utility) will also be part of our moral evaluation. But for Smith utilitarian considerations can only strengthen our motivation but they cannot give us the intrinsic feeling of acting in the right way. For this we need to sympathize with the feelings of an impartial spectator.

In conformity with his sympathy for the industrious and prudent man, Smith's advocacy of the market economy was inspired by his observation that free markets empower industrious individuals against the exploiting upper class. The wealth of a nation is created by the workers and by the middle class and not by kings and the non-productive renter class. The free market economy provided in his view a much better assurance of covering the cost of production, including labor, than the mercantilist policies of government. It is clear that Smith's idea of justice as giving everyone according to his/her effort and contribution is part of his approval of a free market economy.

The ethical and the neoliberal models of economics both apply a teleological mode of reasoning, but in very different ways. While the neoliberal model discards the Aristotelian limits of economics in order to free the *telos* of the market as much as possible, the ethical approach introduces the *telos* of ethics and politics within the field of economics. In line with some late-scholastic philosophers Adam Smith applies Aristotle's political and ethical teleology *in* the world of economics. Concepts as virtues, freedom and justice and moral wisdom that belong, according to Aristotle, to the political sphere become in Smith's discourse part of the economic sphere. The strict demarcation between economics and politics is replaced by a *mixed or hybrid* form of rationality. The new manager must not only be rational. He/she must be fair and virtuous too. The economy must not only be evaluated in terms of growth but also in terms of distributive justice. The hybrid model of 'economics and ethics' transforms the four limits of Aristotle from moral prohibitions into positive ethical and political regulations.

Economic growth or the accumulation of wealth must not be limited in a negative way but positively *combined* with an idea of justice. This effort has a long history in economics. But let me just refer to the more recent attempts of John Rawls (1971) and Amartya Sen (2009) to formulate a theoretical framework that combines economic growth with the idea of justice.

The expansion of money and financial markets must not be prohibited but regulated by a fair-interest theory. Late-scholastic philosophers as Leonardo Lessius (Leuven) and Molina (Salamanca) were the first moral philosophers to develop a full normative theory of interest covering the cost of lending (Bouckaert 1998).

The strict demarcation between economics and politics must be substituted by a *mixed or hybrid* form of political economy exemplified among others in the *Rhineland model* of a social market economy which is quite different from the neoliberal version of political economy.

Because unlimited economic rationality leads to foolishness (A. Sen 1987), economic rationality has to be backed up by practical wisdom, moral deliberation and virtue ethics. Business ethics promotes this new type of ethical leadership.

The neoliberal model of teleological reasoning has been nicely contrasted with the ethical model in the so-called Friedman-Freeman twist of the nineteen eighties (Freeman1984). In Milton Friedman's famous claim that 'the only responsibility of business is to make profit' we find a statement of neoliberal teleology. In contrast to this, Freeman's stakeholder or CSR model applies a mixed teleology combining the aim of profit making in business with the requirement of a fair distribution of profit among the different stakeholders.

However, one of the weak points in the hybrid model of 'economics with justice' is the fact that the economic logic of profit-making and self-interest deeply infiltrates the political sphere. Why should politicians be less opportunistic or less self-interested than ordinary economic man and woman? Aristotle presented a reason in that the strict separation between politics and economics enables citizens to focus on the common good in the public sphere without interference from economic interests. In the non-economic setting of the polis, Aristotelian citizens get the opportunity to develop a higher state of mind. In our current context where economics has invaded the world and commands our use of time and way of reasoning, economic rationality is everywhere. The economization of politics seems to be more powerful than the infusion of ethics in economics. The result is a growing mistrust of politics and political institutions and the incapacity to overcome corruption and opportunism. We need a higher-level-principle of social coordination that enables us to overcome those incapacities and to give the ethical drive in economics a stronger impulse. As Einstein said: we cannot solve our problems with the same thinking we used when we created them. This leads me to a fourth model of teleological reasoning in economics where spirituality as intrinsic motivation of human action plays a central role.

4.4 From Rational to Relational Economics

Human history did not follow the Aristotelian model of economic and social coordination. It was a too narrow straitjacket for the modern idea of social progress based on economic growth, political emancipation and social welfare. But as already said, despite modern progress, the Aristotelian claim for limits reappeared on the scene: limits to growth, limits to the creation of money, limits to the dynamics of markets and limits to rational management. Although we can learn a lot from the Aristotelian warnings, it would be an illusion to turn back to his natural teleology. We will not stop, nor should we, economic development, or the role of financial markets, or the necessity of rational management and the dynamics of new markets such as the digital markets of communication. They are all inherent parts of modern progress and we benefit from them. However, what we can do is to change the meaning and *telos* of our fundamental economic concepts not by an external limit but by an internally chosen limit.

Until now, the idea of hybrid rationality that combines economic growth and distributive justice, has been the most appropriate strategy to enhance and enrich the meaning of economic concepts. But more seems to be needed if we want to overcome the 'failures' of that mixed strategy. I believe that the move towards 'spirituality' in economics and business is a next step to understand and overcome the current paradoxes of economic life (Bouckaert 2011a). It is a move back to metaphysics albeit not to the natural teleology of Aristotle. The move to spirituality in economics is often misunderstood. Some reduce spirituality to being a member of a religious community, other to a psychological tool for high feelings or as a therapy to overcome stress and depression. Of course these may be valuable aspects of spirituality for an individual person. But what interests us here is spirituality as a lever for social transformation and social creativity (Bouckaert and Zsolnai 2007). How can spirituality as a public good transform the economy?

A strong case for a spiritual-based economy is given by pope Benedict XVI in chapter 3 of his social encyclical *Caritas in Veritate (2009).*[3] Let me give some quotes where the pope refers to the *principle of gratuitousness* as the key to introduce spirituality in economics.

Economic, social and political development, if it is to be authentically human, needs to make room for the principle of gratuitousness as an expression of fraternity (n°34, p. 55).

Without internal forms of solidarity and mutual trust, the market cannot completely fulfill its proper economic function (n° 35).

The Church's social doctrine holds that authentically human social relationships of friendship, solidarity and reciprocity can also be conducted within economic activity, and not only outside it or "after" it (n° 36, p. 58).

Action is required not only on improving exchange-based transactions and implanting public welfare structures, but above all on gradually increasing openness, in a world context, to forms of economic activity marked by quotas of gratuitousness and communion (n° 39, p. 62).

How can the *principle of gratuitousness* transform a rational economy driven by self-interest into a relational economy that prioritizes relations of mutual trust, responsibility and co-creativity? Gratuity is based on the logic of gift (Hoevel 2009). Here lies the difference: a rational economy exclusively looks at goods, services, and factors of production as scarce and therefore in need of optimally efficient allocation to maximize welfare, individual or collective. By contrast, a relational economy primary looks at the material world of goods and people as gifts that must be respected and allocated in the most responsible way in order to transform the planet into an *oikos* for all human and living beings. Interpreting our economy as composed of gifts changes the meaning of things. Instead of being perceived as scarce and a matter of hard competition (positional goods), they hold the power of interconnecting people and all living beings (relational goods). The purpose of economics is to create relational goods and to transform the gift of our planet into an *oikos,* a house for human and non-human life. In the encyclical the relational economy is also called 'civil economy' (Bruni and Zamagni 2007) and 'economy of communion'.[4]

The idea of a relational economy is not an exclusively Christian concept. Personalism,[5] Buddhism, deep ecology (Zsolnai and Ims 2005) and other

[3] Although I have some problems with other parts of the encyclical, chapter 3 of which has been strongly influenced by the ideas of Stefano Zamagni, it is a challenging piece of economic philosophy. For an analysis of the encyclical see Bouckaert 2012.

[4] Economy of communion is a concept and a practice launched by Chiara Lubich in 1991 at Sao Paulo and promoted by the Focolare movement.

[5] Philosophers as J. Maritain (1936) and E. Mounier (1936) and especially Jewish philosophers as H. Bergson, M. Buber, S. Weil, F. Rozenzweig and E. Levinas opened a new metaphysical perspective originating from personal experiences of deep interconnectedness and leading to social relations of dialogue, social responsibility and servant leadership. See Personalism (Bouckaert 2011b).

philosophical and religious currents that promote *spiritual humanism* claim a paradigm shift towards a relational economy. I will not deal here with these philosophical backgrounds but instead focus on some consequences and principles. The ethical model of economics views the economy as fair distribution of wealth, combining economic growth with the idea of justice. Yet the relational model of economics aims to integrate spiritual growth in economics. While today material growth claims priority over the quality of interhuman and ecological relations, the aim of spiritual economy is to change this balance. Spiritual growth stands for the development of the inner self connected intuitively to all other living beings and to Life itself. How can we produce goods and services that foster a deep sense of interconnectedness instead of disconnecting people from nature and from their true selves? How do we design indicators that measure public fulfillment and happiness? How does one limit the unbridled drive to always more and bigger and yet develop new and innovative economic activities? Let us again – as we did for the other models of teleology - use the four Aristotelian criteria for a good economy as a reference point, in order to design the specific teleology of relational economics.

Limits to Wealth Accumulation In order to rebalance spiritual and material growth we need a principle that enables us to limit income-based economic growth as the ultimate horizon of economics. In my view the *principle* of *frugality* can help us a lot (Bouckaert 2008). In economics, the frugal and industrious man has been praised by Adam Smith and promoted by Max Weber as the embodiment of worldly asceticism, the protestant driver of early capitalism. Frugality, however, disappeared from the post-war economic scene, giving way to consumerism as a more efficient path to economic growth. Today frugality is again on the scene as part of the idea of sustainable economic growth. But its reappearance remains very ambiguous as long as sustainability is only part of a competitive game to grow faster and smarter than others do. Even if we lower some forms of consumption and limit the use of non-renewable resources, we still may consider our environment exclusively as a means to satisfying our needs and desires. As long as the drive to always more and bigger remains the underlying logic of the system, we miss the idea of spiritual growth. The principle of frugality requires an *art de vivre* with low material consumption and a simple lifestyle in order to open the mind for non-material social, cultural and relational goods. Frugality as detachment from material goods need not imply austere practice of ascetics. A more authentic criterion of frugality is its capacity to disclose and enjoy the intrinsic value of things. The *Slow Food Movement* is a good example. It points the way toward using more qualitative foods and meals, in a more convivial society, while recognizing the ecological limits of the earth. It is a way toward greater joy by accepting limits.

Limits to Money Creation Relational economics does not aim to close financial markets as they are needed to create economic activities and employment. But to overcome the greed of monetary economics we need fundamental corrections in the system. From the seventeenth century onwards, the prohibition of interest, proclaimed for centuries by religious and moral authorities, lost its relevance. Since then interest has been a market-regulated price for money. But the generalization of interest payment was not just an innocuous event. It deeply changed the socio-cultural and economic context. Generalized, market-driven interest payment is only possible in a context of hard competition and endless growth. Indeed, if the average economic growth is lower than the average interest rate, interest can only be repaid through liquidation or by moving debt to future generations. Generalized interest payment is closely linked to the industrial growth obsession of 'always more and bigger'. Moreover, it concentrates wealth in the hands of those who have interest-bearing assets and can invest their money in ventures with a high return on capital. To correct the current system we must reactivate some principles of the older economic wisdom such as the prioritization of the real over the monetary economy, the distinction between lending and investing money, the precedence of public happiness over income growth and the role of cooperative economics. But more is needed. Bernard Lietaer, central banker, university professor and co-designer of the European Currency Unit (the precursor to the euro), is pleading for the creation and promotion of a *complimentary* system of money without interest payment. The aim is not to replace financial markets but to develop diversity, resilience and a spirit of cooperation in the financial system in order to limit the power of banks too big to fail. Lietaer and Dunne (2013) present stories of creative people and communities from all over the world who invent alternative currencies to strengthen local economics, create employment and new social services. The LET's, the PEN exchange (US) or the WIR (Swiss) are nice examples.[6] These complementary currencies are intended to re-balance the yang and ying side of the homo oeconomicus (Lietaer 2001). The rational, yang-sided 'economic man' will finally be challenged and complemented by a relational, yin-sided 'economic woman'. It is this integration of the person as a *relational being* in our economic and financial system which is also aimed at by personalism and other streams of spiritual humanism.[7]

Beyond Markets and Politics Against the tendency to limit the coordination of society to a binary market-plus-state synergy, relational economics calls for a triadic model of social and economic coordination. This is the core idea of *Caritas in Veritate* and of all forms of 'civil economy'. The logic of exchange (giving in order to acquire) is related to markets, the logic of public obligation (giving as a legal duty) to the State and the logic of gift (gratuitously giving) to civil society. The logic of gift is based on the principle of gratuitousness and practiced in voluntary relations of solidarity and fraternity. Before claiming life as a right or a possession, it is

[6]According to Lietaer and Dunne (2013) worldwide over 4000 complementary currencies are brought into use. Alternative currencies are not new. During the crisis of the 1930 's, there were some successful introductions. But most of them did not succeed because national authorities did not accept them as a means for legal payment. One exception is the WIR in Switzerland which is still in use. To-day governments actively support new experiments. Some are designed for the development of local economy and employment such as the LETS (Local Exchange Trading System) which in France are known as *Grain de Sel* (SEL). Others are intended to stimulate local systems of social care as e.g. the 'Caring Relationship Tickets" or *Hureai Kippu* in Japan (1995). A third category of currencies started to meet unmet needs in a local community such as e.g. the PEN exchange in Takoma Park (US).

[7]A fuller treatment of alternative currency is beyond the scope of this paper.

a gift. But the innovative point to make here is the statement that the three principles of coordination are not only necessary for a good society, they are required for a flourishing market economy. The principle of gratuitousness is an inherent part of economics and of politics as well. One of the most original defenders of the triadic model of coordination today is the Italian economist Luigino Bruni: "Life is neither happy nor fully human when liberty and equality are lacking, but the great illusion of market humanism has been to think that one might preserve something authentically human while removing the relationship of fraternity, with its tragic burden of sorrow and suffering. The great challenge of post-modernity will thus be to hold these three principles together while devising and building a three-dimensional humanism "(Bruni 2012: 111).

Beyond Rational Management In his book *A Guide for the Perplexed*, E. F. Schumacher (2004) makes an interesting distinction between convergent and divergent problems (Bouckaert 2013). Convergent problems are problems that can be designed and solved as technical and rational problems. At the end, there is one optimal solution, i.e., there is in a given context and with a given budget one optimal point of supply and demand. Economic rationality is basically formatted for this way of problem solving. Divergent problems, on the other hand, are problems that lead people to different and opposite answers. There is no single optimal solution any more. Schumacher illustrates this with the case of education, where those who are primarily committed to *freedom* will defend non-authoritarian answers to all educational problems, while people primarily committed to *order* will always argue in favor of discipline and obedience on the part of pupils. Such divergent positions cannot be resolved on logical grounds or by optimization procedures. They are based on strong and different value-commitments. To be solved they require a capacity to engage in an empathic dialogue in order to disclose common ground for action. This capacity to overcome diversity and conflict through the search of a higher state of interconnectedness and through the practice of dialogical thinking forms the core of what is today called *spiritual-based leadership* (Bouckaert 2011c; Pruzan and Pruzan Mikkelsen 2007). Its basic characteristics are a deep and personal sense of interconnectedness beyond diversity which is the core experience of spirituality, a talent to empower and to transform people into a co-creative and co-responsible community instead of paternalizing or manipulating them and the gift of imagination to disclose new horizons for future action.

4.5 Conclusion

In this paper we identified four teleological models at work in economic discourse. Each of them has its own teleological view on the nature of economics and the way economics is embedded in a broader social matrix. Of course there is a shared toolbox of concepts. Economics is about the production, consumption and distribution of goods and services. There is no modern economy without money, prices, markets, rational choices, business etc. But the way these concepts are designed, interpreted and applied depends on the way the teleology of economics is perceived and integrated in a broader view of society and history. Economics as a 'moral science' is a way of looking to economics from this broader perspective.

But promoting economics as a moral science today cannot be reduced to going back to the economics of Aristotle or Adam Smith. It is important to realize that these models are conceived and practiced in a specific historical context. Being an answer to the crisis of their time, we have to deconstruct and reconstruct elements of these models into a new paradigm for our time. The credibility of a new paradigm however depends on its capacity to disclose some problems that have been disregarded by a previous model. The reason why we believe in the power of the spiritually based model of economics is its capacity to offer an answer to what we perceive as the most urgent problems of our time. Instrumental rationality and a strong belief in self-interest as basic motivation have been the drivers of modern economic reasoning. They are considered as the main levers behind industrialization, big business and economic globalization. But their success has a dark side. As we can observe, they crowd out the joy of intrinsic human motivation and the principle of gratuitousness and fraternity in economics. They create a 'joyless economy' (Scitovsky 1976) and generate income growth without happiness. Yet even more threatening is the increase of ecological problems and social burn-outs that are related to the overexploitation of human and natural resources. How can we as individuals and communities choose to *limit* this self-interested and self-destructive drive to always more and bigger without destroying the positive benefits of markets and politics.

The emerging paradigm of a spiritual-based model of economics and business provides us at least the right questions and a horizon for new answers. Although its message sounds promising, it still remains a vulnerable and marginal shift in economics. It has to prove its capacity to unlock new layers of energy, motivation and imagination in human beings. It has to demonstrate its validity through example by responsible leaders and entrepreneurs. However the pressure to solve the global ecological and social problems will likely induce leaders to a risky gamble. They can opt for more self-interest, individual and collective, using the power of technology to survive and to destroy their competitors. Or they can choose to change not only their strategies but also their minds. They can choose to be guided not by the *ratio* of self-interest but by the *spirit* of interconnectedness.[8] This is a choice for an open, inner directed and shared teleology in economics.

References

Aristotle. *The Politics* (written 335–323 BC), published in Penguin Classics, 1962, 1981, London.
Benedict, X.V.I. 2009. *Caritas in Veritate*. Vaticana: Liberia Editrice.

[8]The spirit is the human faculty that relates us in a non-conceptual and intuitive way to all living beings and to Life as the transcendent Source in all of them.

Bouckaert, L. 1998. The Ethics of Interest. A Cultural-Historical Perspective. In *Working Across Cultures. Ethical Perspectives for Intercultural Management*, eds. H. Lange, A. Löhr, and H.D. Steinmann, 305–321. Dordrecht: Kluwer Academic Publishers.

———. 2008. Rational Versus Spiritual Concepts of Frugality. In *Frugality. Rebalancing Material and Spiritual Values in Economic Life*, eds. L. Bouckaert, H. Opdebeeck, and L. Zsolnai, 27–45. Oxford: Peter Lang.

———. 2011a. Spirituality and Rationality. In *The Palgrave Handbook of Spirituality and Business*, eds. L. Bouckaert and L. Zsolnai, 18–26. Palgrave Macmillan: Hampshire.

———. 2011b. Personalism. In *The Palgrave Handbook of Spirituality and Business*, eds. L. Bouckaert and L. Zsolnai, 155–163. Palgrave Macmillan: Hampshire.

———. 2011c. Spiritual-Based Leadership. In *Responsibility, Deep Ecology & The Self*, eds. O. Jacobson and L. Pederson, 235–249. Oslo: Forlag 1.

———. 2012. Leadership Ethics and *Caritas in Veritate*. In *The Moral Dynamics of Economic Life. An Extension and Critique of Caritas in Veritate*, ed. D.K. Finn, 83–88. Oxford: Oxford University Press.

———. 2013. Schumacher and the Principle of Responsibility in Economics. In *Responsible Economics. E.F. Schumacher and his Legacy for the 21st Century*, ed. H. Opdebeeck, 209–225. Oxford: Peter Lang.

Bouckaert, L., and L. Zsolnai, eds. 2007. *Spirituality as a Public Good*. Garant: Antwerp.

Bruni, L. 2012. *The Wound and the Blessing Economics, Relationships and Happiness*. New York: New City Press.

Bruni, L., and S. Zamagni. 2007. *Civil Economy. Efficiency, Equity, Public Happiness*. Oxford: Peter Lang.

Freeman, E. 1984. *Strategic Management: A Stakeholder Approach*. Boston: Pitman.

Hoevel, C. 2009. Towards the Paradigm of Gift. *Revista Cultura Economica* 75/76: 89–97.

Lietaer, B. 2001. *The Future of Money*. London: Random House.

Lietaer, B., and J. Dunne. 2013. *Rethinking Money. How New Currencies Turn Scarcity into Prosperity*. San Francisco: Barrett-Koehler Publishers.

Maritain, J. 1936. *Humanisme Intégral*. Paris: Aubier.

Mounier, E. 1936. *Manifeste au service du personnalisme*. Paris: Montaigne.

Pruzan, P., and K. Pruzan Mikkelsen. 2007. *Leading with Wisdom Spiritual-based Leadership in Business*. Sheffield: Greenleaf Publishing.

Rawls, J. 1971. *A Theory of Justice*. Oxford: Oxford University Press.

Schumacher, E.F. 2004. *A Guide for the Perplexed*. London: Harper Perennial.

Scitovsky, T. 1976. *The Joyless Economy: An Inquiry into Human Satisfaction and Consumer Dissatisfaction*. Oxford: Oxford University Press.

Sen, A. 1987. *On Ethics and Economics*. Oxford: Blackwell.

———. 2009. *The Idea of Justice*. London: Allan Lane.

Smith, A. 1759. *The Theory of Moral Sentiments*. Reprint in 1976. Oxford: Oxford University Press.

———. 1776. *The Wealth of Nations*. Published in Penguin Books, 1970, London.

Zsolnai, L., and K. Ims. 2005. *Business within Limits: Deep Ecology and Buddhist Economics*. Oxford: Peter Lang.

Chapter 5
Economic Rationality Versus Human Reason

Laszlo Zsolnai

Abstract First the paper analyses the rationality assumptions of mainstream economics and shows that they are empirically misleading and normatively inadequate. It argues that the world ruled by self-interest based rationality of economic actors leads to 'unreason' from a wider ecological and human perspective. The paper illuminates that human reason requires a different way of economic functioning which implies a redefinition of the final goal economizing.

It is argued that the main goal of economic activities should not be profit-making but providing right livelihood for people. Amartya Sen suggests that economic reason can be understood as reasonableness of preferences, choices and actions. Reason requires that economic activities are achieved in ecological, future-respecting and pro-social ways. Intrinsically motivated economic agents who balance their attention and concerns across diverse value-dimensions are able to do this and show the viability of true economic reason under the circumstances of present day "rationally foolish" economic world.

In the Financial Times and his Apostolic Exhortation "EVANGELII GAUDIUM" *Pope Francis* heavily criticizes the idolization of money and the excesses of global capitalism including the "widespread preoccupation with profits and today's throwaway culture, that enslave the heart and mind of all of us" (Dinmore and Segreti 2013, Pope Francis 2013).

The doctrine of mainstream economics is greatly responsible for the development of the economics-dominated world today where – in words of *John Maynard Keynes* – "fair is foul and foul is fair" because "foul is useful and fair is not" (Keynes 1930).

First the paper analyses the *rationality assumptions* of mainstream economics and shows that they are empirically misleading and normatively inadequate. It argues that the world ruled by self-interest based rationality of economic actors leads to 'unreason' from a wider ecological and human perspective. The paper

L. Zsolnai (✉)
Corvinus University of Budapest, Budapest, Hungary

European SPES Institute, Leuven, Belgium
e-mail: zsolnai@uni-corvinus.hu

P. Rona, L. Zsolnai (eds.), *Economics as a Moral Science*,
Virtues and Economics 1, DOI 10.1007/978-3-319-53291-2_5

illuminates that *human reason* requires a different way of economic functioning which implies a redefinition of the final goal of economizing.

5.1 Economic Rationality

The rational choice model has been widely used in economics, political science and other social sciences as a basic model of human choice behavior. The model states that the agent should maximize her or his utility function to be considered rational.

Agents are considered rational if their preferences are transitive and complete and they choose what they most prefer among the available alternatives.

The rational choice model does not presuppose anything about the preferences people have. They may have self-centered, altruistic or even sado-masochistic preferences. The rational choice model represents a formal theory that says nothing about what people prefer or should prefer. Hereafter this model is referred as the *weak form* of *rationality*.

In economics and also in political science we can find a much stronger version of rationality where the assumptions of self-interest and perfect knowledge are added to the weak form of rationality. Hence we get the *Homo Oeconomicus* model according to which individuals are rational, exclusively self-interested and have perfect knowledge about the consequences of their choices. The Homo Oeconomicus model does have *substantive assumptions* about what people want and the manner in which they want it. This model is hereafter referred to as the *strong form* of *rationality* (Zsolnai 2008).

Herbert A. Simon (1982) has been a relentless critic of the rational choice model for decades. He states that the model has overly strong claims on human beings. Real people have poor cognitive capacity and the information available to them is rather limited in most cases.

Agents in the real world are not capable of maximizing their utility function. Instead of maximizing, they usually make *"satisficing"* decisions. They usually choose the first available alternative that is good enough for them in the sense that it satisfies their aspiration level. This is the main message of the *theory* of *bounded rationality* for which Simon received the Nobel Prize in Economics.

Simon writes, "Faced with a choice situation where it is impossible to optimize, or where the computational cost of doing so seems burdensome, the decision maker may look for a satisfactory, rather than an optimal alternative. Frequently, a course of action satisfying a number of constraints, even a sizeable number, is far easier to discover than a course of action maximizing some function" (Simon 1987: 244).

The question arises of how a decision maker may set the level of criteria that define "satisfactory". "Psychology proposes the mechanism of aspiration levels: if it turns out to be very easy to find alternatives that meet the criteria, the standards are gradually raised; if the search continues for a long while without finding satisfactory alternatives, the standards are gradually lowered. Thus, by a kind of feedback mechanism, or 'tatonement', the decision maker converges toward a set of criteria that are attainable, but not without effort. The difference between the aspiration level mechanism and the optimization procedure is that the former calls for much simpler computations than the latter" (Simon 1987: 244).

During the last decades abundant empirical evidence has been produced by economists and psychologists that shows that bounded rationality is important in real world situations.

Psychologist *Daniel Kahneman* criticizes the rational choice model on the basis of research findings, which indicate that people are *myopic* in their decisions, may lack skill in predicting their future tastes, and can be led to *erroneous choices* by fallible memory and incorrect evaluation of past experiences (Kahneman 2011).

Kahneman differentiates between experienced utility and predicted utility. The *experienced utility* of an outcome is the measure of the hedonic experience of that outcome. The *predicted utility* of an outcome is defined as the individual's beliefs about its experienced utility at some future time. Predicted utility is an *ex ante* variable, while experienced utility is an *ex post* variable in the decision-making process.

According to the rational choice model, decisions are made on the basis of predicted utility. If experienced utility greatly differs from predicted utility then this may lead to sub-rational, or even irrational choices.

The problem of predicted utility raises the question: "Do people know what they will like?" The answer is a definite "No." The accuracy of people's hedonic predictions is generally quite poor.

Experimental studies suggest two conclusions: (i) people may have little ability to forecast changes in their hedonic responses to stimuli; and (ii) even in situations that permit accurate hedonic predictions, people may tend to make decisions about future consumption without due consideration of possible changes in their tastes (Kahneman 2011).

Discrepancies between *retrospective utility* and *real-time* utility should also be addressed. This leads to the question: "Do people know what they have liked?" The answer is again a definite "No." Psychological experiments show that retrospective evaluations should be viewed with greater distrust than introspective reports of current experience.

The results of these studies support the following two empirical generalizations: (1) *The Peak & End Rule*: global evaluations are predicted with high accuracy by a weighted combination of the most extreme affect recorded during the episode and of the affect recorded during the terminal moments of the episode. (2) *Duration Neglect*. The retrospective evaluation of overall or total pain (or pleasure) is not affected by the duration period (Kahneman 2011).

Since individuals use their evaluative memories to guide them in their choices toward future outcomes, deceptive retrospective evaluations may lead to erroneous choices.

Kahneman identifies two major obstacles to the maximization of experienced utility required by the rational choice model. People lack skill in the task of predicting how their tastes might change. It is difficult to describe as rational agents who are prone to large errors in predicting what they will want or enjoy next week.

Another obstacle is a tendency to use the affect associated with particular moments as a proxy for the utility of extended outcomes. Observations of memory biases are significant because the evaluation of the past determines what is learned from it. Errors in the lessons drawn from experience will inevitably be reflected in deficient choices for the future (Kahneman 2011).

Amartya Sen concluded that if real people behaved in the way that is required of them by the rational choice model then they would act like "rational fools."

Sen criticizes both the weak and strong forms of rationality. He refers to the weak form as "internal consistency of choice" and to the strong form as "maximization of self-interest."

He states "It is hard to believe that internal consistency of choice can itself be an adequate condition of rationality. If a person does exactly the opposite of what would help achieving what he or she would want to achieve, and does this with flawless internal consistency (always choosing exactly the opposite of what will enhance the occurrence of things he or she wants and values), the person can scarcely be seen as rational. (…) Rational choice must demand something at least about the correspondence between what one tries to achieve and how one goes about it" (Sen 1987: 13).

Sen uses the term "*correspondence rationality*" to describe the correspondence of choice with the aims and values of the agent. He states that this kind of correspondence must be a necessary condition of rationality, regardless of whether or not it is also the sufficient condition. Correspondence rationality might be supplemented by some requirements on the nature of the reflection regarding what the actor should want and value (Sen 1987: 13–14).

It might well be arguable that rational behavior must demand some consistency, but consistency itself can hardly be adequate to ensure the rationality of choice. Internal consistency is not a guarantee of a person's rationality.

Rationality as self-interest maximization has additional problems. Sen asks, "Why should it be uniquely rational to pursue one's own self-interest to the exclusion of everything else?" Sen argues that the self-interest view of rationality "involves inter alia a firm rejection of the "ethics-based" view of motivation. Trying to do one's best to achieve what one would like to achieve can be a part of rationality, and this can include the promotion of non-self-interested goals which we may value and wish to aim at. To see any departure from self-interest maximization as evidence of irrationality must imply a rejection of the role of ethics in actual decision making" (Sen 1987: 15).

According to Sen, "universal selfishness as actuality may well be false, but universal selfishness as a requirement of rationality is patently absurd" (Sen 1987: 16).

Rationality can be interpreted broadly as the discipline of subjecting one's choice – of action as well as objectives, values and priorities – to reasoned scrutiny. In the light of this definition reasonable economic choices should not necessarily satisfy the criteria of "internal consistency of choice" or "maximizing self-interest". Economic choices should be subjected to the demands of reason (Sen 2002).

Behavioral economist *Robert Frank* developed a model that emphasizes the role of the emotions in making choices. Frank argues that *passions* often *serve our interest* very well indeed because we face important problems that are simply unsolvable by rational action. "Emotions often predispose us to behave in ways that are contrary to our narrow interests, and being thus predisposed can be an advantage" (Frank 1988: 4–7).

Human behavior is directly guided by a complex psychological reward mechanism. Rational calculations are the input for the reward mechanism. "Feelings and emotions, apparently, are the proximate causes of most behavior. (…) The reward theory of behavior tells us that these sentiments can and do compete with feelings that spring from rational calculations about material payoffs" (Frank 1988: 51–53).

The *modular brain theory* supports Frank's ideas. According to the modular theory, the brain is organized into a host of separate modules. Each module has its own capacity for processing information and motivating behavior. Most of these brain modules do not "speak"; they simply do not have language capability. Even more importantly, these non-language modules are *not* equally well connected to the central language module of the brain. Perhaps this is the cause of the seeming disparity between different methods of assessing motivation.

Modular brain theorists view the language module of the brain as the center of our rational consciousness, obsessed with rationalizing all that we feel and do. However, there is a great deal of information that enters the central nervous system that cannot be accessed by the language module. The modular brain theory suggests, "that when economists talk about maximizing utility, they are really talking about the language module of the left hemisphere, however, it does not account for all of our behavior. (…) The rational utility-maximizing language module of the brain may simply be ill-equipped to deal with many of the most important problems we face" (Frank 1988: 205–211).

Frank's main conclusion is that persons directly motivated to pursue their self-interest are often doomed to fail for exactly that reason. Problems can often be solved by persons who have abandoned the quest for maximal material advantage. The emotions that lead people to behave in irrational ways can indirectly lead to greater material well-being (Frank 1988: 258–259).

After a decade-long preoccupation with the rational choice model, sociologist *Jon Elster* developed an alternative theory that he calls the *theory* of *social norms*. (Elster 1989, 2007) Elster contrasts rational action with norm-guided behavior. Rational action is outcome-oriented. Rationality says: "If you want to achieve X, do Y." Elster defines social norms as devices that are not outcome-oriented. Social norms say "Do X" or "Do not do Y" or "If you do X then do Y" or "Do X if it would be good if everyone did X."

"Rationality is essentially conditional and future-oriented. Its imperatives are hypothetical; that is, conditional on the future outcomes one wants to realize. The imperatives expressed in social norms are either unconditional or, if conditional, not future-oriented. In the latter case norms make the action dependent on past events or (more rarely) on hypothetical outcomes" (Elster 1989: 98).

Not all norms are social. There are two requisite conditions for norms to be considered social. First, they must be shared by other people and second, partly sustained by their approval or disapproval. "In addition to being supported by the attitudes of other people, norms are sustained by the feelings of embarrassment, anxiety, guilt and shame that a person suffers at the prospect of violating them, or at least at the prospect of being caught violating them. Social norms have a grip on the mind that is due to the strong emotions their violations can trigger. (…) A norm, in this perspective, is the propensity to feel shame and to anticipate sanctions by others at the thought of behaving in a certain, forbidden way" (Elster 1989: 99–100 and 105).

Elster argues for the reality and autonomy of social norms. By the reality of norms he means that norms have independent motivating power. Norms are not merely ex post rationalization of self-interest. They serve as ex ante sources of action. Autonomy of norms means their *irreducibility* to *optimization*. Norms are *partly shaped* by self-interest because people often adhere to the norms that favor them. However, norms are not fully reducible to self-interest. The unknown residual is a brute fact (Elster 1989: 125 and 150).

Communitarian thinkers criticize the *liberal conception* of the *self* that is at the heart of the rational choice model.

Philosopher *Charles Taylor* has argued that the liberal conception of the self is basically an atomistic conception of the person and that of human agency focusing exclusively on will and freedom of choice. Taylor defends a relational, intersubjective conception of the self that stresses the social, cultural, historical and linguistic constitution of personal identity. By rejecting the voluntaristic conception of human agency he has formulated a cognitive conception that emphasizes the role of critical reflection, self-interpretation, and rational evaluation (Taylor 1985).

Catholic philosopher *Alasdair MacIntyre* defends a teleological and contextualist view of human agency. According to him, moral conduct is characterized by the *exercise* of *virtues* that aims at realization of the good. No agent can properly locate, interpret, and evaluate her or his actions except by participating in a moral tradition or in a moral community (MacIntyre 1988).

In feminist literature the rational choice theory, and especially the strong form of rationality, is often criticized for presupposing an androcentric, male-biased conception of the human person, the so-called *separative self* (Ferber and Nelson (eds.) 1993; Nelson 2006).

In her book "Beyond Self-Interest" *Jane J. Mansbridge* offers an alternative theory of choice that is inspired by feminine values. She distinguishes three forms of motivation, namely *duty, self-interest,* and *love*. Starting with her own case she says, "I have a duty to care for my child, and I am happy by his happiness, and I get a simple sensual pleasure from snuggling close to him as I read him a book. I have a principled commitment to work for women's liberation, and I empathize with women, and I find a way to use some of my work for women as background to a book that advances my academic career. Duty, love (or empathy), and self-interest are intermingled in my actions in a way I can rarely sort out" (Mansbridge 1990: 134).

Mansbridge favors the coincidence of duty and love with self-interest. She says that both forms of non-self-interested motives (empathic feelings and moral commitments) are embedded in a social context, which makes them susceptible to being undermined by self-interested behavior on the part of others. Arrangements are required that generate some self-interested return for non-self-interested behavior to create an "ecological niche" for sustaining such behavior. Arrangements that make the absence of self-interested behavior less costly in self-interested terms increase the degree to which individuals feel that they can afford to indulge their feelings of empathy and their moral commitments (Mansbridge 1990: 136–137).

Based on the criticisms reported above we can say that the concept of economic rationality propagated by mainstream economics is *empirically misleading* and *normatively inadequate*. James March rightly characterized it as the myth of rationality (March 2006).

The conception of economic rationality understood as materialistic self-interest maximization inevitably leads to large-scale ecological destruction, human deprivation and disregard for the interest of future generations.

5.2 Human Reason

According to Amartya Sen human reason requires that an action is based on right motivation, executed by fair processes, and leads to desirable outcomes (Sen 2004). Within this interpretation, economic rationality as we know it is neither intelligent nor ethical by definition.

I argue that economic activities should pass the test of *ecology*, *future generations*, and *society* to be qualified for human reason. This triple criteria require that economic activities should not destroy nature, or violate the interests of future generations, or pose negative impacts on society. Economic actions can be claimed 'reasonable' only if they satisfy all of these criteria.

From the perspective of nature ecological integrity is a central value. The notion of ecological integrity was introduced by American environmentalist Aldo Leopold in his classic *A Sand County Almanac*. He writes: "a thing is right when it tends to preserve the integrity, stability, and beauty of the biotic community. It is wrong when it tends otherwise" (Leopold 1948).

Economic activities might be evaluated against environmental indicators that operationalize the notion of ecological integrity.

Let A be an economic activity. Let E1,...,Ej,...,En be environmental indicators. (n > 1)

Ei(.) is an ecological value function defined as follows:

$$\mathrm{Ej}(\mathrm{A}) = \begin{cases} 1 & \text{if economic activity A is good regarding environmental indicator Ej;} \\ 0 & \text{if economic activity A is neutral regarding environmental indicator Ej;} \\ -2 & \text{if economic activity A is bad regarding environmental indicator Ej.} \end{cases} \quad (5.1)$$

Ei(A) reflects the ecological value of economic activity A regarding environmental indicator Ej.

The following vector represents the ecological value of economic activity A regarding all environmental indicators E1,...,Ej,...,En.

$$E(A) = [E1(A),\ldots,Ej(A),\ldots,En(A)] \tag{5.2}$$

To get an aggregate picture about the ecological value of the economic activity in question we should define weights that show the importance of environmental indicators. Let a1,...,aj,...,an be such importance weights.

It is required that

$$\Sigma aj = 1 \tag{5.3}$$

The aggregate ecological value of economic activity A can be calculated as follows:

$$E(A) = \Sigma aj\ Ej(A) \tag{5.4}$$

E(A) shows the aggregate ecological value of economic activity A. ($1 \geq E(A) \geq -2$).

An economic activity is considered ecological if and only if its aggregate ecological value is positive. That is

$$E(A) > 0 \tag{5.5}$$

How can we evaluate economic activities from the perspective of future generations? We can never know much about the interests of future generations but freedom is a central value here.

Edith Brown Weiss argued that the freedom of future generations is insured by satisfying the following principles: (i) conservation of options; (ii) conservation of quality; and (iii) conservation of access (Brown Weiss 1989).

Considering principles (i), (ii), and (iii) future generations indicators can be created. Let F1,...,Fj,...,Fn be such indicators against which economic activity system can be evaluated. ($n > 1$)

Future generations value function Fj ( ) is defined as follows:

$$Fj(A) = \begin{cases} 1 & \text{if economic activity A is good regarding future generations indicator } Fj; \\ 0 & \text{if economic activity A is neutral regarding future generations indicator } Fj; \\ -2 & \text{if economic activity A is \textit{bad} regarding future generations indicator } Fj. \end{cases} \tag{5.6}$$

Fj(A) reflects the future generations value of economic activity A regarding indicator Fj.

The following vector represents the future generations value of economic activity A regarding future generations indicators F1,...,Fj,...,Fn.

$$F(A) = [F1(A),\ldots,Fj(A),\ldots,Fn(A)] \tag{5.7}$$

To get an aggregate picture about the future generations value of economic activity A we should introduce weights that show the importance of indicators F1,...,Fj,...,Fn. Let b1,...,bj,...,bn be such importance weights.

It is required that

$$\sum bj = 1 \tag{5.8}$$

The aggregate future generations value of economic activity A can be calculated as follows:

$$\sum bj\ Fj(A) \tag{5.9}$$

F(A) shows the aggregate future generations value of economic activity A. $1 > F(A) > -2$.

An economic activity can be considered future respecting if its aggregate future generations value is positive. That is

$$F(A) > 0 \tag{5.10}$$

Economic activities should be pro-social, that is should contribute to the development of people's capabilities.

Amartya Sen proposed to understand people''s well-being in terms of capabilities. Capability is a reflection of the freedom of a person to achieve valuable functioning. Therefore capabilities can be interpreted as a substantive freedom that people enjoy (Sen 1992).

Let G1,...,Gj,...,Gn be capability indicators against which the economic activities can be evaluated. (j > 1)

Let Gj ( ) social value function be defined as follows:

$$Gj(A) = \begin{cases} 1 & \text{if economic activity A is good regarding capability indicator } Gj; \\ 0 & \text{if economic activity A is neutral regarding capability indicator } Gj; \\ -2 & \text{if economic activity A is \textit{bad} regarding capability indicator } Gj. \end{cases} \tag{5.11}$$

Gj(A) shows the social value of economic activity A regarding capability indicator Gj.

The following vector represents the social value of economic activity system A regarding all the capability indicators G1,...,Gj,...,Gn.

$$G(A) = [G1(A), \ldots, Gj(A), \ldots, Gn(A)] \quad (5.12)$$

To get an aggregate picture about the social value of economic activity A we should introduce weights that show the importance of the capability indicators. Let c1,...,cj,...,cn be such importance weights.

It is required that

$$\sum cj = 1 \quad (5.13)$$

The aggregate social value of economic activity A can be calculated as follows:

$$G(A) = \sum cj\ Gj(A) \quad (5.14)$$

G(A) shows the aggregate social value of the economic activity A. ($1 \geq G(A) \geq -2$)

An economic activity system is considered pro-social if its aggregate social value is positive. That is

$$G(A) > 0 \quad (5.15)$$

5.3 Redefining the Final Goal of Economizing

I argued elsewhere (Zsolnai 2011) that profit is neither a necessary nor a sufficient criterion of reason in economic affairs. An economic activity can be reasonable without satisfying the profit requirement. And inversely, the produced profit is not a guarantee that an economic activity is reasonable in a wider ecological and social context.

According to human reason economic activities should be ecological, future respecting, and pro-social. For them (5.5), (5.10), and (5.15) should be simultaneously hold. That is

$$E(A) > 0, \quad F(A) > 0, \quad G(A) > 0 \quad (5.16)$$

From (5.16) we can derive some basic laws of economizing.

The First Law says that

(α) Economic activities should not harm nature or allow others to come to harm.

The Second Law says that

(β) Economic activities must respect the freedom of future generations except where such respect would conflict with the First Law.

The Third Law says that

(γ) Economic activities must serve the well-being of society as long as such service does not conflict with the First or Second Law.

The main goal of economic activities should not be profit-making but providing right livelihood for those who are involved. Human reason requires that this is achieved in ecological, future respecting, and pro-social ways. Intrinsically motivated economic agents who balance their attention and concerns across diverse value-dimensions are able to do this. The Slow Food movement, ethical fashion, fair trade initiatives, and ethical banking show the viability of true human reason within the present day "rationally foolish" economic world.

References

Brown Weiss, E. 1989. *Fairness to Future Generations: International Law, Common Patrimony, and Intergeneration Equity*. Tokyo/New York: The United Nations University/Transnational Publishers, Inc.

Dinmore, G., and G. Segreti. 2013. Pope takes aim at globalization and money worship *Financial times*, 2013 September 23, p 4.

Elster, J. 1989. *The Cement of Society*. Cambridge: Cambridge University Press.

———. 2007. *Explaning Social Behavior. More Nuts and Bolts for the Social Sciences*. Cambridge: Cambridge University Press.

Ferber, M.A., and J.A. Nelson, eds. 1993. *Beyond Economic Man*. Chicago/London: The University of Chicago Press.

Frank, R. 1988. *Passions Within Reason*. New York/London: W.W. Norton.

Kahneman, D. 2011. *Thinking, Fast and Slow*. New York: Farrar, Straus and Giroux.

Keynes, J.M. 1930. Economic Possibilities of our Grandchildren. In *Essays in Persuasion*, ed. J.M. Keynes (The Collected Writings of John Maynard Keynes. Vol. 9.) 1978. Cambridge: Cambridge University Press.

Leopold, A. 1948. *A Sand County Almanac*. Oxford: Oxford University Press.

MacIntyre, A. 1988. *Whose Justice? Which Rationality?* Notre Dame: University of Norte Dame Press.

Mansbridge, J.J. 1990. On the Relation of Altruism and Self-Interest. In *Beyond Self-Interest*, ed. J.J. Mansbridge, 133–143. Chicago/London: The University of Chicago Press.

March, J. 2006. The Myth of Rationality. In *Interdisciplinary Yearbook of Business Ethics*, ed. L. Zsolnai, 17–29. Oxford: Peter Lang Academic Publishers.

Nelson, J.A. 2006: Economics for Humans. Chicago/London: The University of Chicago Press.

Pope Francis. 2013. *Apostolic Exhortion EVANGELII GAUDIUM*. Vatican City: Vatican Press.

Sen, A. 1987. *On Ethics and Economics*. Oxford: Blackwell.

———. 1992. *Inequality Reexamined*. New York/Oxford: Russell Sage Foundation/Clarendon Press.

———. 2002. Rationality and Freedom. Harvard University Press.

———. 2004. *Rationality and Freedom*. Cambridge, Mass: Harvard University Press.

Simon, H.A. 1982. *Models of Bounded Rationality*. Cambridge/London: The MIT Press.

———. 1987. Satisficing. In *The New Palgrave: A Dictionary of Economics*, 243–245. London: Macmillan.

Taylor, Ch. 1985. *Philosophical Papers*. Cambridge, MA: Cambridge University Press.

Zsolnai, L. 2008. *Responsible Decision Making*. New Brunswick/London: Transaction Publishers.

———. 2011. Redefining Economic Reason. In Spiritual Humanism and Economic Wisdom, H. Opdebeeck and L. Zsolnai (eds.) 187–200. Antwerp/Apeldoom: Garant.

Chapter 6
Rediscovering a Personalist Economy

Hendrik Opdebeeck

Abstract The paper suggests that we can rediscover the personalist philosophy in searching for new models for business and economic actions. At the core of Jacques Maritain's "Humanisme intégral" (1936) is the idea that man is a person who is spiritual in nature, endowed with free will, and thus autonomous in relation to the world. For Maritain the community is central: the true goal of the temporal order is thus more than the mere tallying up of individual needs. It concerns the good life of the entire community—the common good or *bonum commune*. But the temporal *bonum commune* is not the ultimate goal, as it is subordinated to what transcends temporal welfare—the attainment of freedom and spiritual perfection of the human person.

Searching for new models for business functioning and economic policy without preventing the flourishing of either the common good or the human person, invites us to rediscover personalism. In a *Journal of Business Ethics* article with the title *Personalist Business Ethics: Insights from Jacques Maritain*, Alma Acevedo writes that although Maritain "is widely regarded as one of the foremost twentieth century personalist philosophers, his contribution has not been sufficiently considered in the business ethics and humanistic management literature" (Acevedo 2012: 197).

6.1 Maritain's Personalism

During the Depression years of the twentieth century personalists like Emmanuel Mounier and Jacques Maritain insisted on the importance of linking our socio-economic system with a spiritual attitude. Emmanuel Mounier who published his *Manifeste au service du personnalisme* (1936), in the same year as Maritain's *Humanisme Intégral* appeared, shared his preoccupation for a spiritual renewal. Johan De Tavernier states that in line with Mounier, Maritain is of the opinion that

H. Opdebeeck (✉)
Centre for Ethics, University of Antwerp, Antwerp, Belgium
e-mail: hendrik.opdebeeck@uantwerpen.be

P. Rona, L. Zsolnai (eds.), *Economics as a Moral Science*,
Virtues and Economics 1, DOI 10.1007/978-3-319-53291-2_6

individualism obliges us to choose between "annihilation" and "a new order of Christian civilization". However the new Christendom will "not be a repetition of the sacral medieval system, but secular and lay" (Tavernier 2009: 376).

At the beginning of this century we see religion re-enter the discourse: "In substance, the radical Enlightenment position in relation to religion, which Kant after a certain fashion subscribed to with his belief in the passage from a Church religion to pure, rational, moral religion, is not a law of history but a hope, a hoped-for prediction that seemed for a certain time to photograph reality, but which today seems to do so to a much lesser extent" (Possenti 2003: 33). In the last decades of the twentieth century with postmodern and deconstructivist philosophy, one relied on the silent presupposition that historically, some kind of secularization had taken place. But today (think at the phenomenon of *IS* or the popularity of Pope Francis) "facing religion's public role—and its increasing influence in the private realm- this assumption seems no longer tenable" (Weidner 2010: 133). Therefore today we are invited to reread religiously inspired personalists like Mounier and Maritain.

Maritain published in various philosophical areas such as metaphysics, ethics, aesthetics and epistemology. It was his socio-political philosophy, however, that was the most influential. Important publications in this field include, among others: *Religion and Culture* (1930a) and *Christianism and Democracy* (1943). *Integral Humanism (Humanisme Intégral)* of 1936 deserves a special place because this book also contains Maritain's anthropological foundation which makes it possible for Maritain to treat a number of problems that belong to what Aristotle and Thomas Aquinas have called 'practical philosophy'. In his *Journal of Business Ethics article*, Acevedo states: "What a human being *is* and why, along with the ethics springing from that ontology and anthropology, are crucial questions that a proper philosophical framework for business ethics and humanistic management must adequately address." (Acevedo 2012: 216).

At the core of Maritain's thought is the idea that man is "spiritual in nature, endowed with free will, and thus autonomous in relation to the world" (Maritain 1936: 18). The notion of individual is used for human beings, animals, plants and microbes. It contains a material component that we have in common with all others, whereas the notion of person is covering the spiritual that, in freedom and love, leads to the other. The claim that the aspirations of the free person are directed toward what transcends man is not simply a less essential, historical form of Christianity. Just as Blondel argued carefully forty years prior, Maritain also departs from the fact that the finality of freedom exists in the natural desire for transcendence, i.e. for God.

Maritain posits in his cultural analysis that the medieval Christian heritage, given its lack of reflection, was bound to fall victim in modern times to what he called "the unhappy consciousness" (Maritain 1936: 82). Because the end point of the dynamism of our will can only be God in Maritain's view, he interprets modern humanism—which shuts itself off from this—as tragic: it is unavoidably a promethean humanism. Although the only alternative for Maritain is a religious humanism, he does show full understanding for his contemporaries who place their lives in the service of ideals that radically transcend them, i.e. in the service of "the God whose name they no longer know" (Maritain 1936: 72). Even so, he introduces a new Christian humanism to them. His humanism acknowledges not only the faults committed against humanity in the name of the Christian God, but also makes the necessary distinctions between the political and socio-economic realm and the domain of beliefs from which the Christians derive their inspiration in order to engage themselves within the realm of the profane. One can state that those thinkers who consider human beings as *subjects* (e.g. René Descartes, Immanuel Kant), or as *individuals* (e.g. Adam Smith), espouse what may be referred to as a *nonpersonalistic* humanism and those who consider them as *persons*, a *personalistic* humanism: "Approaching human beings as *subjects* disregards their spiritual and physical dimensions and discounts the realistic and teleological notions of human nature" (Acevedo 2012: 198–199).

According to Pope Leo XIII, the Catholics had to acknowledge as legitimate aspirations what the previous pope Pius X in his encyclical *Pascendi* (1907) would—in a rather simplistic manner—condemn as modernism. Leo XIII advised the Catholics in the encyclical *Aeterni Patris* (1879) to be inspired by the philosophy of Thomas Aquinas in this thinking. Maritain incorporated this echo of Aquinas. Aquinas was open to the great cultural innovations of his time, namely the pagan metaphysics of Aristotle. He integrated this body of thinking into his Christian synthesis. According to Maritain, the neo-Thomist also needs to be open to modern thinking. That is precisely the task that he sets for himself in *Humanisme Intégral*: to integrate the modern body of thought into a renewed Christian synthesis. Hence today one can state that Maritain's metaphysics of being remains a corrective to metaphysical skepticism. What for instance from Levinas' theories shines forth in the human face is the very depths of the human person that grounds the ethical 'ought': " The human face is only the surface through which a deeper reality resonates" (Gwozdz 2010b: 489)

6.2 The Analytical Rigor of the Aristotalian-Thomistic Tradition

Raised under liberal Protestantism, Maritain became, under the influence of scientism, an atheist. But Bergson, whose lectures he followed, made him realize that reason cannot be reduced to exact scientific views of reality. Bergson believed that there is in the universe an "impulse to life" and that throughout the animal kingdom there may be seen two avenues to knowledge: intelligence, culminating in science, and instinct, culminating in intuition and mysticism. Regardless, Maritain held on to the primacy of objectivity. Science was to submit itself to and to focus upon reality. Maritain wanted to avoid anti-intellectual topics in which a purposeless sentimentality disguised as "intuition" was destroying the sense of truth (Gwozdz 2010a: 560). His position thus gives witness to a sort of Thomistic realism. Further building upon Aristotle's intellectualism, Thomas Aquinas also assigned a primacy to the objective order of reality. Like Aristotle he was convinced that the reason that directed itself to the order of being was simultaneously capable to realize its metaphysical structure.

Likewise derived from Thomism was Maritain's conviction that the problematization of the modern philosophy of consciousness that placed the subject as central contains an idealistic lapse. At the foundation of idealism lies the belief that the subject places a constitutive role in the manner in which the world appears. For Maritain, this philosophy of consciousness meant that man was cut off from the transcendental. Hence his return to an independent ontic order of which man makes up a part and through which he is transcended.

Maritain recognized a similar reaction to idealism and subjectivism in Marxism, more specifically in the dialectical materialism. Moreover, he saw in this method, which strives to describe social developments in an objective manner, an expression of scientism within which he never surrendered the primacy of objectivity. Thus his interest in Marxism was not only motivated by social-mindedness. The humanism that Marxism strove for, however, was atheistic. In order to reach this goal it made use, according to Maritain, of diluted Christian reflections. Because of this last evolution, it was able to offer resistance against Christianity. It thus wanted to make short shrift to the "lie of the higher ideas" and choose for an absolutely realistic immanence. All worthy goals made Marxism dependent upon the analysis of the material condition. In Aristotle's terms the material causality became the first causation in this way. Against this Promethean humanism Maritain posited, as already mentioned, a Christian humanism whereby it was not the God of philosophers who was acknowledged, but the God of Abraham, Isaac, and Jacob. According to the author, the Christian was given the task to save the "humanistic" truths that had been deformed over the past four hundred years. Man was not disowned by God and he did not need to be opposed to God. Man was respected in his relationship to God.

6.3 The Role of Telos

The autonomous authority of the political constitution is a second major point of consideration in *Humanisme Intégral*. The new political structures as they evolved out of the French Revolution were marked by a radical laicization, in which religion was banned to the private realm. As a Christian answer to this situation, one needed, according to Maritain, to disconnect Thomism as metaphysical insight into eternal truths, from the medieval vision of the political life. In contrast to his realistic standpoint, Maritain was here thus indeed in line with modernity. In accordance with Aristotle again, he formulated the political as an autonomous realm with its own laws. Yet, as Aquinas, in line with Augustine, Maritain put forth that man in his personal worth is not tied to a political or economic institution that would lay absolute claims. God alone is sovereign. Maritain refuted thus also any form of totalitarianism. A democratic state respects the freedom of the individual within the general welfare or the *bonum commune* for which the state is responsible.

Subsequently Maritain clearly distinguished between the temporal order and the spiritual order. The temporal order relates to culture and civilization. The spiritual order deals with faith and transcends itself from the temporal order. Yet, both have their specific task. The true meaning of the temporal order lies in the fact that this was simultaneously the kingdom of man and, for a Christian, of God. The world is set free but therefore not yet holy. For a Christian the world is merely moving towards the Kingdom of God. It would be a betrayal of this Kingdom of God if we do not try to bring it into being with all of our power. But we know that our realizations shall always be limited. Maritain points also to Jesus' preference of the poor in order to know in which concrete way we nevertheless can help bring about the Kingdom of God in the temporal order: "Christ himself shall not always be among you, but you will know Him in the poor who you must love and serve as Himself." (Maritain1936: 117)

However, the ultimate goal or telos of the Christian, according to Maritain, is not to make the Kingdom of God through the temporal order of the world. Rather it is to turn this world into a human place to live in. Unfortunately, according to Maritain, the flaws in the world are more prominent than the human striving for the good. This can be seen in capitalism. The mechanism of capitalism in essence is neither bad nor unjust, as Marx thought. Yet, the driving power behind the mechanism of capitalism steadily results in the dissolution of the social fabric and the exclusion of the poor: "The object spirit of capitalism is one that stimulates the active and creative powers as well as the dynamism of man and the individual initiatives, yet it is a spirit which hates poverty and despises the poor; the poor merely exist as mediums of production with an eye towards profit, and not as humans." (Maritain1936: 22)

We can state that Maritain wanted to work out a concrete historical ideal of a new Christianity in which the community aspect was central. The true goal of the temporal order is thus more than the mere tallying up of individual needs. It concerns the good life of the entire community—the *bonum commune*—and this both in the material and moral sense. Consequently this temporal *bonum commune* is not the ultimate telos, but it is subordinate to what transcends temporal welfare (*le bien intemporel*) of the human person—the attainment of freedom and spiritual perfection. Maritain's view on the temporal order therefore is a personalist one. The temporal *bonum commune* that in a given order is a telos in itself remains ultimately intermediate and subordinate to the ultimate goal of the person (Maritain 1936: 140). This position overcomes the antinomy that gives the temporal life of man its typical tension: on the one hand, people are subordinate to the communal work that must be completed and, on the other hand, they are driven by that which is most typical for humans, their eternal calling, above and beyond the communality. In the end, this temporal order is never completed. The definitive balance is never obtained—man is always on the path.

6.4 New Models for the Economy

In April 1936, the year in which *Humanisme Intégral* appeared, the French communist Maurice Thorez in a radio program made a plea to extend a hand to the Catholics in France. New-leftist Catholics around the journal *Esprit* asserted that Christianity could be an important *supplement* to Communism. In this manner, a viable revolutionary movement could become possible that went beyond communism. Emmanuel Mounier, publisher of *Esprit*, expressed in *Révolution personnaliste et communautaire* his admiration for the Marxist method of analysis. Mounier found in Marx a diagnosis of many Christian shortcomings. At the same time, Mounier had many critiques against the one-sidedness of Marx and his totalitarian characteristics.

Maritain, who also got to know Marx's work very well, shows in *Humanisme Intégral* alongside his critique an appreciation for Marx's strong intuition regarding alienation in the modern capitalist society, "the great spark of truth that runs throughout his entire work" (Maritain 1936: 55). Maritain, moreover, pleaded for a property structure, in which alongside private property government participation is built in, in order to care for the human person. In line with Aquinas, the use of individually attained goods needs to benefit the communal welfare of all (the common good). In order to guarantee the benefits of private property to everyone, Maritain, however opted not for a communist state, but for joint ownership and participation in businesses. He articulates industrial ownership in terms of an association of persons instead of an association of capital: "It is not about abolishing private interest, but rather about purifying and bettering it; integrating it into the social structures which look after the general need, and also (and this is the most important aspect), about reforming the private interest into a spirit of unity and brotherly friendship." (Maritain1936: 92)

Maritain poses very clearly that a liquidation of the capitalistic system is necessary in order to make possible an adequate temporal order.[1] A radical change is thus necessary, both on material and moral fronts. All topics are subject to a criterion that is beyond the human realm: the laws of material production, from the dominance of technology over nature and of the yielding of profits from money. Maritain points to the necessity of a certain frugality in the economy, if wellbeing for all is to be attained. It is remarkable how today frugality also is a crucial theme in the discourse concerning the necessary social and ecological transition of our economy (Bouckaert et al. 2008). In a footnote Maritain speaks of the necessity of "a certain poverty": "But even without speaking of the big problems that the progress of science and technology shall cause through the necessity of reducing manpower and the risk of raising unemployment, it is a fact that when everyone disposes of a part of the surplus, this will result in a relative poverty for everyone, with which there will be

[1] Not until 1972 did Maritain elaborate extensively on this in an article "A Society without Money" in 1982, Cahiers Jacques Maritain, Vols. 4–5. The latter publication also appeared in Review of Social Economy (1985).

sufficient but with which luxury shall be difficult." (Maritain 1936:15). Here we have another topic that nowadays also is on the agenda. Think of the publications of authors like Thomas Piketty (2014).

Important also is the question in which way technology, machine, and industry can be made subordinate to man. In contrast to Marx, Maritain does not believe that science offers a way out: technology needs to direct itself toward an ethic of the person. One needs to fundamentally choose between either an essentially industrial civilization or an essentially human civilization. According to Maritain's personalism it is evident that industry is a tool and humanity is the goal: "industry actually is only an instrument and thus dependent upon laws which it itself has not developed." (Maritain 1936: 199).[2] Maritain clearly gives preference to quality over quantity, labor over money, meaning over technology, wisdom over science, communal service of people over individual and collective greed.

6.5 Spiritual Humanism

Maritain does not regard communism as being capable of nipping capitalism in the bud. Communism could only transfer the power of capitalism to the state. In the spring of again 1936, the "red" cardinal Verdier of Paris rallied the French to collaborate with the new order of the *Front Populaire*. However, at the same time, it became clear that a spiritual dimension within an anti-capitalistic revolution was impossible. The atheism in Marx's philosophy—with its ethical, spiritual, and political implications—was the primary obstacle by far. For Maritain atheism and materialism were impossible to separate. Similar to capitalism, communism led towards an idolatry of technological progress and prosperity. As a consequence, Maritain was just as opposed to the teachings of Stalin as he was to the concept of "Ford-ism" in America. Communism, moreover, denied the existence of values that transcended the individual, time or place. At the same time, it regarded man as a collective individual, through which the human being, with its values such as freedom, respect and love, all to readily ended up in the background. The fact that Maritain gave so much attention to the human being in *Humanisme Intégral* does not indicate, however, that the temporal order he works out can be converted to an individual morality. There is a need for knowledge regarding the appropriate social techniques in service of the communal welfare or the *bonum commune*. The ethical principles need to be translated toward the structures.

According to Maritain not only among the intellectual elite, but also among the broad spectrum of the population, one might or might not respond to the proposed profane Christian call. Because of this there is a great need of all types of brands of spiritual re-awakening and it is important that Christians are not dismissive in regard

[2] In *A Society without Money* (1985, p.80) Maritain points out that "the *business world* made up a world apart, having an absolute value of its own, independent of those superior values and norms that give life its human dignity, and which furnish the measure of human life in its wholeness".

to the necessary social emancipation. In addition, Maritain envisions a sort of Copernican revolution in the political activity: "In politics, we need to begin to think, to live, and to act in a Christian way" (Maritain1936: 256). However Maritain is not of the opinion that for the execution of his integral humanism the establishment of a Christian party will be required. Rather, there is a need for one or more authentic political groupings that ultimately act from a similar belief. Not all Christians need to collaborate on this, and also not only Christians,[3] but all who recognize themselves in the proposed realization of a temporal order. It is important that one remains faithful to values such as truth, respect and justice. For Maritain, this isn't a type of religious or apostolic Catholic action such as Pius XI initiated. Rather, a thorough spiritual revolution will be needed, together with a collaboration of laborers and intellectuals. As such, Maritain trusts that one day the indicated changes will occur: "The temporary Christian powers, which the world needs, are in an advanced preparatory phase: it is impossible that one day their influence will not be felt in the world" (Maritain 1936: 293). At the end of his life, Maritain reformulates his pluralistic call in *A Society without Money*: "And it is precisely because this revolution would have as its final end not at all to 'change man', but solely to bring about the most fundamental changes in his social structures that Christians and non-Christians alike (...) could work together for that truly radical revolution, which for me has become an obsession." (Maritain 1985: 79)

The thrust of the discourse of Pope Francis' first encyclical *Lumen Fidei* is strikingly similar to this view of Maritain. The Pope states that "Faith is truly a good for everyone; it is a common good. Its light does not simply brighten the interior of the Church, nor does it serve solely to build an eternal city in the hereafter; it helps us build our societies in such a way that they can journey towards a future of hope. (…). Modernity sought to build a universal brotherhood based on equality, yet we gradually came to realize that this brotherhood, lacking a reference to a common Father as its ultimate foundation, cannot endure. We need to return to the true basis of brotherhood" (Pope Francis2013, ch.51).

6.6 Conclusion

Maritain's *Humanisme intégral* can be summarized as a series of fundamental themes and categories on personalism. After Maritain, these were frequently transformed into various social-political contexts. Foremost the concepts of 'person', 'respect', 'integral humanism', 'community', '(economic) democracy' and 'welfare' became standard values in the post-War Christian corpus of social thought, in

[3]At the end of his life, Maritain reformulates this pluralistic call in *A Society without money* (1985, p.79): "And it is precisely because this revolution would have as its final end not at all to "change man", but solely to bring about the most fundamental changes in his social structures that Christians and non-Christians alike (...) could work together for that truly radical revolution, which for me has become an obsession."

Germany, Italy, and France, among other countries. The works of Maritain also gained significant importance in countries such as Chile and Argentina. For instance, Eduardo Frei popularized the work of Maritain in Chile. As a result, the conservative political Catholicism was suppressed there. The political philosophy of Maritain during and after WWII in the United States provided the Catholics with the foundation of a pluralistic political doctrine. The most striking thing in Maritain's *Humanisme Intégral* is, however, that it deals with a spiritual humanism. Notwithstanding that it deals with a *profane* culture, for Maritain it is essentially based upon a spiritual foundation. Emmanuel Mounier publishing in the same year as *Humanisme Intégral* his *Manifeste au service du personnalisme* (1936) shared Maritain's preoccupation for a spiritual renewal. In essence, Maritain also aspired to a pluralistic democracy. However there can only be talk of a personalist culture when one is open to the transcendent. Precisely this openness creates a possibility to surpass modern rationalism and its technocratic consciousness. One can summarize that rediscovering Maritain's personalism does not mean a plea for a slavish implementation of his theories but for retranslating his analysis in the pluralistic context of our globalised society today.

References

Acevedo, A. 2012. Personalist Business Ethics: Insights from Jacques Maritain. *Journal of Business Ethics* 105: 197–219.

Bouckaert, L., H. Opdebeeck, and L. Zsolnai, ed. 2008. *Frugality, Rebalancing Material and Spiritual Values in Economic Life*. Oxford: Peter Lang.

De Tavernier, J. 2009. The Historical Roots Of Personalism. *Ethical Perspectives* 2009 (3): 361–392.

Gwozdz, T. 2010a. Young and Restless. *American Catholic Philosophical Quarterly* 84 (3): 549–564.

———. 2010b. Metaphysics and Ethics: Levinas, Clarke and Maritain. *International Philosophical Quarterly* 50 (4): 489–500.

Maritain, J. 1930a. *Le docteur angélique*. Paris: Desclée.

———. 1930b. *Religion et culture*. Paris: Desclée.

———. 1936. *Humanisme intégral*. Paris: Aubier.

———. 1943. *Christianisme et démocratie*. Paris: La maison française.

———. 1985. A Society Without Money. *Review of Social Economy* 43(1), April: 73–83.

Piketty, Th. 2014. *Capital in the Twenty-First Century*. Cambridge, MA: Harvard University Press.

Pope Francis. 2013. *Lumen Fidei, Encyclical Letter*. Washington, DC: Usccb.

Possenti, V. 2003 "Religion and Civil Life: Jacques Maritain, a Philosopher in the City" In *Notes et Documents for a personalist approach*, N°68, 33.

Weidner, D. 2010. Thinking Beyond Secularization. *New German Critique* 37 (3): 131–148.

Chapter 7
Happiness and Human Flourishing

Knut J. Ims

Abstract The chapter explores the concept of human flourishing drawing on two traditions, the Aristotelian–Thomistic virtue ethics tradition, and the new research tradition of positive psychology. These traditions may seem very different in origin, but they have some fundamental similarities. Martin Seligman, one of the founders of positive psychology has summed up human flourishing using the acronym PERMA, where each letter indicate one element; **P**ositive emotions, **E**ngagements, **R**elationship, **M**eaning and **A**ccomplishment. Seligman emphasizes the problems of hedonic pleasure and "happyology" in describing human flourishing.

The chapter concludes that the Aristotelian and Thomistic ethics capture the dyadic aspects of human wellbeing: the wellbeing that people experience as they live their lives, and the judgment they make when they evaluate their life. Both employ a virtue ethical perspective, which means that they are concerned about the importance of good character and how to build good characters as part of living in a good society.

In modern economics and business the crucial question is: What does the modern, affluent consumer want? Does he or she want what she should want in order to promote her or his happiness? However, happiness and the good life has to be understood in the perspective of a culture. Then what is a good life in the Western culture? The Gross Domestic Product of a nation does not tell the whole story because GDP is based upon a welfarist approach. GDP gives a one-dimensional materialistic, economic view of human wellbeing, and is very destructive for the natural environment, for pollution. Even when we have a number of 'just background institutions' in the Western world, we have to determine the role of the Government and the role of 'market mechanisms' in order to promote individual well-being and secure the common good.

In the Western world, the market expands continually to new domains in a culture where the individual consumer is assumed to be the "king" through his or her consumer sovereignty. We may well ask which values does the consumer reveal in

K.J. Ims (✉)
Norwegian School of Economics, Bergen, Norway
e-mail: Knut.Ims@nhh.no

P. Rona, L. Zsolnai (eds.), *Economics as a Moral Science*,
Virtues and Economics 1, DOI 10.1007/978-3-319-53291-2_7

the market? This question is essential when we, like Etzioni, assume that we are all embedded in a community; which is nicely put in the formulation "I & We". Etzioni writes: "The individual and the community make each other and require each other. Society is not a "constraint" not even an "opportunity," it is us (Etzioni 1988: 9).

Buscher (2002) gives a number of examples of how the ethics of the market have to be understood in relationship to society's "frame of reference". When economic policy since the 1980s has given the market a dominant influence, an ethical vacuum has emerged. As a consequence, we have to analyze the normative elements of the market to reveal the ideological elements of economic reasoning. Which values do we in fact support if we assume that the economy to large extent is disembedded from society and when the myth of an "ethics-free economic rationality" is not valid? (Etzioni 1988). To explore this question, we have to study a number of assumptions that is taken for more or less granted in our Western culture where the ideal of the 'free enterprise' is hiding in the background.

We will take a critical look on questions such as: Is it ethical to satisfy all kinds of wants? What if the wants are social and environmentally destructive? What if what I want is 'miswanting'"? (Kahneman 2011).

The chapter is divided in two parts. First, some issues on a societal level are described to problematize that markets lead to the greatest good for the greatest number of people. In the second part, we develop the view that citizens need a polity in order to act as responsible consumers.

7.1 Freedom, Market and Governance

The economic problem of production and distribution are intertwined. However, economists have traditionally emphasized the problem of production and let the politicians and other social scientists take care of the problem of distribution. Today the gap between rich and poor citizens has grown to an extreme extent in countries in the West. Only a few Western economists have given much attention to the inequality of income and wealth in the society (Stieglitz 2013; Piketty 2014).

Another problem of distribution is the choice between the share of the production that should be invested or saved for future generations, and how much should be consumed. The more we consume today, the less will be left for the future. Using huge quantities of finite natural resources today will leave nothing to future generations, but the non-intended consequences, often expressed as waste, polluted environments, and a high degree of carbon in the atmosphere, which boost climate change.

There are strong opponents of an active government. Milton Friedman strongly argues for "the power of the market" and against the "tyranny of controls". In their book "*Free to Choose*" Friedman and Friedman (1980) write that the ideas of human freedom and economic freedom working together and came to their greatest fruition in the United States, and they warn about the "overgoverned society". For the Friedmans consumer sovereignty is the sacred principle in the society.

The international trend is a strong belief in the advantage of the "free market". It is demonstrated in the politics of privatization, deregulation, and liberalization from the mid-1980s. Privatization involves the transfer to the private sector functions or services previously performed by the state. Deregulation entails the reduction of government regulations and rules that are applied to the private sector, and liberalization means partial opening up of the economy in response to competitive pressures. Accordingly, the role of the state has diminished and the private sector has expanded (Sales and Beschorner 2006). The consequences are that society is more and more market oriented, and to some extent may be characterized as a "market society" (Sandel 2012).

The paramount value for Friedman is the individual's right to choose what she or he wants. For Amartya Sen this is only one dimension of freedom. For Sen individual freedom is not much of value for individuals that starve or have no capacity to participate in decisions that concerns them. Participation in social life has intrinsic value. Before one can enjoy the freedom of choice, one needs sufficient food and housing, etc. (Sen 1993).

The market as the solution of the problem of production and distribution rest also with the value of private property rights. It involves that private property rights must be easily transferable. The market works when "rights are both privately held and easily transferable." (O'Toole cited in Desjardins 2006: 59). Friedman's position of freedom fits well into the position of market utilitarianism, where 'every person should be free to do whatever he wishes' where his actions do not interfere with the interests of other human beings, and the faith that 'market preserves individual freedom because it depends on voluntary exchange between market actors'.

The image of Homo Oeconomicus that depicts economic agents as rational, self-interest –maximizing beings are misleading (Zsolnai 2013). One implication is that it leads to a belief in massive use of incentives to control or 'guide' human behavior. Altruism, acting for the common good or for ethical commitments does not fit into this model of man. Those assumptions have also a number of bad effects with regard to management practice. (Ghosal 2005).

Economists declare that their goal is to help decision makers towards the goal of efficiency. Seemingly, economic efficiency fits the utilitarian goal of providing the greatest good for the greatest number. But will "an efficient allocation of resources" maximize the economic well-being of all members of society? And if it does, why should we maximize social utility? Efficiency implies optimal satisfaction of consumer preferences given their willingness to pay for different goods and services. However, as a society, and with regard to the environment, should satisfying all the individual preferences be the overriding goal? As Desjardins write: "Why should this be the goal of public policy when we recognize the obvious and acknowledge that many individual preferences are silly, foolish, vulgar, dangerous, immoral, criminal, and the like? Why should we think that satisfying the preferences of a racist, criminal, fool, or sadist is a good thing … What is so good about satisfying preferences?" (Desjardins 2006: 65–66).

When preferences are strange, it is difficult to argue that satisfying preferences is good in itself. Why should we maximize the satisfaction of preferences regardless of their moral worth?

Sandel (2012: 88–90) writes that when market reasoning travels beyond the domain of material goods, it must "traffic in morality". When market reasoning is concerned with material goods, such as cars, toaster, and flat-screen televisions, the objections to satisfaction may be not too strong, but when market reasoning is applied to sex, procreation, child rearing, education, health, criminal punishment, immigration police and environmental protection, it is questionable if everyone's preferences are equally worthwhile. In morally charged arenas, some ways of valuing goods may be higher and more appropriate than others.

Economists uses terms as welfare, utility, or happiness to explain the goal of satisfying preferences. However, it is wrong to believe that satisfaction of preferences always leads to happiness. As Desjardins (2006: 66) writes: "Whether what I want is a good thing depends on what it is that I want". Modern happiness research and Positive Psychology gives us an insight of what make people happy.

Kahneman (2011) demonstrates with the "focusing illusion" that people exaggerate the effect of major purchases or "changed circumstances" on their future wellbeing. For example of buying a new nice car and comparing the car with joining a group of people that meets every week, people believe that the car will increase their wellbeing most. At the start, both experiences will be exciting, but after a while, they will pay less and less attention to the car, The group however, that they attend every week will continue to be exciting. By the fallacy of "What You See Is All That Is" people put too much emphasis on the long term benefits of the new car. This focusing illusion "Creates a bias in favor of goods and experiences that are initially exciting, even if they will eventually lose their appeal" (Kahneman 2011: 406).

7.2 The Aristotelian – Thomistic Tradition and Positive Psychology

Where do we find frameworks that promotes good characters that live good lives in a good society, and where individuals are employed through meaningful work in the context of a fair economy and fair background institutions?

One approach to address these issues is the modern happiness research (Seligman 2002). We find a lot of scientific evidences that very rich people are not happier than people with a moderate income. This phenomenon leads to the so-called "happiness trap", since it contradict common sense thinking, according to which "more is always better".

But what is "happiness"? The word is ambiguous, and its use is manifold as pointed to by researchers (see for example Gilbert 2006). Happiness may mean expressing beliefs about the merits of things, about their position, and not of their feelings. When saying we are happy about, we note that something is a potential source of pleasurable feeling, but we do not feel it at that moment. We could reserve the word "happiness" to a class of subjective emotional experiences that not indicate the morality of the actions that motivated them. However, we might wonder whether the happiness we get from helping a child is better or deeper than the happiness we get from eating an ice cream? In a new study of human emotion, Ketner (2009) find that happiness is found in the rich landscape of positive emotions that until recently remained mysterious to science. Central in Ketner's work stands the emotions of compassion, sympathy and awe, which are programmed into our minds and bodies. As he says "Emotions are signs of our deepest commitments… (They are) intuitive guides to our most important ethical judgments. Our pursuit of the meaningful life requires an engagement with emotions" (Ketner 2009: 34).

The hedonic view of happiness originally developed by Jeremy Bentham is used as the metric for economists to understand happiness as a felicity calculus where pleasure minus pain is the gold standard for a good society. However, such a calculus represents a reductionist view of happiness and it is amoral because it does not take into account the human capacity and willingness to live a meaningful life.

OECD (2013) has developed its "Guidelines on Measuring Subjective Well-being" arguing that data of subjective well-being can provide an important complement to other objective indicators of wellbeing. The OECD framework consists of three concepts of wellbeing: life evaluation, affect, and "eudaimonia" (or flourishing). (OECD 2013, 28–35) This conceptual model gives a richer and more accurate model of human functioning.

Aristotle viewed human life as consisting in the pursuit of ends. The object of Aristotle was to discover the nature of the end towards which man ought to aim, and the ultimate end was described as "eudaimonia", a word usually translated to English as 'happiness'. However, such a translation is not satisfactory since happiness is typically regarded as a state of feeling while the Aristotelian eudaimonia involves a certain kind of activity. Eudaimonia is carrying feeling but it is not in itself a kind of feeling (Aristotle 1925(1980): vi).

Aristotle explores eudaimonia in his "Nicomachean Ethics" (Aristotle 1935). First, he criticizes three popular views about the nature of life (i) a life of pleasure, (ii) a political life which aims at honor, and (iii) the life of money-making. Then he mentions the contemplative life as a fourth way. This requires two conditions. First, the end of human life must be desirable in itself, chosen for its own sake. The other condition is that those activities of the soul had to be in accordance with the rational element in human beings – virtues, either moral or intellectual ones.

Eudaimonia is based upon a judgment of a whole life, while individual actions and projects may be judged as virtuous (*arete*) or not. One statement used by Aristotle is that a swallow does not give a summer, but a summer gives many swallows, meaning that a single good action is not enough to evaluate one's goodness. So Aristotle does not reduce eudaimonia to happiness understood as a particular state or a positive mood. Even if pleasure is taken by a good man in virtuous activity, pleasure cannot be the purpose of man according to an eudaimonic view.

For Aristotle the good man is virtuous, and excels in virtuous actions. Virtues are not external to the good life, but an integral part of it. Amongst the intellectual virtues, wisdom or *phronesis* is essential, and amongst the moral virtues courage, temperance and justice are cardinal. While the intellectual virtues to a large extend are taught, moral virtues is the product of habit (*ethos*).

A virtue may be destroyed either by excess or deficiency. Health may be destroyed by too little food or too much food (Aristotle 1935/1951: 183). It means that too much of a good thing may change the quality of the thing. As Coplestone writes; "all valuational elements, taken in isolation, have in them a point beyond which they are dangerous, that they are tyrannical, and that for the true fulfillment of their meaning (…) there is always a counterweight" (Coplestone 1950: 337–338).

Aristotle also discusses happiness in relation to contemplation. He values contemplation as the noblest of activities because reason is 'the noblest part of us, and the objects of reason are the best of all knowable things" (Aristotle 1935/1951: 265). In particular, to contemplate truth (*theorein*) will give a man the possibility to do it in a continuously way. Aristotle argues that happiness ought to contain a blend of pleasure, and activity in accordance with wisdom (*sophia*) is the most pleasant of all virtuous activities. The 'pursuit of wisdom' (*philosophia*) gives durable and pure pleasures. Contemplation is characterized by self-sufficiency (*autarkeia*) and is seen as the only act that is loved for its own sake.

Aquinas developed the Aristotelian virtue ethical approach further. He introduced three new virtues; the triad of theological virtues; faith, hope and charity.[1] Aquinas might have problems with applying the Aristotelian doctrine of the golden mean for the theological virtues. Why could it be a problem to love God too much? How can St. Francis of Assisi be taken as an example of 'the mean'? (Coplestone 1955: 217). Aquinas was not an admirer of fanaticism. His interpretations of St. Francis were that he did not act out of superstition or of a desire to make a name for oneself. His actions "were performed in response to an invitation of Christ". Aquinas suggests that in one respect there cannot be an excess, however there can be defect. On the other hand, if we consider man's condition and the way he should manifest the love of God, we can talk about a mean. Aquinas had a "respect for the rule of right reason and for the proportion and measure demanded by right reason:" (1955: 218). Coplestone concludes that Aquinas application of the mean was due to his dislike of one-sided exaggerations and his respect for the rule of reason.

Based upon Aristotle, Aquinas made a distinction between act and potentiality which is found in every finite thing. Potentiality is unrealized capacity and indicates a lack of possible perfection. Any finite being is a mixture of potentiality and act. Development is a movement towards the full realization of form (Coplestone 1955: 99). Habits dispose a man to act readily and easily. Good habits are virtues and bad operative habits are vices.

---

[1] Macintyre (1966: 177) stresses that Aquinas cannot mean by the Latin names of the cardinal virtues entirely what Aristotle meant by their Greek equivalents. For example, Aquinas explicitly acknowledges the biblical virtue 'humility'. "…In Aristotle's account of the virtues where anything resembling humility is mentioned, it is a vice….".

Aquinas distinguishes between moral virtues and intellectual virtues. Moral virtue "inclines a man's sensitive appetite to act in accordance with right reason" (Coplestone 1955: 215). Intellectual virtues perfect a man's rational powers. It is not possible to have the moral virtues without the intellectual virtue of prudence, which inclines us to choose the right means to the attainment of the objective good. According to Aquinas, we need virtuous habits to act uniformly, readily, and pleasurably in accordance with right reason (Coplestone 1955: 216).

Baumeister et al. (2013: 505) writes that "some positive psychologists … have revived a conceptual distinction dating to Aristotle between feeling happy and living a good life". The latter is known as eudaimonia. Based upon empirical research Baumeister and his colleagues emphasize that meaningfulness is more central to eudaimonia than feeling good.

Happiness according to positive psychology has been conceptualized and measured in quite different ways: (i) as life-satisfaction, which goes beyond momentary feelings and includes an integrative, evaluative assessment of one's life as a whole, and (ii) as affect balance, which indicate more pleasant than unpleasant emotional states, that is, on how one feels at different moments.

According to Steger (2009) meaning may be defined as purpose, significance or some multifaceted construct. Frankl (1963) emphasized that each person has a unique purpose or overarching aim for life, understood in light of his or her values, and enacted in reflection of his or her community. However, meaning may also be defined from an informational significance point of view. In accordance with this view people experience meaning in life "when their lives make sense". One related view of meaning is a kind of binding the self to the external world. Baumeister and Vohs (2002: 608) argue that "the essence of meaning is connection". While the first two approaches are described as motivational purpose-centered and cognitive significance-centered definitions, there are definitions of meaning in life that combine these two dimensions with an affective dimension, referring to peoples" fulfillment in their lives (Steger 2009: 681).

Baumeister et al. (2013) held that meaning is not personal but rather cultural using the analogy of a large map that is gradually filled in by countless generations. An individual may see himself fitting in a section of this map. Meaning can integrate events across time, and one aspect is that meaning allows people to think about past, future, and spatially distant realties and even the possibilities of these realities (Baumeister et al. 2013: 506). Purpose, implies that present events draw meaning from future ones. It implies that one may be motivated to work toward future goals that is desirable even though the present actions may be highly unpleasant (Frankl 1963). Even if people cannot articulate what it means, they may feel that their life is meaningful if they find it is rewarding in some way. The focus on meaningfulness and the meaning of life implies that it is possible to have a "highly meaningful life that is not necessarily a happy one (e.g. as religious missionary, political activist, or terrorist)" (Baumeister et al. 2013: 506).

A number of studies found that hedonic pursuits produced short-term benefits, while long term pursuits depended more on eudaimonic activities. Seligman (2002) writes about his own experience in one of his classes. He asked his students to engage in one pleasurable activity and one philanthropic activity and write about both. The students found that "The afterglow of the "pleasurable" activity (hanging out with friends, or watching a movie, or eating a hot fudge sundae) paled in comparison with the effects of the philanthropic and kind action". The students told that when "our philanthropic acts were spontaneous and called upon personal strengths, the whole day went better" (Seligman 2002: 9).

Seligman concludes that the exercise of kindness is a gratification which calls on your strengths in contrast to a pleasure which he defines as delights that have distinct sensory and strong emotional components like "raw feels": ecstasy, thrills, orgasm, delight, mirth, exuberance, and comfort." The gratifications are activities we very much like doing, but they are not necessarily accompanied by any raw feelings. They engage us fully, and we become immersed in them. The gratifications last longer than the pleasures as they involve much thinking and interpretation, and they are encompassed by our strengths and virtues (Seligman 2002: 102).

In his recent work on flourishing Seligman (2011) argues that a mood view of happiness will only concern 50% of the world's population who are 'low-positive affective'. Those people may have more engagement and meaning in life than merry people.

In Seligman's view, there is a shift from happiness to wellbeing understood as five elements; Positive emotion, Engagement, positive Relationships, Meaning, and Accomplishment (PERMA). All the elements contribute to wellbeing, but no single element defines it. A short look on these five elements follows:

1. Positive emotions about the past are satisfaction, contentment, pride and serenity. Optimism, hope, trust, faith, and confidence are future-oriented emotions. In comparison with his "authentic happiness theory" Seligman now makes two changes. Happiness and life satisfaction as subjective measures are not any longer the goal of the entire theory.

2. Engagement is also measured subjectively and since flow is a typical activity in this category, the subjective state for pleasure is retrospective. Thought and feeling are typically absent during the flow state.

3. A relationship is about a man's connection to other people. Positive relationships are accompanied either by positive emotion or engagement, or by meaning or accomplishment.

4. Meaning emphasizes belonging to and serving something bigger than the self. It is not only a subjective state. Abraham Lincoln is used as an example since Lincoln was known to be a profound melancholic, but most people may judge his life filled with meaning.

5. Accomplishment pursued for its own sake. This is the drive to exert mastery over the environment. For example, bridge or chess players try to improve in order to learn and to be in flow.

Together with other researchers, Seligman developed a classification scheme and a way of measuring character in 1999. His research group studied Aristotle, Plato,

Aquinas, Augustine, the Old Testament, the Talmud, Confucius, Buddha, Lao-Tze, Bushido (the samurai code), the Koran, Benjamin Franklin, and the Upanishads – some two hundred virtue catalogues in all. "To our surprise, almost every single one of these traditions flung across three thousand years and the entire face of the earth endorsed six virtues" (Seligman 2002: 132). Based upon the writings of the major religious and philosophical traditions, the research group created the following list of virtues: Wisdom and knowledge, Courage, Love and humanity, Justice, Temperance, Spirituality and transcendence.

The contents of the different concepts varied somewhat in different traditions. Humanity in Confucius is not the same as *caritas* in Aquinas. The research group also found that "the commonality is real and, to those of us raised as ethical relativists, pretty remarkable." (Seligman2002: 133).

Seligman regards these six virtues as core characteristics. Viewed together they capture the notion of good character. These virtues may be operationalized in order to be measured, and there are several ways or routes to achieve each virtue.[2] With the notion of signature strengths, strengths of character that a person self-consciously owns, celebrates, and exercises every day in work, love, play, and parenting (Seligman 2002: 160–161), Seligman presents a way each individual may identify, build and choose to use the virtues in the main realms of his or her life (Seligman 2002: 134). Seligman stresses that strengths are not the same thing as talents, since strengths are moral traits, while talents are non-moral, possessed and cannot be chosen in the same way as strengths. A strength involves a choice about when to use it, and whether to build it, or not. The strengths can be acquired by effort and determination by ordinary persons. A strength is valued in its own right and a culture may support strengths by providing institutions, rituals, role models, parables, maxims, and children's stories.

In order to have a good life, a person should use his or her individual signature strengths in daily life. A meaningful life needs an additional component - to use these strengths in the service of something greater than one self. A full life consists in experiencing positive emotions, which may be defined as the pleasant life, plus gratifying activities using your signature strengths, and in addition using your strengths to contribute to something beyond yourself.

Daniel Kahneman (2011) suggests a distinction between experienced wellbeing and remembered wellbeing, referring to two different parts of the self. The experiencing self is the one that answers the question: "Does it hurt now?" The remembering self is the one that answers the question: "How was it, on the whole?" Kahneman's point is that memories are the only thing we can use when we think about what we have done, and our life is seen through the lenses of the remembering self.

---

[2] To give one example of an operationalization of virtues, consider the virtue of wisdom and knowledge. According to Seligman (2002) there are six routes to this special virtue; (1) Curiosity/interest in the world. (2) Love of learning, (3) Judgment/critical thinking/open -mindedness, (4) Ingenuity/originality/practical Intelligence/ street Smarts, (5) Social Intelligence/personal intelligence/emotional intelligence, (6) Perspective. For every route, the researchers developed different statements and the respondents are expected to rate the different items and add the score.

Kahneman and his colleagues developed the so-called ‘Day Reconstruction Method’ (DRM) expecting it would approximate the results of experience sampling (Kahneman 2011: 392). They found many variants of positive feelings in the experience of a moment or an episode like love, joy, engagement, hope, amusements, etc. In a similar way negative emotions come in many varieties, and it is possible to classify most moments of life as ultimately positive or negative. Kahneman's suggestion is that ‘experienced wellbeing’ can inform social policy in multiple ways. For the time being measures of experienced wellbeing are routinely used in large-scale national surveys in USA, Canada and Europe, and the Gallup World Poll has extended these measurements to millions of respondents in more than 150 countries.

7.3 Discussion

The market-based solution to individual, social and environmental problems has major limitations. Willingness to pay is not the only adequate criterion for the allocation of resources. One problem is that market-based solution involves a tendency to systematically ignore the wellbeing of poor and disadvantaged people, future generations, and the natural environment as a whole.

Aquinas appeared as an innovative theologian who applied and developed the Aristotelian framework to Christianity. He used Aristotle as an intellectual instrument, but was not a slave of the Aristotelian framework. Aquinas considered perfect happiness attainable only in the afterlife. For Aquinas the Aristotelian framework was incomplete because it lacked the transcendent. What Aristotle defines as happiness, Aquinas calls temporal happiness or imperfect happiness.

Both Aristotle and Aquinas treat the moral and intellectual virtues as habits by which a man lives rightly. Moral virtues consist in a mean in order to conform to the rule of reason and avoid extremes of excess and defects. They both promoted virtuous behavior, emphasizing the development of man's character. Both insist on the importance of activities that perfect the highest faculty in man, activities directed to the highest and noblest objects.

Aristotle and Aquinas agree that material wealth is needed and desirable, but only to a certain extent. Material means should never take the role of the goal in a person's life. In particular, Aquinas argued that the means will be easily transformed into goals onto themselves. He asserts that man has dominion over exterior things as to their use. But they are to be used for a purpose, serving as *instrumenta* or *adminicula* in man's search for virtue and beatitude (Langholm 1992: 208).

Aquinas feared that exterior things would impede the love and fear of God. Riches have a distinctive feature, “if one seeks more than what is sufficient to sustain life, one is easily entrapped by avarice, which tends to infinity. The desire for external things as a means to a higher end is subject to a natural limit…”…the highest good is such that it is loved the more highly the better one comes to know it, but when the appetite for one material good is quenched, the deluded materialist is already searching for some other thing. Such appetite for inordinate wealth is vicious.....also because it makes man a slave of wealth rather than its master. By placing his end in an infinite quest for worldly riches he makes them his God (for one's God is that in which one places one's end),..." (Langholm 1992: 209).

American psychologist Tim Kasser summarizes the problem of materialistic value orientation in this way: "research shows that the more that people focus on materialistic goals, the less they tend to care about spiritual goals. Further, while most spiritual traditions aim to reduce personal suffering and to encourage compassionate behavior, numerous studies document that the more people prioritize materialistic goals, the lower their personal well-being and the more likely they are to engage in manipulative, competitive, and ecologically degrading behavior." (Kasser 2011: 204).

A number of studies report that religion and faith lead to higher feelings of well-being. Frey and Stutzer (2002) support the view that believing in God and happiness are positively related. They give the following explanations why religion raises happiness: (i) church attendance is an important source of social support, (ii) religion offers an interpretative framework that can instill life with meaning and purpose, (iii) religious people are better able to cope with adverse circumstances, and (iv) church members are on average of better health. (Frey and Stutzer 2002: 59). However, they argue that the causality may be reversed: Happier people are more religious, as in societies in which religion is regarded as important and where participation in church activities is a normal part of social life.

Within the positive psychology literature, there are glimpses of interest in understanding awe, and the importance of awe in people's life. Haidt (2006) introduces a third dimension to illustrate what he calls "Divinity with or without God". Usually we look at a social world as two-dimensional; a flat land where X-axis is closeness and where an Y- axis is hierarchy. However, when you see something extraordinary you might have an overwhelming experience of natural beauty, and you feel lifted up. Haidt's claim is that the human mind perceives a third dimension, a specifically moral dimension, which he calls "divinity" (Haidt 2006: 183).

Haidt cites Ralph Waldo Emerson saying: "He who does a good deed is instantly ennobled. He who does a mean deed is by the action itself contracted. He who puts off impurity thereby puts on purity. If a man is at heart just, then in so far is he God" (Haidt 2006: 191).

Abraham Maslow has studied peak experiences and suggested that all religions are based on the insights of somebody's peak experiences. Maslow finds that peak experiences make people nobler. Maslow also attacks science as becoming as sterile as organized religion. In the late sixteenth century, European scientists began to look down on wonder regarding wonder as the mark of a childish mind. And mature science separates fact rigidly from values and emotions. Maslow concludes that science had helped to de-sacralize the world, and left us with what *is*, rather than what is good or what is beautiful. (See Haidt 2006: 206).

Amartya Sen (1993) warns us of being fetishistic about freedom of choice. We should ask ourselves whether it nourishes or deprives us, whether it enhances self-respect or diminishes it, whether it enables us to participate in our communities or prevents us from doing so. According to Schwartz (2004) the reason is that an overabundance of choice may contribute nothing to the kind of freedom that counts. It may impair freedom by the energy and time we use in selecting between different brands. We could have used this time and energy differently.

Based upon a number of experiments Kahneman (2011) finds that in many cases there are patterns of situations where "More is less". Barry Schwartz (2004) give a number of explanations why this is the case. The problem arises in a market society with an overabundance of choices, for example in a supermarket where you have to choose between one hundred types of cheeses. As the number of available choices increases, the autonomy, control and liberation is in one sense positive. The negative aspects "escalate until we become overloaded". Then "choice no longer liberates, but debilitates. It might even be said to tyrannize" (Schwartz2004: 2)

Money has been the primary goal of many people in Western societies. However, can money buy happiness? Kahneman's answer is that "being poor makes one miserable, and being rich may enhance one's life satisfaction, but does not (on average) improve experienced wellbeing" (Kahneman 2011: 396). Illness for the poor is much worse than for those who have enough money. The average increase of experienced well-being beyond household income of about 75,000 dollars per year was zero. This is a remarkable finding, all things considered. Earning such an income might give occasion to purchase many pleasures. Kahneman speculate whether there may be circumstances that a high income might reduce happiness, and finds that higher income goes together with a reduced ability to enjoy the small pleasures of life, like eating a small chocolate or enjoying an ice cream a warm summer day (Kahneman 2011: 397).

In light of increasing inequality in the USA and Europe – where a small minority are super rich, the middle class has reduced income, while the poor are worst off (see Stiglitz 2013), Kahneman's insights present interesting perspectives. Even if there is a complex relationship between happiness and income, more fairness and more equality would be major positive contributions to increased average happiness in society. We should not forget that a 10% increase in income above the "natural limit" does not count as much as a 10% decrease in income. This follows the general principle that bad things have stronger effects than good ones (Baumeister et al. 2013; Kahneman 2011).

One of Kahneman's main conclusions is that one cannot measure experienced wellbeing without taking goals into consideration. Goals that people set for themselves are essential to what they do and how they feel about themselves. Kahneman argues that we need a combined strategy in which the wellbeing of both the remembering self and the experiencing self is considered (Kahneman 2011: 402). The problem is that the remembering self is sometimes wrong, and, accordingly, we try to maximize our future memories, which are not always the same as our future experiences.

7.4 Concluding Remarks

We have problematized hedonic preferences and indicated that Aristotelian-Thomistic vocabulary implies a self-realization view that is radically different. Kahneman found that wellbeing research was based upon the collection of Gallup data and heavily relied only on the remembering self. After years of investigation, Kahneman developed a complementary way to measure how people are experiencing life from moment to moment. This approach to the good life was not ignored by Aristotle. Aristotle discussed pleasure as part of eudaimonia, and argued that pleasure as a kind of feeling is an important aspect of life. However, when it comes to selecting either pleasure or the ultimate end of life, pleasure has to be subordinated to meaning.

It is interesting to note that new research on happiness also supports Aristotle's reasoning. Baumeister et al. (2013) concludes that meaningfulness appears to be central to the difference between feeling happy and eudaimonia. Happiness is not all that people seek; "meaningful but unhappy life is in some ways more admirable than the happy but meaningless one". (Baumeister et al. 2013: 516) The quest for meaning is the essential part of what makes us human. And meaning requires a certain frame of reference that the market cannot supply. Construction of meaning needs being part of something bigger than oneself – bigger than one's vector of goods and services that can be bought on the market.

Michael Sandel asks: "What is the moral importance of the attitudes and norms that money may erode or crowd out? Would the loss of non-market norms and expectations change the character of the activity in ways we would (or at least should) regret? If so, should we avoid introducing financial incentives into the activity, even thought they might do some good? (Sandel 2012: 90–91).

Economics should be seen as a moral science, where we have to decide the fundamental tradeoff between a sufficient satisfaction of wants, a just distribution of the economic goods and a sustainable production in relation to the ecosystem. It is all political-ethical decisions, that have major impact on the environment and for the future. One of the problems of today is that a small group of the population of the world are behaving unecologically, because they are rich, while the biggest group behave unecologically because they are poor.

Joseph Stiglitz (2013: 228–232) writes that we need to adjust GDP to measure other influences on the wellbeing of a nation than the turnover of goods and money. In particular, we should include national happiness and environmental conservation. GDP is calculating the fuel we consume in a given day, but does not account for the "externalities", the extra carbon emission in the atmosphere, the waste produced or the poison that leaks into the water or destroy the ground. GDP accounts what is easy quantifiable by assigning monetary weights. In this chapter, we have pointed on some of the qualitative factors that are crucial to understand the ecological, social and psychological dimensions of economic activity.

One inspirational source can be found in the small Kingdom in Himalaya, Bhutan, where the Government is committed to implement a policy that promote

"Gross National Happiness'. The Bhutanese government has developed a holistic view of happiness, which is measured in a multi-dimensional way, to secure that the inhabitants have sufficient with material goods to live a meaningful life. The government claim, that if the economic development is not matched with spirituality, there is no development (Alkire 2015). The Bhutanese Government also inquiries into the degree of the social connections and the vitality of the local communities of the (about 700.000) inhabitants in the (Buddhist) culture.

Finally, to what extent does the market logic enhance human wellbeing? The market represents a kind of freedom and autonomy for the single individual where the individual can pursue his or her own self-interests. The market gives opportunities of freedom from interference, a kind of negative freedom. However, markets represents a kind of "Freedom *without and from* responsibility" (Smart 2006). The market is impersonal and needs trust to function in an efficient way, but the trust must be developed in a civil society. Trust cannot be created in an impersonal market. We need virtuous consumers that have capabilities to make wise decisions and, and institutions that can educate the consumers to citizenry to negate the inclination to 'miswanting'. We need communities where citizens can excel their virtues in serving something beyond their selves. However, in Western society we have in fact a surplus of individualism and a deficit of companionship. A number of empirical studies concludes that "humans seem to be genetically wired for community". That one is happier in a community is not just some sentimental affection. McKibben writes "economic efficiency improves if we shift people "from places where they are less productive to ones where they are more productive", but your actual physical health suffers. If you buy everything at Wal-Mart, it's cheaper,… But if you go to the farmers' market, you'll have ten times as many conversations." (McKibben 2007: 110)

References

Alkire, S. 2015. *Well-Being, Happiness, and Public Policy*. Thimphu: The Centre for Bhutan Studies & GNH Research.

Aristotle. 1925. 80 *The Nicomachean Ethics*, Translated with an introduction by David Ross, Oxford University Press, Oxford.

———. 1935/1951. (Containing Selections from the Seven of the Most Important Books of Aristotle, selected and translated from the original Greek by P. Wheelwright). New York: The Odyssey Press.

Baumeister, R.F., and K.D. Vohs. 2002. The Pursuit of Meaningfulness in Life. In *Handbook of Positive Psychology*, eds. S.J. Lopez and C.R. Snyder. Oxford: Oxford University Press.

Baumeister, R.F., Vohs, K. D., Aker, J.L., and E.M. Garbinsky 2013. Some Key Differences Between a Happy Life and a Meaningful Life. *The Journal of Positive Psychology: Dedicated to furthering research and promoting good practice* 8(6): 505–516.

Buscher, M. 2002. Ethics of the Market. In *Ethics in the Economy. Handbook of Business Ethics*, ed. L. Zsolnai. Oxford: Peter Lang.

Coplestone, F.C. 1950. *A History of Philosophy. Volume II Medieval Philosophy*. New York: Dobleday.

———. 1955. *Aquinas*. Harmondsworth: Penguin Books.

DesJardins, J.R. 2006. *Environmental Ethics. An Introduction to Environmental Philosophy*. USA: Thomson Wadsworth.
Etzioni, A. 1988. *The Moral Dimension. Toward A New Economics*. London: The Free Press, A Division of Macmillan, Inc.
Frankl, V.E. 1963. *Man's Search for Meaning: An Introduction to Logotheapy*. New York: Washington Square Press.
Frey, B.S., and A. Stutzer. 2002. *Happiness & Economics. How the Economy and Institutions Affect Human Well-Being*. Princeton/Oxford: Princeton University Press.
Friedman, M., and R. Friedman. 1980. *Free to Choose. A Personal Statement*. New York: Harcourt Brace Jovanovich.
Ghosal, S. 2005. Bad Management Theories are Destroying Good Management Practices. *Academy of Management Learning & Education* 4 (1): 75–91.
Gilbert, D. 2006. *Stumbling on Happiness*. New York: Vintage Books.
Haidt, J. 2006. *The Happiness Hypothesis. Putting Ancient Wisdom and Philosophy to the Test of Modern Science*. London: Arrow books.
Kahneman, D. 2011. *Thinking. Fast and Slow*. New York: Penguin Books.
Kasser, T. 2011. Materialistic Value Orientation. In *The Palgrave Handbook of Spirituality and Business*, eds. L. Bouckaert and L. Zsolnai. Houndmills/New York: Palgrave Macmillan.
Keltner, D.E. 2009. *Born to be Good. The science of a Meaningful Life*. New York: W.W. Norton & Company.
Langholm, O. 1992. *Economics in the Medieval Schools. Wealth, Exchange, Value, Money and Usury according to the Paris Theological Tradition 1200–1350*. Leiden: Brill.
MacIntyre, A. 1966. *A Short History of Ethics. A History of Moral Philosophy from the Homeric Age to the Twentieth Century*. New York: Macmillan.
McKibben, B. 2007. *Deep Economy. Economics as if the World Mattered*. Oxford: A Oneworld Book.
OECD. 2013. *OECD Guidelines on Measuring Subjective Well-being*. OECD Publishing. http://dx.doi.org/10.1787/9789264191655-en.
Piketty, T. 2014. *Capital in the 21st Century*. Cambridge, MA: Harvard University Press.
Sales, A., and T. Beschorner. 2006. Societal Transformation and Business Ethics: The Expansion of the Private Sector and its Consequences. In *The Moralization of the Markets*, eds. N. Stehr, C. Henning, and B. Weiler, 227–254. London: Transactions Publishers.
Sandel, M.J. 2012. *What Money Can't Buy. The Moral Limits of Markets*. London: Penguin Books.
Schwartz, B. 2004. *The Paradox of Choice. Why More is Less*. New York: Harper Collins Publishers.
Seligman, M.E.P. 2002. *Authentic Happiness. Using the New Positive Psychology to Realize your Potential for Lasting Fulfillment*. New York: Free Press.
———. 2011. *Flourish. A Visionary New Understanding of Happiness and Well-being*. New York: Atria.
Sen, A. 1993. Capability and Well-Being. In *The Quality of Life*, eds. M. Nussbaum and A. Sen. Oxford: Clarendon Press.
Smart, B. 2006. Freedom without Responsibility: The Culture of the Market and the Demoralization of Social Life. In *The Moralization of the Markets*, eds. N. Stehr, C. Henning, and B. Weiler. New Brunswick: Transaction Publishers.
Steger, M.F. 2009. Meaning in Life. In *The Oxford Handbook of Positive Psychology*, eds. S.J. Lopez and C.R. Snyder, 2nd ed. Oxford: Oxford University Press.
Stiglitz, J. 2013. *The Price of Inequality*. London: Penguin.
Zsolnai, L. 2013. The Moral Economic Man. In *Handbook of Business Ethics. Ethics in the New Economy*, ed. L. Zsolnai. Oxford: Peter Lang.

Chapter 8
Understanding Financial Crises: The Contribution of the Philosophy of Money

Antoon Vandevelde

Abstract The paper underlines that the origin of money lies more in the religious and legal sphere than in the economic realm. Money was used in the exchange between men and goods and in order to compensate for manslaughter, rather than for facilitating the satisfaction of material needs. 'Vergelding', the conversion of guilt into debt was a means to prevent revenge and violence. But soon unease cropped up: the possibility to express everything that is valuable in monetary terms was felt as a form of violence against the soul of men and things.

Aristotle has tried to fit money in a teleological view of the world, but he was faced with the ambivalence of money. Money was deemed to be good as a unit for calculation and as a means of exchange, but it was distrusted as a value reserve. However, it is impossible to separate the three functions of money, as many utopian reformers of the monetary order have tried. The paper emphasizes that nowadays we experience the violent potential of money in the coercion to pay back our debts. Debts have to be repaid, otherwise the debtor will be destroyed as an autonomous subject. The conflict between various categories of debtors and creditors is the most prominent form of "class struggle" we face in our society. It is also a clash between various conceptions of distributive justice.

In the second book of the Republic, Socrates takes up the challenge launched by Glaucon, one of his disciples. He will explain how a just society should look like (and what should be the proper motivation of a just man). He starts by sketching a functional model of a society, designed for optimizing the need satisfaction of its members. He introduces the principle of division of labor. Each person should develop his natural capacities and specialize in a particular craft. Of course a carpenter cannot eat his production. He should sell his furniture in order to be able to buy food. Hence, money seems to be the result of a kind of natural evolution. Many centuries later, John Locke would say that money has been accepted by tacit consent. Its rationale seems to be entirely functional. It appears within economic society

A. Vandevelde (✉)
Catholic University of Leuven, Leuven, Belgium
e-mail: antoon.vandevelde@kuleuven.be

P. Rona, L. Zsolnai (eds.), *Economics as a Moral Science*,
Virtues and Economics 1, DOI 10.1007/978-3-319-53291-2_8

in order to facilitate economic exchange, need satisfaction and the creation of markets.

Money is a human invention, it is an institution. The Greek term for it, 'nomisma' is derived from 'nomos', rule, law. However, together with markets, it seems to be an evident device within economic society, the result of a quasi-natural evolution. For Socrates' audience this story of a society in which membership is based on one's contribution to the satisfaction of economic needs is a provocation. None of his disciples, sons of wealthy citizens of Athens, is urged to work out of economic necessity, nor will they do out of interest. The satisfaction of material needs is a task for slaves, women and foreigners, not for male citizens and certainly not for (would be) philosophers. In the end Socrates will use his principle of specialization for the defense of a hierarchical society, rather than for the legitimation of a frugal and more or less egalitarian utopia. However, over the centuries, this story has continued to circulate amongst economists as the archetypal foundation of their discipline. Economists belonging to the Austrian school, Menger, von Mises and Hayek, have highlighted the natural origin of markets and money, and the same story can be found in many elementary handbooks of economics.

Anthropologists tell a different history about the origin of money. Contrary to our spontaneous intuitions, money is not rooted in economic functionality. It is not because a story sounds perfectly rational that things really have happened that way. Originally, in most societies, money had been created in temples. For a long time it had primarily been used in religious and legal contexts, rather than as a facilitator of economic exchange. It circulated between men and gods, during religious festivals, at ritual ceremonies like the initiation of youngsters, marriages or funerals, or as gifts at the occasion of solemn visits to relatives. (Servet 1984; Laum 1924) Interestingly, Georg Simmel (1900) reminds of the ancient German appeal to 'mangeld', the habit of paying a monetary compensation to the family of a victim in case of manslaughter or murder. Here money serves to convert guilt into debt. It is used as 'vergelding', as a means to prevent revenge, as a remedy against violence. This is possible because money has the magical capacity to make everything commensurable. It even permits to intermediate between life and death. It establishes general equivalence amongst the most diverse items and concerns.

Of course this is far from evident. The possibility to express everything that is valuable in monetary terms has always been felt as a form of violence against the soul of men and things. Can the death of a family member really be compensated with money? Doesn't this rather illustrate the logic of a society where all authentic values are corrupted by greed? The same token that permits to preempt revenge, violence and war seems to violate our most intimate convictions and commitments as human beings. Kreon was not able to convince Antigone that he had good reasons to posthumously punish her brother Polyneikes, but, undoubtedly, he would also have been unable to undo her resentment by paying a monetary compensation. This is a first illustration of what I call the ambivalence of money. In this paper I will show that money never gets rid of this ambivalence. From Aristotle to contemporary political economists, many theorists have desperately tried to separate its beneficial and its maleficent aspects, but all of them have failed. First I will trace back to

Aristotle's intuitions the long history of monetary trust and distrust. Then I will present my definition of money and of economics. Finally, I will show that recent financial crises can better be understood on the basis of this philosophy of money and I will draw some conclusions about the relation between markets and the scope of democracy. Scientists hate ambivalence or ambiguity, philosophers love it. In this paper I argue that the ambivalence of money is inescapable.

8.1 Aristotle and the Ambivalence of Money

Aristotle was the first to develop a systematic philosophy of money and economics. As is well known, he starts from a teleological conception of the universe. All things aim at their natural goal. This idea lies at the basis of a separate physics for the earthly and for the heavenly sphere. Interestingly, Aristotle thinks within a finite universe. All movement stops when its object reaches its natural destination. This also applies to human beings. In general, they are called upon to develop the essence of humanity, their rational capacities, their insight in the logos of the cosmos. This means that they have to turn away from inferior inclinations and aim at participation in the divine. Paradoxically, the proper aim of human beings is to surpass humanity in the direction of the divine. This teleological way of thinking also applies to common human activities. The idea is that each of our endeavors has a natural or intrinsic goal. Once again, when that goal has been reached, all desire stops. If someone is hungry, he wants bread, but he needs no more than one loaf of bread. Hence, the goal of our activities is also its 'end'. It sounds somewhat anachronistic, but Aristotle could be considered as an ecologist *avant la lettre*, advocating limits to growth.

The problem now is that for a greedy person the desire for money can never be satisfied and has no intrinsic limit. Hence Aristotle's distrust of thc chrematistikè technè, the art of acquiring wealth. It should be strictly subordinate to the oikonomikè technè, the art of making good use of wealth. However, the transgression of this limit is quite tempting for human beings. Aristotle is more realistic than Plato. He admits that some wealth is necessary for human happiness, but an unlimited desire for more wealth makes us into slaves of our greed, and this is as detrimental to our happiness as extreme poverty. For Aristotle all movement 'eis apeiron', all infinite movement, all movement without a proper end, is a cosmic perversion. Hence greed is the very definition of injustice. It is a transgression of 'dikè', the laws of cosmic justice. In this conception, unlimited desire, the absence of respect for natural limits is the very definition of evil. Ethics is nothing else than the respect for natural limits. As such it definitely has some anti-economic flavor.[1] (1) Infinite

[1] That ethics is about the respect for limits has been taken for granted in most societies. In medieval philosophy, divine law was supposed to limit human endeavor. In our contemporary society, we tend to think that the freedom of a person has to (and can only be) limited by the equal freedom for all other human persons.

growth, or endless accumulation of wealth are considered to be unnatural and inhuman.

These ideas form the philosophical background for Aristotle's conception of money. The Philosopher was the first to enumerate the three functions of money, a distinction that is still made nowadays in manuals of economics. First of all, money serves as a measure of value. It permits the comparison of all that is deemed to be valuable and it can be used as a device for calculation. Secondly, as Socrates had already made clear, money serves as a means of exchange. It facilitates economic exchange and it permits the development of markets. And thirdly, money can serve as a store of value. It can be used to store wealth. Now, Aristotle has no problem with the first two functions of money, but for the reasons I mentioned above, he distrusts the third function. While money should remain a mere means for need satisfaction, it risks turning into the ultimate goal of all human activity. Again, this reversal of means and ends is a nightmare for Aristotle. When, for instance a medical doctor aims at earning money rather than at healing his patients, when possibly he keeps his patients dependent on his care in order to make more money, this is evil. It means that natural priorities are reversed, that limits are transgressed and that extrinsic considerations win from intrinsic motivation.

Hence the ambivalence of money. Certainly, it is useful, but it is also dangerous. Insofar as it makes universal commodification possible, it is a threat to ethics, to social hierarchy and to the proper hierarchy of values. If everything can be exchanged for everything, then no inalienable values are left. This is a regime of general prostitution in which no intrinsic value can survive. The problem however is that one cannot separate the three functions of money. In order to function as a means of exchange, money should keep its value over time and it should permit the storage of wealth. Hence the beneficial and the maleficent side of money are as inseparable as the two sides of a same coin.

Aristotle offers an even more original contribution to the philosophy of money. Referring to the story of King Midas, who starves from hunger and thirst because everything he touches turns into gold, he rejects the abstract generality that characterizes money. Basically, money is pure promise. Nowadays, we would say: it is pure virtuality. It has no value on its own, but it can be exchanged against everything. The story of King Midas teaches us however that real wealth is particular, demonstrable, often tangible: it can take the form of a loaf of bread, a glass of water or a gift to a friend. King Midas' mistake is that he takes a mere sign for reality. Hence, when we gather money, we do not accumulate real wealth, but only transitory signs of wealth. Of course, we can dream of a kind of money that could be a perfect and eternal re-presentation of wealth, but this is an illusion. Signs are always treacherous. They suggest more than they can deliver. The paradox is that we can only 'have' real wealth by spending it. Hence the priority of oikonomia – the art of spending money - above the chrematistikè technè, the art of acquiring wealth. Aristotle's doctrine of the various virtues points into the same direction. Friendship is an indispensable condition for happiness. Now, friendship is based on generosity. Moreover in his Nichomachean Ethics, Aristotle praises not just ordinary generosity, he also devotes a separate chapter to *megaloprepeia*, magnificence, the habit of giving great, prestigious gifts, of organizing impressive fiestas and games, of building big temples. Also the virtue of *megalopsychia*, magnanimity, refers to the same apology of gift giving.

Within the philosophical tradition this Aristotelian line of thought has been taken up in a modified way in the medieval praise of caritas. More recently, in twentieth century philosophy, Emmanuel Levinas has defended it strongly. According to Levinas, the proper function of money is that it has to be given away. In this way it may create the most valuable things in life: friendship, community, enjoyment, social appreciation and happiness. More surprisingly the famous economist John Maynard Keynes, by the way an intellectual who knew his classics, seems to struggle with the same ambivalence of money as Aristotle. He also distrusts the third monetary function. Money should circulate, he teaches. When people refuse to spend and save their money for better times, this attitude risks creating a vicious circle of deflation and unemployment. Like many other less well known monetary reformers of his time, Keynes tries to escape the ambivalence of money by devising a kind of shrinking money: money that would lose its value if it is not spent. Nowadays, we live in an unprecedented era of negative nominal interest rates. This is one way of applying Keynes' idea, but of course, historically, the easiest way to depreciate money goes by organizing inflation. Most Keynesians see inflation as the oil of a well-functioning economy. However, in the 1980s it has become clear that this is dangerous. Moderate inflation always risks to degenerate into hyperinflation.

That it is impossible to disentangle the three function of money can also be shown with respect to contemporary economic reality. Suppose I own Italian state bonds. However I receive information that makes me doubt about the ability of Italian government to repay its debts. As a sensible father of my household I will sell these bonds as quickly as possible. I do not want to lose my savings. This is the perfectly rational behavior of a prudent economic actor. However, in doing so, I can as well be accused of speculation against Italian public debt. Or take another example. As a businessman, I know that I will need a certain amount of dollars within three months' time. I insure myself against future uncertainty - a possible increase of the value of the dollar - by buying these dollars now on the term market. However, other economic actors use exactly the same type of transaction in order to earn speculative money. If they think that the value of the dollar will increase, they can make a profit by buying dollars now at a lower price. The international financial system has its own functionality. It should direct money to those places where it can be most efficiently used. However, speculators use exactly the same channels to make a profit as prudent traders. Hence, we cannot escape this conclusion: it is impossible to separate the beneficial from the harmful side of money, the speculative from the acceptable transactions. A consequence of this insight is that every limitation of speculative moves, for example by a Tobin tax, has also an efficiency cost. Regulators will have to weigh up relative costs and benefits of the measures they take.

8.2 Money as Institutionalized Trust

A person who owns money expects to have a reliable claim on a piece of future wealth. This presupposes that, tomorrow, the money I currently own will still be as valuable as today. Hence there should be no inflation at all. One can even show that money presupposes infinite trust in the future. (Orléans 1987) Suppose I save money for my old age. It is rational to do so if I may be sure that my children will accept my money and will be willing to give me goods and services in exchange. Of course, they will do so because they expect their children – my grandchildren - to accept their money, when they will grow old and dependent on the help of others. However, if people start thinking that, at some moment in future, let's say at time t, the younger generation will refuse the money of its predecessors, immediately the whole construction of intergenerational solidarity risks falling apart. The reason is evident: at time t-1 the young generation (that will be old at time t) will refuse the money of the former generation, and so forth. As the consequence of a roll back effect, money will lose its value immediately, here and now.

Now, one could argue that this is mere theory and that, in reality, people do not make such complicated and far reaching calculations. However, if we look back, history shows us ample evidence of the fragility of monetary systems. There have been so many devaluations, phases of hyperinflation, speculative waves, political revolutions and military occupations. The idea of an immutable monetary order definitely is a chimera. If money circulates here and now, this probably stems from the fact that we do not reach the highest standards of rationality in our daily life and that we are subject to shortsightedness.

According to its very logic, money requires infinite trust in the future. Hence it may be no surprise that, for people who are subject to this monetary illusion, it reaches a quasi-divine status in our society. It shares its abstract generality with the god of philosophers.[2] This is what Aglietta and Orléan have called the sovereignty of money. (Aglietta and Orléans 1982, 2002) God or the mammon: the alternative is very much present in the Jewish-Christian tradition. There are indications that religion is the most convincing, perhaps even the only meaningful alternative for consumerism. Money is a fascinating reality. It suggests a form of omnipotence and incorruptibility that is almost inhuman, although money is nothing more than a system of rules resulting from human interaction.

Money should not be identified with gold, or coins, or standardized pieces of paper. These are only superficial forms money takes on. Basically, money is an institution. It is a set of rule systems organizing the appropriation of (signs of) wealth. The basic question to which all types of economic order have to give an answer is this one: what claims on a part of future social wealth can each economic actor legitimately make? For example, one can get money by working. Labor

[2] The God of Christianity is presented as a good father. This is the reason why, probably, he cannot be characterized by the same abstract generality as the god of philosophers (and of many other religions). Hence Christianity seems to be an atypical religion.

relations are organized by labor law. In many countries manual workers fall under other rules than employees or executives. Public servants have other rights and obligations than people working in the private sector. One can also receive money when one is not working, for example when one is involuntarily unemployed. Students can get a scholarship if they fall under particular rules. The rules for getting a mortgage credit are different from the rules for consumer credit. Investment credits, microcredits, credits to countries or amongst banks: they all obey different rule systems. The whole of an economic order is hence a highly complex and differentiated system of rule systems.

Of course this is quite a controversial matter. The rules can be more favorable to the employees or to the employers, to firms or to their clients, to big capital or to small business, to landlords or to their tenants, to taxpayers or to tax authorities, to banks or to their clients, more generally to the net lenders of money or to the net borrowers. Not only class struggle, but many more social conflicts turn precisely around the issue of appropriation. Let's try to be more precise. Economic relations typically take a circular form. They are organized in circuits of strict reciprocity. 'Do ut des.' To each transfer from A to B, there must be a corresponding transfer from B to A. Economic actors try to achieve strict equivalence between what they offer and what they receive. In this sense, economic relations differ not only from altruism, characterized by unilateral gifts, but also from relations governed by more loose forms of reciprocity. The main thing to be organized by monetary rules is the obligation to pay (back). These rules are often quite detailed and they involve overt or latent violence. From an economic point of view, poor people, people without earning power or without money simply do not exist. Also, debts have to be repaid. Otherwise the debtor will be destroyed as an autonomous economic agent: he will go bankrupt. Note that in our analysis, there is no trace of a dichotomy between the monetary and the economic order. The real economy is no more than a set of monetary rules, detailing the obligation to pay (back).

Giving credit (and getting it) is marvelous, it is a most tangible sign of trust. However, credits need to be paid back. Now the pressure to pay back can be too tight or too lax. If the rules are too severe, if even minor temporary difficulties in refunding debts are sanctioned immediately with bankruptcy, there is the threat of deflation and unemployment. Failing firms can contaminate each other and this can lead to the collapse of the economic system as a whole. However, if the constraints are too loose, dubious debts will be refunded. This means that promises are not kept and that the limits the economic agents had agreed upon are not respected: even when an agent does not comply with the monetary rules, he can continue to get access to (signs of) wealth. In this case, the differentiation of the monetary circuits is vanishing and the rules are collapsing. More money will circulate and/or it will circulate at a higher pace. Ultimately, this will result in inflation and possibly in a crash of monetary and financial trust. This is what we call hyperinflation. As we know from the German situation in the 1920s of from contemporary Venezuela, this leads to a sudden and drastic shrinking of economic activity. In that case economic agents will probably seek a new sign of wealth that could credibly be considered as incorruptible. Gold, dollars, land, Chinese state obligations: in principle anything can serve as ersatz money, as the new general equivalent, under the condition that most economic agents put trust in it. Hence monetary authorities have a hard task at steering the system in between the Scylla of deflation and the Charybdis of hyperinflation. Once again, the most crucial question crops up: how can such a fragile institution as a monetary order, organizing the most conflict laden matters in society and threatened by so many uncontrollable contingencies, nevertheless be perceived as absolutely trustworthy? Our analysis of the ambivalence or money implies that there is no ultimate answer to this question. No national or supranational regulation can eliminate once and for ever the vulnerability of an economic (or monetary) order.

8.3 The Risk of a Systemic Crisis

The international financial crisis of 2008 can be understood in terms of our analysis. Readers will remember the sequence of events. In the United States, banks had been lending money to people belonging to the lower middle classes, so that they could buy a house or an apartment. Soon these bankers realized that, probably, these debts would never be paid back. Hence they packed them together under some flashy name and sold them to more naïve clients, bankers, insurance funds, wealthy people. European bankers had forgotten the elementary wisdom that high yields hide high risks. They hardly knew what they had bought, but as all their colleagues had done the same thing, and as interest rates were higher than on similar bonds, they did not ask too many questions. At their turn, they sold these debts to each other and to their clients as 'structured products', yielding a substantial rent. When the truth about the risks attached to the underlying credits became clear, the value of these assets declined suddenly. Private clients owning these dubious credits simply lost their money, but many banks were considered too big to fail. Hence they were permitted to sell their dubious assets to central banks and institutions run by their states. Subsequently some of these states ran into problems and they were permitted to pass on the hot potato to supranational institutions like the European Central Bank and IMF. However, there is no second planet to get rid of these dubious credits.

Actually, two alternative policies are defended by economists and monetary experts. Some of them advocate a very strict policy. They want to prevent the creation of new speculative bubbles by a drastic destruction of dubious credits. Others, like Krugman and De Grauwe, hope that a 'sweet landing' is still possible. They plead for a continued effort of monetary expansion in order to sustain economic growth and in order to slowly digest accumulated debts. The problem is that this remedy boils down to prescribing more of the same recipe that caused the crisis. By continuing to expand the volume of debts circulating around the world, they refuse to eliminate drastically all doubtful debts and probably they even add more of them. In this way, they increase the vulnerability of the system as a whole. Interestingly it is precisely in the attempt to better manage local crises that the risk of a worldwide systemic crisis has been increased. Globalization has had as a consequence that local financial systems have been connected into one big system. Formerly a local crisis had to be solved locally. Nowadays, most walls between the local systems have been dismantled. This has as a consequence that local shocks can better be digested, but also that a coincidence of local problems can contaminate the whole system. Hence, the risk of an uncontrollable systemic crisis increases drastically. I think that this analysis casts doubt on the strategy advocated by Krugman and De Grauwe. Instead of the flight forward, it suggests that prudence is more appropriate.

8.4 Global Markets and Local Democracy

The thesis of the ambivalence of money could inspire pessimism about the possibility of devising an efficient form of regulation of global financial markets. Doubtless, it would be easier if we would be able to neatly separate the beneficial side of money from its maleficent side. Isn't this what we do in the supermarket? We put in our trolley what we like and we leave aside what we do not like. However, societies do not function according to this consumerist model: good and bad are much more intermingled. Nevertheless, the analysis we propose here does suggest some policy advice. In general, this is a plea for institutionalism. As greed will probably always continue to play an important role in financial affairs, it is more efficient to amend the institutional framework within which people operate than to try to amend their psychology. Institutional design should aim at discouraging extremely risky behavior, at minimizing possible harm and at stimulating socially beneficial motivations.

Now, if the vulnerability of the global financial system is due to the decreasing differentiation of the system and to the vanishing of walls between the various subsystems, it could be sound policy advice to reintroduce new walls and clear limits in the system. A transparent separation of saving banks characterized by low risk and low interest rates from investment banks, granting higher yields at the price of high risk, is an example of such a reform. Also, we know that some banks can take up speculative risks that may endanger the financial health of a whole country. The coerced nationalization of Dexia bank in Belgium has increased Belgian public debt drastically. Undoubtedly, this will create additional difficulties in sustaining the payment of pensions in the near future. Other countries like Iceland, Ireland and Spain have had to face analogous problems. Hence a policy of downscaling banks that are supposed to be 'too big to fail' seems advisable. It is remarkable that, despite considerable economic reforms in Europe and in the US after the crisis of 2008, precisely these superbanks have almost immediately started to re-engage in the same speculative activities that in the former years have proven so dangerous. They could do so, because they knew that political and financial authorities will never let them go bankrupt in case they get in trouble. Surprisingly national authorities seem to protect these banks that threaten their stability against the attempt by European instances to downscale them. This is a good example of shortsightedness! Moreover, we know that small players can also create huge deficits by irresponsible behavior. Hence the need for control and regulation of financial markets, preferably on an international scale.

History teaches that regulation will never completely abolish the fragility of the financial system. However, this does not mean that states are inevitably hijacked by global financial markets. Some European countries offer good examples of wealthy, highly competitive economies with a flourishing welfare state and an extensive social security system. It is true that the stability of these institutions is never guaranteed in the long run. Free movement of capital does hinder efficient taxation of revenue from capital and free migration within the EU does create problems of social dumping and does impose a burden on national systems of social security. Hence continuous adaptation to new situations is required. However, the thesis of the inevitable erosion of welfare states by global markets is definitely refuted by empirical evidence.

There are still other lessons to be learned from recent financial crises. If we want to preserve our European model of society with a generous welfare state, or more generally, if we want to preserve an important space for national decision making, then we have to carefully watch over the most important macro-economic equilibria. Excessive public debt, huge deficits of government budget or balance of payments make societies highly dependent on international financial markets and foreign creditors. A few years ago, when financial crisis was hitting hard, the parliament of Cyprus has democratically decided that foreign institutions had to lend their country a huge amount of money without any guarantee that these credits would ever be repaid. Of course they have not received the money. No credit without trust. As I have explained, monetary coercion, the obligation to pay back is the most basic economic law. It is not evident to explain to foreign creditors that one needs money in order to be able to continue a disastrous economic policy, or, in the case of Cyprus, in order to guarantee high interest rates to Russian maffiosi. Without a doubt, the world is not just. Big players are better able to bend the rules to their advantage than little Cyprus. The US has been able to make the whole world contribute to the bankruptcy of Lehman Brothers. However there are also excellent examples of small states that continue to largely keep their fate in their own hands by following a prudent economic policy.

In this respect it may be useful to distinguish between weak and strong states. Weak states are unable to bring about good order in their affairs. Hence, they have to undergo monetary coercion. They cannot escape the violence of money. The reason is that bad governance leads to a vicious circle. Greece has offered a blackboard example: no decent tax raising, inefficient administration, distrust of all state agencies, corruption and clientelism, myopic spending, harming future generations… All these features are closely interconnected. It is because government is so inefficient that revenue raising lacks all legitimacy. Strong states on the contrary benefit from a virtuous circle. They can require a high level of taxation and a high level of compliance to laws and norms in exchange for efficient government. They enjoy high trust on behalf of their citizens for their capacity to organize a generous social security. Moreover financial markets do not fear debt cancellation and grant them low interest rates on public debt. Of course, if we want to preserve democratic decision making within our country, it is utterly important to stay within the group of strong states and not to fall back in the group of weak states.

8.5 Conclusion

A just society is able to shield its members at least partially from the most brutal forms of monetary coercion by limiting the power of money. This can be realized through the organization of an extensive offer of public goods of good quality: the protection of life and property, accessible health care, a decent public school system, an efficient and impartial legal system. Historically this has been one of the most important functions of national states. Probably, in a globalised world, it is a function that should partially be taken over by supranational institutions like the EU. However, also local communities can empower their members and protect them to a certain degree against erratic movements of markets. (Walzer 1983; Sandel 2002)

A sound regulation of financial institutions, a prudent macro-economic policy avoiding excessive deficits and a limitation of the scope of what can be bought and sold on the market place, these are the main strategies that societies can use to protect themselves against the fragility of monetary systems. However it is an illusion that we can ever cancel once and for all times the ambivalence of money and the vulnerability of economic order that is caused by it.

References

Aglietta, M., and A. Orléans. 1982. *La violence de la monnaie*. Paris: PUF.
———. 2002. *La monnaie entre confiance et violence*. Paris: Odile Jacob.
Laum, B. 1924. *Heiliges Geld – Eine historische Untersuchung über den sakralen Ursprung des Geldes*. J.C.B. Mohr Verlag.
Orléans, A. 1987. Anticipations et conventions en situation d'incertitude. *Revue d'Economie Politique* 13 (1): 153–172.
Sandel, M. 2002. *What Money Cannot Buy – The Moral Limits of the Market*, vol. 2012. London: Allen Lane.
Servet, J-M.. 1984. *Nomismata – Etats and origines de la monnaie*. Presses universtaire de Lyon.
Simmel, G. 1900. *Philosophie des Geldes*. Berlin: Duncker & Humblot Verlag.
Walzer, M. 1983. *Spheres of Justice – A Defense of Pluralism and Equality*. New York: Basic Books.

Chapter 9
Economics and Vulnerability: Relationships, Incentives, Meritocracy

Luigino Bruni

Abstract The paper warns that a significant body of philosophical work in virtue ethics is associated with a critique of the market economy and economics. The market depends on instrumental rationality and extrinsic motivation; market interactions therefore fail to respect the internal value of human practices and the intrinsic motivations of human actors. By using market exchange as a central model, mainstream economics normalizes extrinsic motivation, not only in markets but also in social life more generally; therefore economics appears as an assault on virtues and on human flourishing.

Communities and organizations that have preserved their creative and fruitful character over time have been able to live with their vulnerability; they have not eliminated it entirely from their territories but they contained it.

Vulnerability (from *vulnus*: wound), like many true words of the human realm, is ambivalent, because good vulnerability coexists with bad vulnerability, and often the two are intertwined. Good vulnerability is inscribed in all generative human relationships, where if I do not give the other the possibility of "hurting me", the relationship does not reach the depth to be fruitful.

Good vulnerability is what we experience in loving relationships with our children, in friendship, in the primary communities of our lives. Today we know that the most creative work teams are those where people receive an authentic – therefore risky – openness for credit. Generativity in all areas has a vital need for freedom, trust, risk, all of which make the person who grants these vulnerable. Life is generated by relationships open to the possibility of relational wound.

L. Bruni (✉)
LUMSA University, Rome, Italy
e-mail: luigino.bruni@focolare.org

P. Rona, L. Zsolnai (eds.), *Economics as a Moral Science*,
Virtues and Economics 1, DOI 10.1007/978-3-319-53291-2_9

9.1 The Ambivalence of Good Life

The economic, social and anthropological crisis of our time challenges the way mainstream economics has depicted market interactions, their rationality and nature. In the moments of crisis, historical and foundational analyses may be useful in the search of a new synthesis requested by the discipline and the reasons of the common good. In this process that has just started, the greatest task that threatens us is to go beyond the present finance-driven market economy without renouncing however to the achievements of civilization that western economic and social system has delivered in the most recent ages.

In the course of its development, market economy has brought about a change in the nature of human relations. The market has truly become a culture in its own right, an *ethos*, that is more than ethics as we intend this expression to-day, because *ethos* is a custom or a lifestyle that surrounds and informs within itself all dimensions of common life (Bruni 2012a). The market gives birth to and fosters its own sense of being human, in particular the promise of interpersonal relationships without the *"wound" of the other* associated to any genuine communitarian life (Bruni 2012b). It is at this anthropological and relational level that rests the contribution of this paper, that opens with a reflection on the community, and then passing throughout the history of the birth of the modern political economy, to arrive to explore some dimensions of the relation between market and community.

Any reflection on economy, love and vulnerability have to confront the notion of community and its inherent contradictions. The ethos of the market is the main response to the ambivalence of the ethos of the community. On the one hand, individuals living in a community are more likely to establish meaningful relationships and thus to encounter true happiness and humanity; on the other, the community, by its very nature, poses a threat to the individuals' liberties and absolute rights, and consequently to individuality itself.

In sociology the community has been generally described as the main protagonist of the ancient world. Actually, the very idea of community was ultimately foreign to the ancient world, at least in its meaning of cum-munus (i.e. reciprocal gift/obligation). It was, paradoxically, only with the birth of individualism, widely acknowledged as a modern phenomenon, that the community came to be understood in this new, more tragic and proper sense.

In order to show this thesis, let us consider as a starting point the following uncontroversial point: whether tribal or archaic, the ancient community was fundamentally hierarchical and illiberal, and seen as opposed to both an aggregation of free and equal individuals (that we can call society) and a fraternal community. The rise of political economy in the modern era or, from a different point of view, the emergence of modernity out of market economy, marks a time in Western history when we observe the gradual decline of the hierarchical and illiberal community and the parallel affirmation of the individual without community.

Drawing on an interesting etymological account, a large part of today's literature traces the origin of the ambivalent quality of the community, the communitas, back to the word munus (cfr. Latin communitas: from cum + munus). In this view, the cummunitas would mirror the ambivalence of the Latin word munus, which denotes simultaneously a gift and an obligation, and of the Old-English gift which translates as poison in German. This interpretation derives from the groundbreaking "Essai sur le don" written in the early twenties by the French sociologist and anthropologist Marcel Mauss· who studied extensively the ambivalent nature of the gift. His theory of gift was highly influential throughout the twentieth century. In his studies of archaic societies, Mauss showed that what compels the receiver to reciprocate is the spirit of the object, the hau, which is thought to be embedded in the gift. The receiver is thus bound to the giver through the hau, which has been passed to him through the gift. He cannot be released from the hau's "poisonous" spell until the gift has been reciprocated in a way deemed suitable by the giver.

For these reasons the ternary process of giving (giving-accepting-giving back), represents a foundational step of the social process of gift-giving and of the intra- and inter-community cycles of gift-exchange. Gifts affect the inner balance of social relations by generating situations of asymmetry that men – the modern-day individuals especially – find hard to endure. An un-reciprocated gift yields disequilibrium and disorder, whereas human societies have a preference for symmetry. We can read in these terms the extraordinary power of the modern market, which is founded upon the symmetrical exchange of equivalents (or values that are perceived as equivalent by the agents).

The topic of the complex grammar of the munus (the gift that obligates and pretends restitution) has been explored by a number of distinguished scholars, including the French philosophers Derrida and Marion, and the French sociologists of the M.A.U.S.S. movement (Alain Caillé especially). In particular, over the past decade the role of the munus as the primary source of the community's inner ambivalence has been convincingly emphasized by the Italian philosopher Roberto Esposito. In the following pages we attempt to further articulate the meaning of the ambivalence in the terms munus and communitas. But let us proceed one step at the time.

Within archaic communities the gift is always perceived as a social event taking place within groups that bear a recognized sacral connotation. In this context, what is "sacred" is the symbolic dimension in which the "total social fact" (in Marcel Mauss's Essay sur le don) of the gift occurs. In other terms, we could say that the sacred works as an intermediary that accompanies and makes possible the very process of the gift in its basic grammar of giving-accepting-reciprocating. Another essential trait of traditional gift circles is that they are built on reciprocity rather than gratuitousness. This point has been highlighted primarily by Karl Polanyi, whose work was key to the anthropology of gift of the twentieth century. In its basic relational structure, the reciprocity of gift is not fundamentally different, in its social function and relational nature, from the phenomenon of economic exchange or barter – a practice appeared much later than ritual gift-exchange. Through the history of cultures, the difference between gift- and market-exchange can basically be interpreted as a difference in degrees: in the ways of measuring equivalence, in the acceptable delay between gift and counter-gift, in the types of punishment established, rather than a difference in nature.

Therefore, whereas Adam Smith describes primitive man as inclined by nature to "truck and barter" (Wealth of Nations, p. 25), it can be argued on the basis of the anthropological evidence, that the earliest form of exchange between men was not the market nor the barter, but the reciprocity of gifts-munera. The market or the economic exchange emerged long afterwards from the depths of human history as an evolution of gift-exchange. In this context, strangers are not regarded as wholly foreign or different; they are seen at the same time as enemies and guests; as rivals, but also as potential partners in a transaction. In fact, by virtue of their sacral culture, all ancient communities are essentially alike; and this circumstance provides a sort of common ground which makes it possible to connect with each other through a shared symbolic language, to encounter each other, trade or fight.

In the ancient community the political and religious powers are deeply intertwined and no clear separation exists between the religious and political spheres – this is certainly the case for many ancient communities across the Mediterranean, including Rome and Ancient Greece. As noticed by Rudolf Otto and later by Mircea Eliade, the only boundary lies between the sacred and the profane. The sacred community is therefore simultaneously characterized by the absence of a distinction between the political and religious domains, and, as the other side of the same coin, by the existence of an absolute limit between the sacred and the profane, that is the main instrument for governing the life in common.

Hence, the contradictory nature of munus and communitas may be explained as a reflection of the ambivalent nature of the sacred which, as expressed by the Latin word sacer, or the Melanesians' mana, means simultaneously "holy" and "cursed". Thus Aldo Schiavone in this passage on Ancient Rome: "Indeed, the relation between royalty and sacrality […] well documented, in the case of Rome, by the survival, well into the republican era, of the presence of a singular figure, the rex sacrorum, would become a constant in the whole of European history: even Christianity would ultimately rework it in a penetrating and creative way right up to the dawn of the modern age" (Schiavone 2012: 66).

Each and every aspect of the ancient community (even the profane, from which the sacred is distinct) is imbued with sacredness. Everything is symbol: the religious or magic ritual (a distinction extremely tenuous, if not absent, from the archaic world) opens a channel to the holy and becomes the language through which this order is conveyed, thus establishing a connection binding the members of the community to the deities and with each other (cfr. religion, Lt religo: to bind). While invisible to men, this order is more real than it may seem.

The concept of sacred relates closely to that of mediation: every sacred order, every hierophany (i.e. "manifestation of the sacred", to say it with Eliade) requires a system of mediators operating between the community and the deity; inevitably, any possibility of un-mediated contact between the individuals and the deity, or between each other, must be denied, as it emerges in its purity in the traditional cast system. René Girard (1977) in his classic book claims that sacrifice has often been described as an act of "mediation" between a sacrificer and a 'deity'. In fact, sacrifice could be interpreted as ultimately representing a means, an instrumental device enabling the mediator (priest, shaman) to establish a link between the community and the deity within the sacred space. In this perspective, we can argue along with Durkheim that the sacred serves a fundamental social function. Sacral communities are necessarily hierarchical: status is ranked and classified as "high" and "low", "pure" and "impure" in response to the supposed vicinity to the deity and to its order as reflected in history (i.e. priests are typically at the top of the hierarchy; artisans, peasants and slaves at the bottom).

The human community is ordered according to this wholly sacred framework, in which every element gains its meaning from the supreme purpose of preserving the community. Individual members have no autonomy: they are subjected to the sacred community and may even be sacrificed for the sake of a community higher good (or one that is perceived as such by the member and, most importantly, by their chiefs). In an environment that is naturally hostile and characterized by the extreme scarcity of resources, the community's survival and growth inevitably become the highest good. Mechanisms of individual incentives are discouraged through the provision of various types of social bonds and sanctions, thus enhancing solidarity within the community. Figures like the pater familias, the Roman pontifex, Moses in Israel, the Egyptian pharaoh, the Medieval ruler differ in many ways but, from our point of view, they are also very much alike in that they guarantee, by virtue of a sacral hierarchical authority and mediation, the order of the community as a whole.

9.2 The Paradox of the Community

In traditional medieval society the possibility of life in community was closely bound to sacrifice and tragedy. The source of this vision is in Greek thought, predominantly in Aristotle's*Ethics*. Aristotle had grasped a paradox that is at the core of the entire West: a 'good life', or a happy life, is at once civil and vulnerable. As noted in *Nicomachean Ethics* (1169b) "the happy man needs friends"; this is why no one can be happy alone, and why it is impossible to achieve happiness in solitude and in flight from social life and encountering the other. But, if happiness requires social relationships, that is, requires friendship and reciprocity, and if friendship and reciprocity are free acts neither fully or unilaterally controlled by the individual, then our happiness depends on the response of others, on how much they return our love, friendship and reciprocity. If, in other words, I need friends and reciprocity to be happy, then the happy life is ambivalent: the other is my joy and sorrow, my only chance for true happiness, but also he or she on whom my unhappiness depends. The 'good life', the blessing, then depends on others, who however can hurt me.

Conversely, if to avoid this vulnerability and probable suffering I take refuge in solitude and contemplation apart from others (the great neoplatonic alternative), my life cannot fully flourish. This is why the Aristotelian tradition, beyond Aristotle himself, associates the happy life with tragedy. Regarding interpersonal relations, the contemporary thinker Martha Nussbaum states that "these components of the good life are going to be minimally self-sufficient. And they will be vulnerable in an especially deep and dangerous way" (Nussbaum 1986: 344). In this sense social life, the *communitas*, carries the mark of suffering within itself. The Jewish world reminds us, with several great symbols and myths contained primarily (but not solely) in Genesis, that the other is a blessing (because without him or her I cannot be happy), but also that he or she is the one who wounds me and whom I wound in turn (wounding and blessing always have a reciprocal nature).

Pre-modern and ancient thought understood the ambivalent nature of the good life: one cannot be happy without *communitas*, but precisely because of the need for relationship with the other and of his or her presence, the good life is intertwined in various ways with death. In this respect the foundational myths of ancient cities are emblematic. The first city (Enoch) in the Bible was founded by Cain, who killed his brother, and the founding of Rome is associated with the assassination of Remus by his brother Romulus. The idea of the common good in the pre-modern West was not associated with a sum of private interests; it entailed, so to speak, a subtraction: only by giving up and risking something of "one's own" (one's private goods) could one build something that is 'ours' (the common good), which was common to all because it did not belong to anyone. We should, however, quickly note that the pre-modern worldview remained substantially holistic: the community is what is seen, not the individual. The Absolute absorbed everything; individuality did not emerge. There is One, not a manifold. In particular, ancient peoples did not consider the I-Thou relationship, or horizontal inter-subjectivity between equals. The ambivalence of life in community as lived, experienced, and known in flesh had not become a culture, either in the ancient world or in the pre-modern Christian West.

In fact, even the ingenious insights of Aristotle about the need of friends for a good life should be read in a social and cultural context in which the friend is not really a Thou, but an alter ego, another self, as Aristotle states repeatedly: "A friend is another self" (*Nicomachean Ethics*, 1170b)[1]. Indeed, contemporary philosophers like Martha Nussbaum – whose paper, not by chance, opens this issue – are primarily the ones who load the reading of Aristotle's thought on social life with tragedy, but in the original thought of the great Greek philosopher the friend is chosen carefully and selectively precisely to minimize the possibility of negation, or the 'not'. One's friends are very few, because were there many the risk of injury, of betrayed reciprocity, would increase. In this sense, Aristotle's *philia* is selective and exclusive; the *philia* which is at the basis of the life of the polis is a *philia* among small numbers of equals (male, adult, and free, usually united by the same ethnicity, while those of mixed race, farmers, and merchants are excluded, as Aristotle carefully specifies in the first book of the Politics). Friends do bring a certain diversity, but that of the Greeks is a 'positive' diversity among similar; they seek a commonality

[1] A certain philosophy of otherness, from Emmanuel Lévinas to Roberto Esposito, feels that it must overcome this Thou/alter-ego in an external "he/she" that makes relationality open and transcendent: "All the rhetoric of the excess of the other notwithstanding, in a one-on-one comparison, the other is conceivable only and ever in relation to the 'I'. The other cannot be but non-self, its reverse and its shadow" (Esposito 2009: 129).

among themselves into which the 'not' that separates and wounds does not enter; there is no alterity. The polis for Aristotle, and the Greek world in general, was a community of equals, not of the dissimilar (as the Roman *civitas* tended to be), and the whole art of politics was avoiding the suffering due to the Thou-who-are-not-I. Only the polis is a place of relationship between equals, since all other groups that give rise to a polis (the village and the family) are unequal communities. Regarding the family, the basic unit of the state or the polis, Aristotle states that its "primary elements" are "master and servant, husband and wife, father and sons" (*Politics*, 1232b), which are three types of radically unequal relationships. The polis must therefore be the place for these relationships among equals, the culmination – and here lies the paradox of this political vision – of a process of successive aggregations of unequal communities. That is why education is entrusted to the State and "is one and the same for all" (*Politics*, 1337a).

In the ancient world, Greece included, interpersonal relationships were therefore always mediated by an Absolute, by a Third that avoided direct contact between people, symbolized by the community and its representatives. The community is seen as a single organism, to which supreme good all the parts are pre-ordained ("Neither must we suppose that any one of the citizens belongs to himself, for they all belong to the State", *Politics*, 1337a).

I need not enter into deep relationship with you to be happy; my happiness sources from my relationship with the Absolute, with God. The fundamental pre-modern relational structure is thus triadic and unequal. The entire Middle Ages was thus a process of the slow emergence of individuality as a category, to the detriment of the *communitas*. This was a process that unfolded fairly peacefully through the Tuscan civil humanism of the first half of the fifteenth century, which then exploded in a rapid and irreversible proliferation with the Renaissance, the Reformation, the seventeenth century, and the Enlightenment.[2] It is in this cultural process that the rise of modern political economics must be situated.

One of the basic characteristics of modernity was the discovery of the other as a 'Thou', a subjectivity that presents itself to me as different than me, but, at the same time, as a peer. The angel, the mysterious being who fought with Jacob, became the other. Once the Absolute had been eliminated from one's horizon, once the Sun had set, in this 'twilight of the gods' modern humanity lowered its gaze, looked about, and became aware of the existence of the other, of an other-that-is-not-me. In the world of the One – as also in the Medieval Christian world – there was no room for two Absolutes: in the pre-modern world humanity recognized the transcendent Absolute and placed itself on a level of inferiority and submission to Him and his mediators.

[2] In Bruni (2006) there is a reconstructed this historical evolution that led to the rise of modern individualist economics; see this work for further study.

The Absolute no longer exists in the modern world, and humanity finds itself before another like itself, but other than itself, in which every 'I' represents to the other 'I' a 'not', a non-being (if the other-who-is-not-me is, how can I exist?). Here then we have arrived at one crucial moment of this Introduction to this special issue: the discovery of the other by modernity was the discovery of the negative, of the 'not' that true otherness carries within itself. Modern humanity has seen primarily the wound, rather than the blessing, of the other. The reality of the self and of the other-that-is-not-I has not been associated with the positive and with happiness, but with the negative, with non-being, with 'not'. The enthusiasm for the discovery of my existence as a subject (and it was in fact enthusiasm, and legitimate enthusiasm, given the absolute importance of this discovery) was accompanied in modernity by the fear of the existence of the other. At the same instant in which a modern person says 'I' he or she pronounces 'you' fearfully, as if 'you' were negating 'I', and when constrained to say 'you' he or she does everything possible not to recognize this 'you' as an equal, nor is this 'you' considered an indispensable source of his or her happiness. The discovery of the other did not become a means of mutual recognition, but opened a season – still fully developing – of searching for ways to avoid eye contact with the other.

Thomas Hobbes and Adam Smith represent two crucial moments in this epochal process in the social sciences. Hobbes with the Leviathan and Smith with the 'Invisible Hand' of the market sought a replacement for the Absolute as the mediator of the I-Thou relationship. Faced with the 'not' inherent in the discovery of the other, modern political and economic thought has not wanted to confront and traverse that negation, that wound; rather, as a matter of fact it returned to the interpersonal relational structure of pre-modernity, that of I/mediator/Thou, in which the mediator, instead of God, becomes the Leviathan or the Market – which, we should note, play the same role of impeding the passage through the risk that is the other, who comes alongside me as an equal.[3] There is thus a new metaphysics that takes the place of the pre-modern one (as the chosen metaphors themselves suggest: Leviathan is one monster in the book of Job in the Bible).

In Hobbes's politics and Smith's economics there is no direct intersubjectivity, but rather a mediated and anonymous relationality, for fear of the negative and the suffering that a personal 'you' carries in him- or herself. The contract – private for Smith, social for Hobbes – thus became the main instrument of this interaction, where the contract is above all that which is not a gift. But, without genuine and not mediated relationships happiness is full.

The modern social sciences were thus born from the invention of a new 'thirdness' in new mediators, which however does not question the necessity of avoiding a dramatic interpersonal encounter. This new 'third' is no longer the Third (God or *communitas*), nor a third that opens and universalizes the I-Thou relationship, that is, a third who is a 'he' or 'she' (in the fine sense of Emmanuel Lévinas), but a third

[3]There would be much to say regarding the Protestant culture in which both Hobbes and Smith worked; the rejection of mediators in fact created other mediators that, in the long run, are emerging as tyrants no less fierce than those of pre-modern times.

that is immune from our relationship and which reciprocally 'immunizes' us, and that guarantees (or promises) a free zone in which to meet each other without being wounded. In place of a 'Thou', modernity preferred a 'he', a neutral third that prevents our touching and hurting each other, a 'someone' who, with Vladimir Jankélévitch (1970: 781), we could call 'another', or, playing off the semantic richness of the French expression, personne (which can be understood as either 'person', 'someone' or 'no one').

The liberal neo-contractarian theory is representative in this regard, especially in the version by John Rawls. Among its pre-theoretic terms the social contract requires that a 'mutual disinterest' exist for one another (Rawls 1971: 128–9), since feelings, a sense of belonging, friendship and strong bonds are all dangerous, tending ever toward partiality and exclusivity. To be 'just', a broad pluralistic and liberal society needs individuals without ties and passions. The differences between I and Thou are thus addressed by simply removing them; each protects him- or herself from these differences by increasingly sophisticated social and private contracts that do not require a dialogue, much less an interpersonal encounter, but precisely a mutual indifference.

In this sense contractual reciprocity in markets becomes a new form of reciprocity, a radical alternative to that based on a free and reciprocal gift; the gift brings us together since it requires that we find a common ground, which, by definition, belongs to neither of us, whereas the contract makes us immune from each other since what is mine is not yours, and vice-versa.[4] A common ground, especially when a place of relationships among equals, is also a place of conflict and death, a conflict and grief that modernity did not want to accept, renouncing as well – and this is the point – the life-giving fruit of that common ground. Modernity wanted to break the inevitability of this union, though without being able, and by paying a price that is proving too high.

The emergence of modern economics is a crucial moment in the grand 'immunizing' project of modernity, which, from this point of view, aligns itself in close continuity with Machiavelli and Hobbes.

We cannot understand the humanism of modernity without taking economics seriously.

The issue of vulnerability is therefore central: in the economic humanism, vulnerability is considered to be just a cost, something negative to eliminate from our society. The wound of the other is a *benediction-less* wound: "Studying the broad currents of European philosophical thought regarding the definition of what it means to be human, one reaches an unexpected conclusion: the social aspect, the element of life in community, is not generally considered necessary for humankind. However, this thesis is never presented as such; it is rather a presupposition that is never formulated" (Todorov 1998: 15).

Mediation became then a culture, the main project of modernity: non-mediated relationships are bad, because the other is a wound.

---

[4] Roberto Esposito in fact points out that the most radical contradiction is not the one between community and society (as in classic social thought) but between *communitas* and *immunitas*.

There are, then, many key issues of our civilizations where this escape from vulnerability is their main (and often hidden) explanations.

In the second part of the paper I will discuss, briefly, some of these key issues: (i) the neo-managerial ideology, (ii) merit and meritocracy, and (iii) the 'religion' of incentives.

9.3 Manage Vulnerability

Huge empirical literature shows that people cannot flourish at the workplace without receiving and givingrisky and vulnerable confidence (Bruni and Tufano 2016). But the culture of the big global companies today looks for the impossible: it wants creativity from their employees without accepting the vulnerability of relationships. Think of the growing phenomenon of the so-called "managerial subsidiarity", according to which the manager has to intervene in the decisions of a group, taking up the coordination only for those activities that would be worse without his "subsidiary" intervention. Large companies are, in fact, realizing that in order to get the best from their employees they must grant the proper conditions for them to feel free and as protagonists of their own work. No creativity is given except out of freedom, but for subsidiarity to function it is essential that workers and work groups experience genuine confidence – but then they can also abuse it. There are few things on earth that give as much of joy as the participation in free collective action in the company of equals.

In order for the ancient idea of subsidiarity not to remain just a principle to be written only in social reports, it is essential that the management should really trust the work group, and it shouldn't want to control the entire process to prevent abuse of trust and vulnerability. If, however, those who are given "delegation" perceive that in fact this "trust" is just instrumental, a technique to make more profits, subsidiarity stops producing its effects. That's why subsidiarity in companies would need the owners' and not capitalists' assets, where the delegation does not proceed from the top down to the workers, but in the opposite direction (as in politics, where the principle of subsidiarity was born).

When, however, subsidiarity descends from above it becomes something else that only works when and if the owners decide they should, and it is therefore not very resilient to failures of subsidiarity. Only intrinsic motivation associated with the appropriate institutions allows for subsidiarity and for the participatory forms of surviving after crises due to serious abuses of trust. In reality, the *naturally* subsidiary institutions would be the democratic and participative businesses (just like cooperatives), where "sovereignty belongs to the people" indeed, i.e. the workers-members that grant it upwards to their managers and directors.

In other words, subsidiarity and confidence can really work when they are risky and vulnerable. If we were to design a coin of human relations, one side would represent the joys of the free encounter between acts of gratuitousness, and the other would show the many images of our wounds that those joys generated.

But – and here is another paradox of our capitalist system – the culture taught in business schools hates vulnerability and considers it the greatest enemy. And for many reasons. Throughout the centuries, western civilization has formed a clear separation between the places of the good and the bad vulnerabilities. It has not accepted the *ambivalence* and thus created a *dichotomy*. Good vulnerability, capable of generating blessing has been instead associated with private life, the family and the woman, who is the first image of the generative wound. In the public sphere, which is based entirely on the male register, vulnerability is always bad. Therefore economic and organizational life was also based on invulnerability. Showing wounds and fragility in the workplace is only and always a negative value, inefficiency, demerit. The past decades of financial capitalism have amplified the invulnerable nature of work culture in the large global enterprises, where every vulnerability must be ejected.

The best way to eliminate vulnerability inside the community has always been immunity. Immunity is the main feature of the large capitalist enterprises today. Every invulnerable culture is also an immune culture: if I don't want to be hurt in my relationship with you, I have to stop you touching me by building a system of relations that avoids any form of contamination. Immunity is the lack of exposure to the other person's touch. *Immunitas*, as we have mentioned, is the negation of *communitas*: the soul of *communitas* is *munus* (gift and duty) in reciprocity, while that of *immunitas* is reciprocal ingratitude, the absence and the opposite of gift (*in-munus*: anti-gift).

All immune companies are radically hierarchical, because they increase the vertical and horizontal distances between people to prevent them from touching each other, and so manage them and direct them according to the company's purposes. The first function of the hierarchy is not to let people mingle with each other (this is the origin of the Latin word *casta*: not contaminated), not to let them touch whoever is different among them, only those that are similar. In all immune-caste societies it is strictly forbidden to touch those that are different because only members of the same caste can and must touch each other. For this reason, caste-driven companies know little about creativity and innovation, because only biodiversity is always generative.

This lack of touch between different people is at the root of the decay of the elites inside caste societies, including our global enterprises. The beggars' movements of the thirteenth to fourteenth centuries (Franciscans, Dominicans) were the forgers of great innovation and economic, social, political and spiritual generativity, disrupting the early mediaeval order of castes and immunity characterizing their society, because they welcomed the rich and the poor, and people coming from any region or township in the same monasteries. Those new communities were capable of bringing forth some huge innovations because they put merchants and the poor, bankers and craftsmen, artists and mystics together. That biodiversity turned into creativity and innovation, an innovation that was born from not being afraid of wounds or the stigmata of fraternity. Fraternity is anti-immune, as Francis of Assisi tells us by embracing and kissing the leper – solidarity/philanthropy is almost always *immune*, fraternity never.

The social and anthropological origin of every immune-caste civilization is the fundamental distinction between *pure* and *impure*: there are activities, people, things that are pure and can be touched, and others that are impure and can only be touched by the lower castes. But in all immune-caste societies there is also a deep interdependence between the castes. Even *Brahmins* need the *pariahs* (and vice versa), because as a consequence of immunity in these societies the division of labor is radical. This is why the presence of mediators is indispensable, as they have the special function of putting in contact those who cannot touch each other.

The big capitalist enterprises are now the sharpest images of an immune-caste society, and managers are the 'mediators' connecting the various 'castes' of the company without anyone touching the others, the impure ones. Touching is only possible between equals. The members of the "lower" ranks can be touched by superiors only with tools and techniques, not directly. Large companies are less and less mixed, even when people work in open space offices (where they remain well separated in terms of power and wages).

Organizations cease to be generative as soon as we stop meeting and embracing each other, especially the poor and the marginalized. People lose creativity when over the years they reduce contact with those who are different. Something similar is happening to the *elites* of the organizations, institutions, and therefore also to companies: the culture of immunity that leads them not to get contaminated predetermines their sterility and decadence. Much of our generativity, energy and strength depend on being in contact with other humanities, cultures, lives and bodies. Hope and excellence are born and reborn from the promiscuous places of living, from the meeting of the entire humanity of entire people. Therefore, a deep crisis of capitalism is on the horizon, generated by the decay of the impoverished elites and by their immunity and being unfertilized by good vulnerability of entirely human relations. The fear of relational wounds is creating a global culture of immunity, of which large companies are the major global carriers. For this reason, a major challenge of the coming years will be the very survival of organizations. The apotheosis of the immune-invulnerable culture will in fact be the elimination of organizations, the disappearance of the places where people co-habit and co-operate (live and work together), in order to create decentralized production in their place where everyone works at home thanks to the ever more sophisticated technologies. Consumers without shops, banking without banks, online schools without teachers and students, and perhaps even hospitals without doctors and nurses, populated by highly efficient robots and cameras. The final elimination of vulnerability will eventually be reached this way, we will finally have found the tree of life, but it will be a tree without fruits, or with flavorless fruits. And it will be the hunger for tasty fruits to make us still meet, embrace and live.

There is still something more to say about the specific role of managers in the workplace and inside organizations.

Managers are more and more crushed into a real relational stranglehold, one they have failed to give a name to. On the one hand they are subjected to an infinite demand for appreciation that comes from their workers. On the other hand, these managers do not find recognition for their own work. In our daily work there is much more than required by contract. No company is satisfied by mere contract enforcement, and no worker's salary is enough for them to do their best. The company needs exactly what it cannot buy from its workers: their enthusiasm, passions, joy and love of life, their creativity. Their soul and heart. But these human dimensions are derived only and completely from freedom, and therefore the company is only able to have them if they are donated by the workers, because no incentive is a good replacement of the free gift at work – what's more, it usually destroys it. In other words: the company really needs something that the employment contract, with all its typical instruments – incentives and controls – cannot buy, because it can only be given freely as a gift. And there is no gift sustainable without reciprocity. This is the root of the immense, steady and growing demand for appreciation, recognition and attention by workers that remains in most part unfulfilled. This reality that is obvious to all remains mostly silent for lack of words and categories to express it.

The gap between supply and demand of esteem and recognition in business, however, is created and powered by the same culture of large companies and organizations, the ones that ask so much from the workers to make them gradually abandon other areas of non-working life. And in the weaving of these lives into a single dimension, the manager becomes the *first victim* of the same relational illness he himself is contributing to, sometimes unknowingly.

What to do? Studies on wellbeing at the workplace (Bruni and Porta 2016) are beginning to tell us that the first and essential form of reciprocity invoked by the workers is to be "seen" by their leaders, so they could be more present in the places where the work is done. Then, seeing the work and the worker who works, you would also see all the gifts contained in that work. This type of look is the first reciprocity required by workers, a look of attention that would make the essential dimensions of the work visible. They remain invisible because no one looks at them, or because they are not looked at by the right people to see them and recognize them, or because they are looked at with suspicion and an intention to control them. Of course, even the gazes of our colleagues and our own are important, but they are not enough. In communities, including community work, gazes are not all equal, functions and responsibilities count, and one's work must be seen especially by those who have responsibility over one's work. But as it is now revealed by French scholars like Norbert Alter (2009) or Anouk Grevin (Bruni and Grèvin 2016), in modern large organizations the theory and practice of management makes more and more managers unable to see the work because they are "*forced*" to spend their time in the midst of paperwork and computers, to produce charts, indicators, controls; or to do "institutional" evaluation interviews, in which they have half an hour to consider work that is not seen in the daily routine of the twelve months of the year. You can see the traces of work, the operations, but these sophisticated tools do not allow to you see the whole human-spiritual experience of the worker.

And so you end up not assessing the most important aspects of work; these would need the sense of sight above all. The good life that used to be experienced in the efforts and in contradictions and is still there in many small businesses, also depends on the fact that the entrepreneur is working together with their employees, in their company – and that creates solidarity and a virtuous circle of recognition. The best way to recognize the gift that is in every work is to see and acknowledge work in its everyday ordinariness.

But there's even more. Managers too are workers, and they too have a vital need for reciprocity, recognition, and being "seen". In large anonymous companies, however, where the owners are away, fragmented, sometimes non-existent, there is no one "*above*" the manager to see his work, to recognize it, to thank them. They are flooded with requests for attention and reciprocity, but they don't have anyone in turn who should be able to recognize their work and thank for it, which then remains un-recognized, and the organization becomes a major producer of ingratitude, thereby becoming increasingly unsustainable (even when they try to compensate for it by high salaries). So we should learn again to look at work and see it, all the work and the work of all.

To conclude, in Europe we learnt how to work and manage complex operations in homes and monasteries. The first organizations were the deliveries of babies, the cooperation of women for life, for the management of the end of pregnancy, the work of the hands of women who accompanied the pains of birth. Women, hands, life: these are all ingredients that are just too absent from our organizational culture that is entirely based on the male register and lacks the culture of hands and its typical wisdom. Work culture in complex organizations flourished and matured in the abbeys, by centuries of *ora et labora*: the spirit in the service of the hands, allied hands of the spirit that, together, fed work. The top managers of large organizations were trained by reading and copying the codes of Cicero and Augustine. We will cure the relationships in our businesses only if we put them in the hands of new humanistic managers, people who are experts in humanity, capable of listening, of caring, of interiority, of looking after the many travails of organizations. But business schools are focused on the tools and techniques, although they should be teaching their students poetry, art, philosophy, spirituality, having some classes inside factories, and so training them to look at work, feel its smell and true scent instead of the synthetic one of the conference rooms in hotels.

The market of tomorrow will have a vital need for people who are complete, in and outside companies, who can cultivate and activate the fundamental human dimensions we have called gift, reciprocity and soul.

9.4 On Meritocracy

The logic of merit has always been very powerful. We human beings have a deep need to believe that there is a logical and just relationship between our actions, talents, commitment and our results. We like to think that our salary is the result of our quality and our commitment, that the grades we get at school depend on how much we study, that we have earned our awards (the word *meritum* comes from *mereri* meaning: earn, gain). It's natural, it's a real and existing need. The real problem is not so much or only in the idea of merit in itself, but the *answers* we give to the *questions* regarding the recognition of our merits and above all those of the others. The biblical author Qoheleth (9,11) knows this very well: “Again I saw that under the sun the race is not to the swift, nor the battle to the strong, nor bread to the wise, nor riches to the intelligent, nor favour to those with knowledge, but time and chance happen to them all”.

People have always tried to react to this scenario that appears to us as a great display of injustice. In ancient civilizations, the main solution to injustice in the world was to imagine a God who is different from us and follows a fair policy of rewards and punishments. They took the historical fact of inequality and injustice, and gave reality a religious chrism. The apparent injustice was thus turned into an invisible and deeper kind of justice, and the world was given order by finding a religious sense in richness and in their own misfortune or that of others. So those who were rich and powerful were granted the status of ‘blessed’ without calling them for conversion; and those who were poor and unfortunate were sentenced twice: by the misfortunes of life and by God.

The moral need to recognize merit produced an immense sense of guilt in the poorest and the most unfortunate for their own misfortunes. Other forms of religious humanism have instead reacted by imagining that the injustice under the sun would be eliminated in other lives beyond the sun, where the poor but righteous would be rewarded and the rich but wicked punished. The earth is unjust, heaven isn’t. The economic-retributive logic remained, but the horizon of its application stepped out of the historical time span to eternity or at least to another life. Theories about merit necessitate a humanism of morally different individuals, where everyone has their own “card” of actions/rewards. Holistic societies are not meritocratic.

Because of its humanistic and personalistic spirit, meritocratic ideology (which makes merit the criterion to evaluate, classify and order people and organizations) is very charming, seductive and it captures many people. We find it at the centre of the culture of large corporations and multinational banks. Its symbolic technology is of a dual nature. On the one hand large enterprises build a sophisticated system of incentives designed with the aim to identify and reward merit, conceived according to the business objectives. On the other hand, the worker who finds himself in this rewarding mechanism reads his own salary and benefits as a signal of his *meritability*. It is a perfect contract, continuously fed by both sides because it seems mutually beneficial: the company satisfies its need for rationality and ordering reality to its own ends, and the employee meets their need to feel worthy and valued.

It is an ideology that has grown like climbing grass on the retributive tree in the garden of biblical faith, which is experiencing an incredible and growing success in the era of individualistic capitalism. As Max Weber showed us more than a century ago, in Judeo-Christian humanism there is a stream that has interpreted economic success as a sign of election and salvation. The current economic culture has radicalized and universalized that psychological-religious mechanism. It secularized and extended it from the entrepreneur to the entire economic system, production, finance and consumption. The quantity and quality of salaries and incentives (and consumption) become the new indicators of election and predestination for the ‘paradise' of the deserving (meritable). The symbolic-religious dimension of money and success has thus been amplified, radicalized and generalized.

But the worm of this and all pay religious systems is discovered clearly when we leave heaven and descend to the *circles* of purgatory and hell. Merit has a necessary need of demerit. It is a positional and relative reality: the world of the deserving works if merit can be defined, ordered, organized in a hierarchical order, measured and put in a relationship with demerit. Beyond a deserving person there must be someone who is more deserving, and one who is less deserving, below them. It is a perfect caste system, where the *Brahmins* need the *Pariahs*, but cannot touch them to avoid being contaminated by their demerit. The simplest management of demerit is to present it as a necessary step towards merit, as a step of the way, a milestone of the journey. This management works very well with young people, showing them the 'Beloved Mount', telling them that they will be able to climb it only if they can 'grow', although those who propose this scenario know very well that in the 'house of merit' there aren't enough places. And so, when they go through their first failures and the much hoped credit does not flourish according to the pre-set goals, the miracle takes place: the employee has been trained to interpret their own failure as demerit, and so accept their fate in a docile way. The cult is perfect: the 'believer' internalizes religion and implements it independently. And the mass production of guilt becomes the big refuse of our economy, fuelled by aggression, pride and arrogance accompanying the *laudatores* of meritocracy.

Merit is an ambiguous word, rarely a friend of people and the poor – which is even more valid for meritocracy. The evangelic logic of the 'worker of the last hour', one of the most beautiful pages ever written, is a critique of the idea of merit that is no less radical than that of books of Qoheleth or Job. Think about the Book of Job. In the "economic" religions of the past (and also in those of today, in our big enterprises and banks), misfortune and impurities are considered as the effects of a life as a sinner. It is this equivalence that the book of Job does not want to accept – either for himself or for us. From being a rich and powerful man, Job suddenly finds himself unfortunate, impure, and therefore *untouchable*, excluded from all the social castes. This is still the sad fate of entrepreneurs, managers, workers, politicians, priests that, having fallen into disrepair, find themselves not only impoverished, but sitting on a pile of rubble which includes family, friends and health, too. And they immediately end up among the unclean, cast out from the village, away and marginalized by the clubs, associations, groups, confined in social and relational landfills, shunned by all and never touched for fear of being infected by their ruin.

At the heart of the story of Job there is also a religious and anthropological revolution that seeks to overcome the *remunerative* vision of faith (our wealth and our happiness is the prize for a faithful life, ours or that of our fathers), which has also been central in the ethics of capitalism.

This argument against retribution, which is also present in a lot of the prophetic tradition and wisdom, was very valuable among the Jewish people that has always been tempted to read their experience with YHWH-Elohim through commercial categories, starting with the very structure of the Covenant. The faith of Israel is born within the cultures of Mesopotamia, where it was normal to see religion as an *exchange/commercial relationship with a sovereign-God.* Religious practices, in their archaic origin, normally arise as idolatrous practices of a commercial type. Those that manage to evolve and break free from their primordial forms, gradually abandon the logic of *do-ut-des* with respect to the deity. Much of the effort that the people of Israel has made was generated by the process of liberation from a merchant God who gave grace and indulgences in exchange for vows, sacrifices and offerings. Without the prophets, without Job and Ecclesiastes, this process would have imploded, and the religion of Israel would remain one of the many Canaanite cults. But the temptation of an "economic" religion is inherent in every religion, and without the necessary care and attention one may end up back in the ancient idolatrous cults, turning Elohim to a King hungry for offerings and submission statements to grant protection.

So religion becomes a "double game" between the faithful and the gods again, where the sacrifices and vows become the "*currency*" (not only in a metaphorical sense) of this business. An economic religion that has always had (and has) many followers just because it is much too easy, is simply stupid, says Qoheleth – "*the sacrifice [is] of the fools*". The believer is happy to purchase "*merits*" and compensate faults by simple sacrifices, and the administrators of religion draw much economic advantage and control over consciences by fuelling this vile trade. It is not a coincidence that the episode of Jesus with the merchants in the temple (John 2,14-16) is placed at the very beginning of his public life, we can understand it clearly if our point of departure is from these pages of Ecclesiastes. Christianity has had to fight a lot in its early phase to announce a religion of full gratuitousness, and whenever it stops this fight it always falls back to being an ancient idolatrous cult. We need a lot of work and a lot of care not to exit from the horizon of gratuitousness, falling back in the registers of merit and fault.

The Bible's criticism of merit is vital if we want to understand the inherent dangers in a whole social life built on the logic of merit as it is conceived and promoted by companies. We could have imagined another capitalism that's less anchored to retributive religion, and almost certainly would have a less sick planet and more healthy social relationships; but today we must at least prevent its logic from becoming *the* culture of the full scope of social life. Instead, incentives and meritocracy are increasingly occupying many non-economic areas.

The reason for this extraordinary success is easy to understand. We all know that there are many kinds of merit and demerit. There are excellent workers who are bad parents, and vice versa, and we usually live together with merits and demerits of which we are aware, that are revealed only in some decisive steps, sometimes in the last days of our lives when we discover that we have lived a life with few apparent merits but deserved a good embrace of the angel of death. The danger that lurks inside meritocratic ideology is thus very subtle, and usually invisible. Companies have the ability to present themselves as places that reward merit because they reduce the plurality of merit to only those functional to their objectives: an artist who works in an assembly line is not worthy because of his hand that can paint but because it knows how to screw bolts.

The merit of the economy is then easy to reward because it is a simple merit / demerit that's too easy to see and so to measure and reward. Other merits in non-economic areas are much harder to see, and even harder to be measured. This is where the great risk is revealed: given its easy measurability, merit in companies becomes only merit that's 'seen', measured and rewarded in society at large. With two effects: quantitative and measurable merits are over-stimulated, while qualitative and non-productive ones go wasted. It increases the destruction of non-economic virtues that, however, are essential to live well (like meekness, compassion, mercy, humility).

The great task of Christian humanism, at the hearth of Europe civilization, was liberation from the retributive culture that dominated the ancient world, and from assigning guilt to all the misfortunate. We must not resign ourselves to selling it off for the "lentil stew" of merit. We are worth a lot more.

9.5 Incentives

Organizations cannot have the most important virtues they need. The wise ones accept the 'gap' between the desired virtues and those that can be had by their workers, and so they learn to live together with the inevitable need of the human qualities essential for their operation and growth, without trying to replace them with some simpler things.

The first wisdom of each institution is to recognize that they do not control the souls of their members – all virtue is above all a spiritual matter. When this awareness is missing or denied, companies and organizations do not stop at the threshold of the mystery of the worker-person and do their best to fill the 'gap', ending up losing the best part of their workers. The stunning collapse of this form of institutional wisdom is one of the most serious instances of poverty today, because it is presented as a form of wealth, and so it is not fought but powered.

The difference between the virtues required of their members and those available has always accompanied social life, especially in the western world. All good institutions have always been *beggars of virtues*. Monasteries, governments, even the armies had an essential need of the highest virtues of the people, but they knew that these could not be obtained by command or by force: they could only welcome them as free gifts of the soul of men and women. What's new today is the total eclipse of this ancient, wise awareness, especially in the world of big firms that are more and more convinced that they had finally invented the tools and techniques to get all the virtues they need from their workers – all their mind, all their strengths, all their heart – without needing either moral force, or, even less, gifts to be offered. And so they end up with pseudo-virtues.

This mass destruction of virtues has a lot to do with the ideology of incentives. The culture that is practiced in big companies, particularly on the higher levels of direction, is becoming a perpetual worship of the god of incentives, an actual faith whose main tenet is the belief that you can get excellence by people if they are remunerated properly. Meritocracy is born from an alliance with the ideology of incentives, because merit is recognized by building a more and more sophisticated and custom-designed system of incentives to get the most out of every person in order to obtain, if possible, everything. And so they believe that if they 'enchant' people with incentives they can freely do their best (remember that the words *incentive*, *enchantment* and *enchanter* all have the same root). In fact, incentives are not only an unsuitable tool for creating and strengthening the virtues, but they usually destroy them by drastically reducing the freedom of the people. Incentives, especially their latest generation built around the 'management by objectives', look like a contract (and indeed they are), and therefore as one of the highest expressions of the 'freedom of modern people'. But it is enough to look at it a bit more carefully to immediately notice that the freedom of the culture of incentives has nothing to do with the freedom necessary for the development and strengthening of the virtues of real people. That of the incentives is an ancillary freedom which is small and serving the objectives set and imposed by the company's management. It is a lesser kind of freedom, which is very similar to that of a blackbird in an aviary, that of lions in the zoo, although, unlike animals, we think that we are entering freely in our cages and natural reserves. Actually we enter fascinated by the enchanter flute (*incentivus*, i.e. flute), and do not get out anymore.

Let's just think of, for example, loyalty. Only a few words like loyalty are evoked by the corporate culture. It is a key term in job interviews, we find it in the certificates of good conduct, it is an essential part of the repertoire of the ideal employee that every company wants to have. Loyalty is a virtue that makes us able to be faithful to a person, an institution or to a value in situations where our behavior is costly and cannot be observed. Loyalty cannot be established by contract. It's all a matter of the soul. But we all know that in every contract there is an implicit assumption of loyalty, one that we cannot buy, however. Contracts do not establish themselves because they need pacts, and so loyalty and many other pre-contractual virtues. If contracts replace virtues, they end up undermining the ground beneath their own feet.

The basic grammar of loyalty is found in the beautiful episode of Joseph and the wife of the Egyptian Potiphar. While Joseph was in the house of Potiphar, on a day when "none of the men of the house was there in the house", the woman "cast her eyes" on him and said: "Lie with me" (Genesis 39). Joseph answered: "...my master ... has not kept back anything from me except you… How then can I do this great wickedness and sin against [him]?" He made a loyal choice that cost him jail, when the woman he refused accused him of having molested her (Bruni 2016).

For loyalty to emerge, three elements are necessary: a relationship of riskfull trust, a concrete cost that the person has to bear doing or not doing something that would avoid that cost, and – the third crucial element – that the loyal action itself should not be observable. Therefore, the value of loyalty is measured on the basis of what I could have done but I did not do because I wanted to be loyal. Loyalty is the spirit of pacts and promises that live off of visible choices and acts supported by invisible acts and choices. There are words not spoken, things not done, secrets kept inside for the love of someone for a lifetime – they generate, regenerate and do not let our pacts die, including those that are the foundation for the life of enterprises and institutions. Words not said and things not done for which no one will ever say ‘thank you’, but which give moral weight and dignity to our relationships and our entire existence.

It is clear then that the virtue of loyalty cannot be enforced, nor is it possible to create it through incentives. Indeed, the logic of incentives discourages loyalty precisely because it encourages and reinforces visible, controllable and contractual types of behavior.

This opens up a new scenario. Our ability to be loyal is not a constant stock, but varies over time based on the quality of our inner life and on the relational signals that come from the communities in which we live. My choice to be honest here and now will depend on my intrinsic moral rewards but also on the perception that the given company or community is ‘worth’ the costs of loyalty, which can sometimes be very high. Companies cannot create loyalty – because it’s all entirely and only the gift of the person – but they can try to put already loyal people in a position to exercise this virtue there, too.

But it is precisely here that the mechanism of the self-destruction of loyalty and other virtues produced by the logic of incentives is revealed. Big companies and banks have a growing need to control the actions of their members, to be able to predict them and to direct them towards their goals. What they fear more than anything else are the action areas outside the management’s control, the promiscuous border areas; they do not like the houses where “none of the men of the house” is there to control, to manage and to evaluate things. And the reason for this fear and this distrust is the pessimistic anthropology that, beyond words, is the basis of the system of big capitalist institutions. Directors, and even more so the proprietors (and sometimes even unions), think – more or less consciously – that the employee is generally an opportunist and should therefore be checked. In the factories of yesterday this control was very crude and obvious; with the introduction of incentives the same practice got disguised as freedom, but in essence the culture of total control was intensified, because now it gets through even to the soul. This is why the big capitalist organizations reduce the unobservable spaces of action and freedom systematically. And so they also reduce the preconditions for loyalty and many other virtues to be practiced – they all need real freedom and riskfull confidence to stay alive. This creates a radical and progressive creation of contractual ‘loyalty’, which – being observable and controllable – lacks the most valuable part of the virtue of true loyalty. We find ourselves in institutions populated by virtue-bonsais, all controlled and inscribed under the roofs of the businesses themselves. But bonsais do not bear fruit, or if yes, they are tiny and inedible.

All this produces a phenomenon of great importance. These small and manageable ‘virtues’ work well enough for the ordinary situations of business life, but make organizations highly vulnerable in times of great crises, when there would be a great need for the loyalty and true soul of the workers that, however, have been replaced by incentives in the meantime. By eliminating the uncontrollable space of freedom and trust, the ideology of incentives reduces the *small* instances of vulnerability but increases the *big* instances of vulnerability of large companies tremendously, as they are devoid of the ethical antibodies essential for survival in serious illnesses.

Humans are not monkeys. Even though we share 98% of DNA with them, we are much more complicated, complex, symbolic, rich and mysterious than the institutions and businesses think they are. Sometimes we are worse, many times better, but always different. We find feelings and emotions in ourselves that do not allow us to be as efficient as we should. We disperse infinite resources in applications for recognition and respect that – we know – will never be satisfied by the answers we get. We go through physical and spiritual trials, emotional and relational shocks. But we are also able to do things that are much more worthy and higher than those required by the contracts and rules.

9.6 Conclusion

All human communities, whether business, political, communal, or family, are places of life and death, of "blessing" and "wound", in the language of the Bible (Genesis 32).

I am convinced that a good life together plays out in knowing how to identify the critical point of mediation (by the State and the market, in particular). No city could function without rules, contracts, and justice, which are the highest mediation and the indispensable 'thirdness' that all common civil and democratic life vitally requires.

The vast sociological tradition (from Max Weber to Ferdinand Tönnies, to Georg Simmel), to say nothing of the modern philosophical tradition (Hegel would suffice), has grasped, and in a certain manner discovered, with extreme clarity the duplicity and the ambivalence of life together, or the "unsocial sociability" of humanity (Kant). It has discovered the "not," the negative, that is hidden in the other who is like me but who is not me, a tragic negative that lurks at the heart of life together in *communitas*. But, rather than traversing that obscurity, that negative, it has sought escape routes. A major escape route was the invention of the market. One cannot but be amazed that, while modern philosophy came to understand over the course of a few decades – from Hegel to Nietzsche – that flight from the "not" of the other led to nothingness and nihilism, modern economics has been living in its infancy for two and a half centuries. No other age like our age of globalization has been so convinced that it can resolve the contradiction of sociality by trusting in the alchemy of contracts and markets. The great crisis of contemporary economics is concealed in this excessively prolonged infancy, eloquently symbolized by the paradox of unhappiness.

If the extension of contracts and incentive overcomes a critical point, life becomes dismal and, maybe, impossible. If to avoid relational conflicts and pain we design housing regulations, workplaces, and cities that prevent our crossing paths in the halls, stairways, common spaces and the town square, then the cure becomes far worse than the disease. The awareness of such a possible scenario is little in our society, and this lack represents a serious danger for twenty-first century capitalism.

References

Alter, N. 2009. *Donner et prendre*. Paris: La decouverte.

Bruni, L. 2006. Civil Happiness. Economic and human flourishing in historical perspective. Routeledge. London

Bruni, L. 2012a. *Wound and Blessing. Economics, Happiness, Interpersonal Relationships*. New York: Newcity.

———. 2012b. *The Genesis and Ethos of the Market*. London: Macmillan-Palgrave.

———. 2016. *At the Beginning. An Economist Reads the Book of Genesis*. London: MacMillan-Palgrave.

Bruni, L., and A. Grèvin. 2016. *L'Economie silencieuse*. Paris: Nouvelle Cité.

Bruni, L., and P. Porta. 2016. *Handbook of Research Methods and Applications in Happiness and Quality of Life*. Cheltenham: Edward Elgar.

Bruni, L., and R. Sugden. 2013. Reclaiming Virtue Ethics for Economics. *Journal of Economic Perspectives* 27: 141–164.

Bruni, L., and F. Tufano. 2016. *The Transforming Capacity of Trust*. CeDEx Discussion Paper Series.

Doria, P. M. 1710 *Della Vita Civile, s.l.,* Napoli.

Esposito, R. 2009. *Communitas: The Origin and Destiny of Community*. Stanford: Stanford University Press.

Girard, R. 1977. *The Violence and the Sacred*. Baltimore: John Hopkins University Press.

Jankélévitch, V. 1970. *Traité des vertus*, 3 Vols. Vol. II, Les vertus et l'amour. Paris, Bordas.

Nussbaum, M.C. 1986. *The Fragility of Goodness: Luck and Ethics in Greek Tragedy and Philosophy*. 2nd ed. Cambridge: Cambridge University Press.

Rawls, J. 1971. *A Theory of Justice*. Cambridge: Harvard University Press.

Ries, J. 1982. *Il sacro nella storia religiosa dell'umanità*. Milan: Jaca Book.

Schiavone, A. 2012. *The Invention of the Law in the West*. Cambridge: Harvard University Press.

Todorov, T. 1998. *La vita in comune*. Pratiche: Milano.

Part III
Companies and Their Management

Chapter 10
Ethics, Economics and the Corporation

Peter Rona

Abstract The paper analyzes the capacity of corporation for moral agency and concludes that corporations do not have such capacity. Instead, morally unacceptable corporate propensities are better addressed by crafting legal rules that accord with the quiddity of the corporation. Unlike theories that find the source of this incapacity in the purported duty of corporations to maximize shareholder value, and unlike stakeholder theories, the paper proposes, that the incapacity has three sources. First, the interposition of the corporation between the individual or group actor destroys the unity of the actor and the act. Second, corporations, with their power to define roles through binding rules replace the moral self of the actor with the prescribed role. Third, the prevailing economic theory adopts the methodology of the natural sciences and condenses corporate decision making into the quantitative methodology of corporate finance with the result that the numerically expressible trumps qualitative judgment unless the latter is bolstered by binding legal rules.

> It should be clear that corporations are not just macrocosmic versions of humans. They are quite otherwise.
>
> Peter A. French[1]

There is a serious tension between the ontology of the corporation and the various theories attributing moral agency to it. This paper explores this tension and concludes that it cannot be resolved. Instead, the morally unacceptable corporate propensities are better addressed by crafting rules that are homologous with the ontology of the corporation. Unlike theories that find the source of this conflict in the purported duty of corporations to maximize shareholder value,[2] and unlike alternative theories about

[1] French, Peter A. (1995) *Corporate Ethics,* Harcourt, Brace & Co. p. 36.

[2] For an analysis of the doubtful legal foundations of the duty to maximise shareholder value see Stout, L. (2012) *The Shareholder Value Myth,* Berrett-Koehler Publishers, Inc., San Francisco; a contrary view is set out in Mansell, S. F. (2013) *Capitalism, Corporations and the Social Contract,* Cambridge University Press; Vermaelen, T. (2009) "Maximizing Shareholder Value: An Ethical Responsibility?" in Smith, C. and Lenssen, G. (ed.) *Mainstreaming Corporate Responsibility,*

P. Rona (✉)
Blackfriars Hall, University of Oxford, Oxford, UK
e-mail: pzrona@gmail.com

P. Rona, L. Zsolnai (eds.), *Economics as a Moral Science*,
Virtues and Economics 1, DOI 10.1007/978-3-319-53291-2_10

stakeholder value,[3] the paper proposes that the tension stems from three sources: first, the interposition of the corporation between the individual or group actor and the act destroys the moral unity of the action, a unity that cannot be recovered. Second, the corporation, endowed with rule-making powers, legislates the scope and content of authorized and mandated individual and group action, replacing the free will of the actor with the mandate so legislated. Put differently, it replaces the self of the actor with the role prescribed for the actor by the corporation. Third, the prevailing economic paradigm, – analogizing, as it does, the quiddity of its subject to the reality studied by the natural sciences – adopts the methodology of the natural sciences and condenses the discipline guiding corporate decision making, namely, corporate finance, around quantitatively measurable objectives. Because the corporate veil tears the unity of the actor and the act asunder, corporations anchor their key decision-making in the seemingly objective techniques mandated by modern economics and finance.[4] The numerically expressible supersedes qualitative judgment. Corporate officials may, of course, consider value-based issues, but if these cannot be quantified, it is inherently difficult to give them overriding weight unless the issue concerns potential legal culpability.[5] The question addressed in this paper is the extent, if any, to which corporations have room to formulate and pursue ethically meaningful purposes within these constraints – other than those imposed on them externally – and concludes that the scope to do so is insufficient for reducing the gap between corporate conduct and social expectations. Instead of attempting to anchor corporate responsibility to the uncertain foundation of corporate moral agency, the paper proposes that a better approach is the formulation of standards of corporate accountability, expressed as rules, that corporations must meet.

10.1 Introduction

The literature on business ethics addresses ethical issues that arise in the management of the "firm", or even more broadly, of "organizations". There are, of course, many types of firms, such as co-operatives, sole proprietorships, partnerships,

Wiley, which, in turn, is thoroughly refuted in Mayer, C. (2013) *Firm Commitment,* Oxford University Press.

[3] Freeman, R. Harrison, J. Wicks, A. Parmar, B. And de Colle, S. (2010) *Stakeholder Theory: The State of the Art.* Cambridge University Press; Friedman, A. and Miles S. (2006) *Stakeholders: Theory and Practice.* Oxford University Press

[4] The extent to which quantitatively based techniques can be said to to be value free is, of course, doubtful. The contrast made here is between quantitatively expressed information that may be disputed, but cannot be amended by the recipient, and value based, descriptive information, that, by its nature, engages the recipient. For issues related to the separation of 'fact' and 'value' see Putnam, H. (2002) *The Collapse of the Fact/Value Dichotomy and Other Essays,* Harvard University Press; Putnam, H. and Walsh, V. (2012) *The End Of Value-free Economics.* Palgrave.

[5] Michael Bloomberg, founder and CEO formulated the axiom of the Bloomberg Corporation as follows: "You can only manage what you can measure."

family businesses, and corporate bodies such as churches, universities, guilds and municipalities, but the business corporation is quite unlike any of them. Berle and Means in the first paragraph of the first chapter of their seminal book[6] set out the difference:

> Corporations have ceased to be merely legal devices through which the private business transactions of individuals may be carried on. Though still much used for this purpose, the corporate form has acquired a larger significance. The corporation has, in fact, become both a method of property tenure and a means of organizing economic life.

This paper is concerned only with corporations because they are the predominant protagonist of modern economic life, and, as it will be shown, they are unlike other types of firms.[7]

Although the principal features of the modern business corporation – perpetual succession, separate legal personality, centralized management, shared ownership of capital, transferable shares and limited liability – were each known for centuries before its birth in 1856,[8] they were not amalgamated into the limited liability joint stock company now generally called the corporation. The potentialities resulting from the *combination* of these legal powers began to be understood only in parallel with the emergence of the tool based analytic economics during the second half of the nineteenth century that replaced the descriptive moral science known as political economy. By the end of the century the union of corporate powers and analytic economics was consummated, and economic life had a new, man made artifice as its protagonist, operating in accordance with the requirements of an equally man made analytic discipline. These corporate powers were dramatically expanded with the rapid growth of stock market liquidity. The hostile take-over market was born, and with it, the principal characteristic of corporate shares was no longer the relationship between the shareholder and the operations of the corporation, but, rather, its characteristics as currency for the purchase and sale of corporate control.[9] Maximizing shareholder *value* – implying as it does attention to current and future value beyond current market price – was reduced to share *price,* pure and simple. The emphasis of management's responsibility of a publicly listed company shifted

[6] Berle, A. A. and Means, G. C. (1932) *The Modern Corporation & Private Property,* Harcourt, Brace & World, Inc.

[7] The unique features of the modern business corporation are recognised and analysed, among others, in Lawson, T. "The Modern Corporation: the Site of a Mechanism (of Global Social Change) that is Out-Of-Control" in Archer, M. (ed.), (2015) *Social Morphogenesis:* Generative Mechanisms Transforming Late Modernity, New York: Springer; Balkan, J. *(2004), The Corporation: The Pathological Pursuit of Profit and Power,* London: Constable and Robinson Ltd.; Corton, D. (1995) *When Corporations Rule the World,* San Francisco, Berrett-Koehler with Cumbrian Press.A contrary theory is set out in Goodpaster, K. E. (2007) *Conscience and Corporate Culture,* Blackwell Publishing.

[8] For a detailed history see Johnson, P. (2010) *Making the Market,* Cambridge University Press; McQueen, R. (2009) *A Social History of Company Law,* Ashgate Publishing Limited; Taylor, J. (2006) *Creating Capitalism,* Royal Historical Society.

[9] For a detailed analysis of the emergence and the effects of the market for corporate control, see Mayer, C. (2013) *Firm Commitment,* Oxford University Press.

from the profitable management of corporate assets to the continuous maximization of current share price.

The sense that there is something untrustworthy about corporations, that incorporation amounts to some sort of an exemption from the ethical responsibilities of human beings thereby permitting those within it to enjoy privileges not granted to those without, has been with us since well before the enactment of the first modern law on the formation of business corporations in 1859. The idea, that a man-made purpose, namely, profit-making could be pursued by a protagonist devoid of the attributes of human beings, was and continues to be seen by many as something of a swindle, a device for licensing moral turpitude, a means for turning the ancient vice of avarice into the modern virtue of maximizing utility. The law courts spotted the problem well before the birth of the modern business corporation, but could not quite see their way to dealing with a legally competent 'person' that is devoid of a conscience. The authors of a treatise on the laws of corporations[10] cite with approval the words of Chief Baron Manwood in *Tipping and Pexhal's Cafe* (2 Bulstr. 233) to the effect that:

> Corporations are invisible, and immortal, and have no Soul; and therefore no *Subpoena* lies against them, because they have no Conscience nor Soul. None can create Souls but God; but the King creates Corporations, therefore they have no Souls… (a corporation is) a mere capacity to sue and be sued, to take and grant; is *eus rationis;* invisible and immortal, and resteth only in intendment and consideration of law.

Subsequently, a boiled down version of these concerns – namely, that "a corporation has neither a body to be kicked, nor a soul to be damned" – was attributed by Lord Chancellor Eldon to his predecessor, Lord Thurlow, and has achieved the status of an oft repeated legal proverb. As late as 1833, the Parliamentary *Report delivered to the Committee in Aid of Corporate Reform, November 8th, 1833* concluded with the axiomatic formulation, that "there can be no such thing as a perpetual private institution, properly so called. Its immortality makes it public." The attribution of the immortality of the Crown to a body politic or to the Church was one thing; its extension to business transactions was seen as at odds with its quiddity. Mortals have virtues and vices; immortals are useful or harmful. Mixing the mortality of human beings with the immortality of the perpetual institution conflates the virtuous with the useful,[11] giving birth to a monster within which conscience is replaced by the calculus of utility. Immortality, in short, extinguishes the foundation of virtue. Whereas virtuous conduct – without which "the soul (is) to be damned" – justifies the life of the mortal, the life of the immortal is a given regardless of the course it takes. How the ultra-human and extraordinarily effective attributes of the corporation made use of by the humans acting in its name could be reconciled with the virtues and vices of individual behavior remained, and it is claimed here, still remains unresolved.

---

[10] *The Law of Corporations: containing the Laws and Customs of All the Corporations and Inferior Courts of Record in* England (1702) London, various authors.

[11] A parallel move, conflating the virtuous with the useful is the hallmark of nineteenth century utilitarian ethics.

10.2 What Are Corporations?

In one of the influential essays of twentieth century jurisprudence, Professor H.L.A. Hart takes issue with the question:

> The first efforts to define words like 'corporation', 'right' or 'duty' reveal that these do not have the straightforward connection with counterparts in the world of fact which most ordinary words have and to which we appeal in our definition of ordinary words.[12]

He quotes with approval Maitland's famous passage about the indebtedness of the State of Nusquamia in which Maitland asks: "can you convert the position that Nusquamia owed you money into a series of propositions imposing duties on certain human beings that are now in existence?"[13] and answers the question in the negative: "Clearly, you do not think that every Nusquamian owes you some aliquot share of the debt."[14] The search for the "personality" of the State, according to this view, is just as futile as the employment of metaphors in seeking out the "essence" of the corporation. It is clearly not a "fictitious person" in the sense that Sherlock Holmes is a fictitious person any more than a "real person". Building on Maitland's insight, Hart writes:

> Even in the simplest case of all when we say 'X is a servant of Y & Company' the facts which justify the use of the words 'X is a servant' are not *just* the same as the facts which support 'Smith is a servant of Brown.' Hence any ordinary words or phrases when conjoined with the names of corporations take on a special legal use, for the words are now correlated with the facts, not solely by the rules of ordinary English, but also by the rules of English law…

X, the servant of Y & Company is not the servant of a fictitious person in the sense that Watson is the fictitious servant of the fictitious person Sherlock Holmes because Y & Company are entirely real, but are not a person like the real person Brown or like the fictitious Sherlock Holmes. The fictitious characters of literature are described with the ordinary meaning of words, and they could exist in the world as we know it. But a corporation does not and could not exist as a 'person'. It cannot fall in love and marry, catch pneumonia, or serve in the Army,[15] and it cannot come

---

[12] Hart, H.L.A. "Definition and Theory in Jurisprudence" in (1954) 70 LQR 37; reprinted in Hart, H.L.A. (1983) *Essays in Jurisprudence and Philosophy* Oxford University Press. Sealy & Worthington in their *Cases and Materials in Company Law* (2013), tenth ed. Oxford University Press) find to the contrary that "A company is very easily defined. It is the kind of legal entity or corporate body which is brought into being by the registration procedures laid down by the Companies Act…"

[13] In fact, such conversion is not impossible. The series of propositions would specify the duties of the relevant officials to perform specified acts in aid of repayment.

[14] Hazeltine, H.D.,Lapsey, G., Winfield, P,H. (ed.) (1936) *Maitland, Selected Essays* Cambridge University Press pp. 236–7.

[15] Although the Supreme Court of the United States in *Citizens United v. Federal Election Commission* ruled that corporations enjoy freedom of speech much like individuals, it has yet to conclude that corporations could run for elected office. In *Collins Steward Ltd. v. Financial Times Ltd.* [2005] EWHC 262 (QB) the court held that a corporation cannot have hurt feelings.

into being or accomplish anything without the intentional action of human beings. Indeed, without the law attributing legally enforceable significance to human action taken in its name, the corporation cannot exist at all.[16] The converse, however, is also true. There is nothing for the law to attribute in the absence of human action. It is an object of thought before it comes into being,[17] – as Chief Baron Manwood put it, it exists only "in intendment and consideration of the law" – and after it is formed much if certainly not all of it remains mind dependent. The puzzle that the quiddity of the corporation poses stems from this elusive combination of its rule based formation and operation, the mind dependent intentionality of its agents and the objective, factually verifiable objects that this intentionality produces.

The puzzle deepens when we consider, that, on the one hand, not any and all human actions are *legally* attributed to the corporation, and, on the other, that an act may be attributed to the corporation even though no one intended or committed it. They acquire meaning as *acts of the corporation* only if a rule of attribution so provides, but a legal rule of attribution can attribute deeds – with the help of the legal device of 'deeming' so – that, in fact, were not committed by anyone. An act or an event attributed to a corporation need not be grounded in or derived from any individual or group action, let alone any corporate action. For example, in *United States v. Bank of New England*[18] the court concluded, that a corporation can be held guilty of a criminal offence even though no individual officer or employee had committed any crime. A corporation is deemed to possess the sum total of all knowledge of all of its employees, and is deemed to employ the totality of this knowledge to the end that constitutes the criminal *actus reus* even if no one can be found either in the possession of this totality of knowledge or in the act of applying it. In a burst of mysticism the court held that "the corporation is considered to have acquired the collective knowledge of its employees and is held responsible for their failure to act accordingly" even as it recognised, that

> Corporations compartmentalize knowledge,[19] subdividing the elements of specific duties and operations into smaller components. The aggregate of those components constitutes the corporation's knowledge of a particular operation. It is irrelevant whether employees administering one component of an operation know the specific activities of employees administering another aspect of the operation…(T)he corporation is considered to have

[16] Dewey, J. (1926) "The Historic Background of Corporate Legal Personality" *Yale Law Journal*, Vol. XXXV No. 6.

[17] Crane, T. (2013) *The Objects of Thought*, Oxford University Press; Everett, A. (2013) *The Nonexistent* Oxford University Press; Priest, G. (2005) *Towards Non-Being*, Oxford University Press.

[18] United States v. Bank of New England , 821 F.2nd 844. Cited in Hasnas, Ibid. p. 25.

[19] It is, course, at least a question whether corporations 'compartmentalise knowledge' or organise specialised or 'compartmentalised' knowledge. The idea that the corporation somehow breaks up existing knowledge into compartmentalised components – an idea that provides the basis for the court's *ratio* to the effect that the compartmentalised knowledge can be reassembled, and, once reassembled, attributed to the corporation – seems to be fanciful. The view espoused here is the exact opposite. Corporations assemble distinct disciplines and domains of knowledge, such knowledge often arising without any compartmentalisation or aggregation on the part of the corporation.

acquired the collective knowledge of its employees and is held responsible for their failure to act accordingly.[20]

This mechanical notion of knowledge, conflated with objectified information, highlights the problem involved in the attempt to analogize the corporation to the natural person when we bear in mind Polanyi's paradox, to wit, that "we know more that we can say". A corporation only "knows" what can be and is, in fact, documented. But much of our sense of right and wrong depends on the sort of knowledge, including faith, that cannot be turned into objectified information without significant falsification. Any ethical system that goes beyond questions of compliance with the rules of obligations, duties and responsibilities relies on this vast body of inarticulable knowledge, and it is one of the differences between the self and the role.[21] Because corporations are managed by human beings, our expectations of corporate behavior rests on the 'knowledge' of the humans who manage it, but human knowledge cannot be reduced to corporate knowledge, and corporate knowledge cannot be extended so as to coincide with human knowledge. This unbridgeable gap vitiates any theory of corporate moral agency that purports to go beyond rule based, or, to use the technical term, deontological ethics.

In a large number of cases where individuals committed crimes, liability was nevertheless assigned to their employer, the corporation, despite the total absence of any evidence of any corporate action associated with the crime. In The E. F. Hutton case two employees of the brokerage firm defrauded some 400 banks of USD 8,000,000, but instead of holding them responsible, Hutton was allowed to agree to a fine.[22] Similar results obtained in the more recent cases of fraudulent manipulation of the Eurodollar interbank rate by a group of bank employees. The corporate veil, therefore, not only disrupts the unity of the actor and the act, but ascribes meaning to acts, including 'deemed' acts, that could not be ascribed without the disruption of that unity.

A corporation then is not a "person", but does the failure of any and all personification theories defeat the search for a definition of the corporation, as Professor Hart claims, on the ground that the word 'corporation' does "not have the straightforward connection with counterparts in the world of fact…"?

Hart's notion of a definition seems to be restricted to the category of ostensive definitions that obtain meaning by pointing to something to which the word applies. That something in Hart's view must be a 'fact', but he does not define 'fact' either ostensively or otherwise.[23] He assumes that words stand for some *things,* that there

---

[20] Ibid. at p. 856.

[21] See below under 11. for the elaboration of this distinction.

[22] For a survey of cases involving the attribution of criminal responsibility between individuals and their employer corporations see Fisse B. and Braithwaite, J. (1993) *Corporations, Crime and Accountability,* Cambridge University Press

[23] Unless 'fact' is taken to mean the name of a corporeal object, we have an infinite regression under Hart's theory where the putative fact cannot be defined without connecting it to some other 'fact'. Apart from noting the mind- dependent nature of social facts, an exploration of fact formation is beyond the scope of this paper. For an interesting account of fact formation in science see

is a word-object correspondence, which reveals the meaning of words, that meaning can be derived only from the word-object connection, and further, that facts are things. But ostensive definitions, in linking the word with an object – or as Hart has it, with a fact – only identify the object/fact as a paradigmatic sample of the word's correct application. Presumably, Hart would contend that pointing to the Ford Motor Company in response to a request for a definition of the word 'corporation' fails because the Ford Motor Company is not a 'fact', but this use of the word 'fact' seems arbitrary. Why is the Ford Motor Company nothing more than the rules that constitute and govern it, but the motor vehicles it makes more than the laws of physics and chemistry that make their construction possible?

Hart argues that "there is no Caliban out there; there is nothing but the rules", that "to say 'Acme Ltd. cannot do it' suggests that there is an actual person called Acme Ltd. which, because it is a corporation, is different from other people in that it lacks a particular capacity. But the correct analysis is that there is no rule of attribution by which the doing of X by any person would be attributed to Acme Ltd."[24]

In *Meridian Global Funds Management Asia Ltd. v Securities Commission*[25] Lord Hoffmann, delivering the unanimous opinion of the Privy Council, follows H.L.A. Hart and writes

> …a reference to a company 'as such' might suggest that there is something out there called the company of which one can meaningfully say that it can or cannot do something. There is in fact no such thing as the company as such, no Ding an sich, only the applicable rules. To say that a company cannot do something means only that there is no one whose doing of that act would, under the applicable rules of attribution, count as the act of the company.

In contrast, the view taken in this paper is that legal rules give rise to and endow a corporate entity with the ability to generate facts that *cannot be generated by individuals or unincorporated groups of individuals*. The immortality of the corporation, for example, overcomes the extinction of the obligation of the individual upon his death. The management of vast numbers of people across continents is made possible by the rule making legislative power of the corporation dispensing, when coupled with limited liability, with the need for contractual arrangements governing the responsibility and liability of agents in unincorporated arrangements. The protection of corporate assets from the claims of personal creditors cannot be accomplished by contract and agency law.[26]

An individual is legally responsible for the foreseeable consequences of his acts, but there is no such rule either for corporations or for its agents. Corporate management may foresee the deleterious consequences, the likely damage that may result

Fleck, L. (1979) *Genesis and Development of a Scientific Fact,* The University of Chicago Press; Poovey, M. (1998)*A History of the Modern Fact,* The University of Chicago Press.

[24] Lord Hoffmann's letter to the author interpreting Hart's essay, cited above. See also Lord Hoffmann's advice for the Privy Council in *Meridian Global Funds Management Asia Ltd. v Securities Commission* (1995) UKPC 5 (1995) 2 AC 500.

[25] Ibid.

[26] Hansmann, H. and Kraakman. R.R. "The Essential Role of Organizational Law" (2000) 110 *Yale Law Journal* p. 387.

from their actions, but corporate liability depends not on such foreseeability, but on (i) the classification of the action as wrongful, and (ii) the attribution of the action to the corporation. Conversely, the law may attribute legal responsibility to a corporation even in circumstances where individual or group responsibility for the act or event in question cannot be established. In fact, there *is* a Caliban out there even if the legal system, having given birth to it, will only make it responsible for its acts on the selective basis stitched together by the rules of attribution and the principles of agency.

Dealing with the meaning of the word is an epistemological enterprise; dealing with the quiddity of the corporation is an exercise in ontology. In short, the corporation is made *by* language in that it is constructed by the special language of the law, but not *of* language in that it is not reducible to language. The magnitude of the damage from the oil spill in the Gulf of Mexico is not determined by the scope of legal liability for it. A study of how language constitutes and represents the corporation is an epistemological inquiry.[27] The effort to understand the *nature* of corporations – how such catastrophic damage could be caused by corporate action – is an ontological undertaking. Hart proposes that "we put aside the question 'What is a corporation?'" because the word does "not have a straightforward connection to the world of fact, and ask instead 'Under what types of conditions does the law ascribe liabilities to corporations?" implying either that the first question is meaningless, or that the latter question can serve as a substitute for the former in that the answer to the latter will also provide the answer to the former. But an inventory of the types of conditions under which the law ascribes liabilities to corporations will not account for everything that a corporation is or does. It is one thing to claim that only those acts engage corporate responsibility for which there are legal rules of attribution and another to pretend that all other acts are, as a matter of fact, meaningless. Hart's view evades the ontological issue and leads to an epistemological dead end. In defining the corporation the task is not the specification of the circumstances under which liability is attributed to the corporation, but – at least since Hobbes[28] – an exploration of its *authorized roles*. It is these admittedly legally constructed, but factually operative roles – e.g. the owner of property, the party to a contract, the plaintiff or defendant in a lawsuit, the maker or supplier of a product, etc. – that defines the corporation and provides the 'fact' Hart finds missing. Liabilities are ascribed to the corporation on the basis of how the role in question was performed. The problem lies less with the ascription, and more with the role,[29] performed in the name and under the authority of a contrivance with "neither a body to be kicked nor a soul to be damned". Liability is extended not by the expansion of the attribution, but by pushing out the boundaries

---

[27] It is not clear if Hart intends to follow in its entirety Wittgenstein of the *Philosophical Investigations* (1953) Basil Blackwell Ltd. to the effect that objects do not have a determinable existence outside of language, or just take the bit about understanding language through its usage rather than through a search for the meaning of words.

[28] See below, and Pettit, P. (2008) *Made with Words: Hobbes on Language, Mind, and Politics.* Princeton University Press.

[29] For the opposite view see Hart, H.L.A. (1948) "The Ascription of Responsibility and Rights" *The Proceeding of the Aristotelian Society* 49, pp. 171–194.

of the role in question with the help of the legal technique of 'deeming', or the 'constructive' performance of the role, or, at its most extreme, by the deeming of facts that permit a finding of constructive performance.

What Hart and Hoffmann see as a peculiarity of the corporation is not a peculiarity at all, but rather, the defining feature of the law in general. Whereas the basic unit of ethics is the natural person with his innate capacity for thinking, willing and judging, the protagonist of the law – any and every one of its *persona ficta* – is the performer of a legally constructed role, such as a servant, a tenant, a landlord, an agent, a vendor, a CEO, a husband, a forger, a burglar, etc. whose thinking, willing and judging is operative only if it operates within legally defined parameters. But, *as a matter of fact,* each of these role performers also perform other acts, even if in the eyes of the law it is not the natural person, but the performer of a legally recognised role who is at issue. This discrepancy between the doings of the natural person and the acts the role performer has been the graveyard of jurisprudential theories addressing the relationship between the law and ethics, and it has posed acute, but by no means unique problems for theories of corporate agency. *Any* legally recognised and legitimized persona is *ficta*, not in the sense that it is fictitious, but in the sense that it is *made, constructed, contrived* by the language of the law. The corporation is no more 'fictitious' than any other legally constructed role, and the 'personae' of the law are not persons in any ordinary sense of the word, but, rather, *roles,* equipped with legally defined powers, rights, privileges, duties and obligations, all of which, in Hobbesian language, are "made with words". Hart distinguishes the case 'X is a servant of Y Co.' from the case of 'Smith is a servant of Brown' on the ground that "any words when conjoined with the name of a corporation takes on a special legal use", but overlooks the fact that the latter case also takes on the special meaning of the legal use if and only if the role performed by Smith conforms to the relevant legal criteria for 'servant'. If X is a 'servant' of Brown, Brown is the 'master' of X. In fact, there is no difference between the two cases. Both may be read in a legal sense – in which case the issue is the legally determined role of 'servant' , 'master' or 'corporation' – or both may be read in the ordinary sense. Thus, a politician favoring the enactment of an advantage for Hart's Y & Co. may be branded a servant of Y & Co. by his opponents without the name of Y & Co. taking on "a special legal use", and, conversely Brown takes on a special legal meaning if the name is used to specify the identity of the master of X.

Hart's essay was published in 1954. J.L. Austin's William James lectures were delivered at Harvard University in 1955 and published under the title *How to do Things with Words* in 1962.[30] According to the Preface to the first edition, however, the central idea of these lectures, – the theory of what Austin later labeled 'performative utterances' – was set out in "Other Minds" and published in *Proceedings of the Aristotelian Society,* Supplemental Volume XX in 1946, and each year between 1952 and 1954 Austin delivered lectures in Oxford under the title "Words and Deeds".

[30] Austin, J.L. (1962) *How to do Things with Words,* Second edition edited by J. O. Urmson and Marina Sbisa; Harvard University Press, Cambridge, Mass.

As Austin shows, performative utterances can create facts.[31] The declaration that "I take this woman to be my lawful wedded wife" when uttered in the course of a legally sanctioned marriage ceremony together with the parallel declaration of the other party, creates the fact of marriage notwithstanding that the marriage so created has "no counterpart in the world of fact". Similarly, it is perfectly possible to define the corporation as "a body of people, who have legal existence distinct from those who compose it"[32] where securing that 'legal existence' requires the uttering of Austin's performative utterances producing facts that result in the entry of the name of the corporation in the registry of corporations. Whether those facts obtain, whether the name appears in the registry, etc., are all questions of fact, but these facts are different from the ones Hart has in mind. They are mind-dependent, that is to say, they exist not in nature, they do not correspond to something already out there, but arise in consequence of human intentionality, they are, in short, man-made facts. But the set of facts generated by the corporation are different from the set for which attribution rules are available, and that different set constitutes the corporation, Lord Hoffmann's missing *Ding an sich.* A crucial question in the context of the present inquiry, is whether, having granted power to the corporation to legislate the roles to be performed by directors, officers and employees with a scope that exceeds the operation of the attribution rules, what is the justification for requiring attribution rules instead of holding the corporation liable for acts committed and facts generated within the entirety of the scope of the roles so created. Put differently, are attribution rules anything more than devices for avoiding or limiting corporate responsibility for acts committed *in fact* in its name and on its behalf? Does the corporate context alter or displace in some fundamental way – with the help of the requirement for rules of attribution – individual or group intentionality?

10.3 The Self vs. Role Performance

It would have been impolitic for Chief Baron Manwood to recognize at the end of the sixteenth century, that the source of his doctrine was Pope Innocent IV's decretal of 1246,[33] and, possibly, its defense by St. Thomas Aquinas,[34] but his formulation is almost identical with the one set out by this eminent scholar of canon law. In it we find the early, possibly the first description of the corporation as a *persona ficta,* a description inaccurately translated in modern times and giving rise to the disastrous notion of the corporation as a 'fictitious person' or as a 'legal fiction'. Although 'persona' had transmuted by the time of Boethius from the classical Latin

[31] It is hard to see what, if anything in Austin was not already set out by Hobbes.

[32] The New Shorter Oxford Dictionary.

[33] Pope Innocent IV was an eminent jurist. The decretal became a part of cannon law.

[34] Eschman, T. (1946) "Studies on the Notion of Society in St. Thomas: St. Thomas and the Decretal of Innocent IV Romana Ecclesia, Ceterum" *Medieval Studies* 8: 1–42; cited in List, C. and Pettit, P. (2011) *Group Agency,* Oxford University Press.

denotation of 'mask', to the broader sense of the role signified by the mask, – in Boethius' terms, a *naturae rationalis individua substantia,* an hypostasis that possesses a rational nature, – and therefore could be taken to mean a distinct entity with the capacity to play the role in society represented by the 'mask', the sense that it referred to role rather than to a self with a soul remained. This sense of 'persona' is reinforced by the addition of 'ficta', derived as it is, from '*fingere*' – meaning to craft, to make, or to contrive – and certainly not meaning 'fictitious'. The correct translation of the term, therefore, is not 'fictitious person', but, rather, 'contrived entity', or – if we grant that in medieval Latin *persona* increasingly meant 'person' – 'contrived person' or ' a person performing a role'.[35] The opposition set up by the Pope is not between the fictitious and the real – an opposition not encountered in medieval philosophy – but, rather, the Aristotelian distinction between the natural (or God-made) and the man-made. The Pope's Aristotelian pairing is echoed in Chief Baron Manwood's formulation: "None can create Souls but God; but the King creates Corporations". Indeed, the whole point of the decretal is to deny any form of personhood to the corporation, an objective ill served if 'persona' is read as some sort of a cognate of the biological human person, differentiated from it only by its purported fictitiousness.

A few decades later Thomas Hobbes abandons Chief Baron Manwood's metaphysical and theologically well grounded distinction, and instead, proposes a definition of the person in terms of the capacity in which he acts or speaks. "A person is he, whose words or actions are considered, either as his own, or as representing the words or actions of another man, or of any other thing to whom they are attributed."[36] Philip Pettit pithily summarizes Hobbes' radical new claim:

> …there are no persons but spokespersons. Natural persons are spokespersons for themselves, acting and speaking in their own name, and artificial persons are spokespersons for another.[37]

This restatement, amounting to the elimination of the distinction between 'personhood', – that is to say the self – and the 'role' has profound implications. The ethics of the *self* has to do with what it is to live the good life, or what it is good to be; the assumption and performance of a *role* concerns the assumption and performance of obligations and duties, or what it is right to do. The first of these, the right way to be, has to do with a certain quality and direction of the will,[38] an ethical domain well beyond the reach of legally based rules for action. But Hobbes' natural person ceases to be a moral being, a *singulus*; from this point on he is seen only as a representative, an actor, an *universus,* representing himself or others, but always

[35] The thirteenth century customary of Salisbury Cathedral tells the reader what to do when meeting a 'persona' (e.g. the Dean, the Treasurer or the Cantor, and its English version, 'person' meant someone important in the Church.) By the fourteenth century this meaning was captured in the word 'parson'. I am grateful to Richard Conrad O.P. for the elucidation and history of these terms.

[36] Hobbes, T. (first published in 1651) *Leviathan* Ed. E. Curley (1994) Hackett. Quoted in Pettit, P. (2008) *Made with Words; Hobbes on Language, Mind and Politics.* Princeton University Press.

[37] Pettit, Ibid. p.56.

[38] Murdoch, I. (1971) *The Sovereignty of Good,* Routledge, London.

representing and never being, whose acts are made by as well as of language. The self, the *singulus* as the active protagonist of the economy and the locus of moral responsibility is replaced by the *persona ficta* spoken for and represented by the *universus*. A coherent theory of corporate moral agency would either have to show how any one of the ethical theories developed for the *singulus* could apply to both the *universus* – in Hobbesian terms the 'personator' – and the *persona ficta*, the personatee, or develop an ethics specifically for the *universus* and the *persona ficta*. The first of these two alternatives is defeated by the operation of the six attributes of the corporation set out above. Efforts to develop the second founder on Chief Baron Manwood's axiom. But Hobbes' failed attempt to dissolve the distinction between the *singulus* and the *universus* by replacing personhood with 'spokespersonhood' illuminates the proper domain and limitations of Benthamite deontological ethics.It is perfectly feasible to formulate rule based ethical requirements on the rule-contrived corporation, and it is impossible to impose Aristotelian/Thomist teleological ethics on the corporation that requires the operations of a conscience the corporation does not have, because, by definition, it is rule, rather than *telos* based. Conversely, corporate agents, required as they are to obey the rules that constitute the corporation, must subordinate their conscience to the deontological ethics of Benthamite utilitarianism.[39] Corporate agents, while satisfying deontological ethical requirements in the performance of their rule-based roles, are therefore condemned to fall short of the teleological standards expected of them as human beings.

Is the corporation, this 'contrived person', a group capable of group agency? The answer to this question in the literature[40] seems to be unanimously in the affirmative. Disagreement arises only with regard to the capacity of the corporation for *moral* agency. But this analysis is mistaken. Group agency and joint action, as Margaret Gilbert notes, is a matter of joint commitment; corporate action is a matter of performing a role crafted and authorized by the corporation. It may be that the group performing that role has jointly committed to the accomplishment of a shared end, but, unless expressly so specified in the role, it is not that joint commitment that renders their action a corporate action, but, rather, the compliance of the action with the requirements of the rule based role. The joint commitment, if any, is not a matter of a commitment freely made; it is the performance of a role which contains the commitment as a *requirement*. This gap between the moral quality of freely *formulated and chosen* human action and the performance of a predetermined role is the essence of the problem of corporate moral agency, and the nature of the problem is clearly shown by St. Thomas Aquinas.

---

[39] Authorship of deontological ethics is commonly attributed to Kant, an attribution convincingly challenged by Barbara Herman in her *The Practice of Moral Judgment* (1993) Harvard University Press and her "On a Mismatch of Methods" in Parfit, D. (2011) *On What Matters* Vol. Two, Oxford University Press.

[40] See for example Pettit, P. *Group Agency*, Ibid. and the bibliography cited therein.

For Aquinas, as set out in his *Sententia Libri Ethicorum*,[41] an activity may be an *actio*, a self-determined doing, or a *factio*, an event occurring by the operation of forces outside the acting person's mind and will. An *actio* may be carried out by an individual or a group. A group, however, is not a unity (*colligatio*) in the sense that a child *in utero* and its mother is a unity, but, rather, it is a unity of order. He demonstrates the point with the example of an army, the members of which do things that are part of the *actio* but which none of the members can do alone – e.g. surround a town – as well as acts that are solely the acts of the individual soldier that the whole cannot do, such as storming the wall at a particular point. It is therefore the unity of order rather than some feature found in organisms that defines the social group. That unity has two aspects. First, it is the ordering of relationships between and among members, and second, there is the relationship between the group so ordered and the purpose or end for which the association is formed. Of the two, the latter, the Aristotelian *telos* is far the more important. The former is nothing more that the means, the instrumentality for carrying out the latter. Accordingly, for Aquinas, as John Finnis puts it: "Societies as well as individual actions are subjects of *moralis philosophia*[42] precisely because *philosophia moralis* considers human actions (*operationes*) in their relationship to each other and to purpose(s) (*ordinate ad invicem et ad infinem*), and human societies have their distinctive reality, as orders of intelligent, voluntary, purposive action."[43] This theory, conceiving the moral capacity of groups in terms of collective intentionality, rests on the bedrock of Aristotelian epistemology.[44] Capacities are understood by the acts that manifest them, and acts are understood by their objects. Groups are groups because they act in furtherance of a common object, a furtherance in which members of the group choose to participate, and this participation in common in the furtherance of the common object is what endows the group with moral capacity.[45] But does the group consist of only those who actually participated in the action, or is it the larger collection of individuals brought together by some sort of a common *telos*? In the Thomist view, responsibility can only lie with those who committed the act in question. Sharing a common objective becomes morally meaningful only through the acts committed individually or in concert. Fault may be apportioned among members of the group, but it cannot be borne by the *persona ficta.*[46] Sharing a common *telos* creates moral capacity, but moral responsibility becomes meaningful only

[41] *Sententia Libri Ethicorum* (Commentary on Aristotle's *Nichomachean Ethics*), 1271–2. For a detailed exposition of Aquinas' social theory of groups and their actions see Finnis, J. (1998) *Aquinas*. Oxford University Press.

[42] *Moralis philosophia* is one of the four types of Thomist order: (1) the sciences of matter and relationships unaffected by our thinking and studied by natural philosophy, (2) the sciences of the order with which we can sort our thinking, such as logic, (3) the sciences of the order we can bring into our deliberating, choosing and voluntary actions, called *philosophia moralis*, and (4) the sciences of the practical arts that bring order into matter.

[43] Finnis, Ibid. p.27.

[44] Aristotle *De Anima* 2, 4.41a16–22.

[45] Aquinas *Sententia Libri De Anima* ll 6nn. 6–10, lll 14 n 9 (803).

[46] Eschmann, Ibid.

from the acts performed in aid of achieving it. The object of the act gives meaning to it, but moral responsibility resides in the act rather than in the formation of its object. Fault may be apportioned only among those who participated in the act itself, and cannot be assigned to the body corporate precisely because the body corporate cannot act. Its actions are those that can be attributed to it with the aid of some rule of attribution. The Thomist *persona ficta* may be the vessel of the unity of order on which the moral capacity of its members may rest, but only natural persons can act, and moral responsibility is borne by the natural person(s) who acted. Aquinas' unity of order is therefore a long way from the conception of the corporation as a person with the attributes of personhood.

As Magnus Ryan notes, "Roman law, in fact, is obstinately unresponsive to the attractions of treating people as corporate individuals... Canon law had a sophisticated apparatus of corporations, but insisted that no corporation could found itself: it needed a superior to recognize it and appoint its visible, flesh-and-blood spokesman."[47] The unqualified medieval denial of personhood to the corporation was blunted by a series of nineteenth and twentieth century Papal encyclicals – *Rerum novarum* (Leo XIII), *Quadragesimo anno* (Pius XI), *Mater et magistra* (John XXIII), *Gaudium et spes* (Second Vatican Council), and *Laborem exercens* (John Paul II) – that disregarded the ontological singularity of the corporation and sought to formulate principles applicable to "economic enterprises" in general[48] on the basis that the common denominator of all forms of business is the profit motive and the further idea, that the search for profits could and should be channeled toward a "common good".[49] These efforts inevitably, if unintentionally, paved the way for the replacement of the traditional notion of the corporation as the temporary and revocable grant of privileges by the sovereign for the exercise of some powers belonging to the sovereign – a concept that does not confer autonomous personhood on the corporation – with the conception of the corporation as the voluntary association of free individuals, an association with the capacity to give birth to the separate personhood of the corporation. But it is a serious mistake to attribute to an earlier epoch this quintessentially nineteenth century liberal idea, and it is an even more serious mistake to ignore the moral significance of the shift from Baron Manwood's belief that only God can create persons with a conscience to the notion that the law can authorize Tom, Dick and Harry to do so.

While the distribution of profits raises undoubtedly important ethical issues, an understanding of the ontological identity of the participants among whom the distribution is urged along the lines of one theory or another seems indispensable. However one might describe the attributes and propensities of individuals, groups, partnerships, co-operatives, kibbutzes, or corporations on the ground that in "in

[47]Ryan, M. "Bartolus of Sassoferrato and Free Cities" in *Transactions of the Royal Historical Society* Sixth Series, X p. 84.

[48]For a summary discussion of these encyclicals see Cortright, S. A. andNaughton, M. J. (ed.) *Rethinking the Purpose of Business, University of Notre Dame Press.*

[49]Alford, H. O. P. and Naughton, M. J. "Beyond the Shareholder Model of the Firm: Working toward the Common Good of a Business" in *Rethinking the Purpose of Business,* Ibid.

economic enterprises it is persons who are joined together",[50] they cannot all be placed on the same ontological footing, because their quiddity, defined by their roles determines the manner and extent, if any, to which they are so joined. An 'owner', an 'employer', a 'manager' and an 'employee' are all "free and independent human beings created in the image of God",[51] but it is on the basis of their role and not on the basis of this commonality that the distribution of profits will be determined.

There have been three major attempts to overcome the Thomist requirement described above. Peter French has argued that, although admittedly not natural persons, corporations possess all of the relevant properties of "metaphysical personhood".[52] They exhibit the capacity for purpose formation, can respond to reasons, and are rational. However, French does not explain why these alleged corporate properties belong to the corporation rather than those who act in its name any more than the extent to which these properties are constrained by the rules that constitute the corporation and govern its operations. In particular, the corporate capacity for purpose formation, unlike the free will of natural persons, derives from and is defined by the rules constituting the corporation, and a business corporation can respond to reasons only to the extent that such reasons are consistent with its rule-defined purpose, and their rationality. The 'rationality' of corporations is delineated by the rules of corporate finance. There is not corporate rationality outside these rules.

The second effort, developed by List and Pettit,[53] borrows a metaphor from computer science,[54] to distinguish between higher level 'programs' – performing a function similar, but not identical to the Thomist common *telos* – and their lower level 'implementation', fulfilling the role of Thomist *actio*. Based on this distinction,

> the group agent is fit to be held responsible for ensuring that one or more of its members perform in the relevant manner. At the same time, the enacting members of the group are not absolved of their own responsibility…Members have responsibility as enactors of the corporate deed so far as they could have refused to play that part but didn't. The group agent as a whole has responsibility as the source of that deed, the 'planner' at its origin.[55]

They acknowledge that groups are not persons in the ordinary sense of the word, but – borrowing a concept from John Searle[56] – claim that, in the performative sense, they are granted a normative status by the community that can be analogized to personhood. The purpose formation residing with the planners together with the implementation carried out by those who act pursuant to the plan warrant granting the status of performative personhood.

---

[50] *Gaudium et spes* (1965).

[51] Ibid.

[52] French, P. A. (1979) "The Corporation as a Moral Person." *American Philosophical Quarterly* Vol. 16, No. 3.

[53] List, C. and Pettit, P. (2011) (Paperback edition 2013) *Group Agency.* Oxford University Press.

[54] Jackson, F., Pettit, P. and Smith, M. (2004) *Mind, Morality and Explanation: Selected Collaborations,* Oxford University Press.

[55] Ibid. p. 163 (Paperback edition).

[56] Searle, J. R., (1995) *The Construction of Social Reality,* Free Press.

The attempt, however, does not seem to be successful. It assumes that the 'enacting members' work with a tabula rasa, that they have the requisite degree of freedom in forming the purpose of the corporation, and further, that the 'enactors' can refuse to play the part crafted for them by the planners. In fact, compliance with the requirements of corporate finance seriously constrains the scope for purpose formation, and, in fact, performance of a prescribed part can be refused only upon pain of dismissal. Normative status might be adequate grounding for some sort of a moral capacity, but the authors do not overcome the fact that only human beings can act. Presumably, the implementers and the planners are part of the same group, and, accordingly, under the List-Pettit theory they have a dual responsibility, first for implementing, and second, for being members of the group for planning/designing the program. But if they did not participate in the design of the program, why should they be responsible for it when the designers are not held responsible for the implementation?

Is responsibility the consequence of the act committed or is it the result of membership in a group? The Thomist answer clearly sides with the former. The List-Pettit theory attempts to enlarge moral responsibility beyond the act by conflating the two on the ground that, in their view, the group agent meets the three criteria they specify for moral responsibility, to wit, that, (i) the agent faces a normatively significant choice, (ii) the agent has the means and the capacity for making normative judgments about the options, and (iii) the agent has the control required for choosing between the options. But how do these criteria relate to the choice between keeping a job and going unemployed?

The third approach, developed more recently by Peter French and endorsed by Deborah Perron Tollefsen[57] simply denies that personhood is required for a finding of moral responsibility. The approach simply ignores the requirement that moral responsibility requires action and only natural persons can act.

The Thomist conception of the moral foundations of individual and group action would provide a sound basis for the assessment of individual and group action if their actions could be seen as voluntary. But the Papal and Thomist rejection of corporate moral agency rests precisely on the ground that:

(i) corporations are incapable of purpose formation;
(ii) corporate agents are not the vessels of voluntary individual or group intentionality, but, rather, the performers of roles defined by binding corporate rules; and
(iii) regardless of the group agency theory one adopts, the attribution of any group purpose and action to the corporation can be accomplished only through fiat, that is to say, only with the help of a legal attribution rule.

Although the role-defining rules may be seen as adding up to the sort of "order" postulated by Aquinas in that corporate rules do indeed order the relationship among the members, namely the shareholders, the directors, the officers and the employees, it is hard to see in the employee's compliance with a job description the sort of Augustinian free will Aquinas is likely to have had in mind when insisting that

[57] Tollefsen, D. P. (2015) *Groups as Agents*, Polity Press.

participation in the pursuit of a common objective must be voluntary. Second, in what sense is there a shared *telos* among the employees of a large corporation where the individual job description and performance indicator of each employee is set separately? Indeed, it is quite common for corporations to formulate performance indicators so as to foster competition among employees.

With the increasing application of information and robot technology, employees either design or apply systems that operate independently of any "intelligent, voluntary, purposive action" on their part. The whole point of this technological development is the reduction and, ultimately, the liquidation of human intentionality. The ethical issue, although still residing in the individual or group *action*, cannot be assessed without an understanding of the ethical quality of the *role* to be performed. But what is the ethical assessment of a role guided or determined by a software program? How is the operator of that program to be judged when the software seriously curtails or entirely vitiates the scope for his "intelligent, voluntary, purposive action"? What should one make of the actions of the clerk feeding data into Bernie Madoff's systems driven Ponzi scheme?

The contrary view, urged by Seamus Miller[58] among others, is that "the doings of macro-entities, especially organizations, are reducible to the actions of individual persons", and that, accordingly, the individual person performing the act is fully responsible for it. He is right in claiming that group action is the sum of actions by individuals, but which individuals? The legislators who drafted the laws and regulations, the institutional investors demanding the fulfillment of their requirements, the board, senior management, the supervisory agencies, the engineers who deigned the program of VW with which emission data can be falsified, the labor force that installed it, the sales force that sold it, etc.? Miller minimizes the significance of roles and the system within which these roles operate, disregards the effects of the corporate veil, – permitting as it does the shifting of legal responsibility from the agent (whoever that agent might be) to the corporation – and thereby avoids the need to explain how roles are constructed. He ends up with the claim that "a role is simply an abstraction from procedure governed tasks, and the actions that constitute the undertaking of those tasks." This oft-expressed Weberian view is mistaken because the essence of macro-entities is the *system* that co-ordinates and keeps together "the actions of individual persons", and that system is not a part of individual actions.[59] At the same time, the system is the product of anonymous authors who are not accountable.

The view taken here is that a role in the corporate context is a set of duties and authorizations pertaining to a function, defined by rules. The role is the rule-based definition of how a function may or must be performed. The actions performed by individuals or – if one is inclined to agree with any one of the three theories defending the idea of group action – groups, do not fully engage moral responsibility because the three criteria set out by List and Pettit for moral capacity, *pace* List and

[58] Miller, S. (2001) *Social Action, A Teleological Account,* Cambridge University Press.

[59] Lawson, T. (2015) "The Nature of the Firm and Peculiarities of the Corporation", *Cambridge Journal of Economics* 2015, 39, 1–32

Pettit, are not satisfied. In particular, the third criterion is not met, and the first two are also rule constrained.[60] Responsibility for the formulation of the rules cannot be assigned, because these rules and the roles they create are formed both outside the corporation, namely by legislatures, courts and regulators, the technological instruments that make certain roles possible, etc., and inside it by boards.

At the same time, the moral quality of a role, based on its effects, can be assessed, and the assessment can provide the foundations for moral accountability in a manner somewhat analogous to the legal concept of vicarious liability. If the role is constituted so as to permit some act of malfeasance in the course of its performance, the corporation can be seen to be accountable for sustaining a defectively defined role that permitted the commission of the reprehensible act. This sort of accountability, however, is not derived from group agency and it is not a part of any purpose formation on the basis of which the act in question was performed, but, rather, it rests on the rule making powers of the corporation conferred upon it by the legislature. If the corporation has the power to define roles, it should have the duty to define them in a manner that precludes socially undesirable consequences.

10.4 The Rise of Modern Economics and the Rise of the Modern Business Corporation

The history of modern economics is the history of the relentless search for the separation of "value judgments" from "objective facts", and the expulsion of the former from the concerns of the discipline in the effort to render its subject matter resemble as closely as possible the methodology of the natural sciences. Mary Morgan traces this development to the invention of models as the tool of enquiry, the earliest of which is thought to be Quesnay's Tableau Economique of 1767, much expanded by David Ricardo in his "The influence of a Low Price of Corn on the profits of Stock" of 1815 and Chapter ll of his *The Principles of Political Economy and Taxation* of 1817. With the help of models the verbal, descriptive discipline of, for example, Adam Smith or David Hume, is turned into a tool-based kind of knowledge, relying heavily on mathematics, statistics, graphs and diagrammatic representations.[61] As Mary Morgan notes:

> The introduction of this new kind of scientific object – models – involved not just the adoption of new languages of expression into economics (such as algebra or geometry), but also the introduction of a new way of reasoning to economics.[62]

Is the sum and substance of this transformation adequately represented as the adoption of new language of expression and the introduction of new ways of reason-

[60] List and Pettit recognise the difficulty and attempt to deal with it. A refutation of their attempt is beyond the scope of this paper.

[61] Morgan, M.S. (2012) *The World in the Model,* Cambridge University Press

[62] Ibid. p.

ing, is it, in other words, a change in "techniques and method", or is the change even deeper? Is the subject matter of economics in the twenty-first century the same as it had been for David Hume, Adam Smith or even the first, the second or the third model builder, Francois Quesnay, Johann von Thünen and David Ricardo, or did the transformation change, – perhaps starting with Edgeworth's Box – the very subject matter with which the discipline is concerned? In addition to the development of new techniques, did economics invent its own subject matter? The exploration of this question is well beyond the scope of this paper, but a short contrast of a twenty-first century economist, the Nobel laureate N. Gregory Mankiw's description of the subject matter of economics with the one offered by Adam Smith will illuminate the point defended here: in parallel with the transformation of the subject of economics from an ontologically subjective to an ontologically objective subject, the ontologically objective corporation, freed of the subjectivity of humans, was invented. Mankiw writes:

> Economists try to address their subject with a scientist's objectivity. They approach the subject of the economy in much the same way as a physicist approaches the study of matter and a biologist approaches the study of life. They devise theories, collect data, and analyze these data in an attempt to verify their theories.[63]

Adam Smith sees the heart of the subject, his famous human "propensity to truck, barter and exchange" as the necessary consequence of the faculty of reason and speech[64] and elsewhere drives the point home:

> The offering of a shilling, which to us appears to have so plain a meaning, is in reality offering an argument to persuade one to do so and so as it is for his interest…[65]

Seven years after Smith delivered his Lectures on Jurisprudence, Turgot echoes the view that the economy is about thought and speech: "It is a debate between every buyer and seller" about "the opinion and reality of risk."[66]

Mankiw sees the subject as theories about existing, ontologically objective things, while Smith's and Turgot's notion places it firmly in the domain of intentionality. According to Mankiw, the subject of economics is rather like matter, harboring data, which is there to be "collected" for the verification of some causal generalization. For Adam Smith the essence of the subject consists of the "argument to persuade", and its reception by the object of persuasion.

A full exploration of this transformation, or perhaps, more accurately, replacement of the ontologically subjective, mind dependent subject with a reified, ontologically objective and mathematically representable collection of "matter" is beyond the scope of this paper. But the parallel development of modern economics and the corporation merits attention because the question of corporate purpose for-

[63] Mankiw, N. G. (2011) *Principles of Economics,* Cengage Learning 6th edition

[64] Smith, A. (1910) *The Wealth of Nations,* Alfred A. Knopf, New York, p. 12.

[65] Smith, A. (1978) *Lectures on Jurisprudence,* Oxford University Press p. 352. Cited in Rothschild, E. (2001) *Economic Sentiments,* Harvard University Press.

[66] Schelle, G. (Ed.) (1913) *Oeuvres de Turgot et Documents le Concernants,* Ed. P Alcan, Paris 1913, Vol. 3, p. 192.

mation and the ethics of corporate conduct cannot be understood or assessed without a sense of the ideology served by the corporation. Modern economics, with its eschewal of value judgments and its claim to "objectivity" through the formulation of data supported theories, required a protagonist without, in J. S. Mill's words, 'the disturbing cause' of an inherent capacity to formulate value judgments and assume responsibility for the attendant consequences, one whose quiddity could be defined in conformity with the utility maximization theories of the discipline, whose authorized behavior could be conformed to the requirements of model building. Models, in short, abandoned the search for descriptive truth. Instead, modern economics built a surrogate reality where the issue is not what human conduct actually is, but, rather, what it should be in a world of mathematicised rationality.

The removal of corporate conduct from societal ethics and its subjection to the exclusive control of the causal generalizations of modern economics, reinforced by the law gives rise to an agent with unique characteristics. The objective of natural science in its search for law-like regularities is to gain control over nature, to gain predictive power over its behavior. Technological progress, the ultimate practical validation of the natural sciences, rests on the reliability of the predictive power gained through the formulation of law-like regularities. By adopting a similar purpose, economics as a discipline has substituted for its original mission, – the amelioration of the human condition,[67] – a scheme for the control of human behavior in order to promote a particular economic agenda, to wit, the generation of material wealth. In so doing, the "science" of economics has expelled from its purview the meaning and moral significance of human action, and consequently, other values and considerations that are pertinent to the human condition. Economics, in its effort to resemble the natural sciences, claims that it is concerned only with what is, and not with what should be. Its subject matter is thought to be, as John Searle critically observes, "part of the realities of the scientifically investigable world. The doctrine that Savings equals Investment is put on the same footing as the law that Force equals Mass times Acceleration."[68]

But economic activity is purposeful action, undertaken with an end in mind. It is, *par excellence* concerned not only with what is, but, given what is, with what should be done. Corporations are not simply the containers of "facts", but in addition to containing and accumulating facts, the vehicles of organized human action in the pursuit of some goal that, typically, involves the changing of many facts. In specifying what goals accord with its claims of law-like generalizations, microeconomic theory, combining with the power of the law, crafts the perfect agent in the corporation for the execution of its purportedly value free agenda because corporate behavior can be modeled to accord with the requirements of the economic model much more readily that individual behavior. It is the stage upon which human

[67] Rosenberg, A. (1988) *The Philosophy of Social Science*, Westview Press, Boulder.

[68] Searle, J. (2010) *Making the Social World: the structure of human civilization,* Oxford University Press. Searle goes on to note that "It is … a mistake to treat money and other such instruments as if they were natural phenomena like the phenomena studied in physics, chemistry, and biology. The recent economic crisis makes it clear that they are products of massive phantasy."

behavior can be compelled to accord with the requirements of theory, and theory, mimicking the methodology of the natural sciences, dictates the absolute supremacy of *measurability.*

Economic theory posits the utility maximizing agent as its paragon. It is widely thought that the root vice of modern economic theory is the construction of a *homo oeconomicus* who is a grotesque mutilation of the biological human being, and that the way forward is its replacement with a better paragon. But the protagonist of the modern economy is not the individual, but the corporation. The extension of human propensities to the corporation and the search for a better conception of *homo oeconomicus* in order to provide the basis for endowing the corporation with more virtuous properties is a category mistake. Although the work of the corporation is carried out by human beings, it is not their humanity, not their self, but their corporation defined labor that is at play. Their rationality stems not from their nature as human beings, but from their conformity with their corporation defined roles. Accordingly, there is a big difference between the individual and the agent complying with the corporate specifications of the "rational". For the individual it means consistent choices; for the corporation it is measurable efficiency. The individual is granted freedom to pick his preferences as long as he is "rational" in his choices where 'rational' is a synonym for 'consistent'.[69] Utility is whatever he prefers, and any system of rational preferences – defined simply as a set of consistent choices – is legitimate. The corporation, however, has no choice; the only utility it is permitted to choose is efficiency, measured in terms of maximal financial performance. The definition of individual preference is purely formal; that of the corporation is substantive. Just as economics reduces or outright transforms complex phenomena to quantifiable components, the motto of the Bloomberg Corporation – "you can manage only what you can measure" – succinctly expresses the fundamental difference in how humans and corporations manage their affairs.

10.5 The Moral Agency of the Corporation

Some scholars hold that the corporation is a morally competent agent while others think the opposite, but there appears to be a consensus to the effect that the corporation is some sort of a "person". The debate then tends to condense around the three principal views about the 'nature' of this person, namely, the fictitious person theory, the real person theory and the nexus of contracts theory, and within each of these to the search for the location of the moral engine room of corporate action. Is it with the directors, with some or all of the officers, with the committees they form, or with those employees who actually carry out the decisions made by their superiors? The moral capabilities and responsibilities are then adduced from

[69] An examination of the problems with the economist's notion of "rationality" is beyond the scope of this paper. The point being made here is that the usual assumption to the effect that that individual and corporate motivation spring from the same well is not defensible.

characterizations and attributions with which the selected theory equips the corporation.[70] The view taken on these pages is that all three of these approaches are mistaken because all three mistakenly analogize the corporation to the natural person and wrongly attribute to it properties that can be found only in natural persons. These attributions rely entirely on the coercive powers of the law, and lack an independent moral foundation. The distinction between the God-made and the man-made – or, in modern secular terms, the mind independent and the mind dependent – object can be extinguished only in the world of legal artifice.

The use of the corporation as the means through which individual or group action is carried out specifies the quiddity of such action. These specifications have a reflexive effect that further modifies the conduct of the actor – in that their attribution rules both transform and transfer or altogether extinguish, the moral responsibility that would be normally attendant upon such conduct – with the result that corporate action cannot be derived from, reduced to or analogized to individual or social action. The action of a corporate officer or a corporate body Corporate action differs from individual or group action because the interposition of the corporation between the actor and the act constructs a platform for roles that have no parallel in unincorporated social action. In a nutshell, the actions of a mortal human being are the actions of his self (in Baron Manwood's terms, of his soul); the actions of a corporate officer or employee are the fulfillment of a job description (again in Baron Manwood's terms, a role crafted by the King). The moral quality of individual action rests on the singularity, the nonsubstitutability of the actor. The performance of a role is the exact opposite – it is the denial of the singularity of the one performing it.

Corporate action, taking the form of corporate resolutions, internal rules and directives, the activities of committees, etc. amounts to a kind of legislative activity resembling the power of the sovereign, that cannot be had in unincorporated social action.[71] Rule making transforms the intentionality, the ontologically subjective individual or social action into ontologically objective events founded not on the intentionality of the actor but on the binding, impersonal rule that qualifies the action as the action of the corporation. There is a fundamental moral difference between the freely chosen act and the performance of a role intended and defined by another.

Accordingly, the corporation is neither a 'fictive person', nor a 'real person', nor a 'nexus of contracts', but rather, a novel object constituted by legal rules and devices – as Chief Baron Manwood had it, "*eus rationis* which "resteth only in intendment and consideration of law" – many of which have no counterparts or

---

[70] See for example McMahon, C. (1995) The moral Status of Organisations. *Business Ethics Quarterly* 5(3): 541–554; Donaldson, T.(1982) *Corporations and Morality* Prentice Hall, New Jersey; French, P. A. *Collective and Corporate Responsibility* Columbia University Press, New York.

[71] In historical terms, the modern corporation is the fruit of two independent, and in a sense, contradictory sources. The first of these sees the corporation as chartered and therefore created by the State. The second as a particular example of the doctrine of free association. It is this legislative power of the corporation that is bestowed upon it by the State, and that cannot be derived from the doctrine of free association. See Donaldson, T. (1982) *Corporations and Morality* Prentice Hall.

analogies in either social institutions or in other branches of the law, even if admittedly, notions derived from social action or agency law may illuminate their operations.

The special position taken up by the corporation between the actor(s) and the act, the unique, fundamentally undemocratic characteristics of corporate decision-making under the rules with which the corporation operates pose *sui generis* ethical issues that cannot be fruitfully addressed by treating the corporation as an ethically competent agent in a sense analogous to the ethical competence of natural persons any more than by maintaining the opposite. The first approach fails because, as shown above, the corporation cannot be analogized to a natural person. The second fails because corporate action has consequences that have moral meaning. The substantial literature on social action, investigating the necessary conditions for moral agency – an ability to intend and action, an ability to perform an action and the ability to autonomously choose an intentional action[72] – base the answer on their analysis of the applicability of the ethics of individual and group action to corporations, a step made possible only by attributing personhood to the corporation. If corporations are thought to satisfy the criteria for ethically meaningful actions by individuals or groups they are deemed to be moral agents.[73] If not, the idea of corporate moral agency is judged to be a fallacy. But this approach fails to account for the fact that it is *rules*, in particular, role and attribution rules and not the actual facts of the case that determine who, as a matter of law, is deemed to bear responsibility for particular acts and actions. Put differently, corporations are the sum of the rules that constitute them and the facts generated in compliance with those rules as opposed to the capacities and intentions that mark the individual and groups of individuals. Individuals and groups within corporations undoubtedly have the capacity to formulate purposes for the common good, generate social value, take into account society's need, etc., but these capacities are, so to speak, checked at the door, and replaced by the corporate agent who is there to perform the role specified for him/her or them by the rules, adding up to a system of authorized conduct, that constitute the corporation.

Corporate action has serious consequences that are the proper subject of ethical judgment of the *action.* But that action is the product of the performance of many roles. Tracing moral responsibility for corporate action back to the corporate agent or group of agents who caused or participated in causing such corporate action, however, encounters serious difficulties because the intentionality attendant upon the performance of a prescribed role is not the same as the intentionality associated with a freely chosen objective. Aggregating the intentionality in the performance of a large number of prescribed roles is not feasible or meaningful, and the important theories developed largely in the wake of Margaret Gilbert's seminal *Social Action,* instead of focusing on the entirely unique properties of the modern business corporation, classify it as a variant of group agency. List and Pettit, for example, recognize the problem of aggregated intentionality, they nevertheless attribute personhood

[72] See, for example, Rönnegard, D. (2015) *The Fallacy of Corporate Agency.* Springer.

[73] French, P. A. *Collective and Corporate Responsibility.* Columbia University Press; Mansell, S. F. (2013) *Capitalism, Corporations and the Social Contract,* Cambridge University Press.

to the corporation, – even if its "members are less likely to consider the groups as an entity with which to affiliate robustly" – and see it simply as one of unequal power distribution between individuals and groups on the one hand and the corporation on the other:

> There has long been a concern in political theory about actual abuses that companies, churches, and other corporate entities may perpetrate. But much less attention has been given to the problems created by the enormous power of corporations, independent of actual abuses. The assumption seems to have been that when there is no actual abuse, no actual exercise of interference, then all is well. But, unfortunately, this does not follow. The imbalances of power between corporate entities and individuals, and among corporate entities themselves, can threaten relations of respect. They can warp the adjustments of communities to corporations, churches and other institutional powers, sometimes enabling such bodies to have influence that operates as silently as gravity.[74]

List and Pettit believe, that the imbalance can be redressed through appropriate legal means but do not describe what those means might be. The basis of their intuition seems to be the claim that individuals, groups and corporations all possess personhood, and that this common denominator could serve as the basis of redress. But the intentionality of any one or all of the members of the receivables department finds no common denominator with the intentionality of the engineering staff, let alone the intentionality of any one of the shareholders. In what possible sense is John Doe, receivables clerk and the institutional investor, Megaprofits Ltd. with 3% of the shares of the company the member of the same group or a component of the same 'fictitious person'? The former follows procedures designed for the efficient collection of amounts due to the corporation. The second follows procedures designed for making products, and the third is concerned with the prospective returns on its investment. What common intentionality can there be among the worker on oil rig in the Gulf of Mexico doing what is required of him in his job description, the engineers who designed the platform, those who built it, the geologists who designed the drilling and the members of the finance department who set the financial parameters of the entire operation? The personhood of the corporation fails in all but its legal/fictional sense because, as Aquinas had shown, the attribution of a common intentionality to all of the participants of an action is only possible if the participants all subscribe to the end of the action. But singing the company song, "buying into the company ethos", following or contributing to corporate culture does not change the fact that the *actions* of the individuals and the groups employed by the corporation are legitimated not by the pursuit of a voluntarily assumed common purpose or by the intrinsic virtue of such action, but by the rules that apply to it. How compliance with these rules might help achieve the common purpose is of no concern to the agent who performs the role in question. Looking for the actor before an analysis of the *action* – how it came about, how it actually happened – assumes the conclusion, to wit, that there is a morally competent actor behind the action. What is needed is neither the affirmation nor the denial of the legitimacy of

[74] List, C. and Pettit, P. (2011), (2013 paperback edition) *Group Agency* Oxford University Press, p. 184.

extending ethical theories formulated with individuals in mind, but rather, a theory that can deal with the conflict between the ethical and the legal responsibilities of individual officers and employees or groups of officers and employees *not as individuals or groups, but as the performers of roles specified for them by the corporation* and the ethical nature of the consequences of corporate action. It is, of course, quite possible to attribute responsibility to any person or group of persons for, say, the BP oil spill in the Gulf of Mexico, just as it is quite possible to determine what caused the oil spill, but it is not possible to determine responsibility *in fact* if everyone involved followed the rules and performed their assigned roles. Unlike in the case of unincorporated businesses, it is not the intrinsic moral quality of the act committed by the actor that determines his or her moral responsibility, but, rather, the rules defining the actor's role. Although corporate action is undoubtedly initiated and carried out by individuals or groups of individuals, it cannot be entirely derived from or accounted for by the acts of individuals or groups, because it is the product of a system.

Although List and Pettit recognize that whereas the personhood of the corporation rests entirely, in Chief Baron Manwood's words, on 'the intendment of the law', the personhood of the natural person is the fruit of the person's ability to function in any system of social obligation. But they fail to see that corporate influence "operates as silently as gravity" precisely because it operates outside any system of social obligation. The special mathematicised language with which the corporation operates makes it, if not impervious, at least highly resistant to the ordinary language of social obligations. They claim that the excessive powers of the state and the Church could be curtailed by appropriate legal and constitutional measures as a matter of historical fact, and that the similarly situated business corporation could be similarly reigned in. Unfortunately, but not surprisingly, they do not provide any guidance as to how this could be done. *Pace* List and Pettit, business corporations are *not* like the Church or the State because the latter two function in any – and if they function well, in every – system of social obligations whereas the business corporation's only habitat is the system of legal obligations.

In his important study Peter A. French advances the theory that "a *C*orporation's *I*nternal *D*ecision Structure (its CID Structure) is the requisite redescription, the device that licenses the predication of corporate intentionality."[75] The CID Structure consists of "(1) an organizational or responsibility flow chart that delineates stations and levels within the corporate power structure, and (2) corporate decision recognition rule(s)…"[76] French feels compelled to make this move because, in agreement with Donald Davidson's[77] conception of the morally competent agent, a corporation

---

[75] French, P. A. "The Corporation as a Moral Person" *American Philosophical Quarterly* Vol.16, Number 3, July 1979.

[76] Ibid. P.212.

[77] Davidson, D. "Agency", in *Agent, Action, and Reason,* ed. by Binkley, Bronaugh, and Marras (Toronto, 1971). It should be noted, that Davidson and French use the term 'intentionality' in a sense closer to the legal concept of *mens rea* than the sense found in Brentano, Anscombe, Crane or Priest.

would not be a moral agent if "attributing intentions to a corporation (were) only a shorthand way of attributing intentions to the biological persons who comprise (it) e.g. its board of directors."

The analysis offered here differs from French's theory in a number of respects. Rule-made roles, as set out above, –or French's narrower CID Structure – does not "redescribe" anything, but, rather, constrains or altogether eliminates the scope for the voluntary action and freely formed moral judgment of the actor, replaces it with 'value free', numerically expressed criteria, and compromises or altogether destroys the connection between the actor and the act, thereby providing the foundation for attributing legal significance to actual or putative facts that those facts, in the absence of these specialized attribution rules, would not have. There is no scope for the operation of intentionality in this context.[78] Moreover, French does not explain the origins of the CID Structure. Presumably, it is formulated by biological persons, but, if so, how is moral responsibility for its operation, the intentionality thought to reside within it, transferred to the corporation, or, more likely, lost in transfer?

The attempt to found the moral agency of the corporation on its intentionality is mistaken. The view offered below is that the accountability of corporations is not founded on what they intend, but on how they have legislated the roles of individuals and groups in the corporation.

10.6 The Characteristics of the Corporation's System

What, then, is the grammar and the vocabulary of the system with which corporations are constituted and operated? In what particular way are corporations so radically different from other forms for business?

Four legislatively crafted properties of the corporation – perpetual succession, separate legal personality, transferable shares and limited liability – have made it possible for businesses to operate on a scale that would be inconceivable without them. It would not be possible to operate in dozens of countries on a number of continents employing large numbers of people, nor would it be possible to marshal capital on the requisite scale without them. It would not be possible to set up any number of hermetically compartmentalized units, to wit, subsidiaries with which assets and liabilities are assigned and re-assigned. The centralized, hierarchical management structure could not be erected without perpetual succession and the associated concept of separate legal personality. Capital could not be easily and economically mobilized without limited liability and the free transferability of shares. The large capital requirements and scale of operations associated with much of modern technology in manufacturing as well as in services could not be secured. The scale of the operations of any business, however, requires the formulation of a language of communication that is appropriate to that given scale. As the size of a

[78] The terms "intention" and "intentionality" are used throughout this paper in the sense developed by G. E. M. Anscombe (1957) *Intention,* Cornell University Press.

business grows, some form of objectified language increasingly replaces communication based on personal acquaintance. Information must have the same meaning for a large number of people both inside and outside the corporation who have no personal contact with each other. Increasingly sophisticated securities laws and other legislation prescribe what the corporation must disclose about its operations to the world, and, to aid the operations of the capital markets and regulators, the required disclosures are standardized. Management is expected, and, increasingly required by law, to manage the employees objectively, namely on the basis of criteria that exclude subjective judgment. These forces combine to replace the largely verbal forms of communication of smallerbusinesses where everyone knows everyone else, by numerical or quantitative information, where, because numbers are expected to have much the same meaning for everyone, personal acquaintance is no longer necessary. Targets, budgets, financial and individual employee performance reports are all formulated numerically and are designed to conform with the numerical, tool based language of modern economics. The economic theory of the firm supports the rise of modern corporate finance, and the latter provides the foundations for management theory and practice. All three are linked with a common, or at least translatable numbers based concept formation technique and analysis. The grammar of the modern corporation may be said to be the powers with which the legislature equips it in order to remove the limits to its size and the vocabulary may be seen as the numbers based concepts and language with which the corporation exploits these powers.

The claims set out in this paper do not, in any way, gainsay the moral capacities of the directors, officers and employees of corporations, nor is it suggested that there is no such thing as social action. Character and integrity in the management of the corporation does matter, but they are rule constrained and the rules constraining them are based on quantitatively expressible considerations.[79] Management theory and practice has repeatedly shown an ability to accommodate social concerns if those concerns could be translated into measurable units. Conversely, it has been frustratingly resistant to giving due weight to unquantified values even in the face of palpable social pressure. Employment practices responded to ethnic, racial and gender issues with increasingly refined measuring techniques, and better and more detailed numerical standards of the 'environmental footprint' concept has helped nudge the board room door open for environmental issues. But issues such as social justice, indeed, the need to work on building a just society both in the purely domestic and the multinational context of the multinational corporation seems to elicit only a muted response.

[79] Important ideas for building trust in corporations typically end up with proposals for new *rules* for corporate governance. See, For example, Mayer, C. *Firm Commitment*, Ibid.

10.7 Conclusion

The principal conclusion of this paper is that corporations are *sui generis* economic protagonists. They are governed by rules, not values. Intentionality, *telos* or purpose based theories are unlikely to bring about the much desired improvement in societal trust in the business corporation because the quantitative, rule based language developed for the management of corporations is, on the whole, inhospitable to this approach. Corporations cannot be reasonably expected to give up or modify their quantitative tools, because they cannot be managed by non-quantitative means. Indeed, the primacy of rules expressed in quantitative terms is re-enforced by legal sanctions and are embodied in the rules of corporate finance.[80] Methods designed to qualify quantitative results are unlikely to be successful because the scale of corporate operations, the tools for their regulation, and the evaluation of their performance favors the dominance of quantitative measurements that will not, in most cases, mix with the much less easily transmissible and enforceable qualitative considerations. Frustratingly, qualitative issues, absent a radical reformation of economic and legal theory, will tend to lose.

With the disruption of the moral unity between the act and the actor brought about by the corporate veil, there is not much sense in trying to restore it with the help of attributed notions of intentionality. It would be more helpful to place corporate conduct on the footing of the powers with which the legislature equips them. Corporations can be subjected to deontological, or rule-based ethics, but they cannot be forced to comply with teleological requirements. For example, they could be held responsible and strictly liable at law for the consequences of any design defect in the construction of individual and collective roles. Instead of attributing knowledge to the corporation that, in fact, no one has, or responsibility for acts no one had committed – as the *Bank of New England* court had done – responsibility should be based on how the tools at the disposal of the corporation for the design of corporate roles were designed and made use of.[81] These principles were expressed in a different context by Lord Cranworth in the case of *Rylands v. Fletcher*[82] as follows:

> If a person brings, or accumulates on his land anything which, if it should escape, may cause damage, he is responsible, however careful he may have been, and whatever precautions he may have taken to prevent it.

In *Dubai Aluminium Company Ltd. v Salaam*[83] the court made a tentative and inconclusive effort to expand the boundaries of vicarious liability, but fell short of the *Rylands v Fletcher* standard.

---

[80] For a detailed analysis of of the mandatory nature of corporate finance see Ferran, E. and Ho, L. C. (2014) "*Principles of Corporate Finance Law*" (Second edition), Oxford University Press.

[81] In many instances the end result may be quite similar, but the wilful arbitrariness of the *Bank of New England* case could be avoided.

[82] Rylands v. Fletcher L.R. 3 H.L. (E. & I. App) 330 (1868).

[83] 2003 2 AC 366 (House of Lords).

> ...Liability for agents should not be strictly confined to acts done with the employer's authority... it is a fact of life, and therefore to be expected by those who carry on businesses, that sometimes their agents may exceed the bounds of their authority or even defy express instructions...

Instead of drawing the logical conclusion from this premise, the Court proceeded to limit, – as a practical matter, very nearly destroy – its significance, by requiring that the wrongful conduct "*may fairly and properly be regarded* as done while acting...in the ordinary course of the firm's business or the employee's employment. (Italics in the original)

The functional equivalent of Mr. Fletcher's "anything which...may cause damage" is the inadequately or mistakenly defined role. The corporation, this contrivance with its extraordinary powers should be held responsible for whatever damage it causes regardless of intent and regardless of the foreseeability of the damage. Its moral and legal responsibility should stem not from its intent, – it cannot and in fact does not have the capacity form an intent – nor from its actions, but from having legislated with its rule-making powers a potentially dangerous situation and having failed to take measures that would prevent the resulting damage.[84] Conversely, the "deeming" and mysterious attribution notions of the *Bank of New England* case – deeming and attributing as they do events that, in fact, did not happen – should be abandoned. If the corporation is equipped with powers not available to individuals or groups, it should bear all of the consequences, sweet or sour, that the exercise of those powers may produce. These extraordinary and ultra-human corporate powers may be seen as the social equivalent of the dangerous natural substances for which the rule in *Rylands v. Fletcher* was formulated a century and a half ago.

There are some signs of legal theory developing in the direction proposed here. The Bribery Act of 2010 provides in §7 a new corporate offence, consisting of the failure of a corporation to prevent the payment of bribes by any person, including an independent contractor, performing services on its behalf.[85] There seems to be no reason why the principle contained in this Act could not be applied to all acts performed in the name or on behalf of the corporation that result in damage to an individual, a class of individuals or to the common good.

As Colin Mayer notes "While principles of morality are well developed in relation to individuals, they are not in respect of corporations. Indeed, the idea of a moral corporation would be regarded as an oxymoron."[86] The lack of moral principles for corporate conduct, however, is not an oversight. Corporations are objects and objects do not have moral capacities. The idea of a moral corporation is indeed an oxymoron. It purports to attribute to the corporation the undoubted human moral agency of those who are in its employ precisely because the corporation itself has

---

[84] Under this standard employers would be liable for accidents caused by employee drivers out on 'a frolic of their own', but that liability would not preclude a cause of action by the employer against the employee.

[85] A similar but somewhat ambiguous attempt is set out in the Corporate Manslaughter and Corporate Homicide Act of 2007.

[86] Mayer, C. (2013), "*Firm Commitment*" Oxford University Press, p.8.

no such capacity, but the attribution fails because the actions of the employees of the corporation are not based on their moral capacities, but, rather, on their corporation determined roles. Efforts to endow the corporation with moral agency results in confusion, places its agents in an untenable conflict between their roles and their human moral capacities, and renders all the more difficult the definition of corporate accountability.

References

Alford, H., and M.J. Naughton. 2002. Beyond the Shareholder Model of the Firm: Working Toward the Common Good of Business. In *Rethinking the Purpose of Business*, ed. S.A. Cortright and M.J. Naughton. Notre Dame: University of Notre Dame Press.

Anscombe, G.E.M. 1957. *Intention*. Ithaca: Cornell University Press.

Austin, J.L. 1962. In *How to Do Things with Words*, 2nd ed., ed. J. Urmson and M. Sbisa. Cambridge: Harvard University Press.

Balkan, J. 2004. *The Corporation: The Pathological Pursuit of Profit and Power*. London: Constable and Robinson Ltd..

Berle, A.A., and G.C. Means. 1932. *The Modern Corporation & Private Property*. New York: Harcourt, Brace & World, Inc..

Corton, D. 1995. *When Corporations Rule the World*. San Francisco: Berrett-Koehler with Cambrian Press.

Crane, T. 2013. *The Objects of Thought*. Oxford: Oxford University Press.

Dewey, J. 1926. The Historic Background of Cororate Legal Personality. *Yale Law Journal* XXXV(6): 655.

Donaldson, T. 1982. *Corporations and Morality*. Upper Saddle River: Prentice Hall.

Eschman, T. 1946. Studies on the Notion of Society in St. Thomas and the Decretal of Innocent IV, Romana Ecclesia, Ceterum. *Mediaeval Studies* 8: 1–42.

Everett, A. 2013. *The Nonexistent*. New York: Oxford University Press.

Ferran, E., and L.C. Ho. 2014. *Principles of Corporate Finance Law*. 2nd ed. Oxford: Oxford University Press.

Finnis, J. 1998. *Aquinas*. Oxford: Oxford University Press.

Fisse, B., and J. Braithwaite. 1993. *Corporations, Crime and Accountability*. Cambridge: Cambridge University Press.

Freeman, R., et al. 2010. *Stakeholder Theory: The State of the Art*. Cambridge: Cambridge University Press.

French, P.A. 1979. The Corporation as a Moral Person. *American Philosophical Quarterly* 16(3): 207.

———. 1995. *Corporate Ethics*. Fort Worth: Harcourt, Brace & Co.

Friedman, A., and S. Miles. 2006. *Stakeholder Theory and Practice*. Oxford: Oxford University Press.

Gaudium et spes (1965) Second Vatican Council, Holy See

Goodpaster, K.E. 2007. *Conscience and Corporate Culture*. Malden: Blackwell Publishing.

Hansmann, H., and R.R. Kraakman. 2002. The Essential Role of Organizational Law. *Yale Law Journal* 110: 387.

Hart, H.L.A. 1948. The Ascription of Responsibility and Rights. *The Proceedings of the Aristotelian Society* 49: 171.

———. 1954. Definition and Theory in Jurisprudence. *Law Quarterly Review* 70: 37; reprinted in Hart, H. L. A. (1983) *Essays in Jurisprudence and Philosophy.* Oxford University Press.

Haseltine, H.D., G. Lapsey, and P.H. Winfield, ed. 1936. *Maitland, Selected Essays*. Cambridge: Cambridge University Press.
Herman, B. 1993. *The Practice of Moral Judgment*. Cambridge, MA: Harvard University Press.
———. 2011. On a mismatch of methods. In *On What Matters*, ed. D. Parfait, Vol. 2. Oxford: Oxford University Press.
Hobbes, T. (fist published in 1651) *Leviathan*. Curley, E. (Ed.) (1994) Hackett.
Jackson, F., P. Pettit, and M. Smith. 2004. *Mind, Morality and Explanation: Selected Collaborations*. Oxford: Oxford University Press.
Johnson, P. 2010. *Making the Market*. Cambridge: Cambridge University Press.
Lawson, T. 2015a. The Modern Corporation: The Site of a Mechanism (of Global Change) That Is Out of Control. In *Social Morphogenesis: Generative Mechanisms Transforming Late Modernity*, ed. M. Archer. New York: Springer.
———. 2015b. The Nature of the Firm and Peculiarities of the Corporation. *Cambridge Journal of Economics* 2015(39): 1–32.
Mankiw, N.G. 2011. *Principles of Economics*. 6th ed. Cengage Lerning
Mansell, S.F. 2013. *Capitalism, Corporations and the Social Contract*. Cambridge: Cambridge University Press.
Mayer, C. 2013. *Firm Commitment*. Oxford: Oxford University Press.
McMahon, C. 1995. The Moral Status of Business Organizations. *Business Ethics Quarterly* 5(3): 541–554.
McQueen, R. 2009. *A Social History of Company Law*. Farnham: Ashgate Publishing Limited.
Miller, S. 2001. *Social Action, a Teleological Account*. Cambridge: Cambridge University Press.
Morgan, M.S. 2012. *The World in the Model*. Cambridge: Cambridge University Press.
Murdoch, I. 1971. *The Sovereignty of Good*. London: Routledge.
Pettit, P. 2008. *Made with Words: Hobbes on Language, Mind and Politics*. Princeton: Princeton University Press.
Priest, G. 2005. *Towards Non-being*. Oxford: Oxford University Press.
Putnam, H. 2002. *The Collapse of the Fact/Value Dichotomy and Other Essays*. Cambridge: Harvard University Press.
Putnam, H., and V. Walsh. 2012. *The End of Value-Free Economics*. London: Palgrave.
Ronnegard, D. 2015. *The Fallacy of Corporate Agency*. Dordrecht: Springer.
Rosenberg, A. 1988. *The Philosophy of Social Science*. Boulder: Westview Press.
Rothschild, E. 2001. *Economic Sentiment*. Cambridge: Harvard University Press.
Ryan, M. Bartolus of Sassoferrato and Free Cities. *Transactions of the Royal Historical Society* X: 65.Sixth Series
Sealy, L.S., and S. Worthington. 2013. *Cases and Materials in Company Law*. 10th ed. Oxford: Oxford University Press.
Searle, J.R. 1995. *The Constitution of Social Reality*. New York: Free Press.
Smith, A. 1910. *The Wealth of Nations*. New York: Alfred A. Knopf.
———. 1978. *Lectures on Jurisprudence*. Oxford: Oxford University Press.
Stout, L. 2012. *The Shareholder Value Myth*. San Francisco: Berrett-Koehler Publishers, Inc.
Taylor, J. 2006. *Creating Capitalism*. San Francisco: Berrett-Koehler Publishers, Inc..
The Law of Corporations and Inferior Courts of Record in England. 1702. London, various authors.
Tollefsen, D.P. 2015. *Groups as Agents*. Malden: Polity Press.
Vermeulen, T. 2009. Maximizing Shareholder Value: An Ethical Responsibility? In ed. Smith, C. and Lensen, G. Wiley, which is thoroughly refuted in Mayer, C. (2013) *Firm Commitment,* Oxford University Press.
Wittgenstein, L. 1953. *Philosophical Investigations*. Oxford: Basil Blackwell, Ltd.

Chapter 11
Are Business Ethics Relevant?

David W. Miller and Michael J. Thate

Abstract This paper suggests that "the relevance of business ethics" has often been a question of utility, which considers profits, cultural concerns, and social capital regarding organizational health. There are, however, underlying suspicions regarding the relevance of business ethics. In corporate contexts, "ethics" is often conflated with compliance, and becomes the domain of compliance and risk management. This statement is not to disparage compliance officers or their departments. Rather, the point is that there are limits of assigning "ethics" and the valuation of actions as "ethical" to a place or office within corporate contexts. Such approaches will necessarily be reactive to and driven by law, code, and policy.

Another suspicion concerns the relevance of one's personal ethics within an "ethical field." An ethical field is where diverse ethical agents, with differing ethical contexts and convictions, inhabit space. The effect and influence of one's ethical actions or convictions depends on where one lives within a given ethical field. This field approach to ethics stresses that an agent's ethical actions and convictions are enmeshed within social relations. And, of course, power relations within any given field are always asymmetrical. The paper emphasizes that religious ideas can help shape and inform the ethics of peoples and business cultures. Attentiveness to these dynamis is an impactful way to engage business school students and business people to think afresh about ethics as both character and culture. Thinking about ethics through the lenses of the "Right", the "Good", and the "Fitting" can help guide people through ethical grey zones, informing them toward richer and wiser ethical decisions.

The reach of the financial crisis during the 2007–2008 subprime-mortgage disaster remains difficult to overstate. The domino effect and eventual toll on governments, global and domestic financial systems, social institutions, communities, families, and individuals has proven historic. The catastrophe left many questioning how such a thing could have happened. Who and what ideology were at fault? Or was this some inevitable outcome of late capitalism? Amidst all the finger pointing and

D.W. Miller (✉) • M.J. Thate
Princeton University, Princeton, NJ, USA
e-mail: dwm@princeton.edu

P. Rona, L. Zsolnai (eds.), *Economics as a Moral Science*,
Virtues and Economics 1, DOI 10.1007/978-3-319-53291-2_11

posturing of "moral outrage," an interesting body of literature surfaced questioning the role of Business Schools within the crisis (Lorsch et al. 2016).

Kelley Holland suggested that, "with the economy in disarray and so many financial firms in free fall, analysts, and even educators themselves, are wondering if the way business students are taught may have contributed to the most serious economic crisis in decades." (Holland 2009) This naturally lead to many discussions about the place of ethics within business school and undergraduate curricula. David Garvin and Srikant Datar, in conjunction with the commemoration of the 100th anniversary of Harvard Business School in 2008, for example, convened a number of colloquia and workshops addressing the curricular state of affairs within business schools with respect to ethics. (Datar et al. 2010). Their research addressed not only the growing concerns and criticisms of standard models, but also offered analyses and directions for curriculum development. Numerous other studies have appeared as well, offering varying historical analyses, (Khurana 2010; Giacalone and Wargo 2010; Hopper and Hopper 2007) and suggestions for reform (Moldoveanu and Martin 2008).

Such approaches are interesting and indeed welcomed lines of inquiry. And yet, as Michael Grote, professor of corporate finance at the Frankfurt School of Finance and Management, has quipped, so-called "ethics" within the financial sector are often misconstrued and misunderstood as amounting to little more than instructing students to be "good" boys and girls. Grote argues that such moralizing approaches are not only misleading but also unhelpful. A teaching of what he calls 'self-reflection', he argues is a more sustainable option. (See Palin 2013) This paper is in some respects an extension of Grote's critique and proposal of ethics as self-reflection or, as we shall call it, "awareness." Having spent time both teaching in academic environments and working in corporate contexts, we have come to question not only the utility of such moralizing approaches in courses for university students, but also the relevance of this "thing" we have come to call "business ethics" within corporate culture itself.

11.1 The Relevance of Business Ethics

More than simple assessments of benefit and return, we are pressing two underlying (and stylized) suspicions regarding the relevance of "business ethics." First, in corporate contexts, "ethics" is often conflated with compliance, and becomes the domain of compliance and risk management. Compliance officers, of course, perform important roles assessing whether varying actions meet legal specifications, policies and standards. Since the Federal Sentencing Guidelines for corporations went into effect in 1991, "Chief ethics and compliance officers have become trendy in recent years." But as Hannah Clark wrote in her article for Forbes, "some experts fear they act mainly as window dressing." If, after all, one person and their department are in charge of "ethics," where does that leave everyone else? (Clark 2006) She quotes a partner from the law firm Reed Smith who stated that the position of compliance officer and their office amounts to little more than "a mask for the company to hide behind." (Clark 2006) Regardless if one agrees with these statements or not, the chronology of Clark's essay is itself telling. With the appearance of the Sarbanes-Oxley Act of 2002 in the wake of the corporate scandals of 2001 and 2002, many companies "began tripping over themselves to identify potential ethics problems." (Clark 2006) An ethical bubble emerged. Just 2 years after Clark's essay appeared, however the ethical bubble burst—as it has yet again burst after all the moral outrage of 2008/09 (see VW; Panama Papers, big banks manipulating foreign currencies, etc.). The "ethical impulse" within many corporate contexts appears hopelessly reactionary, legalistic, and compliance-oriented. And, as critics have pointed out, compliance officers have functioned more as legal counsel for what is "allowable" than catalysts for cultural change that embodies ethical behaviors and practices.

The point is not to disparage compliance officers or their departments. *They are necessary but not sufficient.* Rather, the point is to stress the limits of assigning "ethics" and the valuation of actions as "ethical" to a place or office within corporate contexts. Such approaches—which fall into the classical ontological school of ethics—will necessarily be reactive to and driven by law, code, and policy. Without considering other schools of ethics, and wider awareness, "ethics" become, at least functionally, that which is allowable and compliant with standards and regulations. Localizing "ethics" in a specific person or department risks the unintended consequence of relieving others of ethical responsibility. This, of course, is not a call to end "business ethics" as such. Rather, we have come to realize that university courses in business ethics and seminars in corporate contexts must confront the challenges such localizing poses for ethical leadership and corporate culture.

The second suspicion concerns the relevance of one's personal ethics within what we refer to as an "ethical field." Put simply, the ethical field is where diverse ethical agents, with differing ethical contexts and convictions, inhabit space. The effect and influence of one's ethical actions or convictions—or the degree to which one is affected by or influenced by the ethical actions and convictions of others—depend upon where one lives within a given ethical field. This field approach to ethics stresses that an agent's ethical actions and convictions are enmeshed within social relations. And, of course, power relations within any given field are always asymmetrical.

For example, imagine a young intern at one of the major Banking Firms on Wall Street is asked to carry out a directive that is "legal" but goes against her personal ethics. What should the intern do? Of all the options open to her—e.g., she could quit, attempt to confront her boss, ask for more information and attempt to share her own convictions, or she could simply carry out the directive—from the perspective of the directive itself, her ethics are functionally irrelevant. The directive will be carried out with or without her. If she removes herself from the situation, there are hundreds, thousands, of applicants waiting to take her place. If, however, the directive was given from the board to the CEO—again, the directive is "legal" but against the CEO's personal ethics—the situation becomes quite different. Her position within the ethical field is higher up. Her ethical convictions will thus tend to carry with them greater social effect than that of the intern. The case becomes more intriguing if the intern in example one and the CEO in example two are the same person separated by time.

After surveying the broad range of distinct approaches to students, the case we have attempted to make with our students is that if "ethics" within business contexts is going to have any bearing upon corporate culture and individual formation, they cannot be reduced to timeless and universal categories right and wrong. Part of the impetus for the course I have been teaching for 10 years on this complex subject is that small decisions now effect big ones later

11.2 Can Ethics Be Taught?

In business school education, one is often faced with a disconnect between "being successful" and "being ethical." Consider the different ranking criteria of business schools in this respect. Bloomberg Businessweek ranked MBA Schools in America according to ethical emphases in late 2012. (Business Week 2012) In 2014, the U.S. News and World Report released its rankings for the best American business schools with no mention of any particular emphasis—ethical or otherwise. (U.S. News and World Report 2014) One would think that these two rankings would have at least some overlap. There was only one. Dartmouth (Tuck) was the sole school that was placed within the top ten of both rankings. Can we infer from this that the top American MBA programs do not value or accent ethics in their curriculum? Or is it even possible for top American business schools to design and teach curricula that is attentive both to skills development and character formation? Whatever the case may be, the question remains, how to teach business ethics effectively—or if they can be taught at all.

The former dean of Harvard Business School, Thomas R. Piper and his colleagues in his amusingly entitled book, *Can Ethics Be Taught?* (Piper et al. 1993) asks a serious question. Can it? They conclude that a major part the answer has to do with where to situate ethics. Is ethics a specialty field in its own right just like finance, marketing, operations, and organizational behavior, or should it be part of each and every discipline and course within business school? This is a helpful series of questions. But the line of questioning cannot stop there. The better question, and the one we seek to address here, is: How can it possibly be taught?

11.3 The Relevance of Religion

We offer a special attempt to tackle the challenge of teaching business ethics. We do so through a somewhat unusual lens: religion.

So how does one teach business ethics to university students? Should we assign Aristotle, Plato, Kant, Mill, and Bentham? Or, have them read and be tested on the

2010 Dodd-Frank Act legislation and its 22,296 pages of related rule releases? The current number of pages in Dodd-Frank are as long as 34 copies of Moby Dick. Frankly, we believe students will learn more about ethics from studying Captain Ahab, Ishmael, and the rest of the crew—or other classic narratives—than Dodd-Frank.

Or should we cast off classic ethical traditions and thinkers, eschew the futility of finding meaning and clarity in modern legislation, and look elsewhere? Some in the emerging fields of neuroscience and neuropsychology suggest that morality is shaped if not driven by our genetics, neurology, and body chemistry. If correct, this requires fresh understandings of classic questions of human agency and personal responsibility. And it complexifies even further our question: how can ethics possibly be taught?

To add to the pedagogical challenge, where does that leave students who come from a diverse ethical field? Or, as noted above, young employees whose personal ethics and sense of values might be stifled if not squashed working for large corporations, simply due to being on the wrong side of asymmetric power? Or the person of good faith and intent who wants to follow all the legislative and regulatory rules, yet finds them unclear, unhelpful, and sometimes even unfair.

The rest of this paper offers a fresh way to teach business ethics, drawing on several millennia of wisdom found in religious traditions. Moreover, our hope is that this pedagogy will help nurture and sustain the positive ethical instincts that we see in the vast majority of students we have had the pleasure of teaching and companies we have had the privilege of advising.

The methodology is called the "Five Questions of Ethics." Together, as an interwoven series of theoretical and practical questions, the first author of this paper has developed a course called, "Business Ethics and Modern Religious Thought." Playfully, students call it, "How to Succeed without Selling Your Soul." Unlike the legal, regulatory, or moral philosophical approaches noted earlier, this course takes a phenomenological approach drawing on the resources of some of the world's great religious traditions, with particular attention to the three Abrahamic traditions.

The course objective is to learn basic ethical theory and develop practical tools for business ethics, with particular attention to the integrative role of religion and spirituality in ethical formation, frameworks, and decision-making. This is applied to contemporary ethical dilemmas faced in organizational life (both for-profit and non- profit entities), drawing on real-time news and the experience—both positive and negative!—of visiting CEOs who represent various faith traditions.

The underlying assumption of the course is that religious thought, whether conscious or not, is a latent variable that often shapes and informs both personal and social ethics. In class, students are exposed to the resources of various religious traditions, that might help address modern business ethics, dilemmas, and leadership, as well as the possible conflicts and other issues that may arise as a result of religious thought applied to contemporary ethical situations.

Importantly, students are reminded that having a personal religious conviction or spiritual orientation is not required for the course. Having respect for those who do is. The class is not about competing truth claims or proselytizing. Nor is it a comparative religion course. Rather it is about understanding and applying wisdom literature, normative teachings on ethics, and insights into human behavior found in varying religious traditions.

We take a phenomenological approach, studying how others apply religious resources to analysis of contemporary business ethics case studies and topics. Students become aware of the resources of their own religious tradition, as well as the traditions of others. They also develop their own ethical decision-making framework and apply it to: impediments to ethical action; decision-making in the "ethical gray zone"; workplace spirituality and ethics; executive compensation; whistle blowing; cheating; bluffing/lying; office romances; off-shore labor; cross-cultural conceptions of ethics; and social media (e.g. freedom of speech, client/data confidentiality, and risk).

The course is organized around "The Five Questions." They are: (Q1) What is ethics?; (Q2) What is the source of your ethics?; (Q3) What is your ethical decision-making framework?; (Q4) What is your public language for doing ethics?; and (Q5) What will you do to stay ethically fresh?

Question 1: What is ethics?

Ethics is about character and culture, not law and compliance. You can have 1000 employees and hire 1000 compliance officers to look over their shoulder, and still will not guarantee ethical conduct (including that of the compliance officers!). So if ethics is about character and culture, that begs the question what is character, and how can universities, MBA programs, and business organizations help develop character? What are intellectual and cultural resources that help shape and inform an ethical person?

But first, let's define our terms. What do we mean by ethics? Think of ethics as having three parts: recognizing, thinking, and acting. First, we need to recognize when an ethical situation is arising; sometimes that is not easy, particularly if 'everyone else is doing it.' Second, we should not rely too heavily on gut feel. It is not as reliable as we think due to many factors, including varying forms of brain bias and subconscious bias. So we need to find fresh ways to think about and analyze an ethical dilemma from different vantage points—and develop practices which form such forms of attention into habits. Finally, after recognizing and thinking, we need to make a decision and take action!

Here is the one-sentence definition of ethics that integrates The Five Questions: *Ethics is the art and discipline of discerning the Right, the Good, and the Fittingaction to take, and having the creativity and courage to do it.*

Let's explore each phrase a bit more carefully:

- "…the art and discipline…"—Ethics is not a rigid formula or legalistic thing, nor is it relativistic. Ethical thinking is both an art and a discipline that draws on rich intellectual traditions.
- "… of discerning…"—Ethics is not just an intellectual exercise. It involves deep reflection, drawing on all our senses, cognition, and experiences.

- "…the Right, the Good, and the Fitting…"—The great ethical traditions are organized into The Right; the Good; and the Fitting. They represent three rich intellectual streams that underpin how we have thought about ethics over the years, analyze dilemmas, and make decisions. Think of these three ethical traditions or accents as lenses. Each lens offers a helpful perspective, but not always a complete one. We see more clearly when we use all three lenses together.

  The three schools of ethics, or The Three Lenses, are:

- The Right—it asks, "What do the rules say?" This school of ethics accents that certain actions are either right or wrong. The determination of right from wrong is generally based on rules, laws, and codes that have been established by authority figures and various institutions (e.g. legal, governmental, and religious systems). These laws often provide a solid ethical foundation, baseline, and clarity. But they can also be rigid, blind to compassion, or "exceptions to the rule." And sometimes, rules lag behind technological developments, and seem unhelpful if not irrelevant. In short, we need the Right lens. It is necessary, but alone it is not sufficient.
- The Good—it asks, "What is the goal or aim of the action?" This school of ethics accents that there are good and bad actions. Ethical decisions are made according to the goodness of the purpose or goal one is trying to achieve. It seeks to do the greatest good for the greatest number, and to serve the common good. It calculates the tradeoffs between benefits and harms. But who determines what the purpose is? And do the ends justify the means if the means are wrong even to accomplish a noble outcome? Like the Right, it is helpful, but alone is not sufficient for ethical decision-making.
- The Fitting—it asks, "What is the appropriate thing to do?" This school of ethics accents that there are fitting and unfitting, or appropriate and inappropriate actions. It relies on the cultivation of values and virtues, and applies them to particular contexts. These are shaped in light of history, humanity, religion, and the cultures in which we live. It accents wisdom, empathy, and character. But it can be vague, and hard to define, measure, or apply.

Many people have a natural predisposition (often subconscious) toward accenting one of these three ethical lenses, often at the expense of the other two. If we rely primarily on just one lens, we suboptimize our ethical decision-making and risk making impoverished ethical decisions by failing to see other aspects of, unintended consequences of, or better solutions to an ethical dilemma.

When used together like a Venn diagram or the lenses of an optometrist's phoropter, the Right, the Good, and the Fitting give us better ethical vision and clarity.

Question 2: What is the source of one's ethics?

To be sure, there are many sources of one's ethics: parents, other family members, teachers, coaches, clergy figures, friends, culture and wider society. But what is the source of society's ethics? In some cases, the sources of social values and normative ethical thought come from metaphysical ideas and religious influences.

To be sure, these can have healthy or unhealthy manifestations, making it all the more important to understand them.

Whether a leader is religiously inclined or not, given that an estimated 90% of the world's population does claim some form of religious identity, it would seem to make intellectual and practical sense to consider how various belief systems shape and inform people's ethics. The class does just that, giving students intellectual permission to explore—in respectful and non-doctrinal ways—how one's world-view (whether Amish or Atheist) might be a constructive ethical resource for modern business dilemmas.

Awareness of the source(s) of one's ethics matters both to individuals and organizations. For many, it helps sustain them in difficult ethical situations. For others it gives a North Star to guide them through ambiguous ethical territory. And finally, one's faith tradition often provides an ethical anchor to ground them amid a sea of ethical relativism and marketplace pressures.

Question 3: What is your framework for decision-making?

Some ethical decisions are black and white and the proper course of action is straightforward (presuming one has the courage to act on it). However, often we find ourselves in the ethical gray zone, where even the most experienced, smart, and values-driven people are unsure what to do. Developing a social decision-making tool that incorporates insights from the Right, the Good, and the Fitting can prove helpful in such situations. The model that the first author of this paper has developed, teaches, and uses in ethics consulting work is called "The Three Lenses Ethical Decision-Making Framework." This provides the discipline to slow us down and ask questions that take us out of our preferred ethical school or lens, thus enriching the analysis, process, and eventual decision, as well as helping to avoid the proverbial problem of unexpected and unintended negative consequences.

So, how does The Three Lenses Decision-Making Framework operative in practice? A scenario was developed with the students to say they are a fresh graduate and working for a top-tier consulting company. They have been hired to advise a prominent bank on whether to it is ethical or not to enter the "same day payday loans" business. The payday loans niche serves mostly poor workers who cannot get a regular loan from a bank due to bad credit risk and low income. Payday lenders give them small loans—sometimes less than $500—to repair their car, cover a medical bill, or help pay their rent. Their next paycheck serves as partial collateral. Yet the fees for missed payments and annual percentage interest rates can be exorbitant, catapulting some into a never-ending cycle of debt.

So using the Three Lenses, we first look at the dilemma and ask questions through the "Right" lens. And we might conclude that—done correctly—the product is completely legal and breaks no rules. So do we conclude, therefore, "Yes, it's ethical"? Not so fast! Just because something is legal does not mean it is ethical. We then ask questions looking at it through the "Good" lens. Here we might reasonably identify benefits for both the customer and for the bank. The customer is loaned desperately-needed cash they otherwise would not receive from a regular bank, and the lender makes a profit. But we could also begin to see potential costs or harms to our customers who fall victim to scandalous interest rates, or who might use the service irresponsibly and fall into an irrevocable cycle of debt. Here is where the "Fitting" lens comes in. Asking questions through the "Fitting" lens might lead us to conclude that although it is legal, and maybe the potential goods outweigh the potential harms, it remains "unethical". Is it fitting or inappropriate to take advantage of the poor by charging usurious fees and interest rates, knowing that many will be in worse shape? Is it consistent with our values and something we are proud to be associated with? Is it virtuous? Is there unacceptable reputational risk to the bank associated with payday lending, even though it is legal and may offer a useful service to some?

Each of these three ethical lenses offers their own focus and perspective. Our ethical vision improves when we use all three lenses. Together, these three lenses help us see wider perspectives and get us out of the limited thinking that equates legal with ethical. It also protects us from our ethical blind spots, brain biases, and other forms of subconscious ethical errors.

Question 4: What is your public language for ethics?

After analyzing an ethical dilemma and coming to a course of action, how do you explain it to and persuade your colleagues or boss, in situations of peer pressure, cultural and religious differences, and diverse ethical fields? It becomes particularly critical to have an effective public language if one's ethical source (Q2) differs from others in the room or geography where one is conducting business. In class we practice not just ethical reasoning (using one's Q3 decision-making framework) but also practice employing public language to articulate one's views in a way that others can hear. For instance, if one's source of ethics is one's religious tradition, using that source, be it the Bible or the Qur'an for instance, might not be deemed authoritative and could be counterproductive, if not offensive to someone from a different tradition or culture.

Q5: How do you stay ethically fresh?

This question is not meant to be sassy or sanctimonious, but to keep us alert, aware, and attentive to our own blind spots or other action traps that might prevent us from doing the ethical thing, or worse, cause us to do an unethical act. In my experience, most people who are punished, fired, or even prosecuted for ethical missteps are good people who slipped up. Many books and articles have been written around the question, "why do good people do unethical things?" In our class on "How to Succeed without Selling Your Soul" we explore what faith resources might serve as tips, techniques, and tools to help us stay ethically fresh. For instance, one CEO has a ritual upon entering his office of turning on an old fashioned brass lamp on his desk. It reminds him of various passages in the Bible where light is a symbol of truth, God's guidance, and justice. Or another CEO who keeps a photo of his grandfather, an illiterate sharecropper, as reminder of grace, dignity, and humility.

Consciously or subconsciously, religious ideas are an important variable that helps shape and inform the ethics of peoples and business cultures. Attentiveness to that is an impactful way, coupled with The Five Questions, to engage students and business people to think afresh about ethics as character and culture. And thinking about ethics through The Three Lenses Decision-Making Framework of the Right, the Good, and the Fitting will help guide us through ethical gray zones, informing us toward richer and wiser ethical decisions. In short, "religious traditions" can be resources for cultivating ethical awareness.

11.4 Conclusion

We have only begun to scratch the surface of important ways to teach business ethics in an age when many find ethics irrelevant or so hopelessly bound by structures and legalism as to be meaningless. Cultural contexts, profit pressures, and differing ethical fields cause numerous challenges. And while religiously motivated geopolitics and violence perpetrated in the name of religion are indeed concerning, we argue that within religious traditions lie millennia of wisdom and guidance for ethical conduct in the field of business, commerce, personal conduct, and interpersonal dealings. Finding appropriate and fresh ways to tap into such resources will not only enrich ethical processes and outcomes as we have argued—they will also enliven our awareness of and respect for religious and cultural differences that often shape and inform our ethical norms and behaviors in today's globalized market and workplace.

Many religions believe that virtuous behavior can be cultivated by studying holy traditions and texts and by emulating those who embody and practice great virtues and wisdom. Indeed, just as elite athletes always seek new techniques or moves, impresario musicians never stop practicing the scales, and world-class companies focus on continuous improvement, so too can we practice and enhance our ethical fitness by an increased disposition toward ethical awareness. Fresh attention to the ethical resources imbedded in various religious traditions might well prove a dynamic tool within our ethical toolkit necessary for our increasingly complex world.

References

Business Week. 2012. http://www.businessweek.com/articles/2012-12-17/mba-rankings-top-schools-for-ethics. Accessed 30 May 2016.

Clark, H. 2006, October 23. Chief Ethics Officers: Who Needs Them? *Fortune*. http://www.forbes.com/2006/10/23/leadership-ethics-hp-lead-govern-cx_hc_1023ethics.html. Accessed 2 June 2016.

Datar, S.M., D.A. Garvin, and P.G. Cullen. 2010. *Rethinking the MBA: Business Education at a Crossroads*. Cambridge, MA: Harvard Business Review Press.

Giacalone, R.A., and D.T. Wargo. 2010. The Roots of the Global Finance Crisis Are in Our Business Schools. *Journal of Business Education* 6: 1–24.

Holland, K. 2009. *Is It Time to Retrain B-Schools?* http://www.nytimes.com/2009/03/15/business/15school.html. Accessed 7 June 2016.

Hopper, K., and W. Hopper. 2007. *The Puritan Gift: Reclaiming the American Dream Amidst Global Financial Chaos*. New York: I.B. Tauris & Co Ltd..

Khurana, R. 2010. *From Higher Aims to Hired Hands: The Social Transformation of American Business Schools and the Unfulfilled Promise of Management as a Profession*. Princeton: Princeton University Press.

Lorsch, J., R. Khurana, and A.W. Lo. 2016. http://www.businessweek.com/debateroom/archives/2008/11/us_financial_cr.html. Accessed 30 May 2016.

Moldoveanu, M.C., and R.L. Martin. 2008. *The Future of the MBA: Designing the Thinker of the Future*. Oxford: Oxford University Press.

Palin, A. 2013. *Financial Crisis Forced Business Schools to Change Curriculum*. http://www.ft.com/intl/cms/s/2/80cba3fc-d9c3-11e2-98fa-00144feab7de.html#axzz39eqWKCt4. Accessed 30 May 2016.

Piper, T.R., M.C. Gentile, and S. Daloz Parks. 1993. *Can Ethics Be Taught? Perspectives, Challenges, and Approaches at the Harvard Business School*. Cambridge, MA: Harvard Business Review Press.

US News and World Report. 2014. http://grad-schools.usnews.rankingsandreviews.com/best-graduate-schools/top-business-schools/mba-rankings. Accessed 30 May 2016.

Chapter 12
Economy of Mutuality

Kevin T. Jackson

Abstract The paper develops a triad of business archetypes. In each archetype, alternative emphasis goes to elements of profitability and financial independence on the one hand, and poverty alleviation and solidarity on the other. Archetype 1: Business enterprises conducted primarily as for-profit institutions to the end of financial sustainability. Financial self-reliance is a precondition of a firm's survival and for remaining capable of continuously expanding products or services to new clientele. Archetype 2: The social and financial missions of business enterprises are merged; a coordination of social and financial functions is at the heart of the "promise" of the company as a sustainable enterprise. Archetype 3: Businesses are run with principal allegiance to social missions – outreach to the poor, environmental rectitude, and other facets of sustainability.

The paper argues that the trio of archetypes also serves as alternative teleological exemplars of the purpose and nature of business. Archetype 1 presupposes the essence of business as profit maximization. Under Archetype 2, business is a means for creating varieties of value for a broad range of stakeholders. For Archetype 3, the purpose of business is serving the common good, with profits secondary and derivative.

Economy of mutuality is presented as a philosophical theory concerning what business is for and the values it presupposes and creates. The theory of economy of mutuality offers a broadened perspective on business, encompassing not just market economy, but also social enterprise and social economy. Economy of mutuality derives from an analysis of alternative prototypes of business enterprise considered in light of higher ends of economic life. The theory maintains that the highest end-state of business, encompassing all such prototypes, is one characterized by reciprocity and integral human development. Seen in comparison to market economy *per se*, economy of mutuality is a more comprehensive conceptual framework for financial and social sustainability.

K.T. Jackson (✉)
Solvay Brussels School of Economics and Management, Université libre de Bruxelles (ULB), Brussels, Belgium
e-mail: Kevin.Jackson@ulb.ac.be

P. Rona, L. Zsolnai (eds.), *Economics as a Moral Science*,
Virtues and Economics 1, DOI 10.1007/978-3-319-53291-2_12

12.1 Introduction

The market economy frame of reference is an orthodoxy, driving mainstream corporate strategy, and setting the stage for how business activity is understood and valued by executives, managers, and numerous other stakeholders in private and public institutions alike. The social economy frame of reference, on the other hand, recognizes economic sectors based upon charities and collective not-for-profit initiatives.

More and more, business managers are cultivating new skillsets together with a deepened understanding of social needs and an enhanced appreciation of the ultimate nature and purpose of business and the real foundations of economic value. As well, firms are being challenged to cultivate new ways of collaborating across the profit-nonprofit divide as traditional boundaries become blurred by new forms of enterprise exemplifying features from both market economy and social economy (Dees 1998; Boyd et al. 2009; Billis 2010). Behind this hybridization of business enterprises is a blending of "commercial exchange logic," characteristic of the for-profit sector, with "gift logic" typified by the nonprofit sector. Whereas the logic of commercial exchange is conventionally driven by principles of profit maximization, mutual gains, and the pursuit of financial sustainability, the logic of gift is conventionally driven by principles of charity, solidarity, and the pursuit of social sustainability. Accordingly, this chapter aims to outline the theory of *economy of mutuality*[1] – a conceptual blueprint for business management oriented to merging financial and social sustainability.

This chapter's discussion will unfold in the following sequence. First the basic idea of economy of mutuality is presented. Second, enterprises are arrayed according to general categories of for-profit (market economy), social enterprise (hybrid economy), and nonprofit (social economy). Readers may refer to Fig. 12.1 for a summary of this arrangement. Then, three distinct ends of business are identified: (1) proximate end; (2) higher pro-social end; (3) the highest end-state. Fourth, an ends-oriented analysis of alternative prototypes is given. The proximate end, considered in the context of a prototype-specific inquiry, reveals the respective aims of separate genres of business enterprises: for-profit enterprises, social enterprises, and non-profit enterprises. The pro-social end aims higher, considering the nature and purpose of business not just from an economic standpoint but from a social point of view. At this level principles of mutual benefit, shared value and gratuitousness are identified as embedded across prototypes in varying degrees. Lastly, the question of what the highest end-state of business is, or ought to be, is explored through a discussion of five key conceptual elements: social solidarity and interdependence,

[1] Economy of mutuality is not to be equated with the idea of "economics of mutuality" (Kay 1991). The theory of economy of mutuality was first conceived in a paper the author presented for the workshop "Teleology and Reason in Economic and Social Affairs," at Blackfriars Hall, University of Oxford in 2014. Some portions of the theory are developed more extensively in "Economy of Mutuality: Merging Financial and Social Sustainability," 133(3) *Journal of Business Ethics*, 499–517 (2016).

EoM: Analysis and Design of Business Enterprises							
Social Economy				Market Economy			
Charities/Non-Profit Enterprises	Hybridized Social Enterprises						For-Profit Enterprises (traditional)
Pure not-for-profit goal	Non-profit with trading / business activity as part of delivery model	Organization working toward financial sustainability (some grants)	Breakeven—all revenues from trading activities	Profits made, but not distributed back into mission	Profits made and (some) distributed to investors; profits likely to be lower due to social mission	Commercial, competitive, and profit maximizing; social value proposition built into business model	Profit-making goal for end of financial sustainability
Full Subsidy	Partial Subsidy		Trade-Offs			Profit-Maximizing	

Fig. 12.1 Analysis and design of business enterprises

cultural capital, *homo reciprocans*, common good, and virtue. The analysis supports the postulate of economy of mutuality (summarized in Fig. 12.2) that the ultimate end-state of business is the promotion of reciprocity and integral human development.

12.2 Economy of Mutuality

Economy of mutuality (EoM) contemplates a new understanding of business enterprise, challenging the assumption that the chief purpose of business is to maximize profit (Duska 1997; Handy 2002, p. 51).

Although it acknowledges the significance of profit as a success indicator, EoM posits that from the standpoint of global sustainability, the pursuit of profit is at the service of a higher purpose.

Broadly speaking, EoM fits within streams of research comprehending economic life as multilayered and occurring in various structures – social, legal, political, cultural – that together form a more complex whole (Polanyi 1944/2001; Hirst 1994; Nee and Swedberg 2005; Buğra and Arğatan 2007; Heinberg 2011). Economy of mutuality draws upon virtue ethics, linking it to classical and neoclassical economic writings, and extending it to contemporary trends in global business (such as microfinance and social enterprises) springing from a sustainability paradigm (Daly and Cobb1990; Wals 2007) and seeking to meld financial and social imperatives of business (Paine 2003). Economy of mutuality sees businesses as key contributors to integral human development, mutuality, and reciprocity.

Market transactions are based on an exchange of equivalents, whether in the form of barter or money. Yet business is not reducible to a system of market exchanges, but flourishes in a wider social context. So EoM gives us some breathing space within and alongside the market. Economic activity is conducted by participants freely choosing to act from motivations other than pure profit-taking, while still creating economic value in the process.

Markets have the important task of letting people use contracts in regulating their relations as they exchange goods and services of equivalent value between them. This is clearly a vital step towards satisfying many needs and desires of market participants. But markets as such are too often disengaged from society. Market-based decisions are not motivated or constrained directly by social custom and legal strictures, not to say ethical norms, and even less, virtue and the common good.

Therefore, EoM sets out some basics for a new way of understanding business: it restates the higher purpose of enterprise, while reflecting upon how business contributes to (or takes away from) the common good of the society in which it is engaged.

Some will challenge the need for this approach on the ground that a stakeholder approach (Phillips 1997; Freeman et al. 2010) already brings about the right balance between business and society. But stakeholder thinking is flawed in accepting at face value the interests and claims of various stakeholder groups independently – in isolation from one another – without considering their deeper connections as part of the larger human community. Unless stakeholder theory is situated in a comprehensive view of humanity, it runs the risk of neglecting to regard each stakeholder as a person that has, not simply external material and instinctive dimensions, but interior and spiritual dimensions as well. (Goodpaster 2011: 13).

12.3 What Is the End State of Business?

Following the spirit of Aristotle's inquiry (Aristotle 1941) about the purpose of human existence, one may in turn query: What is the end-state of business activity? (Abela 2001; Solomon 2004). Is there some characteristic end or purpose or *raison d'être* of conducting business? Otherwise put: what, in general, does business do that is the most valuable?

First one ought to be clear about what one understands "business" to be. To gain clarity, we can look at basic prototypes of business along with proximate ends associated with them. Drilling down further to detect what their respective higher ends are, we will continue to heed the conventional categories established by the prototypes (i.e. for-profit vs. non-profit; financial value vs. social value). But later, in directing our attention toward discernment of the ultimate end, or *telos*, we will, by assuming a holistic standpoint, see a blurring of conventional categorizations to a degree.

12.3.1 Prototypes of Business

Let us consider a trio of business prototypes. In each prototype alternative emphasis is placed upon the elements of profitability and financial independence (market economy) on the one hand, and poverty alleviation and solidarity (social economy) on the other. Here is a quick run-down of each of the three prototypes.

Prototype-A A business is run first and foremost as a for-profit institution with an eye to remaining financially sustainable for the long term. Financial self-reliance is necessary for a firm's survival and it to be capable of continuously expanding its products or services to new clientele. Regardless of how important as a company's social mission may be, it takes a back seat to profit-making capabilities, to make sure the firm serves the interests of its shareholders.

Prototype-B There is a merging of social and financial missions of business enterprises such that a coordination of social and financial functions becomes the core of the company as a sustainable enterprise. Whereas the business firm has a fundamentally economic character, reasonable efficiency in its management is expected: covering operational costs and realizing some form of added value, surplus or profit. On the other hand the emergent sustainability paradigm for business presupposes that companies are expected to uphold and even champion social policies. Nevertheless, while the pursuit sustainability poses challenges for businesses, there is no necessary or incompatibility between the joint pursuit of social and financial objectives.

Prototype-C In this category, businesses are run with principal allegiance to social missions – outreach to the poor, environmental production and promoting other facets of sustainability. The moral justification for business mandates commitment to doing good. Profit is necessary and explicitly intended as a condition to keep doing good. The social outreach objective ought not to be imperiled by corruptive tendencies that sometimes attend market-driven business activities (mission drift, exorbitant interest rates, and group lending abuses with microfinance institutions exploiting indigent people to increase profitability).[2]

The above prototypes embody alternative generic strategic directions for individual business enterprises. Prototype-A exemplifies the strategic orientation of a traditional profit-maximizing corporation such as GE or IBM in the 1970's. Prototype-B, by contrast, expresses the strategic direction of a sustainability ori-

[2] *Mission drift.* Commercially-oriented microfinance institutions (MFIs) are sometimes identified as drifting away from an original mission of serving low-income clients, instead serving better-off clients to improve the financial bottom line (Armendariz and Szafarz 2011). An ethical issue arises insofar as such MFIs are found to be using poor clients mainly as a means to attaining profitability (Sandberg 2012). *Excessively high interest rates.* Interest rates charged by some MFIs can range between 20 and 70% per annum, making them higher than rates commanded by commercial banks (Rosenberg et al. 2009; Sandberg 2012). *Group lending abuses.* Violent collection practices and oppressive forms of group pressure are sometimes used by MFIs for obtaining repayment of group loans (Montgomery 1996; Ghate 2007).

ented firm such as Google.org or Timberland. Prototype-C captures the strategic direction of enterprises such as Grameen Bank and *Focolare*-inspired organizations.

Prototype-A is sometimes held up as the model or ideal for the nature and purpose of business as such. However, today even some profit-maximizing multinational firms are seeking to demonstrate that they can spread value and profits more broadly across their stakeholders and supply chain. An illustration is provided by the food and beverage company Mars. By pairing up with Mars, academics at Said Business School of the University of Oxford are exploring ways that a for-profit business can in effect be a mutual organization, yet without directly sharing ownership (Fearn 2014).

But what is important to grasp is that holding up only one of these prototypes – the for-profit model – as an embodiment of the exclusive or dominant end-point of business is a conceptual error. The mistake consists of falsely attributing goals or ends of specific kinds of business enterprises to the goal or end of business life in general. It is more perspicacious to launch one's inquiry with the full spectrum of business enterprises at one's disposal – across for-profit, social enterprise, and nonprofit varieties – and then inquire as to how best to account for their shared nature and purpose. It is beneficial for us to question and debate what business really is, and ought to be, about. Proceeding from such a broadened outlook, EoM is posited as a moral-economic conception of preconditions of sustainable and inclusive business.

12.4 End-Point Examination of Business Archetypes

Economy of Mutuality makes a distinction between the proximate end, higher end, and ultimate end-state of a business enterprise. By proximate end is meant an immediate purpose of conducting business, as understood within the particular prototype at hand. Here, identifying the immediate purpose of business helps to characterize the prototype, and is taken in a more specific and concrete sense than the purpose revealed in the higher end. But this higher end remains subordinate to yet another end, which is the absolute last end, one "for the sake of which all other things are desired, and which is not itself desired for the sake of anything else" (Aquinas 1273/1972, 1–2, q. 2, a. 8, c).

In terms of how the trio of prototypes has already been specified, it is seen that the proximate end of prototype-A is profitmaking with an eye toward financial sustainability. The proximate end of prototype-B is hybrid development pursued through a melding of financial and social objectives. The proximate end of prototype-C is alleviation of poverty through social outreach. As will be seen, one can discern for each prototype a higher end.

12.4.1 For-Profit Companies

Concerning for-profit, market-based enterprise, reflective economists provide a range of interpretations. For example, Friedman (1962, p. 13) alleges that "the technique of the market place" is "voluntary cooperation of individuals." Similarly, Buchanan and Tullock (1962, p. 103) aver that "[t]he raison d'être of market exchange is the expectation of mutual gains." What can be discerned in these accounts, along with those of countless other economists, is the notion that markets and enterprises operating within them have some general point or purpose – and that is the end of mutual benefit from commercial exchange.

For sure, other economists have stressed how the market creates wealth by exploiting comparative advantage (Ricardo 1817), the division of knowledge (Hayek 1948), and increasing returns to scale (Marshall 1920). Yet all such wealth-producing mechanisms function through mutual benefits arising from activities of trade.

A critic might say that the higher end of market-based, for-profit enterprise is attaining economic freedom. After all, the wedding of market economy to freedom is a recurrent thematic in economics literature. Among its well-known advocates are Mill (1852), Hayek (1948), and Friedman (1962). But this criticism is misleading. It mistakenly takes economic freedom as the liberty of everyone to get at all of what they want, period. But economic freedom, as Luigino Bruni and others have argued, is better understood as the freedom to use one's own possessions and talents as one sees fit, remaining free to trade – under conditions of reciprocity – with those willing to trade in return.

The common core of these understandings is captured by the logic of commercial exchange. For-profit business in a market economy is aimed at the efficient facilitation of mutually beneficial voluntary transactions. Market economy commercial transactions are seen as valuable because individuals want to make them. Business transactions satisfy individuals' preferences not only because such transaction are wealth-creating, but also because the opportunity to make commercial transactions is a form of freedom. So beyond the proximate end of profitability for financial sustainability, we see the higher end of archetype-A enterprise to be the principle of mutual benefit.

An illustration of how an archetype-A business might go about incorporating the concept of mutuality concretely, even without having a formal mutuality configuration, is provided by Mars. In the process of tracing the origins of its supply chain back to 150,000 impoverished cocoa farmers, Mars determined that it had a responsibility to share the fruits of its worldwide financial success with all those involved in its business. Accordingly, the company invested in new technology for cocoa growers that transfigured their way of life. The average cocoa yield tripled, along with associated average incomes. Consequently Mars gained access to more cocoa. Mars launched another mutuality project in Kenya, investigating how people from the poorest communities in Nairobi might be included in the company's distribution and supply chain. A key objective is for Kenyans to access employment and gain entrepreneurial skills. Kenyan youth, it is projected, will benefit as they are able to make income as a local distributor. Mars will benefit, in turn, because their products are marketed and distributed to new communities. (Fearn 2014).

12.4.2 *Hybridized Enterprises*

While hybrids ordinarily work within a market economy by operating a business, their ends are not exclusively financial. Their principal duty extends beyond advancing shareholder interests. Their end is both to succeed (financial sustainability) and to do good for the community (social sustainability). Accordingly, the hybrid enterprise represents a helpful structure with which to meet the needs of business organizations with wider pro-social purposes (Sertial 2012: 271.)

Although the exact structure varies among firms, the hybrid prototype ordinarily links the goals of a for-profit corporation and a nonprofit charity. One illustration of a well-known social enterprise is Google.org, a for-profit company also dedicated to social benefit. Google.com funded Google.org with a grant of three million shares, pledging to contribute one percent of its annual profits to Google.org. A notable feature of Google.org is that, in addition to funding grants to support social causes, it makes for-profit investments, encouraging employees to participate directly in furthering changes in company policy. While elements of Google.org's structure may vary from those of other hybrids, it stands as a noteworthy example of a for-profit enterprise that assumes an explicit pro-social posture.

Further inquiry into the higher end of prototype-B enterprises may be undertaken by reference to emerging models such as Mohammad Yunus' social enterprise (Yunus 2007, 2011) and Michael Porter and Mark Kramer's shared value (Porter and Kramer 2011).

12.4.3 *Social Businesses*

According to Yunus, a social business is "a non-loss, nondividend enterprise, created with the intention to do good to people, to bring positive changes to the world, without any short-term expectation of making money out of it" (Yunus 2007, pp. 265–266). The social enterprise is a hybrid in the sense that it grows and develops as a commercial enterprise. While not intended to make profits for investors, it needs to generate enough income to cover its expenses, which includes providing adequate compensation for managers and employees. Yunus provides a description of the higher end of the social business:

> In its organizational structure, this new business is basically the same as the existing PMB [profit-maximizing business]. But it differs in its objectives. Like other businesses, it employs workers, creates goods or services, and provides these to customers for a price consistent with its objective. But its underlying objective – and the criterion by which it

should be evaluated – is to create social benefits for those whose lives it touches (Yunus 2007: 21–22).

Profits, understood as a surplus of revenues over expenses, are anticipated, yet not returned to investors in the form of dividends. As Yunus puts it:

> The company itself may earn a profit, but the investors who support it do not take any profits out of the company, except recouping an amount equivalent to their original investment, over a period of time. A social business is a company that is cause-driven rather than profit-driven, with the potential to act as a change agent for the world (Yunus 2007: 22).

Yunus advocates a "total delinking from the old framework" of profit-maximization (Yunus 2011: 16). What Yunus offers potential investors, who recoup funds invested while relinquishing a return on investment, is the chance to partake in the logic of gift.

Here the principle of gratuitousness is at work: personal acts of donation creating relationships in which further exchanges of various sorts become possible (Faldetta 2011). Besides the Grameen Bank, Yunus and his associates have diversified into other social enterprises, partnering with companies like Groupe Danone, to market a yogurt product that aims to ameliorate nutritional deficiencies of poor children at an affordable price.

Yunus (2011: 33–56) used the Grameen Bank's expertise in social networking among rural poor to develop Grameen-Danone, an independent social business. Operating with a social enterprise archetype, Yunus shows how it is possible to go beyond conventional thinking about philanthropy and corporate social responsibility (CSR). Groupe Danone is not a donor, and Grameen-Danone is not merely a CSR feature of the Groupe. The new company is independent and autonomous, yet with substantial investment and expertise put up by Groupe Danone. The partnership materialized thanks in large part to Yunus' ability to persuade Group Danone's management that they could not participate in solving social problems effectively within the framework of a traditional profit-maximizing enterprise.

Yunus believes that people who might be donors to various charities or supporters of CSR policies are drawn to investing in social businesses, provided they are well designed and managed to produce and distribute social benefits more efficiently than conventional alternatives.

12.4.4 Shared Value Creation

Porter and Kramer urge bringing business and social good together to create shared value. Stressing that business, operating within the traditional capitalist paradigm, has forfeited social legitimacy, they propose reorienting capitalism to be aimed not exclusively toward corporate profits with tacked-on CSR, but instead at shared value between corporations and community. Currently business is mired in an outmoded approach that thinks of

> value creation narrowly, optimizing short-term financial performance in a bubble while missing the most important customer needs and ignoring the broader influences that determine their longer-term success. How else could companies overlook the well-being of their customers, the depletion of natural resources vital to their businesses, the viability of key suppliers, or the economic distress of the communities in which they produce and sell? (Porter and Kramer 2011: 4).

The conclusion is that a radical alteration of perspective is needed to restore business legitimacy. Under the old model, business distinguished between profit and social responsibility. Shared value, by comparison, is about "creating economic value in a way that also creates value for society by addressing its needs and challenges" (Porter and Kramer 2011: 64). The authors assert that, unlike corporate philanthropic efforts, this alternative approach "is not on the margin of what companies do, but at the center" (Porter and Kramer 2011: 64). Porter and Kramer state that, in contrast to CSR, shared value mandates that all of an enterprise's budget be dedicated to shared value. For it is within shared value that business converges with social needs. Since it brings about a positive impact on a community, shared value turns out to be good for the company as well.

Certainly significant changes need to come about to pave the way for shared value. Company leaders need to be capable of identifying social needs, and be equipped to work collaboratively with members of society toward ends within the scope of their shared interest. Enterprises with a commitment to shared value need to channel efforts at building economic value by creating social value. Some areas where shared value might be created include: healthcare, adequate housing, better nutrition, assistance for aging populations, enhanced financial security, and environmental preservation (Porter and Kramer 2011: 67).

Insofar as enterprises embarked upon creating shared value need to pinpoint social needs, benefits and harms relevant to their respective products, Porter and Kramer advocate creating clusters, "geographic concentrations of firms, related businesses, suppliers, services, providers and logistical infrastructure in a particular field" (Porter and Kramer 2011: 72). Cluster building improves company productivity, competitiveness, and innovation while enhancing the local community (Porter and Kramer 2011: 72).

Summing up, in light of the predominance of hybrid economic logic in social businesses, the higher end of prototype-B enterprise may be specified in terms of both the principle of shared value and the principle of gratuitousness.

12.4.5 Nonprofits

Let us turn to identifying the higher end of prototype-C enterprise, the nonprofit charity. It may be noted that as far back as the fifteenth century, the Franciscans provided philanthropic impetus in the form of the *Monte di Pietà*, a precursor of the modern bank, which grew up not seeking profit, but bringing reform to usurious lending practices and providing charity to the impoverished (Menning 1993: 37).

The public office extended moderate-rate loans to needy people. An underlying rationale was to benefit borrowers instead of providing profits for lenders, representing a lesser evil attached to traditional money lending. The *Monte di Pietà* was dependent upon funds collected from voluntary donations by the financially privileged having no intent to recoup their monetary contributions. Those in need came to the *Monte di Pietà*, contributing some item of value in exchange for the financial loan. The term of the loan extended for one year, representing approximately two-thirds of the borrower's item value. A pre-set interest rate applied to the loan. Any profits realized were applied to offset operating expenses.

As well, the nineteenth century provided for a merging of economic and humanitarian objectives as the bulk of European welfare establishments and hospitals emerged out of spiritual associations.

More recently, the Economy of Communion (EoC) project merits discussion as an enterprise launched in the spirit of this tradition of outreach to the poor. In addition to uniting people to advance social good and fostering a "culture of giving," the Economy of Communion (EoC) project has a peculiar approach to distributing profits (Uelmen and Bruni 2006: 647–648).

Profits from an EoC enterprise are divided into three parts, within the discretion of the business. The first portion goes to the materially poor, often directly linked to *Focolare* networks. The second portion is kept in the firm for reinvestment. The third portion is used to sustain elements of infrastructure that promote and preserve a "culture of giving," which includes programs for education and formation to help people live according to its values. After the owner determines how much to reinvest in the company, the remainder of the profits can be equally divided between assisting those in need, and shaping activities for a culture of giving. To make sure that the needs of the materially poor in *Focolare* communities are met, profits from EoC enterprises have been supplemented by individual donations from *Focolare* members. This division of profits can be viewed as a useful archetype for businesses with a charitable purpose.

Notably, participation in the EoC and sharing profits is voluntary among shareholders and business owners. Neither group is legally bound to give a portion of their profits to the EoC. Instead, a decision to share profits comes from people internal to the business itself. This structure provides the for-profit with the freedom to participate in the EoC to whatever extent it wishes, without needing to conform to rigid guidelines. While this freedom provides for widespread ownership, extending an opportunity to join to many people, it could have a negative impact on shareholders by generating smaller dividends. Consequently, a majority of the shareholders must agree with the ideals of the *Focolare* and be willing to forgo these returns. Potentially this could mean that EoC and other hybrid enterprises following the model would experience difficulty operating as a publicly traded company, or operating in situations where management is separate from ownership. On the other hand, the growth of ethical investment funds within the stock market could provide a means of raising business capital in an EoC model. Alternatively, EoC enterprises could advocate for shareholders to relinquish dividends altogether, donating them to the EoC (Gold 2010: 40).

The EoC departs from standard businesses in several respects. First, pay structure is organized differently in the EoC model. Under the EoC, employers increase wages to reward employees for extra effort extended for the company, and to maximize efficiency of the enterprise. Second, the EoC involves special policies for recruitment. EoC companies, for instance, have as one goal the hiring of more employees and giving employees making mistakes a second chance. The EoC business reintegrates those facing difficulties into the work environment, yet balances this principle with maximizing efficiency maximization. Third, EoC companies use participative management, encouraging workers to participate in decision-making within the business. This might entail organizing councils, meetings, and other formal structures to stimulate communication between different levels of authority. Lastly, EoC enterprises are proactive in cultivating a spirit of solidarity within the enterprise, such as hosting events to increase social interaction among employees including their children as well (Gold 2010: 40).

In consideration of the major driving force of the logic of gift at play in charitable enterprise, the higher end of prototype-C may be specified as the principle of gratuitousness.

To summarize, although on its face prototype-A is often taken to presuppose that business is all about maximizing profits for shareholders, we see that its higher end, in light of the logic of commercial exchange, is the principle of mutual benefit. Under prototype-B, the higher end, in light of a hybrid economic logic, is the principle of creating shared value for a broader range of stakeholders, complemented by the principle of gratuitousness. For prototype-C, the higher end relates to the logic of gift, taking business to be a moral calling whereby the main objective is doing good. Here the higher end is identified as the principle of gratuitousness. It is important to keep in mind that, in moving to consideration of the higher end, and beyond to ultimate end-state, conventional borders between archetypes (profit, non-profit; financial, social) tend to become more fluid. At the same time, the influence of broader principles (common good, gratuitousness, solidarity, interdependence, reciprocity) tends to appear across diverse models.

12.5 The Composition of Economy of Mutuality

We can develop the idea of economy of mutuality further with the help of five key background concepts. Taken together, these key concepts point to the ultimate end-state of business across prototypes – reciprocity and integral human development (Fig. 12.2).

The five key concepts are as follows: (i) solidarity, (ii) cultural capital, (iii) "Homo reciprocans", (iv) common good, and (v) virtue.

EoM: Conceptual Composition			
Transcendent *telos* (across prototypes)	Reciprocity; integral human development		
Philosophical anchors	Social solidarity & interdependence, cultural capital, *homo reciprocans,* common good, virtue		
Pro-social end	Mutual benefit; shared value creation; gratuitousness		
Proximate end	Assistance, welfare	Development	Profitability
Modus operandi	Logic of gift	Hybrid economic logic	Logic of exchange
Sector	Social economy	Crossbreed economy	Market economy
Business Enterprise prototype	Charitable/nonprofit Enterprises (prototype C)	Social Enterprises (hybrids of prototypes A & B; B & C)	For-Profit Enterprises (prototype-A)

Fig. 12.2 Conceptual composition

12.5.1 Solidarity

For Émile Durkheim, social solidarity correlates with various types of society. Durkheim distinguished "mechanical" from "organic" solidarity in his theory of the division of labor (Durkheim 1893). Concerning mechanical solidarity, a society's cohesion stems from homogeneity. People are linked through similar work, educational backgrounds, religious training, and lifestyles.

Mechanical solidarity is normally seen in small-scale societies where kinship bonds of familial networks occur. On the other hand, organic solidarity arises out of interdependence from specialization of work and complementarities between people. This is a development occurring in "modern" and "industrial" societies. Organic solidarity is social cohesion grounded in a dependence individuals have upon one other in more advanced societies.

For J.S. Mill (and others) cooperation in the context of particular businesses was in elemental form a more generalized style of cooperation forming the heart of the division of labor, and hence, of the market (Mill 1848: IV.7.21). Unlike Marxist accounts, Mill interpreted collaboration – not class conflict – as essential to market operation. Mill favored economic democracy rather than capitalism as such. In advocating worker cooperatives over capitalist enterprise he states:

> The form of association, however, which if mankind continue to improve, must be expected in the end to predominate, is not that which can exist between a capitalist as chief, and work-people without a voice in the management, but the association of the laborers themselves on terms of equality, collectively owning the capital with which they carry on their

operations, and working under managers elected and removable by themselves (Mill 1848: IV.1.7).

From the standpoint of today's competitive global economy, Mill's observation is incisive: "there is no more certain incident of the progressive change taking place in society, than the continual growth of principle and practice of cooperation" (Mill 1848: IV.1.7).

Individuals perform different tasks and possess different values and interests. So social solidarity is maintained in more complex societies through interdependence. Such solidarity is seen in contemporary business relationships such as supply chains.

What does solidarity mean in the context of today's globalization? Robert Keohane and Joseph Nye characterize globalization as an increase in networks of interdependence obtaining between people across multi-continental divides (Keohane and Nye 2000: 105). Their characterization emphasizes that globalization, far from being a one-dimensional type of connectedness, is taking place within intricate interdependent webs. Globalization occurs on multiple tiers: technological, environmental, economic (encompassing consumption, finance, investments, production, trade), cultural, social, legal, and political. Given so many patterns of interdependence, a major challenge is to infuse these patterns with solidarity. This may, in turn, be assisted by the growth of cultural capital.

12.5.2 Cultural Capital

Cultural capital solidifies affiliates of human communities and associations. It enables cooperative pursuits to materialize. Cultural capital lifts organizations and business communities up, making them more than a rag-tag group of people each bent on advancing their respective private projects.

Granted that businesses may have the ability to generate wealth, a question lingers: for what purpose? Considering, in light of financial engineering advancements, the momentous technical progress that can be achieved in constructing wealth, what remains unanswered is whether we are left any better than before. Of course, empirical data culled from balance sheets and revenue statements can indicate that a firm has generated greater wealth than the previous quarter. And technological innovation might raise its levels of productivity. But KPIs (key performance indicators) will not provide any indication of whether our character is improved, or whether we are in a state of overall well-being. The intricate issue of to what extent our creative drive guides us toward authentic human betterment cannot be completely comprehended from the perspective of a market devoid of moral-cultural capital. On its own, such a market gives no signals as to whether we are approaching greater alignment with our human nature. Considered apart from cultural capital, the economic system itself does not provide criteria for making judgments distinguishing between higher modes of human satisfaction, based on authentic needs, and lower modes that chase after fake needs and cripple our chances for genuine human fulfillment.

Economy of mutuality presupposes devotion to moral virtues developed within a culture having the ability to ripen the excellence of the whole person. Considered in isolation, neither market nor government can accomplish this. Economy of mutuality reminds us that technical business competence and informed government policies, while imperative, cannot of themselves assemble a good company or a good businessperson.

Culture inculcates a way of viewing the world, of perceiving what is real, of bringing sense to reality. Culture illuminates what we hold sacred, guiding us to apprehend the deepest meaning extending back to our origins and ahead to the future.

Human society is built upon a bedrock of cultural institutions. Family and education are two of the foremost institutions vital for economic society. Family comprises the primary component of human culture; it is the basic unit of society. Education cultivates awareness of and sensitivity toward the world, inspiring a sense of wonder, firing the imagination, and granting moral vision necessary to enlighten scientific, technical and commercial undertakings.

Philosophy, along with religion, the arts, music, literature and other humanities are at the center of culture. These endeavors are concerned with what is most precious and noble in our lives. These wellsprings of higher culture prompt us to engage the deeper significance of our world, pointing beyond drab concerns of everyday things to what is enduring, directing us toward ultimate questions concerning our nature, our purpose and our destiny.

The reason for this stems from a dynamic understood from antiquity: by drawing us back to our purpose, to our authentic nature, to our destiny, higher forms of culture equip us to perceive the whole, not simply the fragments. Culture equips us to assimilate the totality of the cosmos and guides us to comprehend how we fit into it. We grasp the wholeness by being united with elemental cycles of our existence such as living, growing, dying, loving, and working so as to relate them in an organic unity instead of in a subdivided way. Hidden at the center of all cultures deserving of the name is a yen to reunite what is detached.

Perhaps what is needed is a way of connecting one's vocation in business to an ethical outlook on commercial life. This would involve linking:

- business life to communities of virtue;
- generation of goods and services to the end of human flourishing;
- commercial enterprise to the common good;
- employment to the cultivation of excellence and pursuit of well-being in employees.

Straightforward talk about the ways cultural capital inspires and develops virtuous businesspeople can stimulate meaningful discourse across cultures. This may engender some harmony among them. A heightened rapprochement between morality and business may promote more profound interactions among cultures, equipping them to negotiate thorny ideological divergences. Yet it is not plausible to believe that we impart moral wisdom to one another if we simply follow government laws and regulations or mimic technical financial methodologies. In truth, the profit-driven mindset, collective laws and conventional practices, and the econometric worldview are too constraining for the art of business to flourish.

The notion of cultural capital provides a means of explanation for why it is important to interpret the profit motive as something broader than a relentless quest for profit maximization. Most of what is needed to create profit is attainable only through the cultivation and deployment of cultural capital. And although this type of intangible capital is not amenable to being reduced to a specific item on the balance sheet, nevertheless it contains value as a path to enhancing the bottom line.

Therefore, the idea of cultural capital should be brought within the orbit of economic thinking. As with financial capital, a business can build up reserves of cultural capital. It can accumulate this asset by helping to establish relationships of accountability, commitment, fair-dealing, goodwill, mutual respect, and trust, and in the process, helping people to direct their respective talents toward a shared venture. It is a facilitator of human and social capital (Harrison 2012: 2). Likewise, a business can draw upon cultural capital just as it can draw upon these other forms. Yet accomplishing this may require adopting non-traditional styles of leadership and management aimed at a sapiential harnessing of intrinsically valuable human goods.

People are most apt to flourish in the sort of surroundings in which overall social progress and cultural advancement are taking place. Economic growth comes about as a cooperative – not simply an individual – enterprise. The ability of sizeable groups to operate in conjunction with one another generates social trust, one of the essential components of market activity. Francis Fukuyama states that "[t]rust is the expectation that arises within a community of regular, honest, and cooperative behavior, based on commonly shared norms . . . ." (Fukuyama 1995: 26). "These norms," he notes, "can be about deep 'value' questions like the nature of God or justice, but they also encompass secular norms like professional standards and codes of behavior" (Fukuyama 1995: 26).

12.5.3 Homo reciprocans

Many economic theories deploy the ideological construct *homo economicus*. The human person is reduced to an egoistic actor seeking to satisfy his or her subjective ends. Making rational assessments, *homo economicus* sets foot in the market to maximize utility *qua* consumer and economic profit *qua* producer. Hence *homo economicus*, emblematic of market economy, starkly contrasts with the notion of *homo reciprocans* that portrays the human person embedded in social economy, having behavioral inclinations for reciprocity and cooperation with others (Dohmen et al. 2009). Real people do not necessarily pursue only exchanges of equivalent value; their actions sometimes spring from gratuitousness; their exchanges can be prolonged over time (Grassl 2011: 114; Becchetti et al. 2008).

The conceptual model relied upon to portray market economy, embraced by much of the business world, largely overlooks the irreducible complexity of human nature at the core of economics and business (Freeman and Newkirk 2008: 139–143). In actuality, reciprocal human behavior is harmonious with markets. Reciprocity promotes markets and is, conversely, buttressed by market economies (Grassl 2011: 114).

12.5.4 Common Good

Economy of mutuality stresses the purposive nature of business enterprise. As such it is in line with both the methodological approach taken by Aristotle – inquiring into the purposive character of all human enterprises (Solomon 2004: 1023) – as well as with approaches examining the broader purpose of business (Calvez and Naughton 2002; Sison and Fontrodona 2011).

The notion of "common good" is especially germane, denoting something more than the competing interests of selfish individuals and beyond composite interests of special groups. It is the good we all have in common – communal conditions necessary for virtuous pursuit of human fulfillment, flourishing, and perfection by all in society. The common good is an aggregation of collaborative initiatives and shared restraints by which society helps everyone achieve what in the end only each individual can accomplish for herself: shaping a good will and constituting an authentically human self by freely choosing good every time one is given the chance and responsibility to do so.

Thus understood, the common good looks in two directions: to the good of society and to the good of the individuals, since social conditions supply part of the means for human fulfillment. Yet ultimately the two directions are not at odds with one another. Instead they are correlational since "any good of an individual that is a real good is rooted in the good of the community, and, conversely, any common good that is a real good is at the same time the good of all individuals who share in that community" (O'Brien 2009: 29).

At its best, business builds up the common good of society (Solomon 2004; Melé 2009; O'Brien 2009; Sison and Fontrodona 2011). Moreover, the institution of business can be depicted from the standpoint of its own peculiar common good (Sison 2007; Melé 2009). Taken together these propositions mean that business advances the common good of society when it sets about fulfilling the common good of its own (Sison and Fontrodona 2011).

To this point, in the eyes of many classical economists, instead of contravening civil society, the market embodies it. Proper functioning of the market depends on contracts, cooperation, institutions and trust. These elements promote reciprocity. Throughout the classical Latin tradition, economic activity provides a setting where humans manifest their social being, revealing a thirst for camaraderie in relationships of equality and dignity.

For those who see the market as a forum of vicious selfish competition, characterized by excessive gain-seeking behavior of business firms, such characterizations seem quite odd. But a crucial insight EoM contributes is this one: the market starts to look like a robust manifestation of social life once we can discern beneath it a shared sense of common good. This is something going on logically prior to the process of bargaining.

With the support of good and just institutions, with agreements grounded in authentic trust rather than on the basis of deceptive and disingenuous corporate images, market interactions are in a position to assume a wider and more virtuous role. From such a standpoint, EoM acquires nourishment from a tradition of thought common in ancient economies.

12.5.5 Virtue

There is a moral decoupling happening both within business and within wider culture. This decoupling arises from a self-(mis)understanding of business that has unwittingly abandoned the moral virtues in relation to economic life, together with their broader cultural underpinnings. Consequently, it is urgent to consider what is meant by being "good" and "successful" in business, and to clarify the virtues required for being a good businessperson.

Our inquiry is aided by reflecting on cultural capital – the intangible moral resource needed to develop the virtues for achieving excellence in business, whatever one's station. The virtuous businessperson is not only a self-project of individual motivation and effort. Cultivating virtue ultimately depends upon culture – its institutions of family, education, and the arts – to provide formation that fosters excellence.

12.6 The Role of Profitability

Considering business as a human enterprise (Freeman and Newkirk 2008), one finds that deep down, people work to gain a better, fulfilled life for themselves, for loved ones, for the community in which they live. For this betterment to happen, it is vital that individuals working in a free market economy have opportunities to willingly invest whatever talent, vigor, and know-how they possess.

From this dynamic of freely investing themselves, a free people is guided, in Adam Smith's imagery, by an invisible hand toward prosperity and well-being. In this way, we expect that wealth will be created, not just in the short term but in a sustainable fashion. Adam Smith's invisible hand need not be taken to convey anything mysterious. Common sense suggests that by letting people go after their self-interest, unintended yet favorable social outcomes will ensue. In the course of seeking profit, people unwittingly contribute beneficial effects: increasing the overall wealth of society, facilitating technological innovation, fostering peace and civility, enabling workers to get more and improved jobs, bringing people of different lands together to know and respect one another.

Of course, not all motivations underpinning markets are purely self-interested. Nor is the invisible hand a completely reliable check on individual rapacity. Beyond pointing out the importance of pursuing self-interest, Adam Smith stresses the virtues of benevolence and sympathy. (Smith 1759/1976). For Smith, self-interest expressed within the rules of a commercial society is not opposed to virtue. Indeed, character traits associated with the pursuit of long-term self-interest – prudence, temperance, and self-command – are key business virtues (Hirschman 1997: 18–19).

Contemporary market economy represents one component of ideal commercial society. Additional elements are private property, free exchange, democracy and rule of law. Taken together, these components help fuel individual initiative, engaging creative capacities across the population to give those potentials a chance to ignite, express themselves, and lead to contentment and well-being.

Yet the profit motive is seen in wider culture as the end-all-and-be-all of business. Relentless pursuit of profit is praised: "the honor is in the dollar." But the concept of "profit motive" is distorted by narrow economic models. The mindset that sees markets as fueled entirely by self-interest, taking self-interest as the single-minded hunt for profit, misunderstands both "self-interest" and "profit maximization."

Tocqueville discerns an attitude of rational self-interest rightly understood: each person identifies their own self-interest with that of all in the society. When rightly understood, self-interest elevates people above narrow selfish preoccupations. Although self-interest might not instantaneously manufacture virtue, it wields a discipline that "shapes a lot of orderly, temperate, moderate, careful, and self-controlled citizens" (Tocqueville 1863/1994: 527). From Tocqueville's vantage point, a person's rational concern for self gets joined to a broader sense of esteem for various cultural, moral, and legal establishments enabling the wider population to follow their freely selected ambitions, principally through business enterprise.

A virtuous company is not just a "profit machine." Collins and Porras state that

> Profitability is a necessary condition for existence and a means to more important ends, but it is not the end in itself for many of the visionary companies. Profit is like oxygen, food, water, and blood for the body; they are not the *point* of life, but without them, there is no life (Collins and Porras 1994: 55).

Such companies embrace a "core ideology, " or "vital shaping force" which might stem from its origins, as in the case of Sony; or, as with Merck, from a successive generation; or even remain quiescent to be revivified at some subsequent point, as occurred with Ford (Id. p. 54). A virtuous firm might have as its principal motivations professionalism, civic responsibility and customer service, like Housing Development Finance Corporation.[3] Its driving force could be "bedrock values" of personal accountability, respect for the individual, truth, and fair dealing, like Sealed

[3] HDFC (A) Harvard Business School Case No. 9-301-093 (2000).

Air Corporation.[4] It may be spurred on by a commitment to integrity, fairness, fun, and social responsibility, as AES Corporation is.[5]

As with a human being, the organization must have an authentic commitment to its objectives, in a way that is true to its own character and internal nature as a moral agent that is free to choose. It cannot simply mimic the values of other firms, conform to external diktats, or smartly calculate which roster of values will prove to be the most lucrative, trendy or well-liked (Collins and Porras 1994: 75).

No matter how a company articulates its mission, profit maximization normally is not listed as its objectives. Instead, profit is a predictable and reliable side-effect arising in an indirect fashion from the company seeking other aspirations. To situate this thought within the real world of business, we can turn to Collins and Porras' study of companies noted for attaining exceptional long-term performance. The authors note a shattering of the myth that the companies achieving the highest degree of success owe their existence principally to the quest for profit maximization:

> Contrary to business school doctrine, "maximizing shareholder wealth" or "profit maximization" has not been the dominant driving force or primary objective through the history of the visionary companies. Visionary companies pursue a cluster of objectives, of which making money is only one – and not necessarily the primary one. Yes, they seek profits, but they're equally guided by a core ideology – core values and sense of purpose beyond just making money. Yet, paradoxically, the visionary companies make more money than the more purely profit-driven comparison companies" (Collins and Porras 1994: 8).

Narrowing in on profit alone makes an enterprise lose sight of its authentic mission. Conversely, if a firm remains guided by its true objective, profit is produced in due course.

Collins and Porras show how firms that elevate profit to the apex of their business plan actually lose the competitive advantage they were after. Instead of "beating the competition," visionary companies,

> focus primarily on beating themselves. Success and beating competitors comes to the visionary companies not so much as the end goal, but as a residual *result* of relentlessly asking the question "How can we improve ourselves to do better tomorrow than we did today?" And they have asked this question day in and day out – as a disciplined way of life – in some cases for over 150 years. No matter how much they achieve – no matter how far in front of their competitors they pull – they never think they've done "good enough" (Collins and Porras 1994: 10).

The upshot is that the invisible hand is flexible, having a wider range of motion than normally thought. The invisible hand guides in not one but two directions: social good gets generated as a consequence of businesses' quest for profit; as well, businesses' quest for social good generates profit. Economic and moral values, along with financial and social values, are not necessarily at odds with one another

---

[4] Sealed Air Corporation: Globalization and Corporate Culture (A), (B), Harvard Business School Case Nos. 9-398-096, 9-398-097 (1998).

[5] AES Honeycomb (A), Harvard Business School Case No. 9-395-132 (1994).

but instead complementary, in the way oppositions of "yin" and "yang" function as harmonizing forces of holistic Eastern philosophy (Jackson 2004, p. 46).

12.7 Conclusion

The theory of economy of mutuality outlined in this chapter can help us comprehend the blurring of boundaries sometimes seen between "normal" businesses (market economy) and non-for profit or social businesses.

The proximate ends of for-profit, hybrid, and nonprofit businesses respectively were identified at the level of business and economic theories. Higher ends of these various archetypes were then spotlighted, and an account of an ultimate end-state across archetypes was articulated at a deep and broad level. With the help of five conceptual elements – social solidarity and interdependence, cultural capital, *homo reciprocans*,common good, and virtue – it was explained why the ultimate end-state is reciprocity and integral human development.

Among the implications raised by EoM are a reappraisal of boundaries between sectors, along with an appropriate endorsement of new forms of business enterprises. According to this interpretive framework there is no reason to privilege either for-profit enterprise or non-profit enterprise, by crediting either of them with carrying out a more important task or imparting higher moral value. The shift is toward the objective of infusing all prototypes of business enterprise with "pro-social" attitudes.

Another implication of EoM is a call to update outmoded approaches to management entrenched in narrow mindsets threatening to decouple business from its nobler purposes.

Overall, EoM shows how the mode of organization represented by various prototypes of business enterprise is secondary to the higher purpose of a business. The analysis advocates comprehensive moral thinking, inviting business leaders to look at their roles not solely in insular economic terms, but in pro-social terms. From the standpoint of economy of mutuality, while it is acknowledged that for-profit business enterprises have shareholder and stakeholders, they have as well vocations to engage in realistic ways with other institutions in building a better, more sustainable world by promoting reciprocity and authentic human development.

References

Abela, A. 2001. Profit and More: Catholic Social Teaching and the Purpose of the Firm. *Journal of Business Ethics* 1 (2): 107–116.

Aquinas, T. 1273/1972. *Summa Theologiae*, ed. T.C. O'Brien. London: Eyre and Spottiswoode.

Aristotle. 1941. *The Basic Works of Aristotle*, ed. R. McKeon (B. Jowett, Trans.). New York: Random House.

Armendariz, B., and A. Szafarz. 2011. On mission drift in microfinance institutions. In *The Handbook of Microfinance*, ed. B. Armendariz and M. Labie, 341–366. Singapore: World Scientific.
Becchetti, L., A. Pelloni, and F. Rossetti. 2008. Relational goods, sociability, and happiness. *Kyklos* 61: 343–363.
Billis, D. 2010. *Hybrid Organizations and the Third Sector*. Basingstoke: Palgrave Macmillan.
Boyd, B., N. Henning, E. Reyna, D.E. Wang, and M.D. Welch. 2009. *Hybrid Organizations: New Business Models for Environmental Leadership*. Sheffield: Greenleaf.
Buchanan, J., and G. Tullock. 1962. *The Calculus of Consent: Logical Foundations of Constitutional Democracy*. Indianapolis: Liberty Fund.
Buğra, A., and K. Arğatan. 2007. *Reading Karl Polanyi for the Twenty-First Century: Market Economy as a Political Project*. Basingstoke: Palgrave Macmillan.
Calvez, J., and M. Naughton. 2002. *Rethinking the Purpose of Business*. Notre Dame: University of Notre Dame Press.
Collins, J.C., and J.I. Porras. 1994. *Built to Last: Successful Habits of Visionary Companies*. New York: Harper Business.
Daly, H., and J.B. Cobb. 1990. *For the Common Good: Redirecting the Economy Towards Community, the Environment and a Sustainable Future*. London: Green Print.
de Tocqueville, A. 1994. *Democracy in America*, ed. J.P. Mayer, vol. 2 (G. Lawrence, Trans.). London: Fontana.
Dees, J.G. 1998. Enterprising Nonprofits. *Harvard Business Review* 76 (1): 54–67.
Dohmen, T., et al. 2009. *Homo reciprocans*: Survey Evidence on Behavioural Outsomes. *Economic Journal* 119 (536): 592–612.
Durkheim, E. 1893. *The Division of Labor in Society*. New York: Macmillan.
Duska, R.E. 1997. The Why's of Business Revisited. *Journal of Business Ethics* 16 (12/13): 1401–1409.
Faldetta, G. 2011. The Logic of Gift and Gratuitousness in Business Relationships. *Journal of Business Ethics* 100: 67–77.
Fearn, H. 2014. Mars Tries to Share Benefits of Business Without Parting with Profits. *The Guardian*. 4 November. http://www.theguardian.com/sustainable-business/2014/nov/04/mars-business-benefits-without-sharing-profits.
Freeman, R.E., and D. Newkirk. 2008. Business as a human enterprise. In *Rethinking Business Management: Examining the Foundations of Business Education*, ed. S. Gregg and J.R. Stoner Jr., 139–143. Princeton: ISI.
Freeman, R.E., J.S. Harrison, A.C. Wicks, B.L. Parmar, and S. de Colle. 2010. *Stakeholder Theory: The State of the Art*. Cambridge: Cambridge University Press.
Friedman, M. 1962. *Capitalism and Freedom*. Chicago: University of Chicago Press.
Fukuyama, F. 1995. *Trust: The Social Virtues and the Creation of Prosperity*. New York: Free Press.
Ghate, P. 2007. Consumer Protection in Indian Microfinance: Lessons from Andhra Pradesh and the Microfinance Bill. *Economic and Political Weekly* 42 (13): 1176–1184.
Gold, L. 2010. *New Financial Horizons: The Emergence of an Economy of Communion*. Hyde Park: New City Press.
Goodpaster, K.E. 2011. Goods That Are Truly Good and Services That Truly Serve: Reflections on *Caritas in Veritate*. *Journal of Business Ethics* 100: 9–16.
Grassl, W. 2011. Hybrid Forms of Business: The Logic of Gift in the Commercial World. *Journal of Business Ethics* 100: 109–123.
Handy, C. 2002. What's a Business for? *Harvard Business Review* 80 (12): 49–55.
Harrison, L.E. 2012. *Jews, Confucians, and Protestants: Cultural Capital and the End of Multiculturalism*. New York: Rowman & Littlefield.
Hayek, F.A. 1948. *Individualism and Economic Order*. Chicago: University of Chicago Press.
Heinberg, R. 2011. *The End of Growth: Adapting to Our New Economic Reality*. Gabriola Island: New Society Publishers.

Hirschman, A.O. 1997. *The Passions and the Interests: Political Arguments for Capitalism Before Its Triumph*. Princeton, NJ: Princeton University Press.
Hirst, P. 1994. *Associative Democracy: New Forms of Economic and Social Governance*. Cambridge: Polity Press.
Jackson, K.T. 2004. *Building Reputational Capital: Strategies for Integrity and Fair Play That Improve the Bottom Line*. New York: Oxford University Press.
Kay, J. 1991. Economics of Mutuality. *Annals of Public and Cooperative Economics* 62 (3): 309–313.
Keohane, R.O., and J.S. Nye. 2000. Globalization: What's New? What's Not? (and so What?). *Foreign Policy* 118: 104–119.
Marshall, A. 1920. *Principles of Economics*. London: Macmillan.
Melé, D. 2009. Integrating Personalism into Virtue-Based Business Ethics: The Personalist and the Common Good Principles. *Journal of Business Ethics* 88 (1): 227–244.
Menning, C.B. 1993. *Charity and State in Late Renaissance Italy*. Ithaca: Cornell University Press.
Mill, J.S. 1848. *The Principles of Political Economy with Some of Their Applications to Social Philosophy*. London: Savill and Edwards.
Montgomery, R. 1996. Disciplining or Protecting the Poor? Avoiding the Social Costs of Peer Pressure in Micro-credit Schemes. *Journal of International Development* 8 (2): 289–305.
Nee, V., and R. Swedberg. 2005. *The Economic Sociology of Capitalism*. Princeton: Princeton University Press.
O'Brien, T. 2009. Reconsidering the common good in a business context. *Journal of Business Ethics* 85: 25–37.
Paine, L.S. 2003. *Value Shift: Why Companies Must Merge Social and Financial Imperatives to Achieve Superior Performance*. New York: McGraw Hill.
Phillips, R. 1997. Stakeholder Theory and a Principle of Fairness. *Business Ethics Quarterly* 7 (1): 51–66.
Polanyi, K. 1944/2001. *The Great Transformation: The Political and Economic Origins of Our Time*. 2nd ed. Boston: Beacon Press.
Porter, M., and M. Kramer. 2011. Creating Shared Value: How to Reinvent Capitalism and Unleash Wave of Innovation and Growth. *Harvard Business Review* 89 (1/2): 63–70.
Ricardo, D. 1817. *On the Principles of Political Economy and Taxation*. London: Murray, Rogers, Everett.
Rosenberg, R., A. Gonzalez, and S. Narain. 2009. The New Moneylenders: Are the Poor Being Exploited by High Microcredit Interest Rates? CGAP Occasional Paper No. 15. Washington, DC: CGAP.
Sandberg, J. 2012. Mega-Interest on Microcredit: Are Lenders Exploiting the Poor? *Journal of Applied Philosophy* 29 (3): 169–185.
Sertial, H. 2012. Hybrid Entities: Distributing Profits with a Purpose. *Fordham Journal of Corporate & Financial Law* 17:261–297.
Sison, A.J.G. 2007. Toward a Common Good Theory of the Firm: The Tasubinsa Case. *Journal of Business Ethics* 74 (4): 471–480.
Sison, A.J.G., and J. Fontrodona. 2011. The Common Good of Business: Addressing a Challenge Posed by *Caritas in Veritate*. *Journal of Business Ethics* 100: 99–107.
Smith, A. 1759/1976. *The Theory of Moral Sentiments*. Oxford: Clarendon Press.
Solomon, R.C. 2004. Aristotle, ethics and business organizations. *Organization Studies* 25 (6): 1021–1043.
Uelmen, A. and, L. Bruni. 2006. Religious Values and Corporate Decision Making: The Economy of Communion Project. *Fordham Journal of Corporate & Financial Law* 11: 645–648.
Wals, A.E.J. 2007. *Social Learning Towards a Sustainable World: Principles, Perspectives, and Praxis*. Wageningen: Wageningen Academic Publishers.
Yunus, M. 2007. *Banker to the Poor: Micro-Lending and the Battle Against World Poverty*. New York: Public Affairs.
———. 2011. *Building Social Business: The New Kind of Capitalism that Serves Humanity's Most Pressing Needs*. New York: Public Affairs.

Chapter 13
Economic Wisdom for Managerial Decision-Making

Mike Thompson

Abstract The paper argues that Aristotle's "phronesis" can be explained as social practice wisdom, a discursive system linking mind and social practice to produce wellbeing and human flourishing. It uses the contemporary conceptualization of phronesis and its related metatheoretical construct of wisdom principles to bring a practical dimension to wise decision-making. The paper first reviews progress in the understanding of wise leadership within leadership studies and the principles of wisdom proposed by McKenna. Against this taxonomy it then recontextualizes the numerous calls in leadership literature for qualitative, research. It presents samples and interprets the resulting theory based in original material from interviews with 184 managers generated by the Wisdom Project.

The paper concludes that an economic wisdom is present in the minds of managers. Economic wisdom could offer resources for management education and development across all business domains to address the challenges of the VUCA world with a more realistic, holistic and planet-friendly approach.

The search for wisdom in organizational, corporate and governmental practice has become more apparent as the modernist faith in positivist, determinist and objectivist rationality has waned. The case for homo oeconomicus has been eroded since the first serious wounds were inflicted by Amartya Sen (1977) and Kahneman and Tversky (1979). In the past three decades modernist economics has been assailed by psychologists and philosophers who believe that the assumptions of modern economics are fundamentally flawed (Sen 1987; Werhane 1989; Griswold 1999; Brown 1994; Solomon 2006; Raphael 2007). In the words of Bevan and Werhane:

> The flaw seems to be that pure "individualism" is considered to be at the core of Smith's thinking. Stripped of his/her original sociality, the individual becomes a self-centered agent

M. Thompson (✉)
GoodBrand, London, UK

China Europe International Business School, Shanghai, China

University of Victoria, Victoria, BC, Canada
e-mail: mikejthompson@me.com

P. Rona, L. Zsolnai (eds.), *Economics as a Moral Science*,
Virtues and Economics 1, DOI 10.1007/978-3-319-53291-2_13

> and the invisible hand is transformed from a simple metaphor into the concrete hand of the idealized market and Adam Smith's "invisible hand" economics profoundly misunderstood as raw "individualism". (Bevan and Werhane 2015: 330)

The basis of Smith's market society is not only the "self love" in *The Wealthof the Nations* (1776) but also the moral sentiment and "fellow-feeling" in *The Theory of Moral Sentiments* (1790): we are intrinsically social beings and selfish egotistical beings are not typical of homo sapiens. As a consequence, we have unavoidable responsibilities to, and because of, others in commercial dealings (Bevan and Werhane 2015: 327). Elsewhere in this volume, Luk Bouckaert argues that Adam Smith is one of the first moral philosophers to underpin this order with a non-teleological substratum and that Smithian economics is fundamentally relational. Perhaps the starkest contrast between the utilitarian maximizer of twentieth century economics and the more nuanced ontological narratives of human motivation today is brought to life in the fictional and heroic icon of John Galt created by Ayn Rand in her *Atlas Shrugged* (1957). In John Galt Ayn Rand epitomizes the rational ontological outcome of homo oeconomicus who prides himself in self maximization renouncing any concern for the other: "Do you ask what moral obligation I owe to my fellow men? None - except the obligation I owe to myself, to material objects and to all of existence: rationality." (Rand 2007: 1022).

The essential assumption underlying the fictional economic model of humankind is that rationality will inevitably push self interest to selfishness. To recognize the human motivation for sociability and altruism is not to deny the reality of self interest or "self love" as a motivator. Rather it is to say that calculative rationality is not necessarily selfish in seeking one's own advantage to the exclusion of regard for others (Becker1993; Wilson 1998; Midgeley 2009; Thompson 2012). The lack of moral obligation proclaimed by Rand's hero implies that the virtues are irrational and redundant. Thus wisdom as axiomatic to the virtues must also be dismissed as an anachronistic hangover from pre-Enlightenment days. Yet, in contrast to the objectivist claim, twenty-first century globally-connected society consistently calls for responsible behavior by governments, NGOs and companies. The logic of homo oeconomicus outcomes depicted by Ayn Rand would horrify the holders of contemporary norms: "Sweep aside those parasites of the subsidized classroom, who live on the profits of the mind of others and proclaim that man needs no morality, no values, no code of behavior." (Rand 2007: 1014).

The proclamation shows the ugly side of homo oeconomicus in sharp relief but fails to account for the ontological reality that morality, values and codes of behavior are everywhere present in human relations. The calls for practical wisdom and responsible leadership in corporate and public life is a global phenomenon that may be regarded as a post modern twenty-first century Enlightenment. So, for example, the idea that economics is a purely rational science is now widely challenged. Gigerenzer and Brighton (2009) describe "homo heuristicus" as being able to make inferences quickly from a few observations and show that bias can be adaptive and can help to reduce the estimation error. Bank of England economist, Andy Haldane points out that modern macroeconomics and finance has been built on often stringent assumptions about humans' state of knowledge and cognitive capacity.

> In its strongest form, rational expectations assume that information collection is close to costless and that agents have cognitive faculties sufficient to weight probabilistically all future outturns. Those strong assumptions about states of knowledge and cognition have not always been at the centre of the economics profession. (Haldane 2012: 2)

Such acknowledgements of non-rational heuristics and the cognitive capacity assumptions in utilitarian models of economics and behavior are complemented by the widespread contemporary interest in mindfulness (Malinowski 2013; Kongsbakk and Rooney 2016) and spirituality (Thompson 2007, 2011b; Zsolnai2011; Bouckaert and Zsolnai 2011). Recent models of "homo spiritualis" (Thompson 2007), "homo moralis" (Columbo 2009: 743) and "homo empathicus" (Rifkin 2009: 47–81) does not fit John Galt's view of the world. Adam Smith's *The Theory of Moral Sentiments* shows that at the outset of modern economics the "invisible hand" could not somehow be disconnected with concern for the wellbeing of others:

> How selfish soever man may be supposed, there are evidently some principles in his nature, which interest him in the fortune of others, and render their happiness necessary to him, though he derives nothing from it except the pleasure of seeing it. (Smith 1790: 13)

Whilst there can be little doubt that the John Galt archetype lives on into the twenty-first century, he exists under greater scrutiny and stronger competition from leaders motivated by ideals and practices for the common good across all sectors of political, civil and corporate society. The manager today is under insistent and persistent demands internally and externally to make responsible decisions to manage enforcement requirements, geopolitical risks, demands for ethical actions, public criticism and demands from all levels of government.

Such demands not only place a focus on the quality and breadth of the manager and of the General Counsel (Heinemann 2016) but also on the character of the manager: justice, toughness, caring, compassion, honesty, fairness and trust are a commonly cited set of virtues expected of corporate managers.[1] Across the discourses on virtue, wisdom is axiomatic in the quality of un-selfinterested managerial decision-making (Thompson 2011a). Wisdom stands for the integration of knowledge with a developed sense of self- and other-understanding and a developed perceptivity of events and circumstances based on experience or even intuitive insight.

In his *The Age of Discontinuity*, Peter Drucker (1968) asserted that the "knowledge industry" was no longer a secondary industry in the economics classification but was *the* primary industry, "the industry that supplies to the economy the essential and central resource of production." (Drucker 1968: 264). But for Drucker this

---

[1] This is the list of virtues for corporate managers suggested by Robert Solomon but are derivatives of virtues proposed by the ancient philosophers and expounded within a Christian context by Thomas Aquinas. See Helen J. Alford and Michael J. Naughton, *Managing As If Faith Mattered: Christian Social Principles in the Modern Organization*, (University of Notre Dame Press, 2001), chapter 3.

realization led him to raise moral questions for the future of the knowledge economy and the implications for society when scientists and "the men of knowledge" gain power in the knowledge society: "The central moral problem of the knowledge society will be the responsibility of the learned, the men of knowledge." (Drucker1968: 372). The import of Drucker's thesis is that knowledge-based leadership alone is insufficient for the moral challenges that he envisages will emerge from the knowledge economy produced by late twentieth century capitalism. Beyond the evident "moral problems" that Drucker anticipated presciently, organizations face the so-called VUCA[2] challenges that result from globalization, technologization and the digital world. Senior managers are required to meet short-term budgets, reduce risk, excite consumers, engage with stakeholders and, if publicly traded, institutional investors. They are to address climate change targets, demonstrate strategic insight and cope with conflicting compliance and regulatory demands arising from perceived stakeholder rights and environmental exploitation. Keeping ahead with all sources of organizational, market and environmental knowledge based on accurate data is a sine qua non of management, but complex decision-making requires the attributes of wisdom. There are signs that the movement for long-term capitalism is bringing economic wisdom into the knowledge economy (Barton 2011; Polman 2011, 2012; George 2013). Indeed, a diverse group of more than 20 leaders who represent major institutional investors and corporations came together to found Focusing Capital on the Long Term ("FCLT"). Their goal was to develop practical structures, approaches, and ideas to foster longer-term behavior in the investment and business worlds to create value for all stakeholders. Such future-thinking anticipates the wisdom economy in which governmental and non-governmental organizations, institutions and corporations require their "knowledge workers" to act with economic wisdom. For corporations the core business functions of finance, governance, strategy, marketing, HR management, operations, logistics, manufacturing and supply chain will require wise leadership that competes for the future and not just the commoditized world of the status quo. Companies that are competing for the future are already designing tools for economic wisdom management such as the Marginal True Value Curve for the internalization of externalities (KPMG 2014). Competing for the future requires the incorporation of sustainability and ESG measures in the day-to-day strategy and finance functions, a senior team of executives and Boards appointed on merit for their skills and also their track record in wise decision-making. A sign of capitalism for the long-term is evident in Accenture's survey of more than 1000 CEOs, who are already committed to sustainability through their participation in the UN Global Compact and are now implementing action plans to achieve the UN Sustainable Development Goals (Accenture 2016).

Between 2010 and 2012 the Euro-China Centre for Leadership and Responsibility (ECCLAR) at the China Europe International Business School conducted a management wisdom survey of 181 senior managers to gain an insight into the way in which they understood and applied wisdom in the managerial decision-making process (Thompson 2017). The managers were almost exclusively drawn from

[2] Volatile, Uncertain, Complex and Ambiguous.

companies in 21 countries in an enquiry into managers' understanding of wisdom in managerial decision-making.

The survey was an exploration into the experience and dimensions of economic or practical wisdom frequently associated with the Aristotelian term, *phronèsis*. The simplest translation of *phronèsis* is practical wisdom but, in context, is linked to virtuous practice for the achievement of the goal of *eudaimonia* (wellbeing or human flourishing). *Phronèsis* is the practical common sense needed to develop *eudaimonia* through "a true and reasoned state of capacity to act with regard to the things that are good or bad for man" (Aristotle, Nichomachean Ethics VI.5). *Phronèsis* concerns practical judgment, the ability to act virtuously and for the common good in difficult and uncertain situations (McKenna 2013: 15; Grint 2007: 237). *Phronèsis* might be regarded as the process of drawing from *episteme*, which is context-independent intelligence or "scientific knowledge" (Grint 2007: 237) and *nous*, "the insightfulness that makes up for the imprecision of rationality" (Dunne 1997: 15). The possible link between *phronèsis* and *sophia*, the 'other wisdom', is less clear but generally thought to relate to the possibility of acquiring transcendent knowledge intuitively in contemplation (Trowbridge 2011: 151) and, following Socrates, contemplative, esoteric or philosophical wisdom (Robinson 1990: 14).

In returning to Aristotelian *phronèsis* some social sciences scholars have drawn from the contemporary philosophical movement inspired by MacIntyre (1984) and Dunne (1997) to challenge the scientific assumptions that have dominated how professional domains of knowledge have been conceived, practiced, and institutionalized (Kinsella and Pitman 2012). Phronetic research takes a praxeological and axiological approach resonant with MacIntyre's interpretation of practice as the "arena in which the virtues are exhibited and …receive their primary…definition" (MacIntyre 1984: 187). The focus is on human agency and intentionality shaped within particular narratives and, following MacIntyre, a "telos" or a sense of future goals or ends within particular narratives. A phronetic research method was adopted in focusing on human agency in the analysis of findings.

The intent of the management wisdom survey was to explore the nature of the leaders' 'ontological acuity' defined by McKenna and Rooney (2008: 2) as providing "wise leaders with insights beyond the isomorphic tendencies of organizational discourse. Thus, they can evaluate normative practice and its underlying episteme to provide alternative ways of knowing, deciding, and acting." Rooney (2013a: 38–39) argues for close observance of cases, contexts and practice using dialogical and empathetic approaches to ask "how" and to analyze both the narrative and the tacit elements such as emotions, habits, skills and actions. Social Practice Wisdom ("SPW") is not only a research approach but also a re-articulation of Aristotelian *phronèsis*:

> To be practical is to be able to navigate the challenges of thoughtfully and mindfully acting in social life; it means creating long-term well-being through praxis. In this sense, practical wisdom is a way of being that is often far from easy and convenient. (Rooney 2013b: 86).

Social Practice Wisdom is defined by five nested and integrating principles developed by McKenna et al. (2009), revised and summarized by Rooney (2016) in his website:

1. Qualities of mind: An aware, equanimous, and actively open mind. This involves equanimity to understand uncertainty and situated relativities of values, culture, and politics.
2. Knowledge and transcendent ability: Self-knowledge, social, cultural, economic and political knowledge, with insight, foresight, mindsight, and creativity to achieve social excellence and to create well-being.
3. Virtue: Pro-social behavior. Careful consideration and understanding of people's needs, empathy and compassion; including emotional and social needs, to find the right and ethical (virtuous) thing to do.
4. Praxis/doing: Aesthetics,[3] creativity, skill, experience, predispositions, mastery and judgment for responsible use of knowledge, power and communication. This involves knowing why, how, and when to adapt to the environment and why, how, and when to change it.
5. Creating positive and sustainable outcomes for long-term change to the conditions of life: This involves being a galvanizing leader and artful communicator who effects pro-social change with exceptional outcomes.

The methodology and results of the management wisdom survey are reported elsewhere (Thompson 2017) but are summarized here for the purpose of illustrating the extent to which economic wisdom is practiced in managerial decision-making through adopting a phronetic grounded research approach. The aim of the survey was to reveal the habitus of managers, their understanding and application of wisdom in a largely business context. Through an analysis of the language they use, similarities of expression were grouped to identify wisdom constructs. The enquiry might be summarized and framed in one simple question: "How do you, as a manager, understand and apply wisdom?" No a priori definitions were stated, descriptive or normative categories, or theories. The research approach is similar to that adopted by researchers who have sought to identify the virtues in descriptions of managerial excellence "in order to learn and understand their extant virtue language prior to applying theoretical virtue concepts" (Whetstone 2003: 355). Whilst there are elements of a grounded theory approach in illuminating boundaries and categories within the data, there is no theoretical sampling involved in the analysis.

An advisory panel of two strategic consultants and one executive coach designed three survey questions for senior level business leaders defined as C-Suite leaders (or organizational equivalents) and company owners. The questions were:

1. What does wisdom mean for you?

---

[3] The interpretation of Aristotle's use of the term aesthetics in relation to practical wisdom made by Rooney et al. (2010) is that it is the creative art of living with special reference to communicating difficult to convey ideas in everyday social practice, and communicative excellence that creates value for oneself and others.

2. Management decisions are generally acknowledged as requiring fact informed knowledge and a rational approach. In your experience, can you describe how wisdom might add something more to the decision making process?
3. How might someone acquire wisdom?

The selection process for respondents was drawn from the networks of the advisory panel and a CEIBS executive education network. During 2010, 85 Western leaders from 21 countries were surveyed and during 2011, 96 Chinese leaders based in mainland China were surveyed. The majority of the Chinese respondents held senior management positions in mid-sized enterprises (RMB 400m – RMB 600m annual turnover). Of the Western survey participants, 63.5 per cent served companies with annual turnover exceeding €60 million. Participant responses were largely captured via email or hard copy forms but 11 participants were interviewed (Thompson 2017).

In seeking to establish the managers' understanding of wise decision-making it was decided to define the meaning of knowledge as "technical expertise, data, facts" to avoid any potential confusion with the notion of wisdom. Management decision-making was defined as a combination of knowledge and "a rational approach".

The analysis of data was aided by the use of the Leximancer tool which, whilst merging some concepts with synonymous words to maximize their semantic content, does not change the words in the research text, which can be used in the form it takes in the actual sample of data. The initial wave of analysis identified five constructs of wisdom in the data: (i) Humane Character; (ii) Non-rational (intuitive) insight; (iii) Judgment/decision-making; (iv) Problem solving, and, (vi) Smart/knowledgeable. The latter three constructs: judgment/decision-making, problem solving and smart/knowledgeable were grouped under one unifying construct: rational capability.

In seeking to understand the meaning of wisdom to the Chinese participants, the Mandarin word for wisdom provides interpretive insight. Wisdom in Mandarin contains two ideas rather than one: *zhi* 智 (practical intelligence/cognition/knowledge), and *hui* 慧 (enlightened mind/intuition/insight). Chinese participants frequently referred to "IQ" and "EQ" as proxy interpretations of 智慧 in describing wisdom in the decision-making process and it is therefore possible that the blending of the cognitive and non-cognitive capacities of Wisdom is more pronounced by the Chinese participants than the Western participants. Semantically the Mandarin provides for two constructs of wisdom that are confirmed by the understanding of most participants: rational capability and non-rational insight. The third construct of humane character incorporates references to ethics and the explicit mentions of values: honesty, integrity, trust, respect, humility, fairness, dignity, courage, empathy and care.

Whilst the three constructs of rational capability, humane character and non-rational insight are the strongest constructs of wisdom attributed from a textual analysis of the participants' comments, two further categories of attributes are distinguishable in the textual corpora: self-awareness and emotional stability.

To illustrate the meanings of each the five wisdom constructs, example participant responses from Thompson (2017) are reproduced below.

13.1 Rational Capability

In part of his answer to question one, the GM of the Russian operation of a spices company said the following:

> There is a clear difference, as well as overlapping, between wisdom and intellect or logical mind. Being armed with wisdom you are able to get more information from the same set of facts and figures. And you will create a decision, which will be the simplest of the best, or the best of the simplest. And you will make this decision much faster, than simply a clever person could.

The Chief Engineer of a Chinese company answered the same question thus:

> The ability to apply knowledge innovatively, accurately, flexibly and quickly. Have a broad span of knowledge base and know how to apply knowledge effectively.

In both cases, the focus on the role of wisdom is the capability to use reason, logic and intellect to gain a greater knowledge of a situation and apply the knowledge more quickly and effectively.

13.2 Non-rational (Intuitive) Insight

The former GM of an Austrian ice cream division spoke of intuition as an integral part of decision-making: "Wisdom is close to intuition. Insight into what might happen in the future. It combines intuition with logic and applied common sense." And, similarly, the Managing Director of a Chinese-American management consulting group said: "Wisdom comes from the combining of analysis; intuition informed by experience; and the ability to visualize a future state beyond the data." Both refer to wisdom as giving insights beyond the data and logic and even the ability to visualize the future. The Coordinator of a Belgian cultural services network refers to the capacity of intuition as exceeding mental comprehension:

> The intuition is experienced by those who are working with it as exceeding by far the capacities of comprehension of our human mind and, thereby gives a capacity of decision making connected with a much greater quality, to the globality of the factors. It is my personal experience on multiple occasions.

13.3 Humane Character

The EU HR director for an international technology group identifies the ethical desires and preferences of a person who acts with wisdom:

> Wisdom knits together a whole series of intangible things such as character, values, intuition, a feeling of responsibility, a preference for action, a desire for safety and order on behalf of others.

The CEO of a real estate company in Harbin, China referenced three well-known Chinese virtues as part of his description of wisdom. *Ren* focuses on an individual's relationships within the community, defined in terms of sociability, security, and status (Wang and Lin 2009:400) whilst *yi* refers to a sense of moral rightness and discernment: *yi* and *ren* "often work together in unison to define morality and to guide actions" (Ip 2009:464) and the virtue of 诚信 *cheng-xin* meaning honesty and trustworthiness:

> "Zhi" is the ability of acquiring knowledge and experience. "Hui" is the ability of using and comprehending the knowledge. Of course "Zhi Hui" also includes benevolence, justice and honesty. In another word, a person with wisdom must be one who has a very high ethics. But a person with very high ethics, is not necessarily one who is with wisdom.

13.4 Self-Awareness

Twenty respondents used self-awareness and related terms such as reflection, mindful pondering and observing. The CMO of a Chinese technology company sees reflective practice as a continuous an integrated part of decision making: "Logical judgments, rational decision-making, continuous reflection and improvement." The owner of a Canadian consulting company expressed the idea of wisdom being acquired through practices of listening, observing, mindfulness and reflection:

> In my view, wisdom is acquired over time, when one gives conscious attention to being mindful, allowing oneself to engage in reflecting upon issues and upon life overall. Often, gaining wisdom means listening instead of speaking, observing rather than reacting, and certainly, continuing to allow the mind to remain open to endlessly increasing possibilities.

13.5 Emotional Regulation

Emotional regulation as an attribute of wisdom was recognized by eleven participants. The senior manager of a Columbian social bank understood emotional regulation as "the ability to make fair judgments, specially in difficult situations, keeping emotions under control." A divisional manager of a Bulgarian consumer goods company expressed the idea of emotional regulation by wise people through a collection of linked adjectives:

> For me the wisdom includes – life experience (professional and personal), emotional intelligence, tolerance, realism but also many other capabilities necessary to achieve personal balance. The wise people are balanced and sober.

13.6 Conclusions

The findings of the management wisdom survey reported in Thompson (2017) show that senior managers understand wisdom to be practical, rational, ethical and intuitive and that they identify these constructs as intrinsic to decision-making. Although no validity can be inferred from the number of concept mentions from the unprompted responses by participants to the three survey questions, the responses do fit the categories of the five SPW principles developed by McKenna et al. (2009). The evidence for the five SPW principles and the five wisdom constructs above indicate the presence of economic wisdom, in the managerial decision-making process. Such wisdom challenges the narrative of positive economics and its implications for managerial behavior tellingly portrayed by Albert Carr in his *locus classicus*: “Is Business Bluffing Ethical?” (1968).

Although the need for economic pragmatism and logical analysis of facts is recognized as a key feature in managerial decision-making by the survey participants it is clear that the idea of wisdom contextualizes rational capability within a wider range of human attributes that do not fit the modernist faith in positivist, determinist and objectivist rationality. In fact it is difficult to identify the presence of homo oeconomicus in the overall findings at all.

The significance of intuition and nonrational cues in the survey data supports Sternberg’s (1998) Balance Theory of Wisdom in which perspicacity is identified as one of six components of wisdom. In this present study, which relies on unprompted responses, over half of the Western respondents associated wisdom with intuitive insight or “gut feel” or, in the words of GM of a machine tools manufacturer for France and Iberia: “Wisdom adds a non-knowledge, non-rational dimension.” Participants provide a hint of their understanding of what ‘gut feel’ means in, for example, the words of the Global Head of Information Services and Compliance of a governance and compliance multinational, “the unconscious application of patterns that we connect to the present matter at hand.” Exactly what is meant by “gut feel” or “management intuition”(APAC Capital Market Managing Director for a multinational consultancy) in the praxis of wise management requires further research. However, it would not be unreasonable to conclude from the wise management survey that it is a signal that tacit knowledge (Polanyi 1962, 1967) exists in the decision-making process of many managers.

A further conclusion about the nature of practical economic wisdom is that, unlike Rand’s John Galt, they do have a clear sense of “moral obligation” to their fellows. In the words of the EU HR director of an international technology group,

"Wisdom knits together a whole series of intangible things such as character, values, intuition, a feeling of responsibility, a preference for action, a desire for safety and order on behalf of others." Decisions may well be made to maximize happiness but not without reference to the beliefs and intentions of the individual decision-maker or their influence on others in making a decision. As Hauerwas has pointed out, "Our cognitive capacities as moral agents are dependent on our being timeful beings who are able to form our intentions in efficacious ways. But the very efficacy of our intentions is dependent on the content of our beliefs about ourselves, others and our environment." (Hauerwas 1974: 780). This perspective causes business people to ask what kind of persons they are becoming or what kind of corporation they are creating. The Self-awareness construct emerged as a secondary wisdom concept in the survey data but, it is perhaps more forceful if considered as an overlapping construct to humane character in which other-awareness is evident in statements that reflect on how an actor should act or behave in certain situations. As an example, the owner of of a Canadian events company understands wisdom as "operating from a heightened level of awareness and understanding. To be wise is to observe fully before acting, and to refrain from acting, when that is what is best called for."

The management wisdom survey indicates that an economic wisdom is present in the minds of managers. From an optimistic perspective economic wisdom could offer resources for management education and development across all business domains to address the challenges of the VUCA world with a more realistic, holistic and planet-friendly economic approach.

References

Accenture. 2016. *The UN Global Compact: Accenture Strategy CEO Study*. Source: https://www.accenture.com/us-en/insight-UN-global-compact-CEO-study?c=strat_stratsmctwt_10000160&n=smc_0316.

Alford, H.J., and M.J. Naughton. 2001. *Managing as if Faith Mattered: Christian Social Principles in the Modern Organization*. Notre Dame: University of Notre Dame Press.

Barton, D. 2011. *CEOs Can Attract Long-Term Investors*. HBR Blog Network. Source: https://hbr.org/2011/09/how-ceos-can-attract-investors

Becker, G.S. 1993. Nobel Lecture: The Economic Way of Looking at Behavior. *Journal of Political Economy* 101(3): 385–409.

Bevan, D., and P. Werhane. 2015. The Inexorable Sociality of Commerce: The Individual and Others in Adam Smith. *Journal of Business Ethics* 127(2): 327–335.

Bouckaert, L., and L. Zsolnai, ed. 2011. *The Palgrave Handbook of Spirituality and Business*. London: Palgrave.

Brown, V. 1994. *Adam Smith's Discourse: Canonicity, Commerce, and Conscience*. Psychology Press.

Carr, A. 1968. Is Business Bluffing Ethical? *Harvard Business Review* 143: 155.

Columbo, R.J. 2009. Exposing the Myth of Homo Economicus. *Journal of Law & Public Policy* 32(2): 737–765.

Drucker, P.F. 1968. *The Age of Discontinuity: Guidelines to Our Changing Society*. New Brunswick: Transaction Publishers.

Dunne, J. 1997. *Back to the Rough Ground: Practical Judgement and the Lure of Technique*. Notre Dame: University of Notre Dame Press.
George, W. 2013, December. Bill George on Rethinking Capitalism. *McKinsey Quarterly*.
Gigerenzer, G., and H. Brighton. 2009. Homo Heuristicus: Why Biased Minds Make Better Inferences. *Topics in Cognitive Science* 1: 107–143.
Grint, K. 2007. Learning to Lead: Can Aristotle Help Us Find the Road to Wisdom? *Leadership 3*(2): 231.
Griswold, C.L. 1999. *Adam Smith and the Virtues of Enlightenment*. Cambridge: Cambridge University Press.
Haldane, A. 2012. "The Dog and the Frisbee", Speech Given at the Federal Reserve Bank of Kansas City's 36th Economic Policy Symposium "The Changing Policy Landscape". Jackson Hole, Wyoming.
Hauerwas, S. 1974. *Vision and Virtue*. Fides: Notre Dame.
Heinemann, B. 2016, July 26. How the CFO and General Counsel Can Partner More Effectively. *The Daily Alert*, Harvard Business School. Available at: https://hbr.org/2016/07/how-the-cfo-and-general-counsel-can-partner-more-effectively.
Ip, P.K. 2009. Is Confucianism Good for Business Ethics in China? *Journal of Business Ethics* 88(3): 463–476.
Kahneman, D., and A. Tversky. 1979. Prospect Theory: An Analysis of Decision Under Risk. *Econometrica* 1979: 263–291.
Kinsella, E.A. and A. Pitman (Eds.) 2012. *Phronesis as Professional Knowledge: Practical Wisdom in the Professions*. London: Springer.
Kongsbakk, N. and D. Rooney. 2016. Too Busy to Learn: Wisdom, Mindfulness, and Grounding Learning. In *Wisdom Learning: Perspectives on Wising up Management Education*, ed. W. Küpers and O. Gunnlaugson. London: Gower.
KPMG. 2014. *A New Vision of Value*. KPMG International.
MacIntyre, A. 1984. *After Virtue: A Study in Moral Theory*. 2nd ed. Notre Dame: Notre Dame University Press.
Malinowski, P. 2013. Neural Mechanisms of Attentional Control in Mindfulness Meditation. *Frontiers in Neuroscience* 7.
McKenna, B. 2013. *The Multi-Dimensional Character of Wisdom. In Wise Management in Organisational Complexity*, ed. M. Thompson and D. Bevan, 13–33. Basingstoke: Palgrave.
McKenna, B., and D. Rooney. 2008. Wise Leadership and the Capacity for Ontological Acuity. *Management Communication Quarterly* 21: 537–546.
McKenna, B., D. Rooney, and K. Boal. 2009. Wisdom Principles as a Meta-Theoretical Basis for Evaluating Leadership. *The Leadership Quarterly* 20(2): 177–190.
Midgley, M. 2009, April 20. Hobbes's Leviathan, Part 3: What is Selfishness? *The Guardian*. Source: http://www.guardian.co.uk/commentisfree/belief/2009/apr/20/religion-philosophy-hobbes-dawkins-selfishness.
Polanyi, M. 1962. The Republic of Science: Its Political and Economic Theory. *Minerva* 1(1): 54–73.
———. 1967. The Growth of Science in Society. *Minerva* 5(4): 533–545.
Polman, P. 2011. *The Remedies for Capitalism*. McKinsey. Source: http://www.mckinsey.com/en/Capitalism/Paul_Polman.aspx.
———. 2012, June. Captain Planet: An Interview with Unilever CEO Paul Polman. *Harvard Business Review*.
Rand, A. 2007. *Atlas Shrugged*. New York: Penguin Books.
Raphael, D.D. 2007. *The Impartial Spectator: Adam Smith's Moral Philosophy*. Oxford: Oxford University Press.
Rifkin, J. 2009. *The Empathic Civilisation*. Cambridge: Polity Press.
Robinson, D.N. 1990. Wisdom Through the Ages. In *Wisdom: Its Mature, Origins, and Development*, ed. R.J. Sternberg, 13–24. New York: New York, Cambridge University Press.

Rooney, D. 2013a. Empirical Wisdom Research. In *Wise Management in Organisational Complexity*, ed. M. Thompson and D. Bevan, 34–52. Basingstoke: Palgrave.

———. 2013b. Being a Wise Organizational Researcher: Ontology, Epistemology and Axiology. In *A Handbook of Practical Wisdom: Leadership, Organization and Integral Business Practice*, ed. Wendelin Küpers and David J. Pauleen, 79–98. London: Gower.

———. 2016. *The Knowledge Economy, Knowledge Policy, & Wisdom Site*. Source: https://sites.google.com/site/davidrooneyknowledge.

Rooney, D., B. McKenna, and P. Liesch. 2010. *Wisdom and Management in the Knowledge Economy*. London: Routledge.

Sen, A. 1977. Rational Fools: A Critique of the Behavioral Foundations of Economic Theory. *Philosophy & Public Affairs* 6(4): 317–344.

———. 1987. *On Ethics and Economics*. Oxford: Blackwell.

Smith, A. 1790. *The Theory of Moral Sentiments*, ed. R.P. Hanley (2009). London: Penguin Edition.

———. 1776. *An Inquiry into the Nature and Causes of the Wealth Of Nations*, ed. Andrew Skinner (1982). London: Penguin Edition.

Solomon, R. 2006. Free Enterprise, Sympathy and Virtue. *Free Enterprise: Values in Action Conference Series, 2005–2006*. Available at SSRN: http://papers.ssrn.com/sol3/papers.cfm?abstract_id=927482.

Sternberg, R.J. 1998. A Balance Theory of Wisdom. *Review of General Psychology* 2(4): 247–365.

Thompson, M.J. 2007. Homo Spiritualis in Business. In *Spirituality as a Public Good*, ed. L. Bouckaert and L. Zsolnai. Garant: Antwerp.

———. 2011a. A Philosophy and Spirituality of Wisdom-Based Leadership. In *Leading with Wisdom*, ed. M. Thompson and J. Eynikel. Garant: Antwerp.

———., ed. 2011b. *Business, Spirituality and the Common Good*. Russell: Boise.

———. 2012. On Self-interest. In *Spiritual Humanism and Economic Wisdom*, ed. H. Opdebeeck and L. Zsolnai. Garant: Antwerp.

———. 2017. How Managers Understand Wisdom in Decision-Making: A Phronetic Research Approach. In *Wisdom Learning: Perspectives on Wising up Management Education*, ed. W. Küpers and O. Gunnlaugson. London: Gower.

Trowbridge, R.H. 2011. Waiting for Sophia: 30 Years of Conceptualizing Wisdom in Empirical Psychology. *Research in Human Development* 8(2): 149–164.

Wang, C.L., and X. Lin. 2009. Migration of Chinese Consumption Values: Traditions, Modernization, and Cultural Renaissance. *Journal of Business Ethics* 88(3): 399–409.

Werhane, P. 1989. *Adam Smith and His Legacy for Modern Capitalism*. Oxford: Oxford University Press.

Whetstone, J.T. 2003. The Language of Managerial Excellence: Virtues as Understood and Applied. *Journal of Business Ethics* 44(4): 343–357.

Wilson, E.O. 1998. *Consilience*. New York: Alfred A. Knopf.

Zsolnai, L., ed. 2011. *Spirituality and Ethics in Management*. Dordrecht: Springer.

Part IV
Economic Policy and Economic Development

Chapter 14
Catholic Social Thought and Amartya Sen on Justice

Johan Verstraeten

Abstract The paper suggests that Sen's "Idea of Justice" is not only the most inspiring and reasonable response to Rawls' "Theory of Justice" but also an important challenge for Catholic Social Thought. The paper shows that Catholic Social Thought and Sen's Idea of Justice have much in common. It argues that despite the emphasis on individual freedom in Sen's capability approach, the convergence between his approach and Catholic Social Thought is strong. There are several points of resemblance: the role of indignation and emotion, the implications of a realistic anthropology ("seeking institutions that promote justice rather than institutions as themselves manifestations of justice"), freedom as responsibility, human rights as rooted in our shared humanity, valuing religious wisdom in justice theory.

If rationality were to be a church, it would have to be a rather broad church

(Sen 2009, 195)

Catholic social thought[1] is more than a normative framework based on particular faith convictions, papal encyclicals or theology. It is also a dynamic tradition of ethical reasoning about social, political and economic issues. Both as 'permanent

[1] For a definition of the distinction between Catholic social doctrine, Catholic social teaching and 'Catholic social thought' see: Verstraeten 2000.

Official Texts from the Catholic Church (reference is made for all documents to the numbers of the paragraphs and not of the pages).

Leo XIII, Rerum novarum, 1891 in: Michael Walsh, Brian Davis (Eds.): Proclaiming Justice and Peace. Papal Documents from Rerum Novarum through Centesimus Annus, Mystic (Connecticut), Twenty-Third Publications, 1991.

Pius XI, Quadragesimo anno (1931), in: Walsh, Davis, o.c.

John XXIII, Pacem, in Terris, in: Walsh, Davis, o.c.

Gaudium et spes, Pastoral Constitution on the Church in the Modern World, in: o.c.

Benedict XVI, Deus caritas est, Encyclical Letter, Vatican City, Libreria Editrice Vaticana 2005

Francis, Apostolic Exhortation Evangelii Gaudium, Vatican City, Libreria Editrice Vaticana, 2013.

J. Verstraeten (✉)
Catholic University of Leuven, Leuven, Belgium
e-mail: johan.verstraeten@kuleuven.be

P. Rona, L. Zsolnai (eds.), *Economics as a Moral Science*,
Virtues and Economics 1, DOI 10.1007/978-3-319-53291-2_14

learning process' requiring analysis, and as framework of ethical reasoning, it cannot exist without a continuing conversation with the human sciences. Moreover, in order to convince non-Catholics of the reasonableness of its arguments Catholic social thought can't be limited to reiterating its own principles and doctrine. It has only impact on the common search for a more just world in as far as it is in conversation with the leading secular social philosophers of a particular time. In fact it has always done it. In the nineteenth century the encyclical *Rerum novarum* adjusted its Thomist approach with insights from the liberal tradition (defining property as "natural" and "inalienable right"). In the post Medellin era, the official Church' engagement with liberation theology necessitated a critical conversation on Marxism and the idea of class struggle. After Rawls (1971) *Theory of Justice* became an indispensable dialogue partner of Catholic experts in social ethics, allowing them, despite fundamental differences, to demonstrate that the search for justice is reasonable and that making an option for the poor is not merely based on a faith commitment. Realizing justice and opting for the poor are reasonable commitments that can be underpinned with arguments. For example: Rawls' (1971) arguments for the difference principle (economic inequality can only be accepted on the condition that it is also for the benefit of the least advantaged), are an indication that the Christian option is not unreasonable.

With regards to social justice and the economy today, probably the most challenging dialogue partner is Amartya Sen, particularly his book *The Idea of Justice* (Sen 2009), which is not only an outstanding response to Rawls' magnum opus, but also an unavoidable touchstone for the adequacy of Catholic social thought, and this notwithstanding the fact that some experts are inclined to overemphasize the incommensurability between Sen's presumed liberal individualism and the common good oriented communitarian justice approach in papal encyclicals. Symptomatic for this interpretation is Séverine Deneulin's 'Catholic' critique to which Sen himself pays attention (Sen 2009: 244–247).

Without denying fundamental differences between Sen's liberal individualism and the social personalist approach in the Catholic tradition, this article will focus on some underestimated points of convergence between both. In the first part I will outline the most evident of these convergences and, in the second part, I will articulate that even the teleological Catholic 'common good' approach is not completely incommensurable with Sen's concern for the real freedom of the individual.

Francis, Laudato si' Encyclical Letter on Care for Our Common Home, Vatican City, Libreria Editrice Vaticana, 2015

United States Catholic Bishops, Economic Justice for All: Pastoral Letter on Catholic Social Teaching and the U.S. Economy, 1986.

14.1 How Sen's Ideas Corroborate Catholic Social Thinking

Both Catholic social thought, and Sen's idea of justice start from indignation about injustice and from the common presupposition that the experience of injustice constitutes a moral duty to seek reasonable ways for a just alternative. That experience is for both rooted in profound emotions. In *Evangelii gaudium* pope Francis interprets them in the perspective of mercy: "we incarnate the duty of hearing the cry of the poor when we are deeply moved by the suffering of others" (Evangelii Gaudium 193). Theologians such as Edward Schillebeeckx refer to 'negative contract experiences'. Sen starts from the conviction that Adam Smith and David Hume "saw reasoning and feeling as deeply interrelated activities" (Sen 2009: 50).

Both argue, moreover, that moral indignation is a necessary but not sufficient condition and that it need to be followed by moral reasoning. According to Sen "unscrutinized instincts" can have no "unconditional final say" (Sen 2009: 51). But they do matter because "...in celebrating reason, there is no particular ground for denying the far-reaching role of instinctive psychology and spontaneous responses. They can supplement each other, and in many cases an understanding of the broadening of the *liberating* [my italics] role of our feelings can constitute good subject matter for reasoning itself" (Sen 2009: 49–50).

Against skepticism about the very possibility of change, both Sen and Catholic social thought refer to hope. Action for justice or reasoning about it, is not meaningless or in vain. In the Pastoral Constitution *Gaudium et Spes* the Church has expressed its belief that when we have "nurtured on earth the value of human dignity, brotherhood and freedom" all these " good fruits of our enterprise" will be once fully realized and 'transfigured' in the eschaton (GS, 39). It is not meant to be an argument to remain passive, but a motivation for a commitment in the here and now. In contract, Sen's language is not theological at all, but nevertheless he expresses his conviction that it makes sense to believe that 'hope and history rhyme'. His source of inspiration is Seamus Heaney's poem on hope (Sen 2009: 27).

> History says, Don't hope
> On this side of the grave,
> But then, once in a lifetime
> The longed-for tidal wave
> Of Justice can rise up,
> And hope and history rhyme

Sen makes an explicit and CST an implicit distinction between rational solutions and reasonable solutions. Sen is averse to any sort of theory characterized by rationalistic forms of complexity reduction. Hence his convincing critique of rational choice theories and of theories which confuse rational behavior with action based on mere self-interest. Sen also proposes that "serious note of critical scrutiny from the perspectives of *others* must have a significant role in taking us *beyond rationality into reasonable behavior* in relation to other people" (Sen 2009: 197), an idea most relevant to underpin a commitment to indigenous people whose interest are often completely neglected (but strongly defended by Pope Francis in *Laudato si*).

Sen's adequate and complex concept of reasoning matches moreover with one of the basic insights from the Thomist Tradition: "doing good is acting according to reason". Both for CST and Sen human persons are "capable of being reasonable through being open-minded about welcoming information and through reflecting on argument coming from different quarters, along with undertaking interactive deliberations and debates on how the underlying issues should be seen" (Sen 2009: 43).

It is crystal clear that Sen rejects reasoning that excludes the wisdom of religion. He not only takes inspiration from the Hindu tradition, but also from the Gospel. His interpretation of Jesus' story the good Samaritan is most interesting because for him it is not an argument for more charity, or, as Benedict XVI suggested for 'charity primordially among Christians' (*Deus caritas est*, part 2). For Sen the story is about the universality of justice, or, more precisely, the idea of an open impartiality: every human being is 'neighbor' and his or her interests and perspectives need to be taken into account in reasoning about realizing a more just state of affairs in the world (Sen 2009: 171–172). In other words: of the good Samaritan is an argument for a non-Rawlsian and non- parochial neighborhood concept (see Sen 2009: 172, 199).

Both Sen and CST reject ideal solutions for a perfect world. While the Catholic tradition has always been suspicious about dreaming of systems "so perfect that nobody needs to be good" (T.S. Eliot) – an insight based on a profound and realistic understanding of the human condition, – Sen also rejects dreaming of perfect institutional arrangements. He focuses more on" how justice can be advanced" than on "what would be a perfectly just institution" (Sen 2009, 9), and this without denying the role of institutions *as such.* To put it in the words of Sen: "we have to seek institutions that promote justice, rather than treating the institutions as themselves manifestations of justice" (Sen 2009: 82*).* Structures and institutions are not good in themselves. But while Sen judges institutions in in the light of the consequences of real human behavior and "in the light of concrete social achievements" (Sen 2009: 83), official Catholic social teaching doesn't use that expression. It does however go beyond vague references to the human person 'adequately considered' or human dignity in general. For example Pope Francis clearly states that "we are not simply talking about ensuring nourishment or a 'dignified sustenance' for all people, but also their general temporal welfare and prosperity. This means education, access to health care, and above all employment, for it is through *free, creative, participatory and mutually supportive labor* that human beings express and enhance the dignity of their lives" (Evangelii Gaudium 192).

A fifth common insight is that both Sen and CST strongly believe in the universality of human rights as grounded in 'our shared humanity' (Sen 2009: 143). Significant in this context is Sen's reference to the word 'catholicity': "we have reason for some *catholicity* in considering different avenues for promoting" rights as "moral claims" (Sen 2009: 364). Sen's 'catholicity' goes much further than his attention for human rights. It is the basis of his rejection of Rawls 'parochialism' in the Law of Peoples (Rawls 1999), in which Rawls reduces the possibility of applying principles of justice to liberal and decent states. In public reasoning about reducing injustice one should not adopt a closed impartiality (Rawls 1971), but an open impartiality, which requires "taking into account the interests" and also the "perspectives" (Sen 2009: 402) of even the distant "other". Crucial in this regard is the "inclusional broadening" as "the broadening of the collectivity of people whose interests are seen as relevant" (Sen 2009: 199). As such there is room for 'insignificant others' (an idea which matches with liberation theology). Sen urges us to pay attention "to the extent to which different voices from diverse sections of the people can be actually heard" (Sen 2009: xiii). Against Rawls, he also includes poor countries (burdened states) in the reasoning about justice. In contrast with "parochialism", one must look at the world "by the eyes of the rest of mankind" (Sen 2009: 406). "Arguments that may first appear outlandish (…) may help to enrich our thinking" (Sen 2009: 407)

Like *Pacem in Terris* and the Universal Declaration of Human Rights Sen acknowledges not only freedom rights (first generation rights) but also following Pogge and unlike Rawls in the Law of Nations, universal social rights or, in his words, "second generation rights" for the fulfillment of 'imperfect global obligations" (Sen 2009: 381). Sen defines these second generation rights as the long term goals the role of which is "to secure an adequate level of agency and morally basic capabilities for everyone in the world –regardless of nationality, ethnicity, religion, age, gender, or sexual preference" (Sen 2009: 381). Although Sen doesn't refer to human dignity as moral ground for human rights, it is obvious that he rejects any sort of legal positivistic interpretation: Laws must be based on human rights it and not vice versa: while Bentham saw 'rights as a 'children of the law', human rights are according to Sen 'parents of law' (Sen 2009: 363).

14.2 Two More Complex Points of Convergence: Justice and Freedom

One could say that Sen's idea of justice differs from the catholic tradition in so far that it is not directly related to the normative and teleological idea of the common good. But in Catholic social thought the 'common good' can be interpreted in different ways: as the fundamental normative purpose of the state or the world community (the 'universal common good'), or as a means to that purpose (cf. *Gaudium et spes* 26 and 74: "the sum of those conditions of social life" which allow social groups and their individual members "to attain their own perfection"). But there is a third interpretation proposed in *Economic Justice for All* (1986) a pastoral letter on the economy by the US bishops. They interpret the common good as the realization of a participative society: "Basic justice demands the establishment of minimum levels of participation in the life of the human community for all persons", "especially the poor" (Economic Justice for All, 77 and 86).

The US bishops' interpretation is an excellent articulation of what is already implicitly assumed in the broader Catholic tradition. In that tradition (at least since Aquinas) the first point of consideration is the duty or responsibility of citizens to contribute to the common good. Aquinas refers in this regard to the word 'general' or 'legal' justice. In order to avoid confusion with the nineteenth century law positivistic interpretations of 'legal justice', catholic authors such as Taparelli d'Azeglio have introduced the concept of '*social justice*' as a substitute for the concept of legal or general justice. It was officially endorsed in the encyclical *Quadragesimo anno* (1931). More recently the US bishops have enriched the social justice approach, by way of distinguishing two aspects of it: a duty of individuals to contribute and a duty of the society to enable them to do this. On the one hand there is *contributive* justice as duty "to be active and productive *participants* in the life of society". It implies not only a participation in the economy, but also the creation of "goods, services and nonmaterial and spiritual values" necessary for the wellbeing of the whole of society. Hence, not only work matters, but also other human activities such as arts, poetry, conviviality, voluntary work, contemplation, care etc…(Economic Justice for All 1986: 71).

On the other hand, the "duty component" of social justice, expressed in terms of '*contributive*' justice, is connected with a second element according to which citizens must also be *enabled* to make their contribution. Precisely this concern for 'enabling' people to become active participants in the society is one of the major concerns of Sen (who talks about empowering people).

In the Catholic tradition there is a risk to reduce the enabling function, which partially overlaps with the concept of distributive justice, to "the allocation of income, wealth and power in society…evaluated in light of its effects on persons whose basic material needs are unmet" (Economic Justice for All 1986: 71). Particularly in *Quadragesimo anno* the focus is on a distribution of goods. "...the riches that economic-social developments constantly increase ought to be so distributed among individual persons and classes that the common advantage of all... will be safeguarded…" But the text continues with something more relevant: The safeguarding of the common advantage of all is immediately articulated as follows: "that the common good of all society will be kept inviolate. By this law of *social justice*, one class is forbidden to exclude the other from sharing in the benefits... To each must therefore be given his own share of, goods, and the distribution of created goods, which... must be brought into *conformity with the norms of the common good, that is social justice* (QA 57–58)."

In this perspective there is much more than merely a concern for the distribution of goods or the fulfillment of basic needs. Social justice is above all about the realization of a participative society in which citizens are enabled to contribute, and thus to participate. This contribution to the whole presupposes free persons as actors. In the words of the US bishops: "The meaning of social justice [which in the words of QA = the common good] includes a *duty* to *organize economic* and *social institutions* so that *people can contribute to society* in ways respect their *freedom* and the dignity of their labor", and which enables them to become "more capable of *acting intelligently, freely, and in ways that lead to self-realization*" (Economic Justice for All 1986: 72).

The creation of a society in which people can realize their potential with real freedom matches quite well will Sen's capability approach, as well as with Sen's belief in a participative society in which also the poor have a stake as participants in the reasoning about the creation of a just society.

But there is more. A recent evolution in Catholic social thought must be mentioned: a more radical interpretation of the common good in the light of the (preferential) option for the poor. This principle is a result of the dialogue between the magisterium of the Catholic church and liberation theology and, it is recently strongly reaffirmed by pope Francis in his apostolic exhortation *Evangelii gaudium*. This principle has also an objective dimension as realistic assessment of lifestyles, policies, and social institutions in terms of their impact on the poor, who are not only considered as objects of care, but also as subjects of their history. In this Sen's thinking can be useful for Catholic thinking in so far as it contributes to a more substantial articulation of what poverty is (a lack of capabilities to function) and what the concrete implications are of a real option for the poor. Sen interprets development not only in terms of freedom, but also as an 'empowering process' (Sen 2009: 249), an idea which has more affinity with the liberation paradigm than with classical development thinking. The Catholic tradition of thought hesitates between the two (some encyclicals put emphasis on development, other texts and liberation theologians opt for the liberation paradigm). Sen also puts much emphasis on the participation of the poor in democratic decision making. According to him democracy is not primordially a matter of public ballots but 'government by discussion'. This government by discussion requires at a global level "public discussion *of, for and by* the people of the world" (the "by" the people is crucial here, Sen 2009: 328).

A second point for clarification is freedom. On the one hand Sen explicitly rejects the idea that he would defend as sort of radical individualism. It is beyond doubt that Sen focuses mainly on the flourishing of the individual and on the real freedom to choose the sort of life they have reasons to choose and want to achieve. But this doesn't imply that he is a methodological individualist or, that he would underestimate the social dimension of life. Sen himself proves to be very sensitive to this question. In his discussion with Séverine Deneulin, he explains that he would never contend that there is no such thing as the society as a sort of intermediate space between the individual and the state. He only warns against an ideology of the society according to which it becomes a reality apart from individuals, in his words: the "re-establishing of society as an abstraction vis-à-vis the individual" (Sen 2009: 245).

In Sen's perspective, an individual is always interacting with society. He explicitly rejects the presumption "of independence of the thoughts and actions of persons from the society around them" (Sen 2009: 245). His methodological emphasis on open impartiality is, moreover, an indication of the relevance of society and the relevance of "people far and near – in the valuational exercise of individuals" (Sen 2009: 245). As much as the Catholic tradition, Sen emphasizes that freedom has to be as 'freedom with responsibility', that it "makes us accountable for what we do" (Sen 2009: 19) and, that it leads to a behavior that transcends mere self-interest: one has to move from the "pursuit of actual advantage for oneself to promotion of advantage for the community" (Sen 2009: 204).

Apart from this, one must admit that Sen is less group or community oriented than CST. A relevant point in this regard is Sen's warning against the reduction of the identity of an individual to be "merely a member of a group to which he or she belongs" (Sen 2009: 147), but this remark is not an expression of a sort of individualism, but a critical argument against any form or parochialism or nationalistic thinking at the cost of the interests of people outside the group. People can have multiple loyalties: "people can decide on their respective loyalties to different groups" (Sen 2009: 245).

On the other hand there is more room for individual freedom in Catholic social thought than it might appear in some official texts. In the pastoral constitution of Vatican II, *Gaudium et spes*, which is epistemologically the most important Catholic text on social issues and thus a text which serves as a critical touchstone for the interpretation of later official texts, individual freedom is defined in a way which is much more profound than a matter of obedience to the interpretation of moral norms by the magisterium. Most significant is the first part where the council fathers refer to conscience as the 'most secret core and sanctuary' of the human person (Gaudium et spes 16), which is immediately linked with the idea that "only in freedom can man direct himself towards goodness" and that "authentic freedom is an exceptional sign of the divine image within man. For God has willed that man remains under the control of his own decisions…" (*Gaudium et spes*, 17). Although this is directly linked with the search for perfection, loyalty to God, and the need of grace, the text continues unambiguously as follows: "…Man's dignity demands he acts according to a knowing and free choice that is personally motivated and prompted from within, not under blind internal impulse *nor by mere external pressure*" (*Gaudium et spes*, 17). In other words: there is indeed more space for authentic individual freedom in Catholicism than one might think, and as we have pointed out above, the common good requires that individuals are enabled to act according to genuine freedom.

14.3 Conclusion

Far from pretending that Sen's *Idea of Justice* and the Catholic vision on justice simply overlap, I have argued that there is more affinity between both than some Catholic scholars would admit. Even when there is *sensu stricto* no teleological 'common good' approach in Sen's idea of justice, his idea of justice offers as much as the Catholic tradition a realistic and reasonable argument for a participative society in which all citizens and especially the poor are enabled to make a meaningful contribution.

Sen's magisterial work can, moreover, read as a challenge to both Church leaders and economists: if they want to be relevant participants in a debate about *reasonable* steps towards a more just world society, they must abandon absolute truth claims as well as reductionist rational models or "parochialist" ideas. Indeed, paraphrasing Sen, one can say "if rationality were to be a church, it would have to be a rather broad church" (Sen 2009: 195).

References

Rawls, J. 1971. *A Theory of Justice*. Cambridge, MA: The Belknap Press of Harvard University Press, 1999 (revised edition of the 1971 edition).

———. 1999. *The Law of Peoples*. Cambridge, MA: Harvard University Press.

Sen, A. 2009. *The Idea of Justice*. London: Allen Lane (Penguin Books).

Verstraeten, J. 2000. Re-thinking Catholic Social Thought as Tradition. In *Catholic Social Thought: Twilight or Renaissance?* ed. J.S. Boswell, F.P. McHugh and J. Verstraeten (BETL157), 59–77. Leuven: Peeters/University Press.

Chapter 15
The Theological Virtue of Charity in the Economy: Reflections on "Caritas in veritate"

Helen Alford

Abstract Possible connections between the virtue of charity and the economy are explored using key sentences from the third chapter of the encyclical *Caritas in* veritate by Pope Benedict XVI. Without gratuitousness and the unconditional gift operating within normal economic activity, the economy cannot achieve its proper end; while society needs three different sectors to function properly – state, market and civil society – solidarity and reciprocal gift, nevertheless, need to be found in all three. This thinking can be connected with economics on a philosophical level by using the approach of personalism, and on a theological level through practical experience and by using the idea of a theological virtue as a "powerful social resource".

Charity and Economics – such a combination of words would imply to many a text about fundraising, or the need for improved governance on the part of trustees in the charity sector (we may remember the collapse of Kid's Company in 2015, for instance), or perhaps Mrs. Thatcher's various comments about the Good Samaritan, such as the one in a 1968 speech where she said: "even the Good Samaritan had to have the money to help, otherwise he too would have had to pass on the other side" (Thatcher 1968).

If we are talking about charity as a theological virtue, however, our topic is different from these, and one might be forgiven for wondering if there is anything useful that could be said about it in relation to the economy. By the end of this text, however, I hope I will have been able to show with some degree of success (though probably not to the satisfaction of all possible readers) that not only can something useful be said on this point, but even that, in today's socioeconomic context, we would be missing an important aspect of rethinking "economics as a moral science" if we didn't talk about this. In order to get this far without much ado, I will focus my

H. Alford (✉)
Pontifical University of St. Thomas Aquinas ("Angelicum"), Rome, Italy
e-mail: alford@pust.it

P. Rona, L. Zsolnai (eds.), *Economics as a Moral Science*,
Virtues and Economics 1, DOI 10.1007/978-3-319-53291-2_15

comments on the 2009 social encyclical of Pope Benedict XVI entitled *Caritas in veritate*, written to celebrate the fortieth anniversary of a previous social encyclical, written by Pope Paul VI, entitled *Populorum progressio* (Paul VI 1967). In particular, I'd like to focus on the third chapter of *Caritas in veritate* where we find ideas that elicited strong reactions when they first came out, since it is precisely through revisiting these controversial points that we can advance our argument.

Some commentators regarded the ideas in chapter three as "innovative"; others admitted they didn't really understand them. George Weigel, the US biographer of John Paul II, was quite blunt; he drew a sharp distinction between the parts of the encyclical that he thought were written by the Pope and other parts that he attributed to the Pontifical Council of Justice and Peace, and one phrase in particular from chapter three galled him enough that he called it "clotted and muddled" (Weigel 2009). Some years later, I think it has become clearer that this chapter was indeed innovative, even ahead of its time. It was also generative, giving rise to new initiatives like the Blueprint for Better Business (2016). Blueprint is working with a growing number of the FTSE 100 companies, supporting them in rethinking their purpose so that they may promote human dignity and the common good. Not many Papal social encyclicals have had much influence on the FTSE 100 before, even if they have been influential in other ways.

15.1 Innovative Thinking in "Caritas in veritate"

So what was it that people saw as innovative, incomprehensible or "clotted" in chapter 3 of *Caritas in veritate*? Here is the phrase that bothered George Weigel (2009) so much:

> In order to defeat underdevelopment, action is required not only on improving exchange-based transactions and implanting public welfare structures, but above all on gradually *increasing openness, in a world context, to forms of economic activity marked by quotas of gratuitousness and communion* (Benedict XVI 2009, n. 39).

Very similar phrases also appear at two previous points in the same chapter:

> "… economic social and political development, if it is to be authentically human, needs to make room for the *principle of gratuitousness* as an expression of fraternity" (n. 34).

> In *commercial relationships* the *principle of gratuitousness* and the logic of gift as an expression of fraternity can and must *find their place within normal economic activity* (n. 36).

We can treat these sentences as a kind of refrain that keeps coming back in this chapter and that provide a key to unlocking it. In n. 34, the emphasis is on making economic and social development "authentically human"; in n. 36, it is on the need for commercial relationships to include something more in "normal economic activity"; in n. 39, we get the strongest statement: a synthesis of the first too, with the further inclusion of a reference to public welfare, and the whole sentence aimed at "defeating underdevelopment" at the world level. The key part of each of these sentences is the references they all contain to "quotas of", or the "principle of", "gratuitousness", and to "communion", the "logic of gift" and the "expression of fraternity". So the overall message seems to be: we need to expand our vision of the economy so that we can find a place, within economic activity itself, for gratuitousness and the unconditional gift. This is confirmed by other texts from the same chapter, such as the following: "*Without internal forms of solidarity and mutual trust, the market cannot completely fulfill its proper economic function*" (n. 35, italics original). The solidarity and trust need to be "internal" to the economic process, not outside it, or before or after it.

In order to begin to unpack this message, we can start by noting that the last of the three versions of this sentence (from n. 39) includes reference to three aspects of development, "exchange-based transactions", "public welfare structures" and "quotas of gratuitousness and communion", and indeed, there is a threefold logic that runs throughout the chapter.

In n. 38, the encyclical points out that we need three sectors for a healthy society: market, government and civil society. Each of these has a particular strength that the community as a whole needs: in the market, there is "*giving in order to acquire* (the logic of exchange)"; in the public sector there is "*giving through duty* (the logic of public obligation, imposed by State law)" and in civil society there is "an *economy of gratuitousness* and fraternity" (n. 39; italics original). Excluding the civil or third sector is a major mistake: "The exclusively binary model of market-plus-State is corrosive of society, while economic forms based on solidarity, which find their natural home in civil society without being restricted to it, build up society. The market of gratuitousness does not exist, and attitudes of gratuitousness cannot be established by law. Yet both the market and politics need individuals who are open to reciprocal gift" (n. 39).

This works temporally too. It is not that exchange comes first (production through the market mechanism), followed by justice (redistribution and solidarity) and then gratuitousness, but that all need to be present at all times, even if there are different emphases.

Extrapolating from the encyclical itself, we could also think of the market and government as two dimensions on a natural plane, to which gratuitousness adds a third dimension, coming down and going up, opening us up to the transcendent. Such a "three-dimensional model" builds on the idea within the encyclical itself that the particular strengths of each sector are not limited to that sector. Rather, they need to spillover, to cross fertilize and inter-penetrate each other, so that each of the three sectors has three dimensions to its relationships.

At this point we could say that the encyclical is challenging us to imagine a society that is "made in the image and likeness of God", that is, a society modeled on the unity in threefold personal diversity of the Trinity. This is a society which is made up of different parts, but each overflows into the other, uniting them into one.

So let us think for a moment about the ideas of gift and gratuitousness.

The chapter opens with the following text:

> *Charity in truth* places man before the astonishing experience of gift. Gratuitousness is present in our lives in many different forms, which often go unrecognized because of a purely consumerist and utilitarian view of life. The human being is made for gift, which expresses and makes present his transcendent dimension (n. 34).

The text in n. 34 goes on to say that today we tend to ignore the gratuitous dimension of human life; As a result, we "deprive" ourselves of hope, "a powerful social resource", and this leads Benedict on to a few sentences on the theological virtues in general, in which hope is the focus. Hope is a gift that "bursts into our lives", "not due to us". Gift "by its nature goes beyond merit; its rule is that of "superabundance"; it "takes first place in our souls"; it is a "sign of God's presence in us and of what he expects from us".

15.2 Relevance for Economics

What can economic thought make of this? We can usefully split our discussion into two parts, one philosophical and the other theological.

In trying to make a link for business people to the kind of thinking we find in *Caritas in veritate* on a philosophical level, the thought of Jacques Maritain, as presented in texts such as his *The Person and the Common Good*, can be quite helpful (Maritan 1947). Maritain talks about how the human being has two dimensions, not described in terms of body and soul, to which we are accustomed, but in terms of an individual and a personal or relational dimension ("personal" by analogy to the persons of the Trinity who are constituted by relation, sharing one substance). The individuated, or physical, side of the human being is needy and fragile, often in competition with others to satisfy its needs and forming relationships so as to achieve its individual objectives. The relational or personal dimension, which is the spiritual or non-material aspect, is instead constantly transcending itself, overflowing to others and looking for relationships because they are good in themselves, not especially because they are useful to him or her in achieving individual objectives (even if they may also be useful for that). Insofar as we are persons, we find ourselves in relationships which are common goods between us. It is with others, in our relationships (of which friendship is a particular kind) that we search to achieve goals and objectives (build a life together, grow together) so that my relationships are part of who I am, not just useful to me in achieving my individual objectives. Much of what Caritas in veritate says about giftedness is reflected in this personalist philosophy of Maritain, which also gives us a way of understanding interesting empirical results from behavioral economics.[1] Personalist philosophy can help lay a

[1] One example would be the "ultimatum game", where a person (A) is told that she will receive a significant sum of money (say, £500), only if she makes an offer of a part of it to another person (B). B, meanwhile, is also told that A will not receive the sum of money unless he accepts A's offer. According to the classical way of thinking, A will offer the smallest amount possible to get the acceptance of B. In practice, the most commonly offered amount is a 50% split, and the next most

philosophical foundation for linking *Caritas in veritate*, and the Church's social thought in general, with economics.

So far we can say that gift and gratuitousness within human relations are important in making economic systems work. But the encyclical goes further, taking us to a theological level. It argues that markets cannot achieve their economic end without "moral energies" (n. 35) from outside. On our own, we do not have the strength to create a genuinely fraternal and universal community – but this can be "called into being by the word of God-who-is-Love".

Benedict XVI seems to be saying both that we need a third dimension within the economy, that is, a "principle of gratuitousness" that arises from within economic activity itself, and that the economy cannot achieve its own end, and we cannot achieve a genuinely "fraternal and universal community", without this being called into being by Divine love. This second step is much more challenging to economics and business than the first. Is there anything an economist could make of it? A lot hangs on this – if economists and business people cannot access the "wealth" and "richness" of this thinking, then it stays detached from practical economic life.

Firstly, we can find some interesting practical examples. For instance, there are the companies of the Economy of Communion of the Focolare movement.[2] In one of her articles for Theological Studies, Amy Uelmen, a scholar who writes quite a lot about this movement, recounts a particular story. John Mundell, the CEO of an Indiana environmental consulting firm run according to Economy of Communion principles, explained how their long-standing decision to constantly prioritize relationships of love and respect is now helping them through the current financial crisis: "It is as if we have been making deposits in a bank account through our attitudes, our love and our relationships with others in the community. In difficult times, this providence of God acts like a withdrawal that we are able to take to sustain us till things get better" (Uelmen 2010)

So here we have a practical businessman showing that the "providence of God" enriches the "attitudes, love and relationships" within the business so that it is more resilient during times of crisis.

Uelmen's article could be considered to be part of a wider literature in an area that has been called "charisms in the economy". Leading figures who have contributed to this field include the Italian economists Stefano Zamagni, Luigino Bruni and Alessandra Smerilli.[3] These thinkers suggest that many of the key innovations in economic history have been set in motion by charismatic figures or movements in the Pauline sense – people inspired (in all its senses) by a transcendent gift. The

common result is that A offers 40% of the money to B. This kind of result is difficult to explain in a purely individualistic way, whereas, according to a personalist view, we can see that A and B recognize that they have received a gift and that only in cooperating with each other can they achieve both their shared and their individual good.

[2] http://www.edc-online.org/en/

[3] See, for instance, Luigino Bruni and Alessandra Smerilli (2008), *Benedetta Economia: Benedetto di Norcia e Francesco d'Assisi nella storia economica europea*, Città Nuova, with a preface from Stefano Zamagni.

Franciscans created the "monti di pieta", an institution that today would be closest to the microfinance sector but in its structure and functioning is recognized by many economic historians as the forebear of the modern banks; Luca Pacioli, a Franciscan friar, invented double-entry bookkeeping which is at the foundation of modern accountancy; Quakers and Methodists were the pioneers of modern socially-responsible investing, and so on. What drove the foundation of these movements was a desire to live out the Gospel, to love one's neighbor as oneself. The connection between charity and economics in these examples is pretty clear. Even though incorporating charity in its full theological sense into the average economic model today would be pretty difficult, the existence of this literature suggests that there might be ways forward in the future for a fruitful dialogue between theology and economics.

We can also find a point of connection within the encyclical itself, in the idea from n. 34 of the theological virtues as a "powerful social resource" (here the Pope is speaking primarily about hope, but charity isn't excluded). Let us think about the aspect of "power" and then of the "social resource".

St Thomas' treatise on charity could help us understand the power of charity, since he presents it as a virtue, that is, a capacity (or power) to act towards the good, both for ourselves and for others.[4] Charity is created in the soul, a virtue which disposes us to love God and others, animated by divine grace but leaving us free to act (if it were not so, acts of charity would not be our acts; we would be merely instruments being used by God). It is infused into us, creating the capacity within us to love beyond what is possible to nature alone, but in such a way that it builds on the natural way that we do good (that is, through the disposition that a virtue gives us to act well). It is a gift that depends on God, not on our natural goodness or virtue (we can't deserve or earn it), but it can increase "for if it could not, all further advance along the way would cease" (q. 24, a. 4). Charity increases only by its subject partaking of charity more and more (q. 24, a. 5). Charity does not increase by each act of charity, but each act of charity disposes us to an increase in charity (q. 24, a. 6).

So here we can see the idea that in the virtue of charity, God gives us strength to go beyond what is humanly possible for us – it is a source of power in our lives. The next stage, then, is turning this power into a "social resource".

Here we could usefully bring in another gift that the encyclical talks about: truth. Truth, as a "gift", is "greater than we are", and the "truth of ourselves" is "first of all *given* to us". "In every cognitive process, truth is not something that we produce, it is always found, or better, received". Although modern academic disciplines shy away from using a word like "truth", in some way they are all characterized by a "search for truth", which is how they can identify or measure their "development" or "progress". We talk about "discoveries", especially within the sciences, that is, of "uncovering" how something is or works. So if we can bring charity and truth together somehow, perhaps we can have a way of creating a "social resource" out of them.

[4] The full text is available at http://www.newadvent.org/summa/3.htm

Blueprint for Better Business (2016) is an example here. One of the reasons that its position is convincing to business people is that it points out to them that the wisdom from religious traditions (especially virtue ethics and Catholic social thought) converges with scientific results. We may refer again to the ultimatum game, which is an example of a scientific result from behavioral economics. Another example would be from neuroscience, where results are showing that, just as we have an innate predisposition for language, so we have a predisposition towards certain kinds of moral behavior, which can then be formed by us and by our social and cultural context. So neuroscience is producing results that converge with virtue ethics. It is the combination of the insights from the religious and wisdom traditions with the evidence or "truth" of the empirical results from science which is really convincing to business people.

15.3 Conclusion

It is no news to anyone that economics needs to be more reflective about its underlying ideas. Whereas the tradition of jurisprudence is well established in the legal field, economics has no equivalent tradition of self reflection; the nearest we get is the discipline of the history of economic thought. But thankfully, this is gradually changing. In *Caritas in veritate*, however, we are challenged to go further than philosophy, to see what light theological reflection can throw on economics. One of the points of connection between theology and economics that we can find in Caritas in Veritate is the idea of the theological virtues as a "powerful social resource". On a practical level, Blueprint shows that a convincing argument can be made to business people when they can see a convergence between various religious traditions and scientific results. For these, and perhaps for other reasons, Caritas in Veritate has been innovative, at least in relation to the tradition of Catholic Social Thought, or, perhaps better, generative of new initiatives, of new life, rather than "clotted and muddled". There is much more to do at the boundary between economics, philosophy and theology to bring the insights of the latter two to bear on the former, but, thanks in part to Caritas in Veritate, the journey in that direction has begun.

References

Benedict XVI. 2009. *Caritas in veritate.* http://w2.vatican.va/content/benedict-xvi/en/encyclicals/documents/hf_ben-xvi_enc_20090629_caritas-in-veritate.html.

Blueprint for Better Business. 2016. http://www.blueprintforbusiness.org/.

Maritain, J. 1947. *La personne et le bien commun*. Desclée de Brouwer, [*The Person and the Common Good*. Trans. John J. Fitzgerald. New York: Charles Scribner's Sons, 1947.]

Paul VI. 1967. *Populorum* Progressio. http://w2.vatican.va/content/paul-vi/en/encyclicals/documents/hf_p-vi_enc_26031967_populorum.html.

Thatcher, M. 1968. *What's Wrong with Politics*? http://www.margaretthatcher.org/document/101632.

Uelmen, A. 2010. Caritas in veritate and Chiara Lubich: Human Development from the Vantage Point of Unity. *Theological Studies* 71: 29–45.

Weigel, G. 2009. *Caritas in veritate in Gold and Red*. http://www.nationalreview.com/article/227839/caritas-veritate-gold-and-red-george-weigel.

Chapter 16
Ethics of Development in the Age of Globalization

Zsolt Boda

Abstract The paper focuses on three interrelated problems that embody the essential contradictions of the mainstream development ideas in the globalization age. First, development is still mostly defined in materialistic terms, and, as such, it is largely under the influence of mainstream economic considerations. Second, development has remained the problem of 'poor countries' – the 'developed' nations are apparently reluctant to face the development crisis they have caused, although ecological problems made it truly global. The environmental crisis concerns the rich countries as well, meaning a crisis of their development paradigm. Third, although the development project was born as an international one, it has failed to truly unfold as such despite the advent of the 'age of globalization'. Paradoxically, globalization brought about ideas and practice of limited global solidarity and international cooperation, except the field of neoliberal economic policy.

The paper uses the ideas of Denis Goulet who argued that development is, first, an undeniably normative and value-laden concept, and second, that it is a multidimensional phenomenon. That is, development is about creating a better world, and this should include improvements not only in terms of welfare, but also of social conditions, political empowerment, the cultural foundations of self-esteem and ecological aspects. Finally, development is a common endeavor of humanity necessitating global cooperation and effective forms of solidarity between nations and people.

Denis Goulet, the founding father of the interdisciplinary field of development ethics argued that "In ever-new and ever-changing settings, development poses ancient philosophical questions: what is the good life (…), what are the foundation of life in society, and what stance should human groups adopt toward nature? 'Development' provides one particular answer to these questions. (…) What is needed is a critical questioning of the very nature of development and of its declared

Z. Boda (✉)
Centre for Social Sciences, Hungarian Academy of Sciences, Budapest, Hungary

Corvinus University of Budapest, Budapest, Hungary
e-mail: boda@uni-corvinus.hu

P. Rona, L. Zsolnai (eds.), *Economics as a Moral Science*,
Virtues and Economics 1, DOI 10.1007/978-3-319-53291-2_16

goals (…)" (Goulet 1995: ix). Questions about good life have indeed been an age-old concern for humanity, however, development in a modern sense is a much newer project and from the very beginning its "particular answer" has been appropriated by economists. Wolfgang Sachs refers to a 1949 speech by American President Harry S. Truman as a symbolic starting point of the modern development discourse in which Truman set a new political goal: helping to develop the 'underdeveloped' regions of the world (Sachs 1997). The project of development as an international endeavor was born; and its very nature as well as its goals were defined in economic terms, as for Truman development clearly meant material growth.

One can argue that the dominance of economics in the development discourse was a phenomenon of the early decades of developmentalism and that since than the concept of development has been reinterpreted as a complex, multi-faceted one, including social, economic, cultural, political and environmental aspects. There is truth in that view. In fact, prominent and critically-minded economists, like Paul Streeten, Gunnar Myrdal, Amartya Sen and Joseph Stiglitz, to name just a few, have played an important role to relativize the importance of the economic domain in development. Decades of ever-broadening development discourse have brought about many critical ideas, both theoretical, normative and practical enquiries about the ends, the means and the process of development. The ideas put forth by Denis Goulet and others already in the 1960s and 1970s should be evident to everyone dealing with the topic: development is a complex and contested concept with essentially normative nature. It should be also clear that development is not only a problem of the 'underdeveloped' – the global ecological crisis is actually a produce of 'overdevelopment'. Making our societies better in a deep sense is an urging challenge all over the world, and meeting that challenge requires locally embedded, but globally feasible approaches.

However, this paper argues that there is a considerable mismatch between development ideas and the dominant paradigm of development as expressed both by foundational international documents and development practice – more particularly, I will refer to the *Millenium Development Goals* (2000) of the United Nations as the most important development document of the twenty first century. Despite the sophistication of development studies, political action and development practice is still under the influence of old ideas and institutional constraints. The task of development ethics is as defined by Goulet is still relevant: we should keep inquiring about the goals and very nature of development.

This paper focuses on three interrelated problems that embody the essential contradictions of the mainstream development ideas in the globalization age. First, development is still mostly defined in materialistic terms, and, as such, it is largely under the influence of mainstream economic considerations. Development is about achieving economic success in the global economic system. Second, development has remained the problem of 'poor countries' – the 'developed' nations are apparently reluctant to face the development crisis they have caused, although ecological problems made it truly global. Third, although the development project was born as an international one, it has failed to truly unfold as such despite the advent of the 'age of globalization'. Paradoxically, globalization brought about ideas on limited global solidarity and international cooperation, except the field of neoliberal economic policy.

16.1 Materialistic Development

Development in the beginning was almost exclusively defined in economic terms: the problem was defined as how to get the economy grow in order to increase per capita income, measured in GDP and similar indicators (see Rostow 1959). However, even Rostow contextualized economic growth in the modernization processes of the society; and already in 1962 the basic document of the first UN Development Decade stressed that development is more than growth: it should aim at improving the quality of life of people (United Nations 1962).

But it is not self-evident that GDP growth cannot be used as a proxy for increasing quality of life. The high number of people in need (starvation in the 1960s struck almost every fourth person in the world) could alone justify a focus on material goods. The argument sounds plausible that the urgency of unmet human needs justifies the priority on economic matters – fulfilling other development objectives will then follow. Another way economic reasoning tries to maintain control over development issues is to argue that material resources are only means that can be used to promote the politically desirable development objectives. That is, GDP growth is maybe not the same as quality of life improvement, but it can be used for that purpose as a neutral instrument – economics as such is value-neutral and does not force any value choice upon decision-makers (Gasper 2004; Wilber 2010).

The past decades have accumulated a large amount of empirical evidences and analytical arguments against those views. For instance Paul Streeten argued that even high economic growth did not necessary improve the situation of the poorest people in the society (Streeten and Burki 1978). Meeting basic needs necessitates targeted policies which are not dependent on the level of economic growth. But the most forceful critique of economic reductionism came from Nobel laureate Amartya Sen whose oeuvre in large part focuses on issues of development: what is it and how can it be achieved. Sen makes strong arguments against the idea that development problems stems from a lack of economic resources.

First, his studies on famines convincingly demonstrate that hunger is not simply caused by a shortage of food (as material goods) rather it is the result of an interplay between the lack of rights or entitlements to the resources and effective public action addressing the problem (Drèze et al. 1991; Sen 1981). Natural disasters or wars can indeed create food shortages locally and temporarily; but it is very seldom that a whole country be struck by the lack of food. The history of famines shows that elite groups or the power centre generally dispose of enough resources, but they do not share them with those in needs – in some cases (e.g. the Ukrainian famine of the 1930s) political decisions and action are even causing the famine to break out. That is, hunger is not a phenomenon of absolute material shortage but that of unequal access to the resources. If people have the right to material resources, and that right is effectively enforced, they do not need to starve.

However, what can make the elite enforce rights that actually curtail their own privileges? This happens sometime as 'enlightened elites' may link their welfare to the general welfare of their society; however, typically right enforcement needs a political system based on the rule of law and accountability, that is, some form of democracy (Acemoglu and Robinson 2012). Amartya Sen is also arguing that democracy prevents famines because free press and public opinion puts the government under pressure to act in an emergency situation (Sen 1981). The most devastating famines happened in countries under dictatorial rule. These arguments point to the importance of both effectively enforced normative concepts (rights, entitlements) and institutional-political settings in promoting development before the problem of absolute resource scarcity.

Second, Amartya Sen proves that per capita GDP is not a good measure of development; moreover, that GDP growth is neither a necessary, nor a sufficient condition of it. This argument presupposes that the notion of development be dissociated from that of per capita income. For Sen development is related to the quality of life which is best measured in human capabilities: what people can be and do, what is the degree of freedom they enjoy when making choices in life (Sen et al. 1988). This is a clear normative position and echoes what Goulet said about development: that it should be about good life. Sen first used life expectancy as a measure of quality of life. Although he admits that it looks a rather quantitative measure, but it is in fact a complex indicator of the living conditions in a society, including inequalities, access to health and education, the level of crime and so on (Sen et al. 1988). While life expectancy is a good composite measure of many aspects of life quality, a longer life is also to be valued for itself: reaching a certain age is a condition of developing and nurturing capabilities.

What is the relationship between GDP and quality of life/life expectancy? The question seems to be an easy one: people in richer countries enjoy longer lives. However, measure of *level* and measures of *change* should not be conflated; and correlation does not mean causation. It might be that in the actual state of affairs richer countries have higher life expectancy, but does it follow that increasing GDP is the best way to increase longevity in a given country? In fact, throughout the twentieth century in Great Britain changes in per capita GDP and life expectancy has been opposite to each other (Sen 1998). Sen also points to the many deviant cases: rich countries with relatively low and poor countries with relatively high life expectancy (Sen et al. 1988). Following Sen's ideas Anand and Ravallion (1993) empirically prove that GDP growth leads to increasing life expectancy only if the disposable income of the poorest people is increasing and/or income is redistributed through effective public services reaching out to the poor. These conditions are not self-evidently fulfilled even in case of high GDP growth rate. The market does not necessarily reward the poorest – usually the less productive and less organized – segment of the society, and elites are not necessary eager to spend on public services and social policies. Anand and Ravallion's conditions actually requires specific political decisions, policies and institutional arrangements.

Following these findings and arguments we must say that while increasing income may lead to improving quality of life, this effect is conditional. On the other hand quality of life can be improved via community supported programs even at a low income level, as the example of State of Kerala – one of Sen' recurring reference – suggests. The capability set of people can be meaningfully extended, poverty reduced and basic needs met at low income level as well. The capability approach, while having deep philosophical and ethical roots, has also clear policy implications. Let us mention that Denis Goulet's ideas often overlap with Sen's, as both of them define development in terms of growing freedoms of the individual.

It is not my intention to provide a detailed presentation of the oeuvre of Sen or the debates concerning the meaning of development that have characterized the decades of development discourse. The above arguments are meant to illustrate the point that economic reductionism has been under scrutiny for a long time; and that criticisms have not only been of ethical or philosophical nature, but rooted in empirical evidences and advanced by economists. We cannot say that those ideas have not had any effect on policies. Sen himself contributed to the elaboration of the Human Development Index (HDI) at the UNDP which combines life expectancy and an education index with per capita income and which represents a somewhat alternative measure of development compared to GDP. But we cannot say either that economic reductionism would be outdated. Both economists, development experts and politicians still widely use it and refer to GDP levels as the most important development indicator (Peet and Hartwick 2015). While the appropriateness of GDP to measure welfare was already questioned in the 1970s (Nordhaus and Tobin 1972) and later several times (Daly et al. 1994), recently Nobel laureate economists had to argue again against it – with no much success (Stiglitz et al. 2010).

More particularly, development objectives have also been set along economic and material terms. For instance the Millenium Development Goals, using an old and somewhat arbitrary threshold (on this see Wade 2004), defines poverty as earning less than USD 1 per day. That is, poverty is first of all about income, it is not about, say, capabilities.[1] This is not a theoretical problem. The MDGs set the objective to halve poverty so defined, and *2015 UNMillenium Development GoalsReport* proudly announced that the goal was reached. Maybe so. However, the target could be achieved simply by increasing the number of people who live from the market and have financial revenues – as opposed to people living in autarchy or receiving in-kind support from their families or communities (Vandemoortele 2011). Extending markets and financial transactions is certainly part of the neoliberal agenda of today's economic globalization. Whether this leads to poverty reduction and if so, how much, is difficult to see, and not only for the well-known problems of statistical measures (see on this Vandemoortele 2011; Wade 2004). And whether the reduction of income poverty – if so – leads to increasing capabilities is still to be proven.

[1] To do justice to the MDGs: meeting basic needs like eradicating hunger is also an objective, just like increasing school enrollment, improving gender inequalities etc. Reducing income poverty is not the only development goal, but it is the first one.

Summing up, despite decades of both normative and empirical assessments of the limitations of the economic approach to development, the economic reductionism is still influential. Vandemoortele (2011) argues that one of the original intentions of the Millenium Development Goals was exactly to broaden the development discourse which was dominated by economic consideration, and include other aspects and dimensions of development, but they failed to do so. Instead, MDGs themselves reflect the mainstream paradigm based on trade and financial liberalization, and the challenge of development largely remained framed along materialistic and economic terms. Despite decades of reflections on the meaning of development, the most important development policy document of the twenty first century still largely reflects rather old ideas and mainstream economic recipes.

16.2 Whose Development?

None of the MDGs address the rich countries – looks like development is an issue for poor countries only, whose task is to imitate the model of rich countries. As if we were still in the paradigm of Harry S. Truman who almost 70 years ago set the goal of helping underdeveloped regions of the world.

Again, it should be clear since the early 1970s that development as we know it is not *good* in a deep sense, because it is destroying the Earth and the natural environment upon which all life depends. The *Report to the Club of Rome* projected an ecological and disaster to the beginning of the twenty first century, were the actual trends of resource depletion and pollution continued (Meadows 1972). Thirty years later the prospects are not better, in some sense even worse, as anthropogenic climate change has imposed itself as the major menace humanity has ever faced (Meadows et al. 2004). The scientific consensus now is that climate change is happening; that it is caused by humanity; and its consequences will be dramatic in the not too distant future. It is also clear that global warming as well as many other forms of environmental degradation have been caused by two centuries of extensive fossil fuel use, deforestation for agricultural purposes, mining, pollution by modern industries and similar activities – the core of modern development that poor countries are supposed to imitate. Rich countries not only bear the historical responsibility for today's global ecological problems, but even today their per capita resource use and pollution surpass by several factor those of the developing countries. This is a problem of global justice that should first and foremost be repaired on the side of the rich countries (Singer 2004).

There is hardly any new in the above said. In 1987 *Our Common Future*, the report of the Brundtland Commission made a clear case on both the environmental unsustainability of the mainstream development paradigm and the resulting serious global justice problem (Brundtland et al. 1987). At the same time, the report is a political document and such, burdened with some compromises. For instance, while the report provides a forceful critique of the mainstream development it also stresses the importance of global economic cooperation in the form of trade liberalization.

Bernstein argue that the hidden (or not so hidden) neoliberal agenda of the Brundtland Report dominated then the 1992 Earth Summit of Rio de Janeiro and in general, the environment and development discourse of the 1990s (Bernstein 2002). The term 'sustainable development', popularized by the Brundtland Report, has become a mandatory reference in the development discourse, but this has not meant the reappraisal of the development model of globalization. On the contrary. The documents of Rio, Johannesburg (2002) or that of the MDGs make parallel reference to liberal globalization and the need of sustainable development – voiding the latter of its potentially radical content. Because we have good reasons to believe that economic globalization in its present form is by no means compatible with ecologically sustainable development (Daly and Farley 2011).

Let us mention another problem that challenges the development model of the rich countries: that of growing inequality. Recently the work of Thomas Piketty pointed to the fact that the distribution of both income and wealth are becoming increasingly unequal all around the world (Piketty 2014).[2] Piketty argues that the main cause of this phenomenon lies in the inherent logic of global capitalism and capital accumulation. Growing inequality is not only a problem from an egalitarian normative perspective – it is actually at the root of a number of political and social problems. Piketty is warning that increasing inequality may create a hierarchical society where mobility is severely constrained, and this can undermine both the merit-based normative justification of the social order and the actual performance of the society, as talented, but less resourceful people will face reduced opportunities in life. Inequality is undermining democracy, as people have increasingly differentiated access to decisions and decision makers, and the will of the wealthy will prevail (Gilens and Page 2014; Stiglitz 2012). Inequality is also eroding social trust towards both other people and the institutions (Uslaner 2002).

The multiple negative social consequences of inequality have been thoroughly presented by Wilkinson and Pickett (2010). They argue that inequality causes or worsens a number of social problems, like reduced life expectancy, mental illness, obesity, homicide rate, incarceration rate, poor school performance, teenage birth, infant mortality, low social mobility. They actually find that even per capita environmental pollution is positively related to simple measures of income inequality. Their analysis not only describes the positive associations between inequality and the social ills, but, relying on previous empirical studies, reconstructs the mechanisms through which those social problems are produced. We cannot present here in detail the arguments of their influential work. But the implication is quite straightforward: if inequality continues to increase, as predicted by Piketty and others, this will lead to a deterioration of the quality of life in the most developed countries as well. Conversely, if we seek to improve the quality of life, inequality should be reduced. This is not an argument in favor of radical egalitarianism. But, as Wilkinson and

[2] I am referring here to inequalities inside nations. The question about global inequalities is a bit more complicated: on some accounts they have been shrinking in the past decades (mostly due to the growing income in China and some other developing countries), but according to other measures they have been widening (Milanovic 2011; Wade 2004).

Pickett put it, instead of treating social ills through spending on police, prisons, doctors, social workers, psychologists and so, rich countries should devote some effort to reduce income differences between people (Wilkinson and Pickett 2010).

Development should not be only a task for poor countries. Rich countries are not at the 'end of history' either: they can and should increase the quality of life of their people and respond to new challenges, like the one of growing inequality. However, most importantly they need to address at last a fundamental problem stemming from their way of development: the ecological crisis.

The 2015 *Sustainable Development Goals* set by the UN as a follow-up of the MDGs (which were defined for the period of 2000–2015) reflect a move towards the approach advocated here, as they include targets for the rich countries as well.[3] The SDGs speak parallel of poverty reduction and sustainable consumption, making clear that achieving sustainable development sets targets for every nation. However, it is to be seen whether the SDGs indeed represent a new age of development discourse and – more importantly – development practice.

16.3 Global Cooperation and Global Justice

Although Harry S. Truman presented development as a common endeavor of rich countries to help the poor ones, for many years development was rather seen as a task before the national economies and economic policies. This approach is exemplified by the famous 'stages of economic growth' model which describes how factors of production, internal capital accumulation and growing demand can create the conditions of the much need economic take-off in developing countries (Rostow 1959). The model is an idealtypical presentation of the development paths of the Western countries, however, the international context was largely neglected in it – as if countries were stand-alone economic units aiming at maximizing income.

The work of Raúl Prebitsch, Immanuel Wallerstein and others pointed to the role of international economic relations, or more generally the global economic system in influencing individual countries' development opportunities (see Love 1980). Prebisch argued that trade between 'developed' and 'underdeveloped' countries was fundamentally unequal, a thesis than led to two possible conclusions: developing countries should either minimize the economic relations with rich nations or promote new rules for the international economy – ones that reflect the developing countries' needs. Import-substituting economic policies adopted by Latin-American countries were the realization of the former, while for instance the formation of the UN Conference on Trade and Development (UNCTAD), of which Prebisch was the first secretary-general, in 1964 put in practice the latter. Throughout the 1960s UNCTAD argued for international redistribution (in the forms of substantial aid, debt reduction and technology transfer), preferential treatment measures in trade as well as schemes aiming at stabilizing export revenues in developing countries.

[3] See at https://sustainabledevelopment.un.org/?menu=1300.

These claims were directly translated into the document of the New International Economic Order (NIEO) – a resolution passed by the UN General Assembly in 1974 urging for the reform of international economic relations.

It is quite common to interpret the NIEO as an embodiment of some kind of global justice (see Bhagwati 1977) – a claim for a more equitable international economic order, where the unequal distribution of revenues and the inherent inequalities are at least partly counter-balanced. Of course, UNCTAD and NIEO were not able to reform the global economy, but some practical changes still happened. The trading regime (GATT) accepted the Generalized System of Preferences that allowed providing non-reciprocal preferential measures to developing countries. In the Lomé Convention the European Communities set up the STABEX mechanism which offered an interest-free loan for countries of which the export earnings of a group of raw and semi-processed goods fall significantly under the average of previous years.[4]

Another example expressing the spirit of global justice is the concept of the Common Heritage of Mankind, adopted in 1970 by the UN General Assembly. According to the UN resolution, the deep sea bed is the common heritage of mankind, and it must be exploited for the mankind as a whole, taking into particular consideration the interests and needs of developing countries. Obviously the concept embodies moral commitment towards a more equitable international order and international justice (see Anand 2004).

I would argue that the 'justice as fairness' concept and the difference principle of John Rawls are useful conceptual tools for interpreting the normative content of the NIEO, preferential trade measures or the Common Heritage of Mankind.[5] The difference principle demands the evaluation and comparison of entire institutional structures from the point of view of the worst-off persons, or, in the case of the international economic system, the worst-off countries. International institutions and rules are to be arranged so that they are to the greatest benefit of the least advantaged countries; or at least that they are to a greater benefit of the least advantaged countries than of the developed ones.

The concept of justice as fairness has an enormous normative power. It should be one of the guiding principles for international regimes, the complex institutional design of global governance. The development discourse, and to some extent the institutional practice, of the 1960s and 1970s reflected the idea of global justice and solidarity.

However, the decades of developmentalism came to an end by the late 1980s, early 1990s with the advent of the age of globalization (Kalb 2005). The once

[4] Barber and Dickson (1995) argue that the motivation for setting up the European Community's compensatory funds was not informed by the desire to create a more equitable world trading system. Nevertheless, in practice they contributed to some income redistribution in an international scale, and they were actually asked for by developing countries in previous UNCTAD conferences.

[5] John Rawls was reluctant to apply the difference principle to international relations. However, both Beitz (1979) and Boxill (1987) argue that this is a meaningful approach.

widespread discourse on the responsibility of the rich countries to help the poor ones, the ideas on international solidarity, the proposals on the Common Heritage of Mankind or the New International Economic Order reflecting the belief in a more equitable world have all faded away (see Anand 2004). It is not to idealize to 1960s o the 1970s – real development was a scarce good than as well, but at least the development discourse of the age provided a powerful frame to think about the responsibilities of the rich, the needs of the poor and the prospects of a better world. The 1980s brought about important political, economic and ideational changes that had their effects on how we think of the problem of development now. People in poor countries have found themselves in the era of unleashed neoliberal globalization with strongly institutionalized free trade rules and corporate interests. The discourse of global justice was substituted by that of structural adjustment, competitiveness and "the market knows better".

From the development perspective the age of globalization means paradoxically a diminished commitment towards global cooperation – except in the domain of neoliberal economic policies. The World Trade Organization, established in 1994, has become the strongest institutional element in the architecture of global governance, an international organization able to allow sanctions on non-complying parties, with the primary objective of promoting liberal trade policies. While the Doha Round of trade negotiations, starting in 2001 was announced as a 'Development Round', its failure clearly shows a lack of commitment to take developing country needs seriously. The role that the International Monetary Fund and the World Bank played in promoting the so-called 'Washington Consensus' in developing countries is also well known (Van Waeyenberge 2006). In sum, the development model of the globalization era implies that (1) individual countries (2) should integrate their economies into the liberal global economic system (3) and make their institutional and physical infrastructure compatible with the logic of operation of globalization. International cooperation is mostly restricted to institutionalizing neoliberal policies; aid and any other forms of solidarity are of a minor importance and only of supplementary nature. As Denis Goulet put it: "The driving idea behind globalization is free-market capitalism – the more you let market forces rule and the more you open your economy to free trade and competition the more efficient and flourishing your economy will be" (Goulet 2004: 3).

The political goal of liberalizing economic relations has been repeatedly stressed in international development documents, like the Rio Declaration (1992), the Millenium Declaration (2000) and the Johannesburg Declaration (2002). At the same time the idea of global justice has been omitted from the new development discourse. While the concept of sustainable development, popularized by the Report of the Brundtland Commission (*Our Common Future* 1987) was defined along both inter- and intragenerational justice, the Rio Declaration mentions only "shared, but differentiated" responsibility in managing the global commons.

The Millenium Declaration and the Millenium Development Goals (MDGs) that are supposed to herald the new development era are usually interpreted as 'neoliberalism with a human face' (Gore 2010; Vandemoortele 2011). It is not to make a final account of the MDGs program here. Addressing basic needs in the least developed countries; reducing debts; increasing aids are certainly objectives to agree with.[6] But the MDG-paradigm failed to deliver a coherent global development model – countries are stand-alone units with problems to be addressed (Gore 2010). Solidarity is interpreted at the level of donor countries, not at the level of the global economic system.

I would argue that the neoliberal model that became the mainstream development paradigm in the 1980s is still dominant in international documents or the discourses of influential global institutions: countries are seen to be successful as long as they are integrated into the flows of economic globalization. True, the 'great globalization debate' (Kalb 2005) that has been going on since the beginning of the 1990s between globalization critics and globalization supporters has brought up many legitimate arguments against the uncritical application of the neoliberal policies of the 'Washington Consensus'. The global economic crisis starting in 2007 put another deep dent into the neoliberal paradigm. However, the 'post-Washington Consensus' has not been able to take shape as its elements are not clear enough and the ideas of neoliberal globalization are still largely defining development policy discourse and practice (Sheppard and Leitner 2010; Van Waeyenberge 2006). Paradoxically, the 2007 crisis reinvigorated neoliberal institutions like the IMF or the World Bank. Beforehand the IMF struggled with finding a new role in global governance as financial markets provided resources to countries with better conditions than the IMF which was gradually marginalized by globalization itself. But this changed when the G-20 leaders agreed to ensure that the Bretton Woods institutions would have as much as $1 trillion in additional resources to help countries in financial problems (Birdsall and Fukuyama 2011).

The institutional design of global governance and global cooperation still reflect the neoliberal globalization paradigm. Indeed, there are some new developments, but they do not necessarily point towards global solidarity and global environmental justice, rather herald a coming era of increased regional competition and express the concerns of rich countries about their strengthening rivals. The planned Transatlantic Trade and Investment Partnership (TTIP) between the US and the EU, or the Trans-Pacific Partnership between the US, Japan and other Asian countries (excluding China) deserve attention in this respect. On one hand these agreements seek to institutionalize corporate-led globalization as they ensure special rights for corporations, minimizing the possibility of regulating investment and trade by governments. However, they represent a shift from neoliberal policies on the global level, on the other, as they are about creating regional trading blocks and bringing together the rich countries against the rising big rivals, like China, India or Brazil. In a sense these agreements show the ugliest face of corporate globalization (Boda 2015).

---

[6] While the UN is mostly positive concerning the realization of MDGs, independent evaluations are more sceptical. For instance Friedman (2013) argues that while development indicators have been improving in the past two decades, the effect of MDGs cannot be convincingly demonstrated.

16.4 The Ethics of Development

Development is, or should be, about making our life and our world better. As such, it is essentially both a normative and a pragmatic endeavor, involving values and principles, choices about desirable ends and legitimate means. The term 'ethics of development' is almost a tautology, because any serious discussion about development must involve ethics.

Development is a collective endeavor: it is about the objectives, norms and strategies to be followed by a group of people; a society; or, on a final account, by humanity as such. This raises specific problems concerning the procedures of decision making and implementation. Denis Goulet has been particularly sensitive to these issues and stressed that the ethics of development must deal with three basic problems: what are the objective of development; what are the means chosen to achieve those objectives; and what are the procedures through which specific development outcomes will be produced (Goulet 1995). Goulet believed in the potential of participatory decision making and argued for new forms of participation in the development process (Goulet 1989).

The procedural element in the development process is an especially important one, because development is embedded into a system of institutional constraints and power relations (see Sachs1997). From the very beginning development has been defined as a hierarchical, a top-down project, an asymmetrical relationship between those already developed and those in need of development; or between the developers (elites, experts etc.) and the subjects of development (people in poor countries). Who is making decisions on whose behalf? What is the degree of freedom of people influencing decisions and development outcomes directly affecting their lives? These and similar questions are of a paramount importance if we seek to assess the ethicality of the development project.

However, the ambition of this chapter could not be presenting the rich field and the many challenges of development ethics. More particularly, it could not deal with the procedural part of the development project. Its aim was to point to some basic contradictions in today's development discourse and practice – ones that haunt and jeopardize the development project from its very beginnings. An essential problem of development is that it has been taken over by economists who have defined its objective and nature in economic terms. This economic bias reduces the richness of the development challenge and actually may cause a failure on its own terms: economic growth alone has been unable to secure basic needs and improve quality of life. Furthermore, economic growth and materialistic development are at the very root of today's global ecological crisis. Rich countries should face their responsibility in causing the ultimate failure of modernity and reinvent their development model. They should also face their global responsibility and the global justice claims today's development issues raise. Sustainable development institutionalizing both intra- and intergenerational justice could be achieved only through global cooperation based on solidarity and fairness.

These arguments support Denis Goulet's theses on the multidimensional character of development and the need for complex institutional arrangements to serve the objectives of development. He argued that development must be sustainable in economic, political, social, cultural and ecological terms (Goulet 1995). Development should rely on an economic system which is able to generate the necessary material resources for people within the limits of ecological sustainability. Market as an economic mechanism is a useful tool, however, Goulet argued that we should avoid that markets rule the society (Goulet 2004). Markets create inequalities and polarize societies, therefore they must be regulated and complemented by redistributive systems. The viability of institutional arrangements on a final account depends on the sustainability of political processes: how decisions are made, power is distributed and legitimacy ensured. Goulet believed in the potential of local development, that is, bringing the development project the closest possible to communities and people and organize social life at the lowest level – this is sometimes called subsidiarity. However, he was also convinced that the state level cannot be eliminated, otherwise big corporation would take over the organization of social life (Goulet 2004). And he was also repeatedly arguing that development for the humanity cannot be achieved without global cooperation based on global solidarity.

Goulet was aware of the value conflicts that development generates. He distinguished three basic value conflicts (Goulet 2004). The first is about the content of good life. For instance, what is the importance of material values compared to other cultural and ethical ones in the organization of social life? The second bears on the foundation of justice in a polity. What conception of justice is to be institutionalized? What is the importance of individual rights compared to collective decisions? Finally, the third basic value conflict concern the stance society adopts towards nature. Is nature to be used simply as a reservoir of resources or should it be respected on its own right?

Goulet argues that "(t)he provision by a society of satisfactory conceptual, institutional, behavioral answers to these three questions is what constitutes authentic development" (Goulet 2004: 8). There are no easy answers, simple blueprints and one-size-fits-all recipes in development. Economic growth is not a proper answer; globalization isn't either. Development ethics' first task is to raise awareness about the complexity of the development project, which is, as Goulet so eloquently put it, about the quest for good life.

16.5 Conclusion

Development is a never-ending project of humanity: improving the quality of life for everyone. As Goulet observed, even those post-developmentalist critiques who debunk the development as an essentially hegemonic project led by the rich countries and aiming at controlling the rest of the world, ultimately argue for something that is best to be called alternative development (Goulet 2004). It is not the term that should be rejected – it is its content, objectives and nature that should be under scrutiny.

The chapter uses the ideas of Denis Goulet who argued that development is, first, an undeniably normative and value-laden concept, and second, that it is a multi-dimensional phenomenon. That is, development is about creating a better world, and this should include improvements not only in terms of welfare, but also of social conditions, political empowerment, the cultural foundations of self-esteem and ecological aspects. The chapter overviews the state of development in the era of globalization and argues that despite some of its achievements the current development model fails to meet important challenges, like the environmental one. However, this is not accidental: development led by globalization seems to be structurally unable to embody all the necessary social, cultural and environmental aspects. An ethical development certainly requires the transformation of global business and economic regulatory rules, but, more importantly, it also needs a complex social, political and institutional infrastructure that can ensure the translation of the different dimensions of development into decisions and practice.

References

Acemoglu, D., and J. Robinson. 2012. *Why Nations Fail: The Origins of Power, Prosperity, and Poverty*. New York: Crown Business.

Anand, R.P. 2004. Common Heritage of Mankind: Mutilation of an Ideal In *Studies in International Law and History* (pp. 180–196). Dordrecht: Springer.

Anand, S., and M. Ravallion. 1993. Human Development in Poor Countries: On the Role of Private Incomes and Public Services. *The Journal of Economic Perspectives* 7 (1): 133–150.

Barber, J.P., and A.K. Dickson. 1995. Justice and Order in International Relations: The Global Environment. In *Just Environments–Intergenerational, International and Inter-Species Issues*. New York: Routledge.

Beitz, Ch. 1979. *Political Theory and International Relations*. Princeton: Princeton University Press.

Bernstein, S. 2002. Liberal Environmentalism and Global Environmental Governance. *Global Environmental Politics* 2 (3): 1–16.

Bhagwati, J.N. 1977. *The New International Economic Order: The North-South Debate*. Cambridge, MA: *MIT Bicentennial Studies*.

Birdsall, N., and F. Fukuyama. 2011. The Post-Washington Consensus. *Foreign Affairs* 90 (2): 45–53.

Boda, Z. 2015. TTIP: Good, Bad or Ugly. *V4 Revue*, 26/02, http://visegradrevue.eu/ttip-good-bad-or-ugly/.

Boxill, B. 1987. Global Equality of Opportunity and National Integrity. *Social Philosophy and Policy* 5 (1): 143–168.

Brundtland, G., M. Khalid, S. Agnelli, S. Al-Athel, B. Chidzero, L. Fadika, et al. 1987. *Our Common Future: Report for the World Commission on Environment and Development*. London: United Nations.

Daly, H.E., and J. Farley. 2011. *Ecological Economics: Principles and Applications*. Washington, DC: Island press.

Daly, H.E., J.B. Cobb, and C.W. Cobb. 1994. *For the Common Good: Redirecting the Economy Toward Community, The Environment, and a Sustainable Future*. Boston: Beacon Press.
Drèze, J., A.K. Sen, et al. 1991. *Hunger and Public Action*. New York: Oxford Clarendon.
Friedman, H.S. 2013. *Causal inference and the Millennium Development Goals (MDGs): Assessing whether there was an acceleration in MDG development indicators following the MDG declaration*. MPRA Paper No. 48793.
Gasper, D. 2004. *The Ethics of Development: From Economism to Human Development*. Edinburgh: Edinburgh University Press.
Gilens, M., and B.I. Page. 2014. Testing Theories of American Politics: Elites, Interest Groups, and Average Citizens. *Perspectives on Politics* 12 (3): 564–581.
Gore, C. 2010. The Mdg Paradigm, Productive Capacities and the Future of Poverty Reduction. *IDS Bulletin* 41 (1): 70–79.
Goulet, D. 1989. Participation in Development: New Avenues. *World Development* 17 (2): 165–178.
———. 1995. *Development Ethics: A Guide To Theory And Practice*. New York: Apex Pr.
———. 2004. Is Sustainable Development Possible in a Globalized World? *Humanomics* 20 (1): 3–16.
Kalb, D. 2005. From Flows To Violence Politics And Knowledge in the Debates On Globalization And Empire. *Antiviral Therapy* 5 (2): 176–204.
Love, J.L. 1980. Raul Prebisch and The Origins of The Doctrine of Unequal Exchange. *Latin American Research Review* 15 (3): 45–72.
Meadows, D.H. 1972. *The Limits To Growth; A Report For The Club of Rome's Project on The Predicament of Mankind*. New York: Universe.
Meadows, D., J. Randers, and D. Meadows. 2004. *Limits to Growth: The 30-Year Update*. White River Junction: Chelsea Green Publishing.
Milanovic, B. 2011. *Worlds Apart: Measuring International and Global Inequality*. Princeton: Princeton University Press.
Nordhaus, W.D., and Tobin, J. 1972. Is Growth Obsolete In: *Economic Research: Retrospect and Prospect, Volume 5, Economic Growth*, 1–80. New York: Nber.
Peet, R., and E. Hartwick. 2015. *Theories of Development: Contentions, Arguments, Alternatives*. New York: Guilford Publications.
Piketty, T. 2014. *Capital in the Twenty-First Century*. Cambridge, MA: Harvard University Press.
Rostow, W.W. 1959. The Stages of Economic Growth. *The Economic History Review* 12 (1): 1–16.
Sachs, W. 1997. *Development Dictionary, The: A Guide to Knowledge as Power*. Hyderabad: Orient Blackswan.
Sen, A. 1981. *Poverty and Famines: An Essay on Entitlement and Deprivation*. New York: Oxford University Press.
———. 1998. Mortality as an Indicator of Economic Success and Failure. *The Economic Journal* 108 (446): 1–25.
Sen, A., et al. 1988. The Concept of Development. *Handbook of Development Economics* 1: 9–26.
Sheppard, E., and H. Leitner. 2010. Quo Vadis Neoliberalism? The Remaking of Global Capitalist Governance After the Washington Consensus. *Geoforum* 41 (2): 185–194.
Singer, P. 2004. *One World: The Ethics of Globalization*. New Haven: Yale University Press.
Stiglitz, J. 2012. *The Price of Inequality*. London: Penguin.
Stiglitz, J.E., A. Sen, and J.-P. Fitoussi. 2010. *Mismeasuring Our Lives: Why Gdp Doesn't Add Up*. New York: The New Press.
Streeten, P., and S.J. Burki. 1978. Basic Needs: Some Issues. *World Development* 6 (3): 411–421.
United Nations. 1962. *The United Nations Development Decade: Proposals for Action*. New York: UN.
Uslaner, E.M. 2002. *The Moral Foundations Of Trust*. New York: Cambridge University Press.
Van Waeyenberge, E. 2006. From Washington to Post-Washington Consensus: Illusions of Development. In *The New Development Economics: After the Washington Consensus*, ed. K.S. Jomo and B. Fine, 21–45. New Delhi/London: Tulika/Zed Books.

Vandemoortele, J. 2011. The Mdg Story: Intention Denied. *Development and Change* 42 (1): 1–21.
Wade, R.H. 2004. Is Globalization Reducing Poverty and Inequality? *World Development* 32 (4): 567–589.
Wilber, C.K. 2010. *Economics and Ethics*. New York: Palgrave Macmillan.
Wilkinson, R., and K. Pickett. 2010. *The Spirit Level. Why Equality Is Better for Everyone*. New York: Penguin.

Chapter 17
Transdisciplinarity, Governance and the Common Good

François Lépineux and Jean-Jacques Rosé

Abstract Humanity has entered into a stage of its evolution characterized by world unification in a number of domains – a stage which may be called the 'era of globality'. Many issues become global in nature, and the question of the preservation of global common goods is challenging. In order to address current global issues, we need to change our way of thinking: the advent of the era of globality calls for complex and transdisciplinary approaches. It also requires new governance mechanisms to deal with the scale and complexity of global problems. The main argument of the chapter is that based on the principle of subsidiarity, multi-level governance mechanisms should be developed to preserve global common goods. Water provides a relevant illustration of the need for developing such mechanisms. A multi-level, transdisciplinary model is proposed for the governance of water.

17.1 Introduction

The dynamic of globalization, as it currently unfolds, brings about world-wide economic and social integration and closer interconnectedness of peoples and nations. This growing interdependence between the West and the East, the North and the South asks for a reflection on our globalized society, our 'global village' or, more simply put, the entire human family. The increasing number of global issues – from climate change to environmental degradation to social inequalities – entails the elevation of the problems to the global level. The water challenge provides one of the best illustrations of this phenomenon and of the need for innovative governance schemes. It also highlights a new level of the common good: the global common good.

F. Lépineux (✉)
Rennes School of Business, Rennes, France
e-mail: francois.lepineux@club-internet.fr

J.-J. Rosé
Centre Norbert Elias EHESS-CNRS, Marseille, France

P. Rona, L. Zsolnai (eds.), *Economics as a Moral Science*,
Virtues and Economics 1, DOI 10.1007/978-3-319-53291-2_17

The common good can be defined referring to Aristotle's supreme good, by a quote that clarifies the architecture of ends, from concrete practice to the supreme finality (Aristotle 2003, Book I, 1094 a 5, p.5):

> If therefore among the ends at which our actions aim there be one which we wish for its own sake, while we wish the others only for the sake of this, and if we do not choose everything for the sake of something else (which would obviously result in a process ad infinitum, so that all desire would be futile and vain), it is clear that this one ultimate End must be the Good, and indeed the Supreme Good. Will not then knowledge of this Supreme Good be also of great practical importance for the conduct of life?

The concept of common good and its relationship with business has been explored in the business ethics literature over the past 25 years. Velasquez (1992) derives from his analysis that it is not possible to make the claim that multinationals have a moral obligation to contribute to the common good in the highly competitive arena of globalization. Argandoña (1998) views the concept of the common good as a possible theoretical foundation for stakeholder theory. Alford and Shcherbinina (2009) suggest that the common good is the idea underpinning the corporate social responsibility concept. De Bettignies and Lépineux (2009a) analyze three different models of common good: the teleological model, the utilitarian model, and the relational model. Melé (2009) mobilizes the common good principle to integrate realistic personalism into virtue-based business ethics. Sison and Fontrodona (2011) build on the distinction between material and formal parts of the common good; they view profit as the material part and work as the formal part.

The importance of cooperation to achieve the common good is emphasized by several authors. Kaul et al. (1999, 2003) stress that the provision of global public goods calls for the involvement of a number of actors and the cooperation of the spheres of government, business and civil society. Similarly, Sagawa and Segal (1999) uphold the view that businesses and not-for-profit organizations need to develop partnerships to serve the common good; such collaboration can be fruitful for all the parties involved. Crosby and Bryson (2005) argue that collaborative leadership is required to deal with major issues or challenges in a shared-power world. In his analysis of the common good concept, O'Brien (2009) draws a distinction between a descriptive aspect and a prescriptive aspect, and notes that cooperation is "the unifying force of a society" and "the key to both a society's goodness and strength" (O'Brien 2009: 31). De Bettignies and Lépineux (2009b) identify three major determinants that are likely to drive corporations to take the global common good into account: the deterioration of the biosphere, the rise of an anti-globalization sentiment, and the necessity to invent a global social contract. They underline that multinational corporations are co-responsible for the global common good.

Other references in the field of management can be added to this brief review of academic contributions dealing with the common good (e.g. Hardin 1996; Dickie and Rouner 1986; Alford and Naughton 2001; Spence and Schmidpeter 2003; Koslowski 2006). More contributions referring to the common good can be found in other fields: philosophy, law, economics, political science – and in Catholic social doctrine. It follows from a literature review that the necessity to preserve global common goods, as well as the responsibility of business in this respect, calls for further research. The ability of present and future generations to live a decent life relies on the preservation of global common goods like: water, biodiversity, and the climate, regarding which thresholds of irreversibility should not be crossed; and just social and economic structures, respect for spirituality and religious faiths, and the maintenance of peace between peoples and nations.

Water is one of the most vital global common goods – yet, about one billion people do not have access to safe drinking water and suffer all the consequences of this deprivation. As early as 2025, water needed for the global population of eight billion people will amount to 5000 cubic kilometers per year, representing a 25% increase from 4000 cubic kilometers in 2000. Should current trends continue, the situation will worsen, as a shortfall in supply will become unavoidable. To add a word to Gandhi's phrase: "there is enough water for everyone's need, not for everyone's greed". Water issues have the potential to generate serious conflicts between and within nations and regions. Geopolitical tensions regarding water usage have emerged over the last decade in several parts of the world. Water scarcity is already a problem for countries and populations dependent on rivers such as the Jordan, the Nile, and the Colorado; regions in Peru are also clashing over water diversion – to mention only a few examples. Three of the largest countries in the world are significantly impacted: the US, China, and India. The coming decades will see the surge of a global water challenge. States are unable to solve water problems in conventional ways – therefore developing new governance mechanisms becomes necessary. Water companies are the first in line to address this water challenge. That is why it is relevant to envision their possible involvement in multi-level governance schemes aimed at handling water issues.

This chapter is divided into two parts. The first part discusses the advent of the era of 'globality' characterized by world unification in a number of domains, and sheds light on the epistemological dimension of this change of era. We argue that a renewal of our way of thinking is needed. We point out that this new era calls for complex and transdisciplinary thought. The second part takes the example of water as a global common good that requires innovative governance mechanisms. We analyze the Water Manifesto elaborated by the International Committee for a World Water Contract. The paper proposes a multi-level, transdisciplinary governance model based on the subsidiarity principle, involving not only public authorities at all levels from local to global, but also non-state actors such as water companies which could take part in the governance of water resources at various levels.

17.2 The Era of Globality

Humanity has entered into a new phase of its evolution; numerous authors have already undertaken to reflect on this phenomenon, and have proposed various characterizations for it. It is called the information age (Castells 2005), world risk society (Beck 1999), era of information, communication and autonomy (Robin 1989), immaterial society (Gaudin 1988), planetary era (Morin 2008), global empire (Hardt and Negri 2001, 2005), not to mention the already well-known concept of McLuhan's global village (McLuhan and Fiore 1989; McLuhan and Powers 1992) or the concept of modern world-system by Wallerstein (2004). Also we should not forget the vision of world marketization put forward by numerous authors (Beaud 2000; Rifkin 2001), as well as the debate about the Anthropocene initiated by the chemist Paul Crutzen and the age of limits advocated by Latouche (2012).

None of these authors situate the current shift on the same time scale. For some it is a question of a changing time period on a historical scale – comparable to the passage from Antiquity to the Middle Ages, then to the Modern Age. Others consider it in a much longer period of time, notably on the geological scale – the Anthropocene being the new era in which the planet is entering after the Holocene. We adhere to this broad perspective, which we consider as an appropriate hypothesis for two main reasons. Firstly, if it falls to historians of the future to decide how to name the ongoing phase, several factors cause us to think that the neologism 'globality' adequately depicts the current evolutionary period. Globality is distinct from 'globalization'. Globalization usually refers to the financial and economic dimension of human activities on the global level. In our view, the emergence of the era of globality originates from the historical process already at work for at least five centuries, which gradually leads to a world unification. Besides, this change of era can be considered as an appropriate hypothesis for a second reason: if "the future we imagine influences the present we live" (Gatard 2014, p.30), retaining this assumption represents a pragmatic attitude[1] whose finality is to want to transform threats into hope. At the cost of abandoning the blind belief in the ideology of progress (Aron 2010): without denying the positive dynamics of a Western economy which has become an aspiration for most peoples of the planet, but insofar as this dynamics would not crush the wealth constituted by the diversity of civilizations.

It seems that the surge of this new era, which questions the mental and institutional frameworks inherited from the past, cannot be summarized by one single determining factor, but manifests itself as a plurality of upheavals, as much in the order of thought as in that of action or in ends. The phenomenon of world unification represents one of the most remarkable trends of mankind's current evolution. This world unification reveals itself first of all in our perception of the Earth. From the Arctic ice fields to the Antarctic continent, from the depths of Amazon to the remote valleys of Papua New Guinea, and from the Gobi desert to the Okavango delta, every acre of our Earth has been measured, mapped, and indexed, and dozens of satellites sweep the surface of the globe daily to detect its slightest changes. So it is hardly surprising that the world in its globality is more and more commonly called to mind. According to the Gaia hypothesis developed by the geochemist James Lovelock (2000, 2006) the Earth as a physical entity constitutes a living unity; the biosphere and all the ecosystems form a living and inseparable complex system.

World unification is manifested also through the advent of a globalised capitalism dominated by economic actors which are themselves global: large multinational

[1] Both in the Aristotelian sense and in the sense of the contemporary pragmatic philosophical stream.

corporations and global firms whose economic activities exceed the gross domestic product (GDP) of many countries. Over the course of the last decades, the progressive suppression of customs barriers and other obstacles to the circulation of goods and services, consecutive to the cycles of negotiation led by the GATT then the WTO, as well as the liberalization of financial markets and the around the clock functioning of world stock markets, has generated an intensification of commercial exchanges and an uninterrupted flow of capital movements. World unification is also attributable to technological advances, especially the development of new information and communication technologies (NICT). The development of the Internet results in unceasing growth of individuals connected to the worldwide web and a densification of networking between Internet surfers, whereas satellite news chains have engendered worldwide broadcasting of news.

The phenomenon of world unification is an essential trend to grasp the meaning of globality. World unification manifests itself in a variety of ways: the interdependence and interconnectedness of economies, societies and cultures; the awareness that we are a global community living on the same planet; a growing sense of belonging to a whole; the perceived oneness of the human family. A tendency to the uniformity of lifestyles by an alignment to the Western model can be observed in many countries, and a form of global culture conveyed by a number of global companies has appeared. Moreover, and this represents an event that is fundamentally new in human history, the past two decades have seen the emergence of a global civil society (Keane 2003) whose actors are more and more conscious of the common destiny of humankind. The conjunction of all these evolutions – economic, technological, cultural and socio-political – translates an interdependence pushed further by peoples and nations, and calls for a reflection on globality.

The advent of the era of globality is also related to the fact that most of the great challenges humankind is facing are global in every sense of the term. This is the case for the water crisis: its multidimensional nature suggests that complex and multidimensional solutions should be devised to remedy it. Both the states and the international relations system are more and more overwhelmed by global problems – water but also biodiversity, climate change, etc. –, incapable of resolving them if not of comprehending them. That is why the need for innovative governance mechanisms becomes evident. In order to think globality we need to break free from compartmentalization both in the physical, geographic context of the planet, and regarding the more abstract frontiers of knowledge and the various disciplines it encapsulates, as this is a condition to pursue the global common good.

Eventually, the theme of globality and the trend towards world unification resonate in the sphere of spirituality, where numerous faith traditions are profoundly imbued with the ideas of interdependence and interconnectedness. A number of saints, sages, masters and mystics affirmed that nobody is isolated in this world: every human being is connected to others from a spiritual point of view. Every human being carries the world inside them,[2] and our thoughts contribute to forming

[2] Physicists would not deny this affirmation: the matter that forms our bodies contains in variable (and sometimes infinitesimal) proportions, all the elements present on Earth.

the real. This is why the planetary imbalances that characterize our times will not automatically be resolved by external mechanisms of regulation, sophisticated as they may be. The creation of new forms of governance at all levels, from local to global – and their articulation, will be all the more successful as it will be inspired and supported by the inner aspiration of people involved.

Current global issues are not only attributable to regulation failures; they are also fuelled by a way of thinking, and by a conception of reason. A certain way of thinking that has developed in the West since the beginning of modernity is not totally foreign to this situation: a way of thinking that analyses, disjoins and separates, can only produce partitioned and fragmentary thought. In order to fully meet the challenges we face in the globality era, we need to reform the way we think, to break from a certain piecemeal way of thinking, which can only understand fragments. Indeed, the academic community is beginning to perceive that the crumbling of knowledge into a multitude of disciplines, themselves subdivided into innumerable sub-disciplines with impermeable partitioning, can only produce reductionist, mutilated and atrophied thinking, incapable of understanding the stakes of the times.

Globality calls for a profound renewal of our way of thinking. Globality cannot be thought about in separate, disjointed or partitioned analyses but by and in a systematic and macroscopic vision of the whole, which includes and connects the aspects that it seizes (Von Bertalanffy 2013; De Rosnay 1995; Savall and Zardet 2011). Thinking about globality is nourished by the contributions of complexity (Morin 2004, 2008). It requires transdisciplinarity, which allows to discover interdependencies between the different sets of knowledge, and to learn to tie them together. Thinking about globality leads to question our rationality and reason, as they bear part of the responsibility for a number of contemporary systemic crises. Based on a blind belief in reason, the beginnings of modernity were rich in promises of emancipation, and its unfolding allowed for much local progress – in certain parts of science, for such and such countries or social groups. But in the beginning of the twenty-first century, modernity's techno-scientific and economic reason finally reveals to be incapable of regulating the consequences of this progress (Polanyi1983). It has contributed to engender a number of global issues whose scope is expanding: climate change, biodiversity erosion, water crisis and the like. To a large extent, these issues are attributable to the logic of rationality which is freed from any transcending reference and does not have any foundation other than itself. Left thus to itself, could reason escape from its own canting, its misappropriation by the reigning ideologies, its slow slide into the rut of instrumental rationality (Giust-Desprairies et al. 1997)? Could it have avoided its seizure by the devices of economy, bureaucracy and techno-science? In many respects, it is not an exaggeration to affirm that the form of rationality that currently rules the world does not have much that is reasonable (Caillé 1989; Latouche 2001; Maréchal 1997).

On the global scale, numerous current evolutions suggest that reason has transformed itself into the logic of unreason. This process of reversal is not foreign to the surge of totalitarianisms in the twentieth century, as H. Arendt (2013) clearly showed. It is therefore not surprising that in the context of globalization as it currently unfolds, some authors denounce the totalitarian drift of liberalism (Schooyans 1991). For all that, if history teaches us that reason is capable of changing into the logic of unreason, it is not a question of dismissing reason, but to restore it in its integrity, to reestablish it in all the fullness of its faculties. To avert the perils that threaten us while we are entering a new era, we must try re-founding reason, in order that it be able to adequately respond to the challenges of globality. We subscribe to the conclusion of F. Châtelet's work: "Reason has not reached the age of reason. Will it ever reach it? That depends on man and on him alone" (Châtelet 1992).

Rationality has been widely used in economics, political science and other social sciences as a basic model of human choice behavior. The model states that the agent should maximize her or his utility function to be considered rational. Agents are considered rational if their preferences are transitive and complete and they choose what they most prefer among the available alternatives. In many cases the assumptions of self-interest and perfect knowledge are added to the notion of rationality. Hence we get the *homo œconomicus* model according to which individuals are rational, exclusively self-interested and have perfect knowledge about the consequences of their choices (Bourdieu 2000).

This concept of rationality has been criticized on empirical as well as on normative grounds (Simon 1982, 1987; Kahneman 2011; Sen 1987, 2004; Frank 1988; Elster 1989, 2007; Taylor 1985; MacIntyre 1988; Ferber and Nelson 1993; Nelson 2006; Mansbridge 1990; March 2006; Zsolnai 2008). Based on these criticisms we can say that the concept of rationality propagated by mainstream economics is empirically misleading and normatively inadequate. The conception of rationality understood as materialistic self-interest maximization inevitably leads to large-scale ecological destruction, human deprivation and disregard for the interest of future generations. Amartya Sen suggests that reason is a much broader category than rationality. According to Sen (2004), reason is the discipline of subjecting one's choice of action - as well as objectives, values and priorities - to reasoned scrutiny. It requires that an action is based on right motivation, executed by fair processes, and leads to desirable outcomes.

To grasp globality properly, we need a modest reason which is conscious of its limits, fallibility and contradictions. Instead of closed reason, locked up in its ivory tower or in its mental dungeons, we need open reason, flexible enough to move about comfortably in the different dimensions of globality (in its spheres and fields), and ingenious enough – in the sense of G. Vico's *ingenium* – to conceive of their articulations. It is not useless to cite this important Neapolitan thinker from the beginning of the eighteenth century, because if *ingenium* is gladly referred to today, the definition that Vico gave of it in his work is rarely used (Vico 1993(1710): 121–126):

> Ingenium is the faculty of guiding what is separated and diverse toward unity [...] the function of ingenium is to understand the relations of things [...], to see what is convenient, decent, beautiful or shameful, faculty refused to brutes [...] These thoughts give us the occasion to seek out what in man is the inherent ability to know; because man perceives,

> judges, reasons, but often he has false perceptions, he gives blind judgments; he reasons incorrectly. [...] This faculty is ingenium...[3]

To think globality, we need transdisciplinarity, combined with systemic and complex thought. Transdisciplinarity implies that bodies of knowledge that have developed separately and are viewed as distinct from each other should be combined to address global issues such as the water crisis. Transdisciplinarity allows transcending opposing pairs, dualist cleavages, and binary antagonisms – e.g. matter/spirit, particle/wave, logic/intuition – which force us reasoning into a dogmatic stranglehold, and give way to sterile quarrels between defenders of adversary positions in a large number of domains. It seems that the human mind is arriving at a stage where the principle of the excluded middle, whose establishment would, in its time, mark a conquest of reason over the pre-logical mentality, is being brought to completion by another principle, that of the included middle. The adoption of the logic of the included middle, which is one of the three pillars of transdisciplinarity (Nicolescu 2002; Max-Neef 2005), renders possible the passage to a higher level of comprehension, to a broader vision that may re-situate the contradictions experienced at a lower level in a vaster perspective that brings their interactions to light.

Vico inspired Edgar Morin who pursues the same goal of creating a *scienza nuova* (Morin 2008). In order to address the uncertainty and complexity of the planetary era, we need a new way of thinking, mobilizing transdisciplinary approaches that draw on multiple disciplines while questioning the disciplinary organization of knowledge (Morin 1992; Klein 2004; Ramadier 2004). Morin makes a plea for a paradigm shift, that is, a shift from the paradigm of simplicity (a reductive/disjunctive way of thinking) which still dominates our culture, to a paradigm of complexity (a way of thinking that connects) which is emerging (Morin 1990, 1992; Morin and Le Moigne 1999, 2007). This epistemological passage is occurring now and accompanies in the order of knowledge the hypothesis of a change of era whose principal outlines have just been drawn. In particular, the development of complex thought is essential in the field of politics: "It is thus absolutely necessary to develop a complex form of thinking capable of understanding that politics has become multidimensional" (Morin 2008: 95).

Complex thought invites us to reconsider the way we think about governance with its various levels, from the individual and elementary level of self-governance, to the level of global governance. The continental, national and regional levels are concerned, – as well as the level of megacities whose numbers will only continue to grow over the next 20 years, – and the local level. Instead of thinking in silos – each level being addressed by a disciplinary silo –, what is needed is a systemic view of all governance levels, capable of conceiving the complex interplay between levels and their articulation. As important as and maybe even more important than the creation of innovative mechanisms at all these levels, are the relations that will be established between them, as well as the capacity of actors at every level to apply

[3] Our translation.

the principles of responsibility and subsidiarity, which will determine their efficiency.

Complexity is a pillar of transdisciplinarity, which straddles the borders of knowledge; both mobilize the resources of a renewed reason whose contours we have just attempted to sketch. When a number of global issues of the twenty-first century – including forced migrations, environmental crises, and water – call for transdisciplinary approaches (Max-Neef 2005), they also require multi-level governance mechanisms to handle global common goods of vital importance. Complex thought and transdisciplinarity are necessary to design new, multi-level governance mechanisms that preserve global common goods. Water – an essential global common good – provides a good illustration of the development of such mechanisms.

17.3 Water as a Global Issue

Water is a major issue of the era of globality because the survival of mankind depends upon its availability. It is a vital common good, one of the most precious ones (Petrella 2001, 2008; Barlow 2009). It may even be considered as a fundamental human right (Barlow and Clarke 2003). There is no difference between human beings when it comes to water: we all need a daily amount of water to live decently. Access to drinking water is therefore a universal problem. This is all the more true at a time when fierce competition is going on for freshwater resources in many parts of the world. International institutions such as the United Nations are mobilized to reduce water-related risks; initiatives such as the Sustainable Development Goals (SDGs) exemplify their concern and commitment. The SDGs include an objective for clean water and sanitation – goal 6: "Ensure access to water and sanitation for all" (United Nations 2016). While more than 40% of the global population is affected by water scarcity, 2.4 billion people in developing countries are still deprived of basic sanitation facilities.

Combined with food security issues that have occurred in recent years – e.g. hunger riots in Haiti, protests in Egypt, flour and bread rationing in Pakistan and rice shortages in Thailand and the US, water shortages can and will have destabilizing effects on societies. It is likely that drinking water scarcity will create a new category of refugees: water refugees, who will add to climate refugees. The worsening of the water crisis may also be destabilizing for economic reasons. A report commissioned by HSBC and produced by Frontier Economics in June 2012 warns that the world's economic growth is likely to be severely affected by water scarcity in a context of competing demands for freshwater resources. Fifty percent of the global population is predicted to live in water stress areas by 2050. The report stresses that policy reform is needed to address future water shortages: steps should be taken to improve water resource management and reduce water waste so that the stability of water supply may be ensured throughout the world. Low-income countries could gain a return on investment of $5 for every $1 invested in access to safe water and sanitation; achieving universal access could result in gains of over

15% of annual GDP for concerned countries (e.g. Democratic Republic of Congo, Nicaragua). The report also insists that the global water challenge is multidimensional: activities such as agriculture, mining, manufacturing, tourism, recreation, transport, and fisheries, vitally depend on the quality of water resources (Frontier Economics & HSBC 2012).

There is a duty to hand on to future generations a livable planet. If we wish to preserve a livable planet, we should not forget that water is the basis of life. In this context, Riccardo Petrella and the Global Committee for the Water Contract have worked out a proposal for action called *The Water Manifesto*, with a view to creating a global water contract. The initiative is supported by diverse groups of citizens from Africa, Latin America, North America, Asia and Europe. The Water Manifesto illustrates the complexity of drinking water distribution and clarifies the need for transdisciplinary approaches. The Manifesto is based on well-founded principles, five of which are listed below (Petrella 2001, 2008; Global Committee for the Water Contract 1998):

- Water 'the source of life' belongs to all the inhabitants of the Earth in common;
- The right to water is an inalienable individual and collective right;
- Water has to contribute to the strengthening of solidarity among people, communities, countries, genders, generations; [...]
- Water policy implies a high degree of democracy at the local, national, continental and world level;
- Access to water necessarily takes place through partnership. It is time to go beyond the logic of 'warlords' and economic conflicts for the domination and conquest of markets.

The text of the Manifesto fully acknowledges that water is the basis of life, indeed *the source of life*. It places the emphasis on access to water as an inalienable right. Water is not a commodity – the Manifesto rejects the commodification of water which leads to water-related wars as numerous states instrumentalize water for geopolitical reasons. Nor is it a marketable good to be conquered by water lords so as to maximize profits on the planetary battlefield. The Manifesto emphasizes that water belongs to the economy of common goods and sharing, not to the economy of competition and private accumulation. Providing drinking water is a matter of solidarity; inequalities cannot be tolerated in this respect. Water is a '*respublica*' which calls for participatory democracy – citizens not private interests must be at the centre. Local communities, cities, basins and regions need to get involved. Providing access to water for all is a matter of multi-level governance: "It is up to society as a whole and at the different levels of social organization to guarantee the right of access, according to the double principle of co-responsibility and subsidiarity" (Global Committee for the Water Contract 1998). The Manifesto mentions numerous levels and actors of governance, and explicitly refers to the subsidiarity principle which is required in any attempt to design multi-level governance schemes. Regarding prices, the progressive pricing of drinking water based on the quantity used should start beyond the indispensable minimum, in order to cover the fundamental needs of the poorest and reach the objective of water for all. These are the rules which, according to the Manifesto, can foster decentralized, sustainable management of water that meets the needs of present generations while preserving water resources for future generations.

In order to realize its vision the Water Manifesto formulated several proposals (Petrella 2001; Global Committee for the Water Contract 1998):

- the creation of a 'Network of Parliaments for Water'
- the promotion of information campaign, awareness raising and mobilization
- the establishment of a World Observatory for Water Rights.

A new legal framework is to be defined, especially at the world level, in order to legalize water as a vital patrimonial good, common to all humanity. The Manifesto points out three important challenges: modernizing water distribution systems in megacities; reforming irrigation systems in intensive industrial agriculture, and deciding a moratorium on the construction of large dams. The aims of the Observatory for Water Rights will be to collect and disseminate rigorous information on water access, supporting partnerships and solidarity.

Drinking water is a key issue of the globality era, since human beings highly depend upon its availability. The global water crisis requires new ways of thinking and acting involving systemic and complex approaches. It illustrates the need to conceive innovative governance mechanisms in a transdisciplinary perspective (Thill and Ezin 2002). The Water Manifesto rightly addresses water as an urgent and highly complex issue of utmost importance. Providing access to drinking water for all in a sustainable way represents a problem interwoven with many ecological, economic, social, cultural and ethical issues. This complex challenge constitutes a critical test to demonstrate the viability of multi-level governance serving the global common good.

Global water issues cannot be solved by states alone, by technical progress alone, or by the market mechanism alone. New governance schemes are required. Besides global governance, other levels of governance should be employed as well. What is needed is a multi-level governance system, based on the principles of co-responsibility, subsidiarity and cooperation. Political science literature has been dealing with multi-level governance in the context of the European Union for the past 20 years. There is wide agreement that governance in the EU has become multi-level. The EU has moved away from state-centric governance (Marks et al. 1996), allowing the problem of the division and sharing of sovereignty in a multi-level system of governance to be discussed (Börzel and Risse 2000). Yet there is no consensus about how multi-level governance should be organized (Hooghe and Marks 2003). The concept of multi-level governance fits with the changing role of the nation state in a post-Westphalia world. It relates to the dispersion of central government authority to public authorities located at other territorial levels and to non-state actors. As explained by Bache and Flinders (2010: viii):

> In recent years the concept of 'multi-level governance' has located itself at the centre of debates concerning the future of nation states and the reallocation of powers both upwards to supranational organizations and downwards to sub-national levels.

Fragmented state functions are reorganized as is the case in the European Union whose character as a system of multi-level governance has strengthened through the deepening of European integration.

Fairbrass and Jordan analyze the development of multi-level governance in Europe in the field of environmental policy (Fairbrass and Jordan 2010: 147):

> The European Union has created some of the strongest and most progressive environmental policies of any polity in the world. This remarkable achievement has been accomplished with the involvement of a variety of state and non state actors at different levels of governance, ranging from the local to the global. Clearly, the EU's own supranational institutions, such as the Commission, Parliament and Court have played a decisive role in this policy development. So too, have a range of national and subnational actors encompassing central government departments, regional and local government authorities, national regulatory agencies, and many private and voluntary sector, non-state actors such as firms and environmental interest groups.

The European policy regarding biodiversity is a successful example of multi-level governance with the involvement of sub-national, national and supranational actors. Environmental groups such as the Royal Society for the Protection of Birds, Birdlife International and the WWF contributed to elaborate the 'Birds Directive'.[4] This example illustrates the relevance of multi-level governance to handle a global common good. It also suggests that multi-level governance requires the application of the subsidiarity principle.

Subsidiarity is a principle of political and social organization which deals with the articulation and coordination of various levels of governance. The idea of subsidiarity goes back to Aristotle and Greek thought; it has been developed by Thomas Aquinas in the thirteenth century and modernized by the Christian social doctrine in the twentieth century (Clergerie 1997). For the past three decades and especially since the Treaty of Maastricht (1992), this idea has appeared in political debates regarding the evolution of European institutions. The subsidiarity principle may be defined as follows (D'Onorio 1995: 12–13):

> In accordance with this principle, it is up to each level of authority to assume all the duties conferred upon it without needing to resort to a larger-scale authority. Intervention of the higher level in the competences of the subordinate level is justified only [...] in the case of a deficiency or default of the subordinate.

Subsidiarity favors responsibility on the part of multiple actors and aims to bring power closer to the people by leaving to each degree of authority the exercise of its own competences. Its application requires the adoption of the principles of co-responsibility and cooperation by all actors involved.

We propose a multi-level, transdisciplinary governance model involving not only public authorities but also non-state actors at various levels, and realizing the subsidiarity principle. The model is illustrated by Fig. 17.1.

The governance axis encompasses all levels from global governance to self-governance, while the 'transdisciplinarity' axis comprises several disciplines: philosophy, political science, economics and management, and spirituality. Water occupies the center of Fig. 17.1, at the intersection of the two arrows: water issues fall within all governance levels, and all the disciplinary fields appearing on the horizontal axis can contribute to the design and efficiency of water governance.

---

[4] Directive 79/409/EEC on the conservation of wild birds.

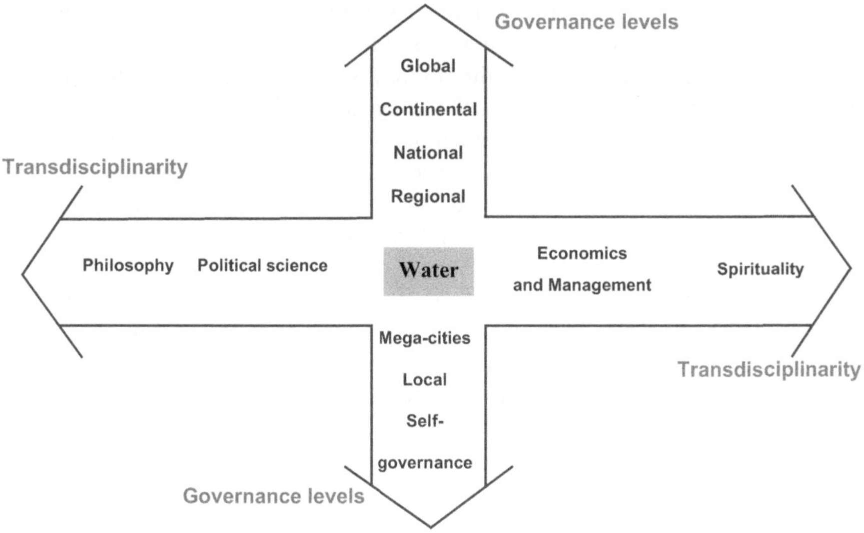

Fig. 17.1 The multi-level, transdisciplinary governance model

Figure 17.1 may be relevant also for other global common goods – such as biodiversity or climate – which can similarly be positioned at the center.

All governance levels represented on the vertical axis of Fig. 17.1 are concerned with water or drinking water issues.

The water crisis is emerging as a priority issue for the world as a whole. Global governance in this respect is still embryonic, although several United Nations agencies are dealing with water challenges, notably the United Nations Environment Program, the United Nations Development Program, and the World Health Organization; the World Trade Organization is involved with these challenges as well. The World Water Council created in 1996 brings together UN and intergovernmental organizations, governments, private firms, international NGOs, and civil society groups. Its mission is "to promote awareness, build political commitment and trigger action on critical water issues at all levels" (World Water Council 2016) and it organizes the World Water Forum every third year. Although the World Water Council is more a think tank and a multi-stakeholder platform than a governance body, it might prefigure what a global governance institution dedicated to water could look like.

The continental level of governance primarily concerns the European Union, which has elaborated a doctrine about subsidiarity with a view to implementing multi-level governance in the EU. Other continents and subcontinents are concerned as well, as far as water resources need to be shared between countries – for instance South America, Middle East, or South Asia. The creation of parliaments for water at the continental level, as advocated by the Water Manifesto, would represent a significant step forward for the establishment of water governance bodies.

The national level refers to the about 200 states that exist today. Nation-states were traditionally viewed as the guarantors of the common good; this is not true any more as no single country can address today"s global problems alone. But even though they cannot – alone – ensure the safeguard of global common goods, states still have a responsibility to maintain public welfare services and systems; therefore national governments will remain an essential actor of water governance.

The term 'regional' is understood here in the infra-national sense (e.g. the '*Länder*' in Germany or the '*régions*' in France). The regional level of governance seems to be the most appropriate to manage river basins.

Mega-cities refers to the 600 cities of more than 1 million inhabitants that will exist by 2020, most of which will be in developing or emerging countries. Water companies are particularly concerned with this level of governance as they supply water to cities and mega-cities. The challenge for them is to provide access to water to all inhabitants.

The local level is that of local government which may want to involve business or civil society organizations in the governance of water in a given territory.

Self-governance, when it comes to water preservation, refers to each citizen's ability to restrict their needs in accordance with available resources.

The 'transdisciplinarity' axis includes five disciplines that may relevantly contribute to the elaboration of water governance schemes, and to their efficiency.

Philosophy nurtures the streams of business ethics, corporate social responsibility, and wise management (Rosé and Lépineux 2013). It stimulates the reflection on the common good concept and the subsidiarity principle.

Political science deserves to be present on this axis as reflections on multi-level governance have been developed mainly by political scientists; governance is primarily a political science subject.

Economics and management are interested in problems associated with the provision of public or common goods. A growing number of management scholars discuss the idea that businesses are starting to assume a political responsibility (Palazzo and Scherer 2008; Scherer et al. 2014). The concept of (global) corporate citizenship is developing: corporations may be seen as (planetary) citizens (Crane et al. 2008; Schwab 2008), responsive to the communities in which they exist.

Spirituality is included as well, as global common goods usually convey a spiritual dimension (Bouckaert and Zsolnai 2012). This is particularly the case for water which incorporates both a material and a spiritual value for many communities. In a spiritual perspective, humankind cannot overcome the water needs of billions of people with materialistic, one-dimensional approaches. But the inner aspiration of a significant number of people can facilitate the peaceful search for sustainable solutions to the water crisis. History has shown that the personal engagement of spiritually-driven individuals may be decisive when it comes to fundamental social change (Bouckaert and Zsolnai 2012). The global water issue leads us to move away from individualistic welfare understood as the satisfaction of material desires, toward a more holistic conception of community well-being.

It is now increasingly recognized that the provision of global common goods requires the cooperation of various actors, belonging to the spheres of government, business and civil society. Specialized, sustainability-oriented networks and multi-stakeholder initiatives including actors from the three spheres are important drivers of corporations' adoption of corporate social responsibility or sustainability policies and approaches. Business organizations such as water companies could also make important contributions to governance schemes fostering co-responsibility between multiple actors. In the context of a scarcity of water resources in numerous regions of the world, water companies are co-responsible for providing access to drinking water to all. This responsibility rests on them wherever they operate, notably in cities of emerging or poor countries. Participation in multi-level governance mechanisms could be a way for water companies to manifest their engagement to manage water resources in a sustainable way – thereby assuming their share of the necessary effort to preserve this global common good.

The question may arise as to whether these private actors acknowledge that water is a global common good, not only a marketable commodity – and whether they adhere to the principles of co-responsibility and cooperation. In a transdisciplinary perspective, there is no fundamental contradiction: water can be both a global common good and a marketable good if it is sold at a price that most users can afford and an indispensable minimum is provided freely to the poorest who cannot afford to pay for it. Similarly, there is no contradiction between drinking water distribution and adherence to the principles of co-responsibility, subsidiarity and cooperation; these principles allow water companies to meet stakeholder expectations and provide access to drinking water for all in a sustainable way. Water companies could take part in the elaboration of policies regarding the provision of drinking water to all the population of a city, megacity or region – which means that nobody should be deprived of access to drinking water, and the price for this service should be reasonable given the level of economic development of the concerned area.

17.4 Conclusion

Humanity is currently facing global problems and risks which may worsen in the near future. These include the degradation of natural ecosystems; violations of basic rights in many parts of the world; the sharpening of social inequalities within developed and developing nations; problems linked to population growth; the phenomenon of migration including the new category of climate refugees; the lack of food, basic instruction and health care, and the systemic risk of a global 'crash'. Drinking water scarcity is only one among a series of global issues; yet it is of vital importance for about one billion people with no access to drinking water.

Water – one of the most crucial problems of humankind today, which conveys both a material and a spiritual dimension – is an example that illustrates the relevance of complex and transdisciplinary approaches in tackling crucial global issues. The discussion about the global water challenge highlights the need to change our way of thinking. The advent of the globality era implies a paradigm shift: the adoption of complex and transdisciplinary thinking is required.

Cooperation between the three spheres (government, business and civil society) is essential to ensure that global common goods are well managed and successfully preserved. Multi-level governance mechanisms based on subsidiarity and co-responsibility are required to solve the water crisis and to avert the perils that are looming ahead. Through their involvement in governance schemes at different levels, water companies can take part in the elaboration of water policies that safeguard this global common good. Besides, businesses of all kinds cannot ignore global issues such as the water crisis, as they are – and will increasingly be – directly or indirectly impacted by it. They are attentive to water risks, to water management, and to the evolution of water governance schemes, should these involve private water companies. Eventually, like water, other global common goods including biodiversity and climate require collaborative solutions between a variety of actors: the multi-level, transdisciplinary governance model that we suggested for water could be applied to other globalcommon goods as well.

References

Alford, H., and M. Naughton. 2001. *Managing as if Faith Mattered. Christian Social Principles in the Modern Organization*. Notre Dame: University of Notre Dame Press.

Alford, H., and Y. Shcherbinina. 2009. Corporate Social Responsibility and Common Good. In *Business, Globalization and the Common Good*, ed. H.-C. de Bettignies and F. Lépineux, 63–82. Oxford: Peter Lang.

Arendt, H. 2013. *The Origins of Totalitarianism*. Lenox: Hard Press Publishing. First edition 1951.

Argandoña, A. 1998. The Stakeholder Theory and the Common Good. *Journal of Business Ethics* 17 (9–10): 1093–1102.

Aristotle. 2003. *The Nichomachean Ethics*. Cambridge, MA: Harvard University Press.

Aron, R. 2010. *Mémoires*. Paris: Robert Laffont.

Bache, I., and M. Flinders, ed. 2010. *Multi-level Governance*. Oxford: Oxford University Press.

Barlow, M. 2009. *Vers un pacte de l'eau*. Montreal: Editions Ecosociété.

Barlow, M., and T. Clarke. 2003. *Blue Gold, the Battle Against Corporate Theft of the World's Water*. New York: Routledge.

Beaud, M. 2000. *Le basculement du monde*. Paris: La Découverte.

Beck, U. 1999. *World Risk Society*. Cambridge: Polity Press.

Börzel, T.A., and T. Risse. 2000. Who is Afraid of a European Federation? How to Constitutionalize a Multi-level Governance System. In *What Kind of Constitution for What Kind of Polity?* ed. C. Joerges, Y. Mény, and J.H.H. Weiler. San Domenico: European University Institute.

Bouckaert, L., and L. Zsolnai, ed. 2012. *The Palgrave Handbook of Spirituality and Business*. London: Palgrave MacMillan.

Bourdieu, P. 2000. *Les structures sociales de l'économie*. Paris: Le Seuil.

Caillé, A. 1989. *Critique de la raison utilitaire*. Paris: La Découverte.

Castells, M. 2005. *The Information Age – Economy, Society and Culture*. 3 volumes. Oxford: Blackwell.

Châtelet, F. 1992. *Une histoire de la raison*. Paris: Editions du Seuil.

Clergerie, J.-L. 1997. *Le principe de subsidiarité*. Paris: Ellipses.

Crane, A., D. Matten, and J. Moon. 2008. *Corporations and Citizenship*. Cambridge: Cambridge University Press.

Crosby, B.C., and J.M. Bryson. 2005. *Leadership for the Common Good: Tackling Public Problems in a Shared-Power World*. San Francisco: Jossey-Bass.

De Bettignies, H.-C., and F. Lépineux. 2009a. Business and the Global Common Good: An Interdisciplinary Approach. In *Business, Globalization and the Common Good*, ed. H.-C. de Bettignies and F. Lépineux, 27–61. Oxford: Peter Lang.
De Bettignies, H.-C., and F. Lépineux. 2009b. Can Multinational Corporations Afford to Ignore the Global Common Good? *Business and Society Review* 114 (2): 153–182.
De Rosnay, J. 1995. *Le macroscope – Vers une vision globale*. Paris: Editions du Seuil.
Dickie, R.B., and L.S. Rouner. 1986. *Corporations and the Common Good*. Notre Dame: University of Notre Dame Press.
D'Onorio, J.-B., ed. 1995. *La subsidiarité – De la théorie à la pratique*. Paris: Téqui.
Elster, J. 1989. *The Cement of Society*. Cambridge: Cambridge University Press.
———. 2007. *Explaining Social Behavior. More Nuts and Bolts for the Social Sciences*. Cambridge: Cambridge University Press.
Fairbrass, J., and A. Jordan. 2010. Multilevel Governance and Environmental Policy. In *Multi-level Governance*, ed. I. Bache and M. Flinders, 147–164. Oxford: Oxford University Press.
Frank, R. 1988. *Passions within Reason*. New York: W.W. Norton.
Ferber, M.A., and J.A. Nelson, eds. 1993. *Beyond Economic Man*. Chicago: The University of Chicago Press.
Frontier Economics/HSBC. (2012). Exploring the Links Between Water and Economic Growth. Report commissioned by HSBC and produced by Frontier Economics, London. http://water.issuelab.org/resource/exploring_the_links_between_water_and_economic_growth.
Gatard, C. 2014. *Mythologies du futur*. Paris: L'archipel.
Gaudin, T. 1988. *Les métamorphoses du futur*. Paris: Economica.
Giust-Desprairies, F., A. Lévy, and A. Nicolaï (eds.). 1997. La résistible emprise de la rationalité instrumentale. *Revue Internationale de Psychosociologie* IV(8).
Global Committee for the Water Contract. 1998. Water Manifesto, www.gdrc.org/uem/water/WATER_MANIFESTO.doc.
Hardin, G. 1996. The tragedy of the commons. In *Business and Society*, ed. B. Castro. Oxford: Oxford University Press.
Hardt, M., and A. Negri. 2001. *Empire*. Cambridge, MA: Harvard University Press.
———. 2005. *Multitude – War and Democracy in the Age of Empire*. New York: Penguin Books.
Hooghe, L., and G. Marks. 2003. Unraveling the Central State, but How? Types of Multi-level Governance. *American Political Science Review* 97 (02): 233–243.
Kahneman, D. 2011. *Thinking, Fast and Slow*. New York: Farrar, Straus and Giroux.
Kaul, I., I. Grunberg, and M. Stern, ed. 1999. *Global Public Goods: International Cooperation in the Twenty-First Century*. Oxford: Oxford University Press.
Kaul, I., P. Conceiçao, K. Le Goulven, and R.U. Mendoza, ed. 2003. *Providing Global Public Goods: Managing Globalization*. Oxford: Oxford University Press.
Keane, J. 2003. *Global Civil Society?* Cambridge: Cambridge University Press.
Klein, J.T. 2004. Prospects for Transdisciplinarity. *Futures* 36 (4): 515–526.
Koslowski, P. 2006. The Common Good of the Firm as the Fiduciary Duty of the Manager. In *Global Perspectives on Ethics of Corporate Governance*, ed. G.J. Roussouw and A.J.G. Sison, 67–76. New York: Palgrave MacMillan.
Latouche, S. 2001. *La déraison de la raison économique. Du délire d'efficacité au principe de précaution*. Paris: Albin Michel.
———. 2012. *L'âge des limites*. Paris: Mille et une nuits.
Lovelock, J. 2000. *Gaia – A New Look at Life on Earth*. Oxford: Oxford University Press.
———. 2006. *The Revenge of GAIA – Earth's Climate Crisis and the Fate of Humanity*. New York: Basic Books.
MacIntyre, A. 1988. *Whose Justice? Which Rationality?* Notre Dame: University of Notre Dame Press.
Mansbridge, J.J. 1990. On the Relation of Altruism and Self-Interest. In *Beyond Self-Interest*, ed. J.J. Mansbridge, 133–143. Chicago: The University of Chicago Press.
March, J. 2006. The myth of rationality. In *Interdisciplinary Yearbook of Business Ethics*, ed. L. Zsolnai, 17–29. Oxford: Peter Lang.
Maréchal, J.-P. 1997. *Le rationnel et le raisonnable*. Rennes: Presses Universitaires de Rennes.

Marks, G., L. Hooghe, and K. Blank. 1996. European Integration from the 1980s: State-Centric V. Multi-Level Governance. *Journal of Common Market Studies* 34 (3): 341–378.
Max-Neef, M.A. 2005. Foundations of Transdisciplinarity. *Ecological Economics* 53 (1): 5–16.
McLuhan, M., and Q. Fiore. 1989. *War and Peace in the Global Village*. New York: Touchstone Books.
McLuhan, M., and B. Powers. 1992. *The Global Village: Transformations in World Life and Media in the 21st Century*. Oxford: Oxford University Press.
Melé, D. 2009. Integrating Personalism into Virtue-Based Business Ethics: The Personalist and the Common Good Principles. *Journal of Business Ethics* 88 (1): 227–244.
Morin, E. 1990. *Science Avec Conscience*. Paris: Editions du Seuil.
———. 1992. From the Concept of System to the Paradigm of Complexity. *Journal of Social and Evolutionary Systems* 15 (4): 371–385.
———. 2004. *La méthode*. 6 volumes. Paris: Editions du Seuil.
———. 2008. *On Complexity, Advances in Systems Theory, Complexity, and the Human Sciences*. Cresskill: Hampton Press.
Morin, E., and J.-L. Le Moigne. 1999. *L'intelligence de la complexité*. Paris: L'Harmattan.
———, ed. 2007. *Intelligence de la complexité. Épistémologie et pratique*. Colloque de Cerisy: Editions de l'Aube.
Nelson, J.A. 2006. *Economics for Humans*. Chicago: University of Chicago Press.
Nicolescu, B. 2002. *Manifesto of Transdisciplinarity*. New York: State University of New York Press.
O'Brien, T. 2009. Reconsidering the Common Good in a Business Context. *Journal of Business Ethics* 85 (1): 25–37.
Palazzo, G., and A.G. Scherer. 2008. Corporate Social Responsibility, Democracy and the Politization of the Corporation. *Academy of Management Review* 33 (3): 773–775.
Petrella, R. 2001. *The Water Manifesto. Arguments for a World Water Contract*. London: Zed Books.
———. 2008. *Le manifeste de l'eau pour le XXI^esiècle. Pour un pacte social de l'eau*. Montreal: Editions Fides.
Polanyi, K. 1983. *La grande transformation. Aux origines politiques et économiques de notre temps*. Paris: Gallimard.
Ramadier, T. 2004. Transdisciplinarity and Its Challenges: The Case of Urban Studies. *Futures* 36 (4): 423–439.
Rifkin, J. 2001. *The Age of Access – The New Culture of Hypercapitalism, Where All of Life Is a Paid-for Experience*. New York: Jeremy Tarcher.
Robin, J. 1989. *Changer d'ère*. Paris: Editions du Seuil.
Rosé, J.-J., and F. Lépineux. 2013. From the Financial Crisis to Wise Management: The Relevance of the 'Return to Aristotle'. In *Wise Management in Organizational Complexity*, ed. M. Thompson and D. Bevan, 68–84. London: Palgrave MacMillan.
Sagawa, S., and E. Segal. 1999. *Common Interest, Common Good: Creating Value Through Business and Social Sector Partnerships*. Cambridge, MA: Harvard Business School Press.
Savall, H., and V. Zardet. 2011. *The Qualimetrics Approach*. Observing the Complex Object: Information Age Publishing, Charlotte.
Scherer, A.G., G. Palazzo, and D. Matten. 2014. The Business Firm as a Political Actor: A New Theory of the Firm for a Globalized World. *Business & Society* 53 (2): 143–156.
Schooyans, M. 1991. *La dérive totalitaire du libéralisme*. Paris: Editions Universitaires.
Schwab, K. 2008. Global Corporate Citizenship. *Foreign Affairs* 60 : 107–118.
Sen, A. 1987. *On Ethics and Economics*. Oxford: Blackwell.
———. 2004. *Rationality and Freedom*. Cambridge, MA: Harvard University Press.
Simon, H.A. 1982. *Models of Bounded Rationality*. Cambridge, MA: MIT Press.
———. 1987. Satisficing. In *The New Palgrave: A Dictionary of Economics*, ed. J. Eatwell, P. Newman, and M. Milgate, 243–245. London: Palgrave Macmillan.
Sison, A.J.G., and J. Fontrodona. 2011. The Common Good of Business: Addressing a Challenge Posed by «Caritas in Veritate». *Journal of Business Ethics* 100 (1): 99–107.
Spence, L.J., and R. Schmidpeter. 2003. SMEs, Social Capital and the Common Good. *Journal of Business Ethics* 45 (1–2): 93–108.

Taylor, C. 1985. *Philosophical Papers*. Cambridge: Cambridge University Press.

Thill, G., and J.-P. Ezin, ed. 2002. *L'eau, patrimoine mondial commun. Co-expertise scientifique et participative et gouvernance*. Namur: Presses universitaires de Namur.

United Nations. 2016. *Sustainable Development Goals*. New York: United Nations. http://www.un.org/sustainabledevelopment/sustainable-development-goals/.

Velasquez, M. 1992. International Business, Morality, and the Common Good. *Business Ethics Quarterly* 2 (1): 27–40.

Vico, G. 1993. De l'antique sagesse de l'Italie. Paris: Flammarion. First edition 1710.

Von Bertalanffy, L. 2013. General System Theory: Foundations, Development, Applications. George Braziller, New York. First edition 1969.

Wallerstein, I. 2004. *World-Systems Analysis: an Introduction*. Durham: Duke University Press.

World Water Council. 2016. http://www.worldwatercouncil.org/.

Zsolnai, L. 2008. *Responsible Decision Making*. London: Transaction Publishers.

Part V
Conclusions

Chapter 18
Agenda for Future Research and Action

Peter Rona and Laszlo Zsolnai

Abstract This concluding paper summarizes the main messages from the book about the restoration of economics as a moral science. It is argued that economics, unlike the natural sciences, does not have an ontologically objective subject, because economic life, unlike matter, is the product of human intentionality. Economic phenomena are always necessarily incommensurate because they occur in historical time and space.

People make their economic decisions by employing practical knowledge (or wisdom). Practical knowledge is the human capacity for the reflective and critical evaluation of our reasons for action. It is the totality of our capacities – including feelings, tastes, experience, impulses and rational reasoning – ordered and filtered to critically evaluate sources of our lives we engage and deploy in making decisions. Accordingly, economics is a form of practical knowledge or reason.

Gift and gratuitousness are basic facts of human life. Persons, communities and organizations are endowed with natural, social, cultural and spiritual wealth as free gift. In their economic functioning they should acknowledge, preserve and enrich their material and non-material heritage. The adequate response to gratuitous giving is gratefulness and generosity toward those who provided the gift.

This concluding chapter summarizes the main messages from the book about the restoration of economics as a moral science. One set of propositions we developed relates to research and addresses how it is possible to incorporate intentionality and ethics into economics as a discipline. The other set of our propositions concentrates on practice and seeks to find answers to how new ethical models of economic action and policy can be developed and implemented. We hope that our propositions – be they imperfect and incomplete in their present form – will inspire both research and action in a meaningful way.

P. Rona (✉)
Blackfriars Hall, University of Oxford, Oxford, UK
e-mail: pzrona@gmail.com

L. Zsolnai
Corvinus University of Budapest, Budapest, Hungary

European SPES Institute, Leuven, Belgium
e-mail: zsolnai@uni-corvinus.hu

P. Rona, L. Zsolnai (eds.), *Economics as a Moral Science*,
Virtues and Economics 1, DOI 10.1007/978-3-319-53291-2_18

1. Economics, unlike the natural sciences, does not have an ontologically objective subject, because economic life, unlike matter, is the product of human intentionality. The objects of economics are objects of thought – in the words of Thomas Hobbes are "made with words" – that come into being through language and perception that posits them as its objects. The tool-based language of modern economics, expressed in the form of models constitutes its own reality and does not represent an objective reality outside it. A clear distinction between theory and its objects cannot be drawn because the objects of economics are the product of theory.
2. Intentionality is a constitutive and irreducible element of economic phenomena. Unlike the objects of the natural world, economic objects are mind-dependent. Intentionality is then intertwined with reflexivity, because the variables of economic events affect each other through the agency of human beings, who are both the objects and the subjects of those events. Economic phenomena are always necessarily incommensurate because they occur in historical time and space.
3. People make their economic decisions by employing practical knowledge (or wisdom). Practical knowledge is the human capacity for the reflective and critical evaluation of our reasons for action. It is the totality of our capacities – including feelings, tastes, experience, impulses and rational reasoning – ordered and filtered to critically evaluate sources of our lives we engage and deploy in making decisions. Accordingly, economics is a form of practical rather than theoretical (in Kantian terms "pure") knowledge or reason.
4. In economic life ontologically different types of agents function. People acts as persons having free will and conscience. Organizations – be they incorporated or unincorporated – act as artificial persons with varying degree of moral capabilities. Economic interactions are ontologically different when they occur between persons, between organizations, or between persons and organizations. Ontologically different economic interactions cannot be described by one single model. Distinct strategies should be developed for improving the ethicality of interactions between ontologically different types of agents.
5. Contrary to the atomistic assumption of mainstream economics about economic agents relationality plays a primary role in economic life. The major determinant of the economic agents' choices is the impact of the decisions on the network of their relations with others. By their choices and actions economic agents maintain and reinforce, initiate and develop or break and destroy their relationships with other agents. Identity and self-knowledge is crucial in managing the agents' nexus of relationship. Good, meaningful and mutually beneficial relationships contribute significantly to the well-being of the agents and increase the sustainability and competitive advantage of their functioning.

6. Economic agents harbor heterogeneous motivations. Some of them are prosocial, others are antisocial while the rest consists of self-interest. Motivations of economic agents are partly stable but may change by the context of behavior. Belief systems, including economics influence the motivations of economic agents as well as the construction of context within which they act. Virtuous circles should be developed where prosocial dispositions and supportive social contexts help to form positive economic behavior. Practicing virtues is important because it stabilizes pro-social behavior and/or modifies endogenously the preferences of agents.
7. In well-functioning market exchange economy, political governance and social reciprocity work together in a balanced and concerted way. Exchange-based transactions, public welfare structures and quotas of gratuitousness and communion are needed to serve the common good, that is to attain social wellbeing, inter-generational justice and ecologicalsustainability.
8. Gift and gratuitousness are basic facts of human life. Persons, communities and organizations are endowed with natural, social, cultural and spiritual wealth as free gift. In their economic functioning they should acknowledge, preserve and enrich their material and non-material heritage. The adequate response to gratuitous giving is gratefulness and generosity toward those who provided the gift.
9. Human happiness and wellbeing is a multifaceted and complex phenomenon. Aristotelian and Thomistic ethics adequately capture the dyadic aspects of human wellbeing: the experience of people as they live their lives, and the judgment they make when they evaluate their life. Good and virtuous character is a precondition of human flourishing. Modern happiness research and positive psychology revealed that hedonic pleasure plays a limited role in determining human flourishing. Meaningfulness has a much bigger role in it which involves integrating past, present, and future of the person and is linked with purpose in life.
10. The corporation was born as the device for severing the unity between the actor and the act. Due to this severance, responsibility has become coterminous with legal liability or the management of competing interests among shareholders and other stakeholders. The positivist economic theory, when combined with the function performed by the corporate veil destroys the unity between the action, the actor and the moral responsibility for the action with the result that the corporation must do without the basis for a morally authentic life. Despite the often heroic efforts of ethically minded CEOs the ethical prospects of corporate functioning is rather limited because the actions of its agents are the product of rule-based roles. Unincorporated organizational forms have a greater capacity to function in ethical, social and environmental friendly ways.

11. Different business archetypes can be identified in economic life. Archetype 1: Business enterprises conducted primarily as for-profit institutions to the end of financial sustainability. Financial self-reliance is a precondition of a firm's survival and for remaining capable of continuously expanding products or services. Archetype 2: The social and financial missions of business enterprises are merged; a coordination of social and financial functions is at the heart of the "promise" of the company as a sustainable enterprise. Archetype 3: Businesses are run with principal allegiance to social missions – outreach to the poor, environmental rectitude, and other facets of sustainability. The archetypes express alternative strategic orientations for individual business enterprises, namely profit-maximization, sustainability-orientation, and serving the common good.
12. Money is extremely powerful but ambiguous institution. Its basic functions as a unit for calculation, means of exchange and reserve for value cannot be separated from one another. The potential of money for coercion and violence, and its morally corrupting power cannot be easily neutralized. Ethical banks and sustainability oriented investment initiatives are heroic efforts to resolve the inherent contradictions of money and monetary systems in economic life.
13. The existing economies function with a considerable justice deficit. In order to produce material wealth they accumulate and continuously create socio-ecological burden for the poor and marginalized people, for nature, and for future generations. Mainstream economics bases economic actions and policies on individual preferences and the only conception of justice is the efficient allocation of resources. The resulting state of affairs is the increasing social inequality, deprivation of large number of people and destruction of the biosphere, including climate change and biodiversity loss.
14. Justice is a multifaceted concept. No single totalizing theory can capture the complexity of it. We need to explore multiple justice claims and synthesize them into a "justice matrix". A multidimensional understanding of justice requires reinventing the models of economic action and policy on the basis of the socio-ecologically embedded person who has both self- and other-regarding goals and preferences. Economic rationality should be replaced by a broader conception of reason which requires that an action is based on right motivation, executed by fair processes, and leads to desirable outcomes.
15. Global common goods such as climate stability, biodiversity, water and the like are crucial for the survival of humanity. They require new governance mechanisms to deal with the scale and complexity of the problem. Based on the principle of subsidiarity, multi-level governance mechanisms should be developed to preserve global common goods. The current development model led by global corporations fails to meet this important challenge. Ethical development models require the transformation of business functioning and economic regulatory rules. It also needs a complex social, political, and institutional infrastructure that embraces the environmental, human, social, cultural and spiritual dimensions of development and translates them into decisions and practice.

Index

A
Akerlof, G., 12, 35, 36, 40
Alford, H., 16, 17, 225–231, 250
Altruism, 12, 25, 35–37, 48, 81, 101, 200
Anthropology, 16, 22, 27, 40, 70, 108–110, 118, 122, 126
Aquinas, T., 16, 70–72, 74, 84, 85, 87, 88, 141, 143–145, 147, 155, 180, 219, 260
Aristotle, 7, 12, 25, 44, 70, 83, 97, 111, 144, 166, 178, 203, 250
Assisi, St. Francis of, 84, 117
Atkinson, A.B., 22
Augustine, 72, 87, 120
Austin, J.L., 140, 141

B
Balance Theory of Wisdom, 208
Becker, G., 27, 32, 200
Bentham, J., 83, 166, 219
Bhutan, 91
Bible, 112, 114, 123, 127, 171
Blackfriars Hall, University of Oxford, 14
Blueprint for Better Business, 226, 231
Boda, Z., 17, 243
Boethius, 141
Bouckaert, L., 12, 13, 54, 74, 200, 201, 262
Boulding, K., 3, 11, 23
Bounded rationality, 29, 58, 59
Brown Weiss, E., 64
Brundtland Commission, 238, 242
Bruni, L., 14, 25, 34, 51, 54, 108, 116, 119, 125, 181, 185, 229
Buber, M., 30
Buddha, 87
Business, 13, 15–17, 32, 34, 43, 49, 50, 54, 55, 70, 74, 79, 99, 101, 116, 119, 121, 123, 126, 132–134, 145, 146, 149–152, 154, 156–160, 163–172, 176–195, 202, 204, 208, 209, 226, 228, 229, 231, 246, 250, 262–264, 274
Business archetypes, 15
Business ethics, 15, 70, 164–167, 172, 250

C
Capability, 16, 61, 65, 92, 152, 179, 205, 206, 208, 219–221, 236, 237, 272
Capital, 5, 34, 45, 57, 73, 101, 117, 131, 177, 202, 239, 252
Capitalism, 52, 73, 75, 117, 118, 121–123, 127, 183, 187, 202, 239, 242, 252
Caritas in veritate, 16, 51, 53, 225–231
Catholic Social Thought, 16, 216–222, 231
Catholic University of Leuven, 12, 14, 16
Character, 8, 12, 14, 15, 23, 25, 28, 34, 37, 47, 54, 62, 63, 74, 79, 81, 82, 84, 86–88, 91, 98, 101, 103, 107, 110, 111, 113, 117, 133, 135, 151, 153, 154, 157–158, 166, 168, 169, 172, 176, 178–180, 188, 191–194, 201, 205, 207, 209, 217, 230, 237, 245, 251, 254, 259, 273
Charity, 16, 24, 84, 176, 182–186, 218, 225–231
Chief Baron Manwood, 134, 136, 141–143, 153, 156
Christianity, 70, 72, 73, 88, 110, 123
Cicero, 120
Civil economy, 12, 25, 51, 53
Civil society, 53, 92, 191, 227, 250, 253, 261–264

P. Rona, L. Zsolnai (eds.), *Economics as a Moral Science*,
Virtues and Economics 1, DOI 10.1007/978-3-319-53291-2

Coase, R., 24
Cobb, J., 177
Common good, 13, 16, 17, 25, 44, 50, 74, 76, 79, 81, 108, 112, 145, 154, 160, 169, 177, 178, 186, 189, 191–192, 195, 201, 203, 216, 219–222, 226, 228, 249–251, 253, 257–264, 273, 274
Common Heritage of Mankind, 241, 242
Community, 22, 48, 62, 73, 80, 99, 107, 146, 178, 207, 219, 227, 237, 253, 271
Complexity, 5, 191, 217, 245, 254, 256, 258, 274
Confucius, 87
Conservation, 64, 91
Consumer sovereignty, 79, 80
Corporate accountability, 161
Corporate finance, 132, 146, 147, 158, 159, 164
Corporate social responsibility (CSR), 49, 183, 184, 250, 263
Corporation, 7, 14, 32, 121, 131–161, 164, 167, 179, 182, 183, 193, 202, 209, 243, 245, 250, 253, 262, 263, 273, 274
Crowding-out effect, 31

D

Daly, H., 177
Decision making, 15, 60, 104, 105, 132, 205–207, 221, 244
DeMartino, G.E., 11
de Tocqueville, A., 193
Development, 26, 50, 65, 72, 84, 98, 108, 138, 164, 177, 202, 220, 226, 233, 253, 274
Development ethics, 233, 234, 244, 245
Drucker, P., 201, 202
Durkheim, É., 111, 187
Duty, 33, 53, 62, 117, 131, 135–137, 140, 142, 148, 149, 182, 217, 219, 220, 227, 258, 260

E

Easterlin's paradox, 33
Ecological integrity, 63
Ecology, 13, 17, 22, 51, 52, 55, 57, 63, 64, 66, 67, 74, 89, 91, 234, 238–240, 244, 246, 259, 273, 274
Economic activity, 4, 13, 17, 23, 51, 52, 63–66, 91, 101, 151, 178, 191, 226, 229, 253
Economic agents, 12, 13, 24, 25, 31, 67, 81, 101, 272
Economic approach to human behaviour, 27–30
Economic efficiency, 39, 81, 92
Economic interactions, 12, 272
Economic phenomena, 6, 272
Economics, 3, 12, 21, 44, 58, 69, 79, 95, 108, 132, 164, 176, 199, 215, 225, 234, 249, 271
Economics as a moral science, 3, 11, 23, 55, 225, 271
Economizing, 58, 66–67
Economy of communion (EoC), 51, 185, 229
Eliade, M., 110
Eliot, T.S., 26, 218
Elster, J., 61, 62
Emerson, R.W., 89
Emotional regulation, 207–208
Entitlements, 166, 226, 235
Ethical field, 15, 165, 167, 171, 172
Ethical gray zone, 168, 170, 172
Ethics, 5, 11, 21, 44, 60, 70, 80, 97, 108, 131, 164, 176, 201, 215, 231, 233, 250, 271
Ethos, 84, 108, 155
Etzioni, A., 11, 80
Eudaimonia, 34, 44, 83, 85, 91, 203
Euro-China Centre for Leadership and Responsibility (ECCLAR), 202
Evangelii gaudium, 8, 45, 57, 217, 218, 221
Exchange, 4, 5, 12, 14, 17, 23, 26–28, 30, 33–38, 44, 46–48, 51, 53, 81, 96, 98, 100, 104, 109, 123, 150, 176, 178, 181, 183, 185, 186, 190, 193, 226, 227, 253, 273, 274

F

Fictitious person, 135, 141, 152, 155
Finnis, J., 144
Fitting, 15, 85, 168
Flourishing, 13, 14, 16, 34, 45, 46, 54, 69, 79–92, 104, 111, 116, 120, 122, 178, 189–191, 203, 221, 242, 273
Focolare, 180, 185, 229
Foucault, M., 39
Frame of reference, 80, 91, 176
Frank, R., 60, 61
Franklin, B., 87
Freedom, 12, 13, 16, 33, 37, 39, 47, 49, 54, 62, 64–66, 70, 72, 73, 75, 80–82, 89, 92, 116, 119, 125, 126, 147, 152, 168, 181, 185, 216, 217, 219–222, 236, 237, 244
Freeman, E.M., 49
French, P.A., 146, 147, 153, 154, 156, 157

Freud, S., 38
Frey, B., 31, 89
Friedman, M., 49, 80, 81, 181
Frugality, 52, 74
Future generations, 53, 63–66, 80, 88, 104, 251, 258, 259, 274

G
Gandhi, M. K., 251
Gaudium et spes, 145, 217, 219, 222
General Agreement on Tariffs and Trade (GATT), 241, 253
Gift, 12, 33, 51, 96, 108, 176, 226, 271
Girard, R., 110
Global common goods, 17, 249–251, 253, 257, 259–264, 274
Global economy, 188, 234, 238, 240–243
Globalization, 17, 29, 30, 55, 102, 127, 188, 202, 233–246, 249, 250, 252, 255
God, 34, 70, 72, 84, 88, 89, 96, 100, 113, 114, 121, 123, 124, 134, 142, 145, 153, 171, 190, 222, 227, 229, 230
Good, 8, 12, 23, 44, 58, 73, 79, 96, 107, 142, 164, 177, 225, 233, 249, 272
Good life, 13, 45, 73, 79, 84, 85, 87, 91, 108–112, 119, 127, 142, 233, 236, 245
Good Samaritan, 218, 225
Goulet, D., 233, 234, 236, 237, 242, 244, 245
Governance, 17, 32, 80–82, 104, 202, 208, 225, 241, 243, 249–264, 273, 274
Gratuitousness, 12, 17, 33, 51, 53, 55, 109, 116, 123, 176, 183, 184, 186, 190, 226, 227, 229, 271, 273
Greenspan, A., 47
Gross Domestic Product (GDP), 79, 91, 235–237, 253, 258
Gross National Happiness, 92

H
Happiness, 7, 13, 22, 33, 34, 44, 52, 53, 55, 62, 80–92, 97–99, 108, 111, 113, 114, 122, 201, 209, 273
Hart, H.L.A., 135, 137–140
Hayek, F., 96, 181
Heaney, S., 217
Hobbes, T., 4, 33, 114, 115, 139, 142, 272
Holocene, 252
Homo oeconomicus, 12, 21, 30, 32, 53, 58, 81, 152, 199, 200, 208
Homo reciprocans, 177, 186, 190–191, 195
Hui, 205, 207
Human Development Index (HDI), 237
Human person, 13, 62, 69, 71, 73, 142, 190, 218, 222
Hume, D., 22, 149, 217
Hunger, 22, 98, 118, 235, 257

I
I & We, 80
Identity, 12, 22, 23, 25, 27, 29, 30, 34–36, 62, 140, 145, 170, 222, 272
Ims, K.J., 13
Incentives, 14, 26, 27, 31–33, 81, 91, 107–127
Intentionality, 4, 5, 8, 136, 141, 144, 147, 148, 150, 153–157, 159, 203, 271
Invisible hand, 12, 13, 23, 24, 28, 46, 114, 192, 194, 200, 201

J
Jackson, K., 15, 16, 195
Jesus, 73, 123, 218
Justice, 14, 16, 30, 35, 49, 50, 52, 76, 84, 87, 97, 121, 127, 158, 190, 201, 207, 215–222, 226, 227, 237, 238, 240–245, 273, 274

K
Kahneman, D., 35, 59, 80, 82, 87, 90, 91, 199
Kant, I., 70, 71, 127, 166
Kasser, T., 89
Keynes, J.M., 3–5, 8, 57, 99
King M., 98
Kolm, S., 37, 38
Krugman, P., 102, 103

L
Lao-Tze, 87
Laudato si, 216, 217
Law, 15, 27, 29, 45, 66, 67, 70, 72, 74, 75, 96, 97, 101, 104, 133–136, 138–141, 145, 148, 151, 153, 154, 156, 158, 159, 165, 168, 169, 190, 193, 218–220, 227, 236, 250
Leopold, A., 63
Lépineux, F., 17, 250
Leviathan, 114, 142
Levinas, E., 51, 71, 99
Liability, 15, 133, 137–139, 149, 157, 159, 160, 273
Liberal individualism, 216

Limit, 3, 15, 27, 35, 38, 44–47, 49, 50, 52, 53, 55, 58, 73, 88, 90, 97–99, 101, 103, 105, 110, 133, 138, 141, 143, 157, 158, 160, 165, 171, 216, 234, 238, 245, 252, 255, 273
Livelihood, 67
Locke, J., 95
Lord Chancellor Eldon, 134
Lord H., 138, 141
Lord T., 134
Love, 24, 33, 62, 70, 73, 75, 84, 87, 88, 97, 108, 111, 119, 122, 125, 135, 192, 200, 229, 230

M
MacIntyre, A., 62, 84, 203
Managers, 16, 26, 45, 47, 49, 116, 118–120, 122, 146, 176, 182, 188, 201, 202, 204, 205, 207–209
Mandeville, Bernard de, 24
Mankiw, N.G., 150
Mansbridge, J.J., 62
March, J., 63
Maritain, J., 13, 69–76
Market, 5, 12, 23, 43, 51, 79, 96, 108, 133, 166, 175, 200, 227, 237, 252, 273
Market society, 81, 90, 200
Marx, K., 30, 45, 73–75
Maslow, A., 89
Mauss, M., 109
Mayer, C., 132, 133, 158, 160
McCloskey, D.N., 11
McKibben, B., 92
Meaningful life, 83, 85, 87, 92
Menger, C., 96
Meritocracy, 14, 107–127
Mill, J.S., 5, 8, 151, 181, 187, 188
Millenium Development Goals (MDGs), 234, 237–239, 242, 243
Miller, D.W., 15, 148
Modular brain theory, 61
Money, 4, 14, 36, 44, 57, 74, 83, 95, 122, 135, 178, 225, 274
Moral agency, 131, 137, 143, 147, 152–157, 160
Moral corporation, 160
Moral economics, 11–17
Morin, Edgar, 251, 254, 256
Motivations, 12–14, 23, 25, 26, 28, 30–32, 35, 38, 47, 48, 50, 55, 60–63, 67, 72, 83, 85, 95, 98, 103, 116, 152, 172, 178, 192, 193, 200, 201, 217, 222, 241, 273, 274
Mounier, E., 51, 69, 74, 77
Mutuality, 15, 176–195
Myrdal, G., 234

N
New International Economic Order (NIEO), 241, 242
Non-overlapping magisteria (NOMA) principle, 39
Non-tuism, 34
Nussbaum, M., 111, 112

O
Oikos, 12, 44, 45, 51
Opdebeeck, H., 13, 69–77
Otto, R., 110

P
Pacioli, L., 230
Pascal, B., 24, 33
Passion, 23, 60, 115, 119
Peak experience, 89
Person, 12, 26, 47, 60, 69, 81, 95, 107, 134, 164, 178, 206, 216, 228, 235, 272
Persona ficta, 140, 141, 143–145
Personalism, 13, 51–53, 70–77, 250
Personhood, 142, 145–147, 154–156
Petrella, R., 257–259
Philanthropy, 33, 86, 117, 183, 184
Philia, 112
Phronesis, 16, 84
Piper, T.R., 166
Plato, 26, 44, 86, 97, 166
Polanyi, K., 30, 109, 137, 177, 208, 254
Pontifical Council of Justice and Peace, 226
Pope Benedict XVI, 51, 226
Pope Francis, 8, 45, 57, 70, 76, 217, 218, 221
Pope John Paul II, 145, 226
Pope Paul VI, 226
Positive emotion, Engagement, positive Relationships, Meaning, and Accomplishment (PERMA), 13, 86
Positive psychology, 13, 82–92, 273
Practical knowledge, 7, 8, 271, 272
Price, 5, 23, 37, 46, 48, 52, 54, 99, 103, 115, 133, 134, 149, 182, 258, 263
Profit-making, 49, 67, 134, 179, 180
Pro-social behavior, 12, 38, 204, 273

Purpose, 4, 5, 7, 8, 11–14, 16, 21, 23–25, 28, 29, 36, 43, 45, 51, 71, 83, 85, 88, 89, 111, 117, 132–134, 144–147, 149–151, 154, 155, 159, 169, 175–178, 180–182, 185, 188, 189, 191, 194, 195, 204, 219, 226, 235, 238, 273

Q
Qoheleth, 121–123
Quadragesimo anno, 145, 215, 220
Quality of life, 235–237, 239, 240, 244, 245

R
Rational choice, 27, 29, 31, 32, 38, 54, 58, 59, 61, 62, 217
Rational fools, 60
Rationality, 4, 7, 13, 14, 27–29, 31, 34, 49, 50, 54, 55, 57–66, 80, 100, 108, 121, 146, 151, 152, 199, 200, 203, 208, 215, 217, 222, 254, 255, 274
Rawls, J., 16, 49, 115, 216, 218, 241
Reason, 5, 11, 26, 43, 57, 71, 80, 96, 108, 146, 170, 176, 203, 215, 231, 235, 252
Reciprocity, 12, 24, 28, 30, 33, 35–40, 51, 101, 109, 111, 112, 115, 117, 119, 120, 177, 181, 186, 190, 191, 195, 273
Reflexivity, 6, 272
Relational good, 12, 30, 33, 34, 51, 52
Religion, 70, 72, 89, 100, 110, 116, 122, 123, 166–172, 189, 218, 219
Rerum novarum, 145, 215, 216
Responsibility, 11, 15–17, 25, 29, 38, 49, 51, 92, 119, 131, 133, 137–139, 141, 143–149, 151, 153, 154, 156, 157, 159, 165, 167, 181, 183, 184, 191, 193, 194, 202, 207, 209, 215, 219, 221, 238, 242, 244, 250, 254, 257, 260, 262–264, 273
Ricardo, D., 30, 149, 150, 181
Right, 7, 15, 26, 47, 53, 76, 81, 101, 108, 135, 163, 178, 200, 216, 235, 255, 274
Risk, 15, 26, 40, 55, 74, 98–100, 102–103, 107, 112, 114, 116, 124–126, 150, 164, 165, 168–171, 178, 201, 202, 220, 251, 257, 263, 264
Robbins, L., 4, 39
Rona, P., 3–9, 14, 132–161
Rosé, J.-J., 17, 249–264
Rostow, W.W., 235, 240

S
Sachs, W., 234, 244
Sandel, M., 81, 82, 91
Sartre, J.-P., 34
Schillebeeckx, E., 217
Schumacher, E.F., 54
Schwartz, B., 90
Searle, J., 146, 151
Self, 6, 12, 22, 46, 57, 70, 81, 111, 132, 164, 179, 199, 216, 227, 233, 252, 272
Self-awareness, 205, 207, 209
Self-esteem, 17, 31, 246
Self-interest, 12, 13, 23–26, 28, 31–33, 35, 38, 39, 47–49, 51, 55, 57, 58, 60–63, 81, 92, 192, 193, 217, 221, 255, 273
Self-love, 200
Seligman, M., 13, 82, 85–87
Sen, A., 11, 13, 16, 25, 49, 60, 63, 65, 81, 89, 199, 216–222, 234–236
Shareholders, 15, 131, 133, 145, 147, 155, 179, 182, 185, 194, 195, 273
Shareholder value, 131, 133
Simmel, G., 96, 127
Simon, H.A., 58, 59
Slow food movement, 13, 52, 67
Smith, A., 13, 23–25, 29–31, 44, 46–50, 52, 55, 71, 110, 114, 135, 140, 149, 150, 192, 199, 201, 217
Social norms, 29, 61, 62
Society, 7, 14, 22, 45, 63, 74, 79, 95, 108, 133, 169, 178, 200, 219, 227, 233, 249
Socrates, 44, 95, 98, 203
Solidarity, 15, 24, 37, 51, 53, 100, 111, 117, 120, 176, 179, 186–188, 195, 227, 235, 241–245, 258, 259
Spiritual humanism, 52, 53, 75–77
Spirituality, 50, 54, 87, 92, 120, 167, 168, 201, 251, 253, 260, 262
Sraffa, P., 30
Stakeholder value, 44, 132
Stakeholders, 15, 16, 25, 44, 49, 132, 176, 178, 180, 186, 195, 202, 250, 261, 263, 273
Stiglitz, J., 91, 234
Streeten, P., 234, 235
Subsidiarity, 17, 116, 245, 251, 257–261, 263, 264, 274
Sustainability, 15, 52, 176, 177, 179–182, 202, 245, 263, 272–274
Sustainable Development Goals (SDGs), 202, 240, 257

T
Taylor, C., 62
Teleology, 12, 14, 16, 43–55, 62, 71, 97, 143, 148, 159, 176, 216, 219, 250

Telos, 4, 14, 43, 44, 49, 50, 72–73, 143, 144, 146, 148, 159, 178, 203
Thatcher, M., 225
Thate, M.J., 15, 164–172
Theological virtues, 16, 84, 225–231
Theology, 16, 17, 84, 142, 215, 219, 221, 225–231
Thomism, 72
Thompson, M., 16, 200–209
Titmuss, R., 31
Tönnies, F., 127
Trade, 13, 17, 23, 24, 28, 30, 32, 67, 91, 110, 123, 169, 181, 185, 188, 202, 238, 240–243, 261
Transatlantic Trade and Investment Partnership (TTIP), 243
Transdisciplinarity, 17, 249–264
Trinity, 227, 228
Truman, H.S., 234, 238, 240
Trust, 24, 38, 39, 51, 76, 86, 92, 97, 100–102, 104, 107, 116, 125–127, 158, 159, 190, 191, 201, 205, 207, 225, 227, 239

U

Ultimatum game, 35, 36, 228, 231
UN Conference on Trade and Development (UNCTAD), 240, 241
UN Global Compact, 202
United Nations (UN), 202, 234, 235, 237, 240, 241, 243, 257, 261
Universal Declaration of Human Rights, 219
Utility, 4, 12, 15, 21, 33–36, 43, 48, 58, 59, 61, 81, 82, 134, 151, 152, 164, 190, 255

V

Value, 4, 21, 44, 60, 75, 79, 96, 109, 131, 166, 175, 200, 217, 233, 235, 255, 274
Value creation, 183–184
Vandevelde, T., 14, 96–105
Verstraeten, J., 16, 215–222
Vico, G., 255, 256
Virtues, 3, 12, 21, 48, 62, 79, 98, 110, 134, 169, 189, 200, 228, 250, 273
Virtue ethics, 12–14, 25, 26, 49, 84, 177, 231
von Mises, L., 96
VUCA world, 16, 202, 209
Vulnerability, 14, 102, 103, 105, 107–127

W

Wall street, 47, 165
Wallerstein, I., 240, 252
Washington Consensus, 242, 243
Water crisis, 17, 253, 254, 256, 257, 259, 261, 262, 264
Water Manifesto, 251, 258, 259, 261
Wealth, 6, 29, 44–49, 52, 53, 80, 88, 96–98, 100–102, 104, 110, 122, 124, 150, 151, 181, 188, 192, 194, 200, 220, 229, 239, 252, 271, 273, 274
Weber, M., 33, 52, 121, 127
Welfare, 13, 17, 45, 46, 50, 51, 72–76, 82, 104, 185, 218, 226, 227, 236, 237, 246, 262, 273
Wellbeing, 14, 16, 25, 26, 74, 79, 82, 83, 86–92, 119, 201, 203, 220, 273
Whately, R., 39
Wisdom, 8, 16, 29, 45, 75, 84, 102, 120, 167, 190, 199, 215, 231, 272
World Trade Organization (WTO), 242, 253
World Water Contract, 251

Y

Yunus, M., 182, 183

Z

Zamagni, S., 11, 12, 22–40, 51, 229
Zhi, 205, 207
Zsolnai, L., 11–17, 57–67, 81, 201, 262, 272–274

9783319532905